Contents

CW01499107

Latin American and Caribbean International
Institutional Law

Marco Odello · Francesco Seatzu

Editors

Latin American and Caribbean International Institutional Law

Editors
Marco Odello
Law and Criminology
Aberystwyth University
Aberystwyth
UK

Francesco Seatzu
Facoltà di Giurisprudenza
University of Cagliari
Cagliari
Italy

ISBN 978-94-6265-068-8   ISBN 978-94-6265-069-5   (eBook)
DOI 10.1007/978-94-6265-069-5

Library of Congress Control Number: 2015937753

Published by T.M.C. ASSER PRESS, The Hague, The Netherlands www.asserpress.nl
Produced and distributed for T.M.C. ASSER PRESS by Springer-Verlag Berlin Heidelberg

Printed on acid-free paper

Springer Science+Business Media B.V. Dordrecht is part of Springer Science+Business Media
(www.springer.com)

Contributors

Mª Ángeles Cano Linares is Profesor Titular of Public International Law and International Relations at the Rey Juan Carlos University in Madrid (Spain). She has cooperated with various universities, including Paris X, San Martín (Buenos Aires), Medellín (Colombia) and La Habana. She publishes in areas related to international peace and security, human rights, integration processes and migration. Recent publications include: Cano Linares, M.A. and Díaz-Silveira Santos, C., *La acción exterior del sistema de integración centroamericana*, 2012; and Cano Linares, M.A. and Trinidad Núñez, P., *Grupos vulnerables y desfavorecidos. Protección contra su explotación laboral*, 2011.

Alana Lancaster is a Lecturer in the Faculty of Law, University of the West Indies Cave Hill Campus (Barbados) serving as the Course Director of International Environmental Law, Caribbean Energy & Gas Law, Caribbean Environmental Law, and Equitable Remedies. Alana's research is heavily interdisciplinary, and she is currently conducting research on the law and policy concerning ocean governance and the transboundary management of natural resources in the Caribbean region, trade and environmental law, climate change law, renewable energy law and the role of blue carbon science in the management of the Caribbean's coastal resources. Alana is also involved in collaborative research relating to comparative marine and environmental (CARICOM/EU), human rights and the environment, eco-health and water law.

Eugenia López-Jacoiste Díaz is Adjunct Professor in Public International Law, Deputy Dean and Director of the European Documentation Centre at the University of Navarra (Spain). She has conducted research in various international institutions, including the *Max Planck Institut für ausländisches öffentliches Recht und Völkerrecht*, Heidelberg. Her publications include *El Banco Mundial, el Fondo Monetario Internacional y los derechos humanos*, 2013; *La política de seguridad y defensa en Europa*, 2006 and *Actualidad del Consejo de Seguridad de las Naciones Unidas: La legalidad de sus decisiones y el problema de su control*, 2003.

Marco Odello is a Reader in Law at the Department of Law and Criminology, Aberystwyth University (UK). He publishes and teaches in the areas of Public International Law, Human Rights, Humanitarian Law and International Organisations. His recent publications include: Odello M. and Seatzu F. (eds), *Armed Forces and International Jurisdictions*, 2013; *Il diritto dei rifugiati*, 2013; Odello M. and Seatzu F., *The UN Committee on Economic, Social and Cultural Rights*, 2012.

Florabel Quispe Remón is Profesora Ayudante in Public International Law at the University Carlos III of Madrid (Spain). Her publications include: Bustamante Alarcón R. and Quispe Remón F., *Derechos humanos y lucha contra la impunidad: el caso Fujimori*, 2011; and *El debido proceso en el derecho internacional y en el sistema interamericano*, 2010.

Francesco Seatzu is a Full Professor of International and European Union Law at the University of Cagliari (Italy). He authored *The UN Committee on Economic, Social and Cultural Rights: The Law, Process and Practice*, 2012 (with M. Odello); *The World Bank Inspection Panel*, 2007; *Insurance in Private International Law: A European Perspective*, 2003; co-edited *Natural Resources Grabbing: Erosion or Legitimate Exercise of State Sovereignty?*, 2015 (with A. Bonfanti and F. Romanin Jacur); *Foreign Investment, International Law and Common Concerns* (with T. Treves and S. Trevisanut, Routledge, 2013); *Armed Forces and International Jurisdictions*, 2013 (with M. Odello); *Tradition and Innovation in Private International Law*, 2005 (with L. Pereznieto Castro and T. Treves). Professor Seatzu is the author of several articles in public and private international law published in Italy and abroad.

Jill St George is a Lecturer in Law at the University of the West Indies, Cave Hill Campus (Barbados). Having been called to the Bar of England and Wales, Jill worked as a Research Assistant on a number of funded research projects in the UK before moving abroad in 2011. Jill's areas of teaching and research include Public International Law and Criminal Law, with a focus on gender-based violence and regional policy harmonisation in the Caribbean.

Abbreviations

ACHR	American Convention on Human Rights
ACS	Association of Caribbean States
ACTO	Amazon Cooperation Treaty Organization
ADB	African Development Bank
AFTA	Asian Free Trade Association
AIS	Andean Integration System
ALADI	Latin American Integration Association
ALBA	Bolivarian Alliance for the Peoples of Our America
ALCUE	Latin America and Caribbean and European Union Summits
ANCOM	Andean Common Market
APC	Andean Presidential Council
ASA	South American-African cooperation
ATJ	Andean Tribunal of Justice
CA	Cartagena Agreement
CABEI	Central American Bank for Economic Integration
CACM	Central American Common Market
CAF	Andean Development Corporation
CAFTA	Central American Free Trade Agreement
CAN	Comunidad Andina de Naciones/Andean Community
CARICOM	Caribbean Community
CARIFTA	Caribbean Free Trade Association
CCJ	Caribbean Court of Justice
CDB	Caribbean Development Bank
CELAC	Community of Latin American and Caribbean States
CEPAL	Commission for America and Caribbean
CET	Common External Tariff
CFP	Common Foreign Policy
CJAC	Court of Justice of the Andean Community
CMC	Consejo del Mercado Común
CPC	Comisión Parlamentaria Conjunta
CSME	Caribbean Single Market and Economy

CSN	Comunidad Sudamericana de Naciones/South American Community of Nations
CU	Customs Union
EC Dollar/XCD	Eastern Caribbean Dollar
ECCB	Eastern Caribbean Central Bank
ECCBA	Eastern Caribbean Central Bank Agreement
ECCM	East Caribbean Common Market
ECCU	Eastern Caribbean Currency Union
ECLA	United Nations Economic Commission for Latin America
EU	European Union
FCES	Foro Consultivo Económico Social
FONPLATA	Fondo Financiero para el Desarrollo de los Países de la Cuenca del Plata
FTAA	Free Trade Area of the Americas
FTAs	Free Trade Agreements
GMC	Grupo del Mercado Común
GNI	Gross National Income
GOAC	Gaceta Oficial del Acuerdo de Cartagena
HDI	Human Development Index
IADB	Inter-American Development Bank
IBERPYME	Iberoamerican Program for Inter-institutional Cooperation for the Development of Small and Medium-sized Businesses
IDA	International Development Association
IIRSA	Initiative for Regional Infrastructure Integration
ILC	International Law Commission
ILM	International Legal Materials
IO	International Organisation
JPC	Joint Parliamentary Commission
LAC	Latin American and Caribbean
LAFTA	Latin American Free Trade Association
MCC	Mercosur Commerce Commission
Mercosur	Southern Common Market
MIPYMES	Micro, Small and Medium-sized Businesses
NAFTA	North American Free Trade Association
OAS	Organization of American States
OECS	Organization of Eastern Caribbean States
Parlatino	Latin American Parliament
POP	Protocol of Ouro Preto
PYMES	Small and Medium-sized Businesses
RTA	Regional Trade Agreement
SACN	South American Community of Nations
SAFTA	South America Free Trade Area
SELA	Latin American Economic System/Latin American and Caribbean Economic System

SICA	Central American Integration System/Sistema de la Integración Centroamericana
SRDBs	Sub-Regional Development Banks
TCCJ	Treaty Creating the (Andean) Court of Justice
TFUE	Treaty on the Functioning of the European Union
TPR	Permanent Tribunal of Revision
TUE	Treaty of the European Union
UN	United Nations
UNASUR	Union of South American Nations
UNCTAD	United Nations Commission for Trade and Development
WISA	West Indies Associated States
WTO	World Trade Organization

Introduction: Mapping the Field of Latin American and Caribbean Institutions

Preliminary Remarks

The American continent represents a very interesting example of different forms of international organisations (IO) for different reasons. Historically, the continent has developed inter-state structures since the early nineteenth century. Over time various organisations have been created and replaced by other institutions both at regional and sub-regional levels.[1]

The original historical evolution of Latin American cooperation developed during and after the independence process from Spain. Simon Bolivar, the leader of independence in Spanish Latin America, envisaged the political unity of Latin America as a means to defuse regional conflicts, to establish the predominance of a regional international law, and to reduce the vulnerability of the Latin American countries to the actions of some powers, in particular Spain, Great Britain and the United States of America (USA).[2] The initial inter-State cooperation took the form of regular congresses usually called Hispanic-American or Latin American Congresses,[3] moved then into Pan Americanism, and finally to the present Inter-American System, represented by the Organisation of American States (OAS).[4]

The continent also shows different types of organisations that combine very different countries, often linked by geographical vicinity and cultural similarities, as in the case of the Andean Community or some Central American and Caribbean organisations. The presence of the USA is certainly a relevant factor in the

---

[1]Mace 1988, pp. 404–427.

[2]See: Belaúnde 1967.

[3]This term was used from the First Congress of Panama in 1826, when still some American territories were under Spanish colonial domination, until 1889 when Brazil joined the meetings organzsed by Spanish-speaking American countries.

[4]See: Stoetzer 1993, Chapters 1 and 2; Ball, 1969, pp. 3–21; Inter-American Institute of International Legal Studies 1966.

development or failure of many forms of IOs in the continent.[5] This element was in part based on the 1823 Monroe's Doctrine, and later reaffirmed by the USA foreign policy towards the continent and individual countries. However, the hegemonic role of the USA, with its economic and military power is not the only reason for some of the shortcomings of the various attempts to create functioning international institutions within the continent.

The approach of many countries in the region, including a strong nationalistic feeling, the protectionist economic policies of some governments, depending on the period of time, the political crisis and instability that affected several countries, particularly in the 1960s and 1970s, the military juntas which governed several countries in Latin America since the end of World War II until the late 1970s, are all relevant factors that have limited the forms of institutional cooperation, and have often undermined their development towards forms of stronger integration.

In this sense, if we compare the experience of several past and existing IOs in the Americas and the European continental experience, it is possible to see how European countries, which have many more cultural, linguistic and historical differences, have moved much faster towards forms of economic, political and legal integration. The main examples of the European Union (EU) and the Council of Europe (CoE), with the variety of institutions, courts and legal integration, including economic integration, are certainly unknown in the context of the American continent. Some examples of recent developments in the case of the Andean Community and the MERCOSUR may show some similarities with the developments of the EU; for instance the introduction of international adjudicatory bodies for dispute resolution and the introduction of the Andean Passport. However, despite the formal adoption of certain legal agreements and institutions, these developments look more as a copy on paper of the EU system rather than as an effective system of profound integration.

The present book addresses, from an international legal perspective, some of the relevant sub-regional institutions and organisations that are presently established in the Latin American part of the Western Hemisphere, following some criteria that are defined below.

Criteria of Inclusion and Exclusion

The original idea for this book was to develop a better understanding of the existing forms of institutional integration at the sub-regional level in the Americas. During the development of the project, some selection criteria have emerged, so that the book could take a more defined shape and offer the reader some understanding of the complex picture that is presently characterizing the various international institutions within the Latin American and Caribbean (LAC) parts of the continent.

---

[5]Langley 2010.

It has been relevant to identify more clearly the organisations and institutions that operate in the Western Hemisphere. The pan-continental organisation is the OAS which derives from an evolution of nineteenth century alliances and cooperation within the American continent, and includes today the great majority of States in the region, from North to South America.

However, the great experience and developments of the OAS have not been included in this study, as it may deserve a more specialist approach and also adequate space to properly address the various areas that are covered by its constitutive treaty and its various institutions and organs. For this reason, the OAS has been excluded *a priori* from this study.

If we look at the various institutions and organisations that are present in the Latin American part of the continent, we can find a great variety of examples over the past 50 years.[6] First of all, they are all in the LAC part of the continent. The Latin American and Caribbean choice is based on the fact that the great variety of existing institutions is mainly developed in that sub-region. There are different names used to classify certain regions and sub-regions in the world. Certainly, in the Americas, the geographical locations of North, Centre and South are often used. However, there are also different ways to identify certain regions. We intend for Latin America the portion of the American continent, which for historical and geographical reasons has been identified from Mexico to south Argentina and Chile (*Tierra del fuego*), mainly the Magellan straight. The sub-region includes also the Caribbean and Central American sub-regions,[7] which encompasses not only Spanish speaking countries, but also French, Dutch and British overseas territories. This definition is based on the Latin influence on the continent at the time of colonisation (Latin languages such as Spanish, Portuguese and then French), where the results of imposition of cultural and ideological models were certainly not autonomously developed, but reflected the influence of colonial powers in the region.[8]

In determining which institutions were to be included in this study, two main criteria were relied upon. The institutions included in this volume satisfy the following requirements. In the first place, all the organisations have, as their main purposes, the development of some or all of their member countries. Although some of the constitutive treaties are worded mainly in terms of economic development, others contain measures for social development as well. As will be seen in specific chapters, clear-cut separations between the two are almost impossible

---

[6]On the peculiar features of the LAC region, see among others: Centro Latinoamericano para la Competitividad y el Desarrollo Sostenible (CLACDS) del INCAE y el Instituto para el Desarrollo Internacional de la Universidad de Harvard (2000); Pennetta 2013; Schelhase 2011, p. 175 ff.

[7]On the peculiarities of the Central American sub-regions, see: Vuskovic 1983, p. 36 ff. For a full discussion of this issue, see: Woodward 1999, p. 20 ff, who also stresses the potential of the Central American states for political union.

[8]Zanatta 2010, p. 233 ff.

to draw and there is often a wide overlapping and interdependence between the two notions of development. Second, they are all established under international law, therefore they are international intergovernmental organisations and they have been created by states by means of international treaties, which are also their legal basis and confer upon them corporate personality. Therefore, other institutions, which are based on governmental departments, national public corporations, private multinational corporations and other forms of cooperation have been excluded from this book.

The main focus of this book is to deal with what is often referred to as International Institutional Law or Law of International Organisations.[9] The different institutions and organisations are mainly examined from the legal point of view. The scope is therefore to provide the reader with a good panorama of the rules and principles that govern the structures and functioning of international organisations within the Latin American geo-political context. Therefore, this study does not address other issues that are often related to the analysis of international relations within the context of structured institutions, in particular the relationship and possible tensions between the institutions and their member States. Also, this work does not address the political, social and economic contexts where institutions are operating. This is a relevant element that can shed light on the potential success and/or failure of inter-state cooperation. However, it should be the object of a separate study. The aims, purposes and functions of the organisations under consideration are certainly taken into consideration, as they are a fundamental part of the institutional *raison d'être*, the justification, of each individual organisation. They are often part of the foundational charter or treaty which created the organisation and they are essential elements that provide the general guidelines and powers of individual organs of each organisation. However, a detailed analysis of the policies and functions of international organisations requires a different type of research that goes beyond the limits of the present work.

Organisation of the Volume

Not all the existing organisations that are presently active in Latin America have been included in the present work. Also, past organisations or others which are not any more active, but still formally existing, have not been considered in this work. Examples of these are the Rio Group, the Latin American Parliament (Parlatino) and the Bolivarian Alliance for the Peoples of our America (ALBA).[10] The reason for this selection is that this book would like to provide the reader with an updated and useful contemporary study on the forms of international institutional organisations in the sub-region.

---

[9]See, among others: Schermers and Blokker 2011; White 2005; Amerasinghe 2005.
[10]See: Santulli 2012.

Apart from the mentioned criteria for selecting certain organisations, it is not always easy to further classify international institutions. Different criteria can be used, including chronological, historical, fields of activities, aims and purposes, etc. Therefore, the organisations that have been addressed follow certain criteria.

The main criteria for selecting existing organisations have been based on the number of member states, the extent of their aims, going from broader to narrower organisations. However, we are aware that this is not the only possible option, as other ways of organising the volume would have been equally feasible. The structure of the volume is as follows:

1. Latin American Economic System (SELA)
2. Latin American Integration Association (ALADI)
3. UNASUR
4. Latin American Sub-regional Development Institutions
5. Andean Community
6. Southern Common Market (MERCOSUR)
7. Pacific Alliance
8. Caribbean Community (CARICOM)
9. Organization of Eastern Caribbean States (OECS).

The volume is divided into nine main chapters, and this brief introduction focuses on individual Latin American sub-regional organisations. The editors have sought to make this work an integrated volume rather than merely a set of essays. In achieving this aim, they have circulated drafts of relevant papers to contributors when appropriate, during the process of revision, in order to facilitate cross-referencing and discussion on disputed concepts.

Chapter 1 looks at the Latin American Economic System (*Sistema Económico Latinoamericano*—SELA) which since 1975 includes 25 Latin American and Caribbean (LAC) nations which established a permanent system for intraregional economic and social cooperation, in order to coordinate and consult on the positions of those countries in relation to third countries and other international organisations.

Chapter 2 considers the Latin American Integration Association (ALADI) which replaced the Latin American Free Trade Association (LAFTA), the first incarnation of regionalized trade in South America, replaced by the 1980 Montevideo Treaty creating a new association, the Latin American Integration Association (LAIA or ALADI in Spanish), currently including 12 states of the region. This chapter considers that the integration envisioned by ALADI is challenging because it relies on other existing institutions, but without altering the pre-existing legal structure of trade relationships. It looks at the challenges of regional integration in Latin America and the possible legal structure that may implement economic integration.

Chapter 3 deals with the Union of South American Nations (UNASUR), which represents one of the most recent attempts of regional integration. The adoption in Brasilia, in 2008, of the Treaty establishing the UNASUR is the end of a process that led to the establishment of a framework of cooperation and integration among several South American States. UNASUR opens a new phase in the efforts made by South American States to achieve some of the objectives that have been on the agenda of Latin American international relations. The relevance of UNASUR is that it tries to achieve a more comprehensive, legal, institutionalised and developed framework of cooperation. In particular, this new development of institutionalisation foresees a gradual integration process that also involves two major existing organisations, MERCOSUR/MERCOSUL (*Mercado Común del Sur*) and the Andean Community of Nations (CAN).

Chapter 4 considers the specific case of Latin American sub-regional development institutions. This type of multilateral organisation is playing a rapidly increasing role in the supply of development finance and technical assistance to the countries of the LAC region. Evidence is also to be found in the following two circumstances. First, like reserve pooling institutions sub-regional multilateral organisations in general and international sub-regional banks in particular are helping countries of the region to mobilize financial resources for productive activities. Second, and even more significantly, sub-regional multilateral development organisations are helping the LAC countries to increase their role and level of integration in international capital and financial markets while also strengthening their internal capital markets. For instance, they are improving their funding conditions and issuing bonds in Latin American currencies.

Jointly with global multilateral financial institutions, international sub-regional development banks are also supporting LAC countries in the current financial crisis by supplying liquidity. Therefore, for these and other reasons, the wealthier countries of the LAC region, such as Brazil and Mexico, have allocated and still continue to allocate increased resources to these organisations, and have also in several circumstances taken their views into consideration in their own action plans and programmes. However, though surprising, the wide and fast-growing role of sub-regional multilateral institutions in the international financial system has as yet received very little attention from an international legal perspective.

The overall goal of this chapter is to fill this gap, and therefore to critically review the experience of LAC countries with international sub-regional development and financial cooperation. Starting from the premise that this experience has been one of the most successful in the developing world (though uneven in terms of country coverage and services provided), the chapter will show that the Andean sub-region has been particularly successful in establishing sub-regional multilateral institutions in the fields of development and finance. The chapter will also indicate that development financing in the LAC region has been wider in scope than cooperation in monetary matters. In doing so, it will stress in particular that the two most successful sub-regional financial institutions, namely the Andean Development Corporation (CAF) and the Central American Bank for Economic Integration (CABEI), have shown the capacity to supply services to member countries in a timely way, with counter-cyclical effects and on a wider scale relative to other types of multilateral financing.

Indeed, the genuine sense of ownership of these organisations by member states, preferred creditor status, and professional management is reflected in very healthy portfolios, even in the face of default by member countries. This is so even though the services of these institutions could be broadened to support also the growth and integration of the physical infrastructure and macro-economic policy coordination. Concerning its overall structure, this chapter is divided into two main parts. In the first part, it will ascertain and critically discuss and evaluate, from an international legal perspective, the relative position of international sub-regional financial institutions within the LAC region, focussing both on their financial role and on how they provide a set of tools to channel financial resources, technical assistance and knowledge to countries of this region. In the second part, through a consideration of the structure and functioning of the CABEI and CAF the chapter will elaborate recommendations and draw some conclusions about the international sub-regional institutions in the fields of development and finance that operate in the LAC region, and how they can better enhance sub-regional cooperation and promote collective action.

Chapter 5 analyses the Andean Community (*Comunidad Andina de Naciones*—CAN). This quite unique example of integration process in the LAC region represents probably the closer type of international organisation with structures similar to the EU. The Andean Community is also the result of an evolution which originated with the Andean Pact and with subsequent amendments to the original treaty and protocols has become today the Andean Community. This organisation includes some elements of supranational bodies, a legal system and a specific judicial body, which provide a relevant example of legal structures which tend to go beyond the mere rhetoric of integration which is typical of other institutions in the region.

Chapter 6 addresses the 'Common Market of the Southern Cone', commonly known as MERCOSUR. This organisation, jointly with the Andean Community, includes the main countries of the region, and it has been for many years a good example of international cooperation among the countries of the Southern Cone (Argentina, Brazil, Paraguay, Uruguay) and Venezuela (since 2012). The first and main objective of MERCOSUR is trade liberalisation, more precisely the creation of a free trade area between its members and the implementation of a *sui generis* common market. This chapter takes the EU and the North American Free Trade Association (NAFTA) as points of reference, since a conceptual comparison between a MERCOSUR-type free trade area and a NAFTA-type free trade area or an EU-model customs union may demonstrate the relative uniformity of these types of trading conglomerates but also their functional and taxonomic diversities. The chapter assesses MERCOSUR's main achievements and shortcomings in the areas of socio-economic cooperation and sub-regional integration, and the effective achievement of its objectives, including, from an international legal perspective, the latest developments within MERCOSUR.

Chapter 7 analyses the Pacific Alliance, the most recent tool of LAC integration, which was established by the so-called 'Framework Agreement' signed on the occasion of the 2012 Summit of Paranal. The Alliance realizes a shift of focus in the economic strategy of integration applied for instance by MERCOSUR, which was grounded on the establishment of an outward-looking Common

Market. The inherent tension/contradiction between the normative institutional architecture and declared economic and social objectives has been the true 'leit-motif' of the Latin American and Caribbean experiences of integration since 1980 when the Latin American Integration Association (ALADI),[11] the first 'real' experience of integration in Latin America was pursued under the Treaty of Montevideo. This trend was confirmed by the Asuncion Treaty, which created the MERCOSUR.[12] Moreover, it was further confirmed by the 2012 'Framework Agreement' which establishes the Alliance. All these agreements were aimed to establish areas of regional economic integration in Latin America. In the 'Framework Agreement', nevertheless, this incompatibility is more evident, because the economic commitment for creating a common space for the movement of goods, services, capitals and people has been more emphasized than on former occasions.

Chapter 8 is devoted to the Caribbean Community (CARICOM), addressing a specific organisation in the Caribbean sub-region. The Treaty of Chaguaramas, establishing the CARICOM became operative in August 1973; there were great expectations that at long last there was in place an institutional framework for economic integration in the Caribbean. This invariably implied that the challenge of market fragmentation would be an issue of the past and intra-regional commerce would also be enhanced. Forty years and more after the entry into force of the Treaty of Chaguaramas (and 12 years after the entry into force of the Revised Treaty of Chaguaramas), not much progress has been made in terms of the economic integration and de-fragmentation of Caribbean markets. Issues abound at present as to whether the CARICOM, one of the world's oldest still-functioning regional economic institutions, would ever be able to survive and if it does, whether it would at last plug the Caribbean region into the grid of global commerce. This chapter holds that there are still some weak areas in the institutional and normative framework of the Revised Treaty of Chaguaramas that could not properly support market integration. It suggests that the CARICOM needs to play a greater role in ensuring that this weak framework is further strengthened.

The final chapter looks at the Organisation of Eastern Caribbean States (OECS) and at its institutional evolution. The 1981 original agreement was not conceived as a platform for a political or economic union, and consequently did not commit its member states to achieving such a union in time. By the year 2000, however, OECS states began to explore the fundamentals of some form of economic union, as well as a closer integration in other policy areas. In January 2011, this vision became a reality, with the entry into force of the 2011 Revised Treaty of Basseterre, which transformed the structure and operation of the union into a modern regional trade agreement (RTA), which may be viewed as a variant of the Treaty of the European Union.

---

[11]See Chap. 2 of this volume.
[12]See Chap. 6 of this volume.

Final Remarks

On the basis of the findings described in the individual chapters a number of general considerations can be drawn. We perceive to be useful, at the outset, to briefly stress the variety of approaches in the field of institutional cooperation adopted by the main organisations, which is the central theme of this collective work, as developed in the single contributions.

There is a long and well-established experience in different forms of international institutional cooperation. This means that states in the LAC region are familiar with this type of international framework and the normative structures that are associated to these institutions, but still show underdeveloped forms of integration.

The Andean Community provides a good example of how Latin American countries can follow the path of gradual integration. This is true despite the fact that the Community is still a quite undeveloped model of supranational integration, at least if compared to the EU experience. In fact, the EU provides the most sophisticated example of existing integration process from a legal perspective.[13]

At this point it is worth asking whether the Andean Community might represent a model to follow for sub-regional integration in the LAC region. Our answer is positive, due to the fact that the Community has proved to be able to achieve some forms of integration through institutional cooperation.[14] If generally adopted, this model would reduce the number of existing inter-governmental sub-regional organisations, which would be followed by adhesion of new members to the existing ones, or eventually to a possible fusion of the main sub-regional organisations, in particular the Andean Community and the MERCOSUR. If supported by the political will of individual states in the LAC region, this process would contribute to avoid an overlapping of institutions and structures, it might also rationalise the financial implications and, most importantly, ensure the efficient functioning of remaining sub-regional structures, as the EU example shows.

However, recent developments in the LAC region, such as the case of the Pacific Alliance, seem to go in the opposite directions due to the fact that the Pacific Alliance does not seek to create a customs union or a common market. Yet, the Alliance can mainly be considered as a free-market alternative to the less dynamic and rather protectionist MERCOSUR, a comparable organisation in terms of size and economic weight. Unlike the Andean Community, this new organisation established in 2012, does not adopt a supranational normative model leading to integration in a technical sense, but rather applies a more traditional

---

[13]See: Augenstein 2013; Biondi and Eeckhout 2012; Craig and de Búrca 2011.

[14]See, for instance: CAN, Andean Council of Foreign Ministers, Association of the Republic of Argentina, the Federative Republic of Brazil, the Republic of Paraguay and the Eastern Republic of Uruguay, States Parties of MERCOSUR, with the Andean Community, Decision 613, Lima, 7 July 2005, at: http://www.comunidadandina.org/ingles/normativa/D613e.htm. Accessed 17 September 2014.

approach of inter-state cooperation under international law. In other words, the Alliance's approach is mainly inter-governmental and pragmatic.

Parallel to this trend we can identify a more integrationist attitude within the UNASUR framework, as evidenced in the Preamble to its constitutive treaty which states that 'South American integration should be achieved through an innovative process, which includes all the accomplishments and progress achieved so far by the MERCOSUR and CAN processes, as well as the experiences of Chile, Guyana and Suriname, going beyond the convergence among them'.[15]

Nevertheless, the integrationist approach of UNASUR is, in some way, narrowed by the reference, in the same Preamble of its constitutive treaty, to the 'unlimited respect for sovereignty and the territorial integrity and inviolability of States'.

The same treaty includes in its objectives and purposes a broad set of cooperation areas, from citizenship to energy integration and from financial integration to consolidation of a South American identity,[16] however, there is no evidence of adequate legal and institutional support in the architecture of the organisation.

Marco Odello
Francesco Seatzu

References

Amerasinghe C F (2005) Principles of the Institutional Law of International Organizations. 2nd rev. ed. Cambridge University Press, Cambridge

Augenstein D (ed.) (2013) 'Integration through law' Revisited: The Making of the European Polity. Ashgate, Farnham

Ball M M (1969) The OAS in transition. Duke University Press, Durham, N.C.

Belaúnde V A (1967) Bolívar and the Political Thought of the Spanish American Revolution. Octagon Books, New York

Biondi A and Eeckhout P (eds) (2011) EU Law after Lisbon. Oxford University Press, Oxford

Centro Latinoamericano para la Competitividad y el Desarrollo Sostenible (CLACDS) del INCAE y el Instituto para el Desarrollo Internacional de la Universidad de Harvard (2000) Centroamérica en el siglo XXI: una agenda para la competitividad y el desarrollo sostenible: bases para la discusión sobre el futuro de la región. Banco Centroamericano de Integración Económica, AVINA, at: http://www.incae.edu/EN/clacds/publicaciones/pdf/cen1000agenda.pdf. Accessed 11 December 2014

Craig P and de Búrca G (eds) The Evolution of EU Law. Oxford University Press, Oxford

Inter-American Institute of International Legal Studies (1966) The Inter-American System. Oceana Publications, Dobbs Ferry

Langley L D (2010) America and the Americas: The United States in the Western Hemisphere. 2nd ed. University of Georgia Press, Athens

---

[15]UNASUR Treaty, signed in Brasilia, 23 May 2008, entered into force on 11 March 2011, Preamble, at: https://treaties.un.org/pages/UNTSOnline.aspx?id=2. Accessed 11 December 2014.

[16]UNASUR Treaty, articles 2 and 3.

Mace G (1988) Regional Integration in Latin America: A Long and Winding Road. International Journal 43(3): 404–427

Pennetta P (2013) Consideraciones sobre los procesos de integración regional en Europa y América Latina. Cultura Latino Americana. Annali 15: 181–206

Santulli C (2012) Retour à la théorie de l'organe commun: réflexions sur la nature juridique des organisations internationales à partir du cas de l'Alba et de la Celac, comparées notamment à l'Union européenne et à l'O.N.U. Revue générale de droit international public 116: 565–578

Schelhase M (2011) The Changing Context of Regionalism and Regionalization in the Americas: Mercosur and Beyond. In: Shaw T M, Grant J A, Cornelissen S (eds), The Ashgate Research Companion to Regionalisms, Ashgate, Farnham, pp. 175–192

Schermers H G and Blokker N M (2011) *International Institutional Law: Unity within Diversity.* 5th rev. ed., Martinus Nijhoff Publishers, Leiden

Stoetzer O C (1993) The Organization of American States. 2nd ed. Praeger Westport: Conn.

Vuskovic P (1983) Economic Factors in the Evolution of Central American Societies. In: Fagen R R, Pellicer de Brody O, Aguilar Zinser A (eds) The Future of Central America: Policy Choices for the U.S. and Mexico. Stanford University Press, Stanford, pp. 35–45

White N D (2005) The Law of International Organisations. 2nd ed. Manchester University Press, Manchester

Woodward R L (1999) Central America, A Nation Divided. Oxford University Press, Oxford

Zanatta L (2010) Storia dell'America Latina contemporanea. Laterza, Bari

Chapter 1
The Economic System in Latin America and the Caribbean: A Commitment to the Development of the Region's Nations

Florabel Quispe Remón

Abstract This chapter looks at the Latin American Economic System (*Sistema Económico Latinoamericano*—SELA), which since 1975 includes 25 Latin American and Caribbean (LAC) nations which established a permanent system for intraregional economic and social cooperation, in order to coordinate and consult on the positions of those countries in relation to third countries and other international organizations. The origin, structure, institutions and functioning of SELA are addressed in the first sections. Then the chapter looks at specific areas of regional and extra-regional cooperation. These areas include economic and technical cooperation but also address the needs of small- and medium-sized businesses in LAC states.

Keywords Intraregional cooperation · Panama Convention · IBERPYME · MIPYMES · Small- and medium-sized businesses · ALCUE summits · South American-African Cooperation (ASA)

Contents

F. Quispe Remón (✉)
Department of Public International Law, University Carlos III, Madrid, Spain
e-mail: fquispe@der-pu.uc3m.es

© T.M.C. ASSER PRESS and the authors 2015   1
M. Odello and F. Seatzu (eds.), *Latin American and Caribbean International Institutional Law*, DOI 10.1007/978-94-6265-069-5_1

1.1 Introduction

Once the new Nations of Latin America achieved independence, their aspiration to unite in order to face any external attack was a persistent goal. This Bolivarian dream, however, was never fulfilled. The concept of integration, as it is known today, had its origins in the Latin America of the 1960s when, through the *Tratado de Montevideo* (Montevideo Treaty) in 1960, the *Asociación Latinoamericana de Libre Comercio* (ALALC, Latin American Free Trade Association) was first established; it became la *Asociación Latinoamericana de Integración* (ALADI, Latin American Integration Association)[1] 20 years later, and it still exists today.

Since then, given its scarce achievements, new subregional groups have been created according to their geographic location, with the hope of producing better results. This is how the *Comunidad Andina de Naciones* (CAN, Community of Andean Nations)[2] was created in 1969, the *Mercado Común del Sur* (MERCOSUR, Southern Common Market)[3] in 1991. Finally, in 2007, in order to form a unified block among the region's countries, the *Unión de Naciones Suramericanas* (UNASUR, Union of South American Nations),[4] which includes all of the countries that are members of the previously mentioned processes, was established.[5] All these processes shared the common objective of gradually and progressively establishing a strong Latin American common market. That is, they were based on trade and economic growth.

Latin American countries are conscious of the importance of working as a unified block, realizing that the road to reaching their goals will be smoother if they join forces. The synergy of States becomes more and more relevant to achieving objectives on a regional level and, even more, in the international context. For this reason, in 1975, 25 Latin American and Caribbean (LAC) states considered it necessary to establish a permanent system for intraregional economic and social cooperation, in order to coordinate and consult on the positions of the different countries before third countries, to create the *Sistema Económico Latinoamericano* (SELA, Latin American Economic System).[6] It is important to study this regional body, which has been functioning for more than three decades, in greater depth, as it is scarcely known in comparison with those mentioned above. In order to do this, it will be necessary to delve into its origins, its objectives and priorities, its organic structure, how it works and the work it has carried out during the years it

---

[1]See Chap. 2 in this book.

[2]See Chap. 5 in this book.

[3]See Chap. 6 in this book.

[4]See Chap. 3 in this book.

[5]A complete study of the integration processes in Latin America can be found, among others, in the special issue: Mundo Nuevo, Revista de Estudios Latinoamericanos, Universidad Simón Bolivar, Instituto de Altos Estudios de América Latina, Caracas Año II, N° 4 (Julio-Diciembre 2010); Quispe Remón 2010, at 259–292.

[6]See: Bond 1978; Zagaris 1978; Marinas Otero 1978.

has existed. This analysis will offer a general vision of its evolution, its effectiveness, the fulfilment of its objectives and its impact on the development of Latin America and the Caribbean.

1.2 The Origin of the SELA and Its Constitutional Treaty

In 1975, when states were negotiating the *Sistema Económico Latinoamericano* (Latin American Economic System),[7] known today as the *Sistema Económico Latinoamericano y del Caribe* (SELA, Latin American and Caribbean Economic System),[8] the Latin American countries' goal was to establish a permanent system of intraregional economic and social cooperation, for consulting and coordinating the different positions of America, whether before international bodies or before third countries or groups of countries. Their commitment was to create a permanent system that would include all of the nations in the region and that would make use of all of the agreements and principles adopted until that time by the countries of Latin America, as well as to achieve the economic and social development of its members. In addition, they considered it essential to create greater unity among the countries of Latin America in order to guarantee actions of solidarity in the area of intraregional economic and social cooperation, as well as to increase the region's negotiating power.

The treaty through which SELA was created, clearly established that all of the activities of this permanent system of intraregional coordination would be carried out based on the principles of equality, sovereignty, the independence of the Member States, solidarity, nonintervention in internal issues, reciprocal benefits and non-discrimination. A foundation of respect for the economic and social systems freely chosen by each of the countries was also included.

At the time SELA was created, given that some of the processes of integration in the region were incomplete, the Member States also considered it necessary to strengthen and complement those processes that were ongoing in many countries, through the joint promotion of programmes and projects specifically geared towards development. In fact, due to this commitment, even with the complex and ever-changing situation of regional integration, in the words of the current Permanent Secretary of SELA, as mandated by the Latin American Council, the Permanent Secretariat of SELA "maintains a constant monitoring and analysis of the evolution of the Latin American and Caribbean integration processes, with an emphasis on the institutional modifications that have taken place in the pre-existing structures and on the new initiatives that have been put in motion in recent years".[9]

---

[7]Panama Convention establishing the Latin American Economic System (SELA). Adopted on 17 October 1975 at Panama City, entry into force on 7 June 1976. 15 ILM 1081 (1976).

[8]In November 2005, the Latin American Council, during the XXXI Ordinary Meeting, agreed to modify the name without changing the SELA acronym.

[9]Rivera Banuet 2010, at 19.

SELA came about as a result of the Reunión de Panamá (Panama Meeting), held from July 31 to August 2, 1975, in which 25 nations reached a consensus regarding its creation, and approved its Constitutional Treaty.[10] The Panama Convention, as the document is known, was registered with the General Secretary of the United Nations through the Government of Venezuela, its trustee.

SELA's constituting document may be reformed by means of a proposal made by any of the Member States, once it is approved by the Latin American Council. The Convention does not have an expiration date. It will be in effect indefinitely. However, any of the Member States may renounce its membership by means of written communication to the Government of Venezuela, which will transmit it as quickly as possible to the other Member Nations. Ninety days after the notification is delivered to the Venezuelan Government, the Convention will be declared null and void with respect to the renouncing Nation. While it is true that the Government of Venezuela is the trustee of the Constituting Treaty, it seems surprising that a Nation must renounce its membership to the Government of Venezuela and not before a SELA body. As a regional international organization, it has a permanent structure which allows it to function, even though it does not have its own territory. And it has its own legal status, different from that of each of the countries.[11] In fact, according to the Panama Convention, the SELA, its bodies, the civil servants of the Permanent Secretariat and Government Representatives will enjoy privileges and immunities that are necessary for carrying out their functions in all of the territories of each of the Member States, and the corresponding agreements will be made with the Venezuelan government and the other Member States (Article 37). This is an example of one of the manifestations of its legal status. In addition, SELA can sign international treaties (Headquarters Agreement signed by SELA and Venezuela, March 27, 1978).

According to its constituting treaty, the SELA "is a permanent regional body for consultation, coordination, cooperation and joint economic and social promotion, with an international legal status, made up of sovereign Latin American nations".

The SELA has its headquarters in Caracas, Venezuela, and is made up of 28 Latin American and Caribbean countries. Grenada, El Salvador and Costa Rica were the most recent countries to become members, joining in 2008, 2009 and 2010 respectively. A large number of the Member States joined during the 1970s,

---

[10]The 25 nations (Argentina, Bolivia, Barbados, Brazil, Colombia, Costa Rica, Cuba, Chile, Ecuador, El Salvador, Grenada, Guatemala, Guyana, Haiti, Honduras, Jamaica, Mexico, Nicaragua, Panama, Paraguay, Peru, Dominican Republic, Trinidad and Tobago, Uruguay and Venezuela) which signed the Panama Convention constituting the SELA (October 1975) were slow to ratify it, which delayed its taking effect.

[11]See: Díez de Velasco 2008.

with Paraguay joining in the 1980s and the Bahamas and Belize becoming members in the 1990s.[12] SELA's official languages are Spanish, French, English and Portuguese.

It can be noted that in 1990, 70 % of the total population of the SELA countries (427 million) was concentrated in Brazil, Mexico, Colombia and Argentina. Twenty years later, in 2010, that percentage was almost the same, although the total population of the SELA nations had increased to 571 million inhabitants. As a means of comparison, we can point out that in 2009 the European Union (formed by 27 countries) had approximately 500 million inhabitants and the United States, around 307 million inhabitants.

Each of the 28 Member States presents a different reality as a result of its different economic, social and developmental idiosyncrasies. In order to characterize the level of development of the SELA countries, the 2010 Human Development Index (HDI), prepared by the United Nations Development Programme (UNDP), has been used due to its broad focus.

Table 1.1 presents information on the population (in millions of inhabitants) and the HDI for the years 1990 and 2010 for each country, in order to visualize its evolution. In addition, there is information regarding gross national income (GNI) purchasing power parity—PPP—in 2008 US$.

Graph 1.1 shows that the HDI and GNI are correlative, thus following the same tendency. It should be pointed out that only three countries surpass US$ 20000 in GNI and that of those, two have the highest GNIs (Bahamas and Barbados). At the other extreme, Haiti presents both the lowest GNI and HDI of the system.

SELA's objectives are mainly the promotion of regional cooperation in order to achieve complete, self-sustaining and independent development, particularly by means of activities designed to bring about better use of the region's natural, human, technical and financial resources through the creation and promotion of Latin American multinational companies. These companies may be set up using government, semi-public, private, or mixed funding and their national character can be guaranteed by the respective Member States. Their activities would be subject to the jurisdiction and supervision of the national governments. These companies would: increase the capacity for negotiations to acquire capital and technological goods; promote cooperation among the member countries in the area of tourism; stimulate cooperation for the protection, conservation and improvement of the environment; collaborate with those countries that face situations of economic emergency, as well as those emergencies caused by natural disasters; and cooperate in any other activity that may contribute to achieving the economic, social and cultural development of the region.

---

[12]Argentina (10/01/1977), Bahamas (25/03/1998), Barbados (4/06/1976), Belize (6/03/1992), Bolivia (7/06/1976), Brazil (14/05/1976), Chile (18/10/1977), Colombia (18/06/1979), Costa Rica (28/10/2010), Cuba (14/01/1976), Ecuador (2/04/1976), El Salvador (29/10/2009), Grenada (25/11/2008), Guatemala (2/11/1976), Guyana (17/01/1976), Haiti (17/03/1977), Honduras (14/06/1976), Jamaica (4/04/1976), Mexico (14/01/1976), Nicaragua (2/02/1976), Panama (4/12/1975), Paraguay (19/09/1986), Peru (29/04/1976), Dominican Republic (4/06/1976), Suriname (27/07/1979), Trinidad and Tobago (7/06/1976), Uruguay (16/03/1977) and Venezuela (14/01/1976).

Table 1.1 Population data (Pop), human development index (HDI) and gross national income (GNI) of SELA member countries (*Na* not available)

Country	Pop 1990	Pop 2010	HDI 1990	HDI 2010	GNI 2008
Argentina	32.5	40.7	0.682	0.775	14.603
Bahamas	0.3	0.3	Na	0.784	25.201
Barbados	0.3	0.3	Na	0.788	21.673
Belize	0.2	0.3	Na	0.694	5.693
Bolivia	6.7	10	Na	0.643	4.357
Brazil	149.6	195.4	Na	0.699	10.607
Chile	13.2	17.1	0.675	0.783	13.651
Colombia	33.2	46.3	0.579	0.689	8.589
Costa Rica	3.1	4.6	0.639	0.725	10.870
Cuba	Na	Na	Na	Na	Na
Ecuador	10.3	13.8	0.612	0.695	7.931
El Salvador	5.3	6.2	0.511	0.659	6.498
Grenada	0.1	0.1	Na	Na	7.998
Guatemala	8.9	14.4	0.451	0.56	4.694
Guyana	0.7	0.8	0.472	0.611	3.302
Haiti	7.1	10.2	–	0.404	949
Honduras	4.9	7.6	0.495	0.604	3.750
Jamaica	2.4	2.7	0.62	0.688	7.207
Mexico	83.4	110.6	0.635	0.75	13.971
Nicaragua	4.1	5.8	0.454	0.565	2.567
Panama	2.4	3.5	0.644	0.755	13.347
Paraguay	4.2	6.5	0.557	0.64	4.585
Peru	21.8	29.5	0.608	0.723	8.424
Dominican Rep.	7.4	10.2	0.56	0.663	8.273
Suriname	0.4	0.5	–	0.646	7.093
Trinidad and Tobago	1.2	1.3	0.66	0.736	24.233
Uruguay	3.1	3.4	0.67	0.765	13.808
Venezuela	19.7	29	0.62	0.696	11.846

Source Created by the author based on 2010 Human Development Report by the United Nations Development Programme

A second objective is to support the processes of integration in the region and generate activities coordinated to those processes, or with the SELA countries, especially those actions that tend towards harmonization and convergence, always respecting those commitments that have been made as part of each of the processes.

Another objective is to promote the design and execution of economic and social programmes and projects that are of interest to the member countries. SELA also includes among its objectives to act as a mechanism for consultation and coordination in Latin America for the adoption of common positions and strategies on economic issues in international bodies and forums and before third countries

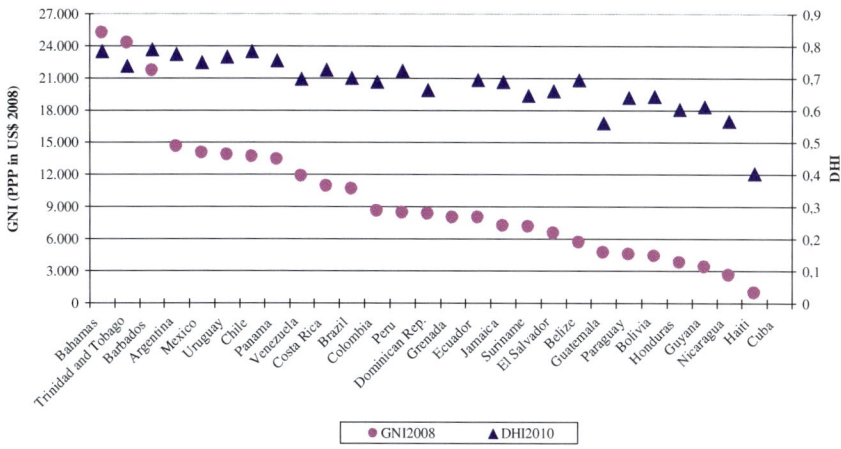

Graph 1.1 Gross national income and human development index for SELA countries (*Source* created by the author based on data from the 2010 Human Development Report published by UNDP)

and groups of countries. Finally, according to its constituting treaty, SELA has, within the context of its objective of intraregional cooperation, to provide a means of assuring preferential treatment towards relatively less developed countries and special measures for countries with limited markets and those whose geographic condition affects their development, while keeping in mind the economic conditions of each of the Member States.

1.3 SELA's Structure and Operation

As a regional organization, SELA has a solid permanent structure that allows for its day-to-day work to go on. This organizational structure consists of the Latin American Council (the Council), the Action Committees (the Committees) and the Permanent Secretariat (the Secretariat).

1.3.1 The Latin American Council

The Council is made up of representatives of each Member State,[13] with voting rights, and it meets once a year in a regular meeting (during the first trimester of

---

[13]Besides choosing a representative, each government may name the advisers and delegates it considers necessary.

the year) at the ministerial level (preceded by a preparatory meeting)[14] and in an extraordinary meeting, ministerial or not, when it is considered necessary (decided at the ordinary meeting or at the request of one-third of the Member States). The Council's meetings are held in the Permanent Secretariat's Headquarters (Caracas, Venezuela), unless it is decided by consensus to meet in another venue.

Their decisions are made by consensus when the subject is general policy, the interpretation of and proposals for amendments to the organization's Constituting Convention, and the approval of common positions and strategies; other decisions, such as the approval of the budget and SELA's work programme, are decided by a two-thirds majority of the members that are present, or by an absolute majority of the Member States, depending on the case, as is stipulated in the Constituting Treaty (Article 17).

This is SELA's highest governing body and it has the task, among others, of establishing the body's general policies; approving its Regulations and that of the other bodies; electing and removing the Permanent Secretary and the Adjunct Permanent Secretary; establishing and approving the body's budget and finances; making decisions regarding the interpretation of SELA's constituting document, the amendments proposed by the Member States and adopting the measures necessary for their execution; considering and approving the Permanent Secretariat's reports, proposals and work programme; examining, orienting and approving the activities of SELA's various bodies; adopting the measures needed to achieve the organization's objectives; considering the Action Committee's reports; approving the Member Nation's common positions and strategies regarding economic and social themes before third parties, whether they be international organizations, other countries, etc. However, it must be clearly stated that this body cannot, under any circumstances, adopt decisions that affect the national policies of the Member States.

The Latin American Council was created by the Panama Convention, as previously mentioned, but its internal regime is ruled by its Regulations[15] as are those of its subsidiary bodies. Nevertheless, if a case that is not foreseen in the Convention or the Regulations should arise, it would be resolved by the Latin American Council.

---

[14]The preparatory meetings of the Latin American Council are private and geared towards reaching agreements on planning the agenda; on recommendations regarding specific topics on the agenda; the possible establishment of commissions or working groups; and other subjects that facilitate the Council's meeting.

[15]The Latin American Council's Regulations were approved by the Latin American Council in its Decision N° 1, adopted at its I Ordinary Meeting, held in Panama, on October 17, 1975 and ratified at its First Extraordinary Meeting, held in Caracas, Venezuela on January 14, 1976.

1.3.2 The Action Committee

This is a body created by the Panama Convention and its operation is governed by the Action Committees' Regulations[16] and if a situation that is not foreseen in the Regulations should present itself, it will be resolved by the Latin American Council. The Action Committees will be made up of more than two of SELA's Member States that are interested in carrying out joint programmes and projects on specific themes. Thus, the main objective is to carry out the specific cooperative studies, programmes and projects between the Member States and the preparation and adoption of joint negotiating positions, as long as these are compatible with SELA's objectives, do not have discriminatory effects and do not create a conflict that would be detrimental to other Member States. The Action Committees may create Working Groups or adopt the operating procedures they consider necessary for achieving their objectives.

The temporary functions of these Action Committees end when they have concluded their tasks or when the number of States that are party to them falls to fewer than three. The fulfilment of the objectives that have to do with regional cooperation, through the Action Committees, is only obligatory for those Member States that are participating in them.

The Action Committees are formed by the representatives of the Member States that are interested in participating, based on the subject to be dealt with. Each Action Committee establishes its own secretariat, which will be in charge of supporting and coordinating the Action Committees' tasks and will act as an intermediary between the Committee and the Permanent Secretary. The Member States that are not participating may attend the Plenary Meetings of the Action Committees as observers.

The Action Committees' Regulations allow any State participating in the Action Committee to propose its withdrawal from the Committee at any time by means of a written document directed to the other Member States that are part of the Committee and to the Permanent Secretary. The withdrawal will take effect 90 days after the Permanent Secretary has received the notification; nevertheless, the State that withdraws will be responsible for all of the obligations that it may have assumed up until the time of the notification of its withdrawal. The Regulations, however, stipulate that the Member States that participate in an Action Committee may, by consensus, establish different rules regarding the withdrawal of a Member State from the Action Committee.

The Action Committees are constituted through a decision made by the Latin American Council, a decision made by the interested States, or a proposal made by the Council's Permanent Secretary. Once constituted, the Committees must

---

[16]Approved by the Latin American Council in its Decision Number 5, adopted in its First Ordinary Meeting, held in Panama October 17, 1975 and ratified in its First Extraordinary Meeting held in Venezuela in January 1976.

inform the Permanent Secretary, so that she/he can then inform the other Member States. The Committees must report to the Permanent Secretary on their advances and the results of their work, and they must present an annual report regarding their activities to the Council. In addition, the Member States may request information from the Permanent Secretary regarding the Action Committees' operations whenever they consider it pertinent.

The economic support for the creation of the Committees corresponds to the Member States that participate in them. This means that when a Committee concludes its activity, the participating Member States must adopt the necessary measures to repay any debts and to liquidate the Committee's funds and assets. The commitments adopted by the Action Committee imply financial obligations on the part of the participating Member States only.

1.3.3 Permanent Secretariat

The Secretariat's headquarters are in Caracas, Venezuela. This body is the technical administrative body of the organization. It carries out the functions assigned to it by the Panama Convention, the Permanent Secretariat's Regulations[17] and the assignments conferred on it by the Latin American Council, in the same way as other previously mentioned bodies do. It is directed by a Permanent Secretary, who is elected by the Latin American Council for a 4-year period, and who must be a citizen of one of the Member States. She/he will be in charge of the technical administrative personnel needed to run the Permanent Secretariat.[18] She/he will have a voice in the Latin American Council, but not a vote. The Permanent Secretary will have an Adjunct Permanent Secretary who will help with the coordination and supervision of the various units that are part of the Permanent Secretariat.

Among others, the responsibilities of the Permanent Secretariat are to carry out the functions assigned to it by the Latin American Council and, when appropriate, execute its decisions; to propose to the Council programmes and projects of common interest that will have an impact on achieving the organization's objectives; to facilitate the activities of the Action Committees and to contribute to the coordination among them, including helping to carry out the corresponding studies, presenting the financial reports to the Latin American Council for its consideration; subject to the Council's approval, to promote and agree upon certain actions to carry out studies, programmes and projects with international bodies

---

[17]It has 37 articles. It was approved by the Latin American Council in its Decision N° 145, adopted at the VIII Ordinary Meeting, in Caracas, August 23–25, 1982.

[18]According to Article 28 of SELA's Constituting Treaty the Permanent Secretary may be re-elected once, but not for consecutive periods, and cannot be substituted by a person of the same nationality.

and institutions, basically those that are regional, or national (of the Member States and other countries) in character; to prepare an annual report on its activities to submit for the consideration of the Latin American Council at its Ordinary Meeting and coordinate, during this period, the presentation of the Action Committees' reports, apart from the direct reports that the Committees present to the Council. The Permanent Secretariat may hire consultants, preferably citizens of the Member States, for brief periods, in order to carry out specific functions that may be transitory in nature.

The Permanent Secretary is the legal representative of the Permanent Secretariat and when the Latin American Council deems it so, she/he is the legal representative of SELA. She/he is responsible to the Latin American Council for adequately fulfilling the Permanent Secretariat's responsibilities. Neither the Permanent Secretary nor the Secretariat's staff may receive instructions from any government, national or international body with regard to the fulfilment of their duties. The responsibility for directing the Permanent Secretariat falls on the Permanent Secretary, who must carry out her/his assigned duties in an efficient manner; manage the staff's tasks in carrying out the Permanent Secretariat's functions; oversee the use of immunities and exemptions that the civil servants of Permanent Secretariat enjoy under the Agreement signed by the Member States; select and hire the Secretariat's administrative and technical personnel. The Secretary is the "guardian" of SELA's funds insomuch as she/he is in charge of collecting the Member States' contributions, administering them and executing SELA's budget. At the end of each ordinary period of sessions, the Permanent Secretary will be responsible for preparing and distributing to the Member States' representatives the provisional agenda for the following ordinary period. This agenda will include the topics proposed by the Council, by the Action Committees and Member State of the Council, and the Permanent Secretariat, accompanied by an explanatory memorandum, so that at the beginning of the period of the following session, the Council may approve them by an absolute majority.

Summing up, the organic structure of the Permanent Secretariat must be fully authorized to handle SELA's objectives as a permanent regional body for consultation, coordination, cooperation and joint economic and social promotion programmes.

1.4 SELA's Restructuring and Its Priorities

SELA's Constituting Treaty notes that its objective is to create a permanent forum for consultation, coordination, cooperation and joint economic and social promotion for Latin America and the Caribbean.[19] This is an objective that has not changed in all the years of SELA's existence; however, time and the region's

---

[19]See: Diaz Müller 1981.

situation have not remained static. Therefore, given the Panama Convention's size and flexibility, the Latin American Council considered it necessary to reconsider its priorities, which included:

- The adaptation of the organization's functions to the new regional reality and the establishment of priorities according to the needs of the current Member States.
- Respond to the challenges presented by the current dynamic in international relations and the growing economic difficulties of the Member States.
- Answer the need to recover SELA's unifying power in order to gain a larger and better presence on the international scene.
- Recognize the importance of commitment and political will to strengthen SELA in order to speed and deepen regional integration and cooperation.
- Redefine the work priorities, keeping in mind the objective: effective integration and cooperation among the Member States and their insertion into the international economy.
- Create a mechanism for monitoring that guarantees greater efficiency in the implementation of the annual budget and the Permanent Secretariat's annual work programme.[20]

These priorities are included in the guidelines established by the XXVIII Latin American Council in its Decision N° 440.[21]

The Decision establishes the restructuring of SELA, its working methods, the lines of action for presenting the Permanent Secretariat's Work Programme, financing and budget, the unpaid quotas, institutional issues and work.[22] It prioritizes integration and development in Latin America and the Caribbean, and the themes of common interest and the disposition for effective cooperation among the Member States, taking into account the situation of those countries that do not have sea access and small island nations. Keeping in mind the objectives laid out by this organization and in the hope of reaching those objectives, the Decision classifies work areas according to three aspects:

- intraregional relations,
- economic and technical cooperation and
- extra-regional relations.

---

[20]Decision N° 440 (see note below) clearly defines the lines of action that must guide the preparation of the Annual Work Programmes that the Permanent Secretariat carries out; among them we find describing the activities and the cost these imply, explaining the priority level of each action, keeping in mind the benefit it will bring to the Member States or the urgency of its implementation, and explaining the actions connected to each of the proposed tasks and the costs.

[21]SELA, Decision N° 440, XXVIII Ordinary Meeting of the Latin American Council, Caracas, Venezuela, April 7–9, 2003.

[22]See Decision N° 440, Articles 1–7.

Several actions have been carried out along these lines. These include Work Programme Projects[23] for a specific year that deal with the three aspects mentioned, as well as the organization of seminars and congresses to evaluate those points of interest that may allow for effective and efficient relationships, both among the nations that make up SELA as well as at the international level with other nations that are not part of SELA, and with other international organizations, in order to establish effective economic and technical cooperation.

1.4.1 Area of Intraregional Relations

At the internal level, the Council made it clear in the Decision that the priority in the Permanent Secretariat's next Work Programmes would be integration and cooperation among SELA's Member States. The organization would adopt actions designed to contribute to complementarity, convergence and the full implementation of the regional and subregional processes of integration of the Member States, especially offering assistance to the smallest countries, economically speaking, and to those that were the least economically developed.

In addition, they established that the impact of the specific decisions adopted by the Latin American and Caribbean Heads of State and of Governments regarding the regional integration process would be evaluated by SELA, and if the Latin American Council approved the measure, the Permanent Secretariat could monitor the decisions. They highlighted the importance of the exchange of experience and information from the impact studies regarding financial and trade policies, on situations such as migration, and national development and social policies related to Latin American and Caribbean integration, in order to collaborate on the search for solutions to the vulnerability of the region's economies. Thus, for example, the subject of the Work Programme Project for 2011 in the area of Intraregional Relations is: integration and development policies in Latin America and the Caribbean. Six specific projects have been proposed:

- The first is related to support for integration in Latin America and the Caribbean. A deepening of the coordination and convergence.
- The second refers to integration in Latin America and the Caribbean in the area of health.
- The third is about knowledge and Information and Communication Technology (ICT) for development and integration.
- The fourth concerns the development of a regional software industry in Latin America and the Caribbean.

---

[23]Since 2004, the Work Programme Projects include SELA's three priorities. A certain number of projects, with their corresponding activities and objectives are established for each priority.

- The fifth contemplates the development of a one-stop service for foreign trade in the context of facilitating international and paperless cross-border trade.
- The sixth focuses on an exploratory analysis of growth trends and their long-term social effects in Latin America and the Caribbean.[24]

1.4.2 Area for Economic and Technical Cooperation

As can be seen in its Constituting Document, one of SELA's priorities is to promote cooperation, both bilateral and multilateral, with international bodies and countries donating to the region. In the area of cooperation, the priorities are decided by a common agreement made by the Member States, taking into consideration the sense of complementarity with regard to the already existing projects. We can gather from Decision N° 440 that SELA's activities in the area of development will be carried out on a horizontal level, preferably, where the organization will act as a focal point in order to foment technical cooperation among the region's countries. SELA will continue to be an exceptional forum for regional consultation and coordination on this subject.

These efforts are oriented towards attracting external resources for financing programmes and project in certain areas related to the Work Programme. In addition, the hope is to provide technical assistance for preparing high-level meetings for the State or States with the smallest economies or that are least economically developed who request it. They encourage the exchange of experiences and information on national policies, especially those of the greatest transcendence in macroeconomic coordination, the struggle against poverty, and the areas of inclusion and international cooperation. SELA highlights the importance of having a System of Latin American and Caribbean Innovation and Competitiveness and, thus, sets up discussions aimed at establishing scientific and technological information networks.

Within this context, the Work Programme Project 2011 reflects the priorities suggested by the Member States on this subject.[25] As in the other documents, their interest is basically oriented towards those aspects that were previously mentioned, which are already being developed in the Project. In the area of economic and technical cooperation, three projects are proposed:

- The first is oriented towards strengthening economic and technical cooperation in Latin America and the Caribbean.
- The second refers to technical assistance to contribute to the economic and social development of Latin America and the Caribbean.

---

[24]See SELA 2010a.
[25]Ibid., pp. 20–43.

- The third is related to the Iberoamerican Programme for Inter-institutional Cooperation for the Development of Small and Medium-sized Businesses (Programa IBERPYME).

In SELA's first project the objective was to advance in strengthening economic and technical cooperation, for which it had to contribute to developing a closer relationship between the national focal points of international cooperation in Latin America and the Caribbean; also, to promote the exchange of experiences among its authorities; to promote South–South cooperative activities between Latin America, Africa and Asia.

   Along these lines, and in order to establish a setting for the exchange of ideas and experiences, and to progressively strengthen South–South cooperation, the Permanent Secretariat of SELA has been promoting meetings between cooperation directors, not just regional directors, but also extra-regional directors (from Asia and Africa). The central theme for the 2007 International Meeting of Directors of Cooperation was dedicated to "Cooperation for countries that are highly vulnerable to natural disasters" and the assessment of a possible "Cooperation Program for the integration and development of Latin America".[26]

1.4.3 Area of Extra-Regional Relations

The importance of designing a proposal for negotiation from the perspective of Latin America and the Caribbean in relation with international bodies and financial markets can be seen in the provisions of Decision 440. They highlight the importance of carrying out a "systematic analysis of the impact of external debt and international financial flows on the economies of the Member States, as well as the impact these factors cause on development and the sub regional processes of integration, the technology gap and the transfer of technology."[27] Taking into account the great changes seen in the world economy in recent times, SELA wishes to contribute to the understanding of multilateral trade negotiations, putting emphasis on their impact on development and regional integration, and if the government requires it, with approval from the Latin American Council, facilitate its participation in various international economic forums and negotiations. Therefore, in this area:

- The first project refers to the VI Bi-regional Summit of Madrid, the recessive dynamic in some European countries and perspectives for economic relations between Latin America and the Caribbean, and the European Union.
- The second project is centred on the evolution of, and perspectives regarding, economic relations between the United States and Latin American and Caribbean countries.

---

[26]Ibid., pp. 13–14.
[27]See Decision N° 440 (n. 21 above), Article 4.III.2.

- The third project is related to international trade, the multilateral trade system, and the development of Latin America and the Caribbean.
- The fourth project refers to the diversification of Latin America and the Caribbean's external economic relations.[28]

In this way, in spite of its intraregional relations, it is possible to see that SELA has an interest in developing relationships between its Member States and other international organizations, such as the European Union (EU). The economic relationship between the European Union and the Latin American and Caribbean region is not a new subject. Because of its great political, economic and financial weight, the European Union plays a leading role in the various forums where basic aspects of the international agenda are dealt with, giving the Union's relationship with Latin America and the Caribbean special importance. This is the case of the Latin America and Caribbean and European Union Summits (ALCUE). Within this context, in the part of its Work Programme Projects related to extraregional relations, SELA includes an analysis of the economic relationships between the European Union and Latin America and the Caribbean, and the particular relevance that the European Union has in this context. Therefore, SELA's Permanent Secretariat's Work Programme for 2007 included monitoring the state of the relations between the two regions as part of the evaluation of the results of the IV Bi-regional Summit held in May 2006 in Vienna. The idea was to analyse the results and implications for the economic cooperation relations between the regions and to make proposals to SELA's Member States suggesting possible joint activities with a view to the following Summit, which was held in Lima, in 2008. In the same way, the programme examined the interrelationship of trade policy, the negotiation of trade agreements and regional integration in LAC, where the divergence of the majority of the region's governments' official positions with regard to trade policies, trade agreements and regional integration can be seen.

It should be made clear that the European Union has no direct relationship with SELA as a permanent regional body, but SELA's Member States do participate in the ALCUE Summits.

Relations between Africa and the Caribbean are practically nonexistent, although there is an incipient relationship between Africa and the countries of South America, and the intention of developing it.[29] An initiative by Brazil and Nigeria has established a forum for South American-African cooperation (ASA) between the African international organization African Union (UA) and the Union of South American Nations (UNASUR). Two important meetings have been held through this union, in Abuja, Nigeria in 2006, and in Isla Margarita, Venezuela in 2009. The First South America–Africa Summit, whose objective was to consolidate the process of cooperation in various areas of common interest, as well as their strategic association, concluded with the Abuja Declaration and Plan of

---

[28]SELA 2010a, pp. 44–49.
[29]CEPAL 2008.

Action,[30] in which the participants highlighted the need to explore the opportunities for cooperation in different areas (agriculture, trade, energy, the environment, health, etc.), as well as to foment and activate bilateral agreements between countries in the areas of trade, airline service and agriculture. In the Second South America–Africa Summit, they approached the themes of multilateral cooperation: human rights, democracy, governability, agriculture, rural development and water resources, energy, the development of infrastructures, etc., and they concluded with the New Sparta Declaration.[31] The third Summit took place in Malabo, Equatorial Guinea, in 2013.

Undoubtedly, ASA is an important initiative in the relationship between South America and Africa, which must be maintained and consolidated through the necessary actions, because it is a forum for cooperation that seeks the development of both regions. However, it must be pointed out that the Caribbean, Mexico and Central America are not included in ASA.

In addition, some of the South American countries have fledgling bilateral agreements with Africa; Argentina, Cuba, Chile, Colombia, Mexico, Uruguay and Paraguay have a Preferential Agreement signed in 2004 with the Customs Union of Southern Africa, and in 2010 signed a Free Trade Treaty with Egypt and a Framework Agreement with Morocco. All of this takes on importance, because "foreign trade of the two regions adds up to 9 % of the total in the world."[32] In political terms, for example, Venezuela maintains diplomatic relations with almost all of the countries in Africa, and even created a Vice Chancery for Africa in 2005; many African countries have diplomatic representation in Latin American countries. Added to this, the visits made by Heads of State to African countries, and vice versa, are a clear demonstration of the rapprochement and interest in maintaining relations that benefit both regions.

It should be noted that SELA's objectives in its various areas of priority are numerous and probably very difficult to explain exactly, because they include diverse participants with different realities. Nevertheless, this does not constitute an impediment for making the effort needed to achieve and strengthen an effective relationship among the Nations of South America (and, ideally, the Caribbean) and the Nations of the African continent. In this context, SELA has prepared a document called *Las relaciones de América Latina y el Caribe con África: situación*

---

[30]First Africa–South America Summit, Abuja, 26–30 November 2006. Abuja Declaration, ASA/Summit/doc.01(I), at http://cancilleria.gob.ec/wp-content/uploads/2014/10/Abuja-Declaration.pdf. Accessed 12 January 2015.

[31]Second Africa–South America Summit (II ASA), 26–27 September 2009, Isla de Margarita, Nueva Esparta State, Bolivarian Republic of Venezuela. Issued the Declaration of Nueva Esparta, at http://www.voltairenet.org/article162310.html. Accessed 6 January 2015. See also: SELA 2014.

[32]Ibídem. From this study, it results that the main actor in international trade from both regions is Mexico, occupying the 15th position in the world; Brazil is in the 21st place; and the main African actor, in the 36th place in the world, is South Africa. Also, it appears that Chile and Brazil are the biggest investors from Latin America and the Caribbean in Africa, South Africa and Algeria in Latin American and the Caribbean.

actual y áreas de oportunidad (Latin America and the Caribbean's relations with Africa: current situation and areas of opportunity), which starts by indicating that both regions share the challenges of growth, development, reduction of poverty and increasing competitiveness, and therefore they have a common interest in offering their inhabitants education, health and employment, and improved levels of economic and social well-being. This document offers an analysis of certain institutional, economic and trade, and cooperative aspects to give a vision of the current situation and of the challenges for the future in the relations between Latin America and the Caribbean, and Africa, as well as highlighting those areas where advances have been made and the opportunities for the establishment of a successful bi-regional relationship in the long term.[33] It points out the current situation is ideal for strengthening the relations between the two regions and would lead to great benefits for both. In order to put the proposals made in the document into practice and strengthen the existing bilateral or regional relations, they consider that SELA may be the proper forum and regional mechanism for Latin American and the Caribbean.

It should be noted that relations between Latin America and the Caribbean, and Asia have also been the object of a study by SELA[34] which explained in a report the current situation and the challenges, as well as the possibilities for developing trade, financial and cooperative relations between Latin America and the Caribbean, and the Asia-Pacific countries.

1.5 Small- and Medium-Sized Businesses: A Priority for SELA

SELA is a pioneering organization in showing its concern for the development of small- and medium-sized businesses in the region. However, it should be pointed out that there are other organizations that support the businesses as well, as is the case with ALADI and the *Comisión Económica para América Latina y el Caribe* (CEPAL, Economic Commission for Latin America and the Caribbean), which comes under the United Nations umbrella, among others.

Faced with the need to create an Ibero-American programme that would spur cooperation among the various institutions, both public and private, to support the development of small- and medium-sized businesses, the Ibero-American Heads of State and of Governments, in the setting of the VIII Ibero-American Summit held in Porto, Portugal in October 1998, decided to create the Ibero-American Programme for Inter-institutional Cooperation for the Development of Small and Medium-sized Businesses (IBERPYME). The creation of this

---

[33]SELA 2014.
[34]SELA 1999.

programme originated with SELA, whose concern in this area has been reflected in the projects that have been carried out since the 1990s, and in the signing of the Cooperation Agreement with the Spanish Agency for International Cooperation (AECI) in 1996.

In fact, in 1999, due to SELA's experience in this area, the governments decided that SELA's Permanent Secretariat would assume responsibility for constituting the Programme's Management Unit. This meant that the Permanent Secretariat would, from the beginning, take charge of organizing the work, managing the interests and needs of the participating states, and administer the agreed-upon programmes and activities. In addition, it was decided that the Government of Venezuela would act as the official representative of the programme and, with support from the governments of Spain and Portugal, adopt the measures necessary to assure its success.

This is a programme that is carried out and administered by SELA and assigned to the *Secretaría General Iberoamericana* (SEGIB—Ibero-American General Secretary). Since its establishment, the programme has contributed to the development of organizations and institutions that support micro-, small-, and medium-sized businesses (MIPYMES) throughout the countries of Ibero-America.[35]

The objective of the IBERPYME Programme is to contribute by developing the institutional capacity of government and business entities that carry out support programmes for PYMES (small- and medium-sized businesses) in order to contribute to increasing their competitiveness with a view to internationalization. This is achieved through a series of activities (training courses, seminars, etc.) directed towards public and private companies that work with small- and medium-sized firms. Another objective of the IBERPYME Programme is to contribute to the process of internationalization of Ibero-American companies, by reporting on the successful experiences and contributing to the training of those individuals involved in exportation processes.

It is essential that businessmen and women, government workers, organizations and other entities connected with MIPYMES be aware of the innovative experiences that can be adapted to their situations, by reinforcing the existing structures that generate the exchange of experiences with other Ibero-American business people or civil servants during meetings, visits, etc.[36]

The Work Project Programme for 2007 makes it clear that the general objective of the IBERPYME programme "is to contribute by developing the institutional capacity of the governmental and trade-union agencies that run support programmes for MIPYME, so that by the design and implementation of programmes and actions, we can help the increase the competitiveness of the MIPYMES, with

---

[35]See: Informe General Programa IBERPYME: 1999–2011, XXXVII Reunión Ordinaria del Consejo Latinoamericano, Caracas, Venezuela, 19–21 October 2011, SP/CL/XXXVII.O/Di No. 29 -11 at: http://www.sela.org/attach/258/default/Di_No_29-Informe_General_Programa_IBERP YME_%281999-2011%29.pdf. Accessed December 15, 2014.

[36]SELA 2007, pp. 16–18.

a view to their internationalization."[37] Furthermore, through the various Work Programme Projects of recent years, IBERPYME's positive results in developing micro-, small- and medium-sized businesses throughout Ibero-America, by giving them support and assistance, can be seen. Therefore, both SELA and SEGIB intend to deepen the role that this Programme has in supporting intermediary private and public organizations in the region, as well as MIPYME companies that have participated in their activities throughout these years. They hope that the IBERPYME programme will become a reference point for everything related to public policies and activities designed to support MIPYMEs in Ibero-America, while at the same time facilitating the exchange of knowledge, experience and analysis among the main actors in the region that are responsible for making decisions and formulating policies related to MIPYMEs. To that end, they have established various activities to be carried out.[38]

Summing up, it is possible to say that a latent concern for SELA, in addition to the PYMES, is to stimulate cooperation, and that this cooperation to be really effective. To this end, SELA's Permanent Secretariat prepared a document entitled *Visiones, enfoques y tendencias de la cooperación internacional para el desarrollo: Hacia un marco conceptual y práctico latinoamericano y caribeño* (Visions, focuses and trends in international cooperation for development: Towards a conceptual and practical Latin American and Caribbean framework) in which we can find the general framework for the main trends and current discussions related to international cooperation for development from the Latin American and Caribbean point of view.[39] There is one aspect of the report's conclusions that should be highlighted, as it will be essential to achieving any of the group's objectives; since the idea is to go before other nations and bodies as a single region, its members must present a common position. "Latin America and the Caribbean should deepen their efforts to achieve more unified postures at the intraregional level (and, ideally, consensus at the regional level) on those issues that are key to the system of international cooperation for development that most interest their region; for example, the democratization of multilateral financial bodies, international finance for development, the millennium development objectives and South-South cooperation".[40] By means of documents such as those that have been mentioned, SELA has offered a general panorama to those aspects that are essential to achieving adequate cooperation and fulfilling the longed-for integration of the countries of Latin America and the Caribbean.

---

[37]Idem, p. 16.

[38]See SELA 2007, pp. 21–23.

[39]SELA 2010b.

[40]Ibid., pp. 49–50.

1.6 Final Considerations

SELA is a regional body that has been in operation for more than three decades, with 28 Member States, 25 of which are founding members, and with more than 570 million inhabitants. Few organizations in the region can boast this size, nor the fact that no Member States have dropped out along the way.

SELA's objective is to promote a system for consultation and coordination in order to establish common positions and strategies in economic issues for Latin America and the Caribbean before other countries or international organizations. SELA's work is also oriented towards stimulating cooperation and the integration of Latin American and Caribbean countries.

During its years of existence, SELA's work can be seen through the projects it has carried out, mostly through its Permanent Secretariat, to achieve the objectives established in its constituting documents, focusing its work areas on three issues: intraregional areas, extra-regional areas and economic and technical cooperation.

Undoubtedly, one of the most relevant aspects of its existence has been the establishment and later on the restructuring of its priority areas, that, divided into projects and activities, allow for greater control and monitoring of the objectives and, in addition, give continuity to its work over time.

Making the proposals defined by SELA more effective is a task that corresponds exclusively to the Member States and, as is true in any international agreement, it requires commitment and political will to carry them out, especially in a region that has maintained positive growth rates in these times of economic crisis. In this context, SELA may constitute the proper instrument for concerted action, in a globalized world that is organized in blocks, to achieve the longed-for improvement in the quality of life for its citizens, of both the current and future generations.

References

Bond R D (1978) Regionalism in Latin America: prospects for the Latin American Economic System (SELA). International Organization, 32: 401–423

CEPAL (2008) África y América Latina: perspectivas de cooperación intrarregional. E/CEPAL/G. 1198

Diaz Müller L (1981) El SELA y las empresas multinacionales latinoamericanas en el marco del desarrollo regional. UNAM, Instituto de Investigaciones Jurídicas, México D.F

Díez de Velasco M (2008) Las Organizaciones Internacionales. Tecnos, Madrid

Marinas Otero L (1978) El 'sistema económico latinoamericano' (SELA). Revista de política internacional, 159: 137–143

Quispe Remón F (2010) Problemas y perspectivas de procesos de integración en América Latina. International Law, Revista Colombiana de Derecho Internacional, 10: 259–292

Rivera Banuet J (2010) 50 años de integración de América Latina y el Caribe: Evolución y perspectivas. Mundo Nuevo, Revista de Estudios Latinoamericanos, 4: 15–54

SELA (1999) Informe sobre las relaciones económicas de América Latina y el Caribe con Asia-Pacífico. Permanent Secretariat, Instituto para la Integración de América Latina y el Caribe, at http://www.asiayargentina.com/pdf/Sela-1.PDF. Accessed 15 October 2014

SELA (2007) Proyecto de Programa de Trabajo para el 2008. XXXIII Reunión Ordinaria del
    Consejo Latinoamericano Caracas, Venezuela 26-28 November 2007, SP/CL/XXXIII.O/DT
    Nº 4-07. http://www.sela.org/attach/258/EDOCS/SRed/2007/11/T023600002667-0-Proyecto
    _Programa_de_Trabajo_2008_.pdf. Accessed 16 December 2014
SELA (2010a) Proyecto de Programa de Trabajo para el año 2011. XXXVI Reunión
    Ordinaria del Consejo Latinoamericano Caracas, Venezuela, 27-29 October 2010.
    SP/CL/XXXVI.O/DT Nº 4-10 at http://www.sela.org/attach/258/EDOCS/SRed/2010/09/
    T023600004341-0-Proyecto_Programa_de_Trabajo_2011_-_XXXVI_RO_CLA_-_
    Oct._2010.pdf. Accessed 10 December 2014
SELA (2010b) Visiones, enfoques y tendencias de la cooperación internacional para el desar-
    rollo: Hacia un marco conceptual y práctico latinoamericano y caribeño. XXI Reunión
    de Directores de Cooperación Internacional de América Latina y el Caribe, Paramaribo,
    Suriname, 29-30 July 2010, SP/XXI.RDCIALC/DT Nº 4-10, at http://www.sela.org/attach/25
    8/EDOCS/SRed/2010/07/T023600004271-0-DT_4_Visiones_enfoques_y_tendencias_de_la_
    cooperacion_internacional.pdf. Accessed 2 November 2014
SELA (2014) Nuevas modalidades de relacionamiento económico y cooperación entre
    América Latina y el Caribe y África. Reunión Regional sobre las Relaciones Económicas
    y Comerciales de América Latina y el Caribe con el área del Pacífico, la India y África.
    Caracas, Venezuela y 10 de octubre de 2014. Doc. SP/RRRECALCPIA/DT N° 3-14 at
    http://www.sela.org/attach/258/EDOCS/SRed/2014/10/T023600006095-0-DT_3_Nuevas_
    modalidades_de_relacionamiento_economico_y_cooperacion_entre_America_Latina_y_el_
    Caribe_y_Africa.pdf. Accessed 15 November 2014
UNDP (2010) Human Development Report. *The Real Wealth of Nations: Pathways to Human
    Development.* 20th Anniversary Edition. UNDP, New York
Zagaris B (1978) The Economic System of Latin America (SELA): An Innovative Mechanism
    for Less Developed Countries. Comparative Law Yearbook, 2: 117–148

Chapter 2
The Latin American Integration Association

Eugenia López-Jacoiste Díaz

Abstract This chapter considers the Latin American Association in the context of different backgrounds and main goals within the regional economic integration processes. It also looks at the various types of agreements that are developed within the region and new forms of partnership. The institutions of ALADI are also considered in the context of the legal framework that develops external relations with other institutional partners in Latin America. The chapter considers the role of ALADI in relation to other existing regional and sub-regional agreements, such as the Andean Community, Mercosur and NAFTA, and their relationships as a factor of integration and cooperation.

Keywords LAFTA · Andean Community · MERCOSUR · ALADI · GATT · Economic integration · Open agreements · Partial agreements

Contents

This chapter has been written as part of a larger research project called 'The reform of economic international institutions', project number DER2010-20414-C02-01 (subprogram JURI), which is funded by the Spanish Ministry of Science and Innovation.

E. López-Jacoiste Díaz (✉)
Department of International Law, University of Navarra, Navarra, Spain
e-mail: ejacoiste@unav.es

2.1 Introduction

Ever since their independence, Latin American countries have attempted to join together both politically and economically.[1] Moreover, in Bolivar's view, regional unity was a necessity to maintain their newly gained regional independence from Spain. He envisaged the political unity of Latin America as a means to defuse regional conflicts, to establish the predominance of a regional international law, and to reduce the vulnerability of the Latin American countries to the actions of the great powers, especially Great Britain and the United States.[2] While Latin America's independence changed the region's political structure, it also transformed the economic landscape. The region's mercantile economies began modernization by instituting reforms that would allow them to compete in the industrialized world and would facilitate trade liberalization and regional integration. At the onset of the Great Depression, however, their export-reliant economies began to sink into recession as foreign demand decreased. Only government protection and foreign assistance prevented a complete collapse of the economy. The need to protect and shield industries in order to create a viable economy was addressed in the years following World War II by convincing leaders to adopt import substitution policies on both a national and, subsequently, regional basis.[3] Some authors believed that 'Latin America's economic difficulties stemmed from [*inter alia*] [...] lack of capital, excessive concentration of power in the hands of the wealthy, an inefficient system of land tenure and inadequate domestic markets'.[4]

Most Latin American countries implemented far-reaching structural reforms in the 1980s, based on the triad of free markets, free trade and privatization. In short, the inward-looking import substitution industrialization approach to development was replaced by an outward-looking strategy, as Latin America decided to become part of the global economy. This economic reform programme was initially stimulated and promoted by the International Monetary Fund and the World Bank. Indeed, it was reasonable to reach a new trade policy, i.e. a new import substitution model which involves replacing imported goods with domestic goods. This keeps money within a nation's or trade region's borders, preventing foreign producers from profiting at the expense of the domestic industry. Import substitution necessarily involves raising tariffs on imports to protect nascent, national industries, which, in theory, will give national industries an advantage in supplying the country with goods previously imported from abroad. Nevertheless, one of the problems of implementing this import substitution policy was that the Latin American national markets did not have enough demand to support these newly

---

[1]Baquero-Herrera 2005, pp. 156–158.

[2]Mace 1988, p. 405.

[3]ECOSOC, Economic Commission for Latin America, UN Doc E/CN.12/89 (14 May 1950) *Desarrollo de la America Latina y sus Principales Problemas,* describing plans for establishing viable economies in Latin America.

[4]Radway 1981, p. 7 discussing development of Latin America's infrastructure.

'substituted' industries. Given the policy objective, regional integration was to cover the limitations of the import substitution model through the creation of a regional market. The approach was to eliminate internal barriers to trade and to maintain or increase high levels of external protection and expand industrial planning at the regional level. The explicit goal was to divert third-party imports to intra-regional production and export. The sustainability of the initiatives depended on successfully opening national markets to intra-regional trade.

Successful integration, however, will only be accomplished with a significant change to the *status quo* that takes into consideration problems encountered in the past in order to change the political will of the Latin American states, including such issues as national, regional and international economic reform.

Conceptually, there are two different channels on which trade and economic integration among countries can occur. We call these two mechanisms integration by markets and integration by agreements. Integration by markets focuses on the notion that economies can join together through the use of the marketplace, i.e. allowing the private sector to be the vanguard of trade integration. This can also be described as regional integration via *de facto* agreements. In contrast, integration by agreements focuses on trade integration via the use of formal or *de jure* trade treaties. This channel of integration emphasizes the primacy of legal instruments to further economic integration among countries. These two instruments of integration are closely related and indeed are ultimately complementary. Integration via markets without formal regional trade agreements can create uncertainty among businesses since the legal foundations are not sufficiently clear and transparent. Integration by agreements can be vacuous if the underlying economic factors are not favourable for integration.

Latin America has primarily used formal regional trade treaties as the main channel of integration in preference to integration via the market. Nevertheless, in recent years, new models have been developing in order to strengthen internal markets because this can give stronger political bargaining power to the outward-looking economic-oriented forces within the country.

In 1960 the Treaty of Montevideo was signed, creating the Latin American Free Trade Association (LAFTA), a free trade area allowed by Article XXIV of the General Agreement on Tariffs and Trade (GATT). The LAFTA represents the first incarnation of regionalized trade in South America. This intergovernmental organization was replaced by the 1980 Montevideo Treaty creating a new association, the Latin American Integration Association (LAIA or ALADI in Spanish). Currently it is made up of 12 states: Argentina, Bolivia, Brazil, Chile, Colombia, Cuba, Ecuador, Mexico, Paraguay, Peru, Uruguay and Venezuela. Altogether they represent 20 million square kilometres and more than 500 million people. Today, while referring to the Latin American economies several other regional organizations are also included: the Andean countries (Bolivia, Colombia, Ecuador and Peru),[5] MERCOSUR (Argentina, Brazil, Paraguay and Uruguay)[6] and the NAFTA countries (Canada, Mexico and United States).

---

[5]See Chap. 5 in this book.
[6]See Chap. 6 in this book.

In the international legal order there is no legal provision that prohibits a State from participating in more than one organization. International organizations can be complementary in their objectives and functions. In this context, the significance of ALADI has to be noted in the creation of a 'real political will in trade integrations' that will lead to some of its member states establishing new partnerships to achieve greater integration, but without withdrawing from the ALADI system.

In light of this chapter, we will focus on the study of ALADI. It is important to analyse what ALADI is today, taking into consideration its political and economic background as well as its development from the 1990s until today. To reach these aims it is worthwhile studying its structural organization, working methods and some of the many agreements among the ALADI members. This chapter posits that the integration envisioned by ALADI is difficult because it relies on existing institutions, but without altering the pre-existing legal structure of trade relationships. It concludes that regionalism is only beneficial to Latin America if an organization is given the necessary legal power to implement economic integration.

2.2 Economic, Political and Institutional Background of ALADI

Since the General Agreement on Tariffs and Trade, (GATT 1947) has been ratified, there have existed a set of international trade obligations and rules applicable to contracting members states aimed at the reduction of tariffs and other trade barriers. One of the most important ideas underpinning the GATT (and today World Trade Organization) framework is the idea that bilateral and trade agreements can lead to the ultimate facilitation of international trade. This idea, included in the GATT in 1947, was that the GATT provision itself should not prevent, as between the territories of the contracting parties, the formation of a custom union or a free-trade area or the adoption of an interim agreement necessary for the formation of custom unions or free trade areas.[7] Thus the international trading regime that was created in the 1940s specifically promotes regional trade agreements. As expected, such regional trade agreements developed all over the world and particularly in the Western Hemisphere.

After Word War II, the Latin American economies have significantly increased. Their raw materials (such as meat, sugar, cocoa) were in high demand in European markets. This European economic need moved Argentina, Brazil, Chile, Mexico, Paraguay, Peru and Uruguay to sign the first integration treaty (1960 Montevideo Treaty). This Latin America Free Trade Association (LAFTA) agreement aimed at greater economic integration through expansion of their national markets

---

[7]General Agreement on Tariffs and Trade 1947, 55 UNTS 194, Article XXIV with some specific limitations.

and of their reciprocal trade. A few years later, Colombia, Ecuador, Bolivia and Venezuela joined the Montevideo Treaty. The treaty's stated goal was to gradually eliminate trade restrictions on imports from member states and to guarantee a free trade area among its member states. The 1960 Montevideo Treaty created, as a preliminary step for future trade integration, a free trade area formed by reciprocal multilateral agreements whereby two or more countries agree to limit or to eliminate all import tariff and duties between them. With such agreements the signatory states attempt to establish an economic grouping of states similar to a customs union as a previous commitment for the future common market.

This free trade area should be fully operational for 12 years (that is, until 31 December 1972). This deadline was postponed until 31 December 1980, because during that period the signatory states had been unable to identify the national goods that should have been included in the free trade area. Thus, the 1969 Protocol of Caracas modified that deadline until 31 December 1980, considering that 20 years was reasonable to reach those goals. Evidently, it was planned to carry out the integration process gradually through a list system which would reduce taxes and tariffs on certain goods progressively.

Discontented with the slow pace of liberalization, five members of the group (Bolivia, Chile, Colombia, Ecuador and Peru) established the more ambitious Andean Pact in the late 1960s.[8] Indeed, the Andean Group split from LAFTA. In 1969 they decided to form their own sub-regional common market in reaction to their frustration with that association. They opted for a sub-regional common market for their manufactured goods wherein sub-regional industries could grow in strength as they took advantage of more economies of scale but were still protected from the industries of the first-generation developed countries. At that time, the Andean Community benefited from the mistakes made by LAFTA, which attributed to its early success.[9]

From the Economic Commission for Latin America's point of view and for many observers, both outside and inside the region, LAFTA was intended and believed to be a 'magic elixir' that would reform the economic structure and improve general welfare throughout the region. Unfortunately, LAFTA never got off the ground. Moreover, early results suggested that the pieces of the 'trade-pie' were not cut equally.[10] Indeed, countries with 'larger national markets and more diversified industries were reaping most of the benefits [of LAFTA]'.[11] Instead of trade increasing the well-being of all, LAFTA improved conditions for a few, while others—such as Chile, Colombia and Peru—began running trade deficits.[12] LAFTA was producing on a regional scale the dominance-dependency relationship

---

[8]Venezuela joined this Group in 1973 and Chile withdrew in 1976.

[9]Middlebrook 1978, p. 64.

[10]Mace 1988, p. 412 where he states that the integration process is not creating equal benefits for member countries and attributes the initial failure of regional agreements to 'local factors'.

[11]Mace 1988, p. 412.

[12]Porrata-Doria et al. 2005, pp. 7–12, noting that Chile, Colombia and Peru began trade deficit within first 3 years of LAFTA.

characteristic of North–South relations in general which many developing countries criticized with increasing vehemence. The most frustrated countries were those mid-way up the developmental chain because they had intended LAFTA to stimulate their economies and industrial growth.[13] Thus, in 1969 Chile, Colombia, Ecuador, Peru and Venezuela decided to form their own sub-regional common market in reaction to their frustrations with LAFTA.

Briefly explained, LAFTA had trouble accomplishing its goals because members insisted on negotiating concessions on a product-by-product basis. Moreover, LAFTA's failure to stimulate growth resulted mainly from two factors: first, LAFTA's structure was built on governing trade among its member countries rather than on creating trade opportunities for all members. Second, LAFTA agreed to agree on lowering trade barriers in the future; it was therefore merely a framework for agreeing to tariff reductions at a later date. Then, at the time of its signing no trade was liberalized. It was hoped that, through bilateral negotiations countries with widely divergent interests could find mutual benefit through concessions that fitted in with each country's priorities. Moreover, the tight schedule of the tariff negotiations meant that if one round failed subsequent rounds necessarily would fail as well. But these limitations did not mean the economies of the LAFTA nations did not prosper and grow; rather, the causes of this prosperity were primarily extra-regional in nature and not a result of regional integration efforts. Moreover, some authors see other deficiencies as well. Professor Porrata-Doria lists four causes of LAFTA's failure: (1) a lack of understanding of the purposes for entering into LAFTA; (2) the lack of regional trade on which LAFTA could act to facilitate free-trade; (3) an unworkable framework; and (4) a lack of an institution capable of building consensus between the members.[14]

2.3 The Main Goal of ALADI: A Common Market for the Region

LAFTA eventually ended in failure, and in 1980 was replaced by the Latin American Integration Association (ALADI). The new Montevideo Treaty was signed at the same time by all LAFTA member states. Considering the reasons for the failure of LAFTA, ALADI replaced it with a different, more streamlined structure and more realistic objectives and mechanisms and indeed, intended to put some of LAFTA's inherent problems right. Both organizations, LAFTA and ALADI, have a very similar legal nature. Both Montevideo treaties are regional multilateral treaties under international law, open to the admission of any Latin American state. Both Montevideo Treaties aim for trade integration, although

---

[13]Bennet 2008, p. 108.
[14]Porrata-Doria et al. 2005, pp. 13–14.

through different mechanisms. Such different mechanisms are essential to understand the differences between LAFTA and ALADI and why ALADI supposedly works successfully.

Unlike LAFTA, the 1980 Montevideo Treaty establishes a long-term and gradually common market with no strict deadlines. Compared to a single free trade area, ALADI is more of *an association* among countries. Article 1 clearly states that the contracting parties intend to continue the integration process and to promote economic and social development, as a harmonious and balanced development of the region. According to Article 2, ALADI aims to develop the following basic functions: promotion and regulation of reciprocal trade, economic complementation and development of acts of economic cooperation that will contribute to expanding markets. To achieve its final objective, countries shall take into account the following specific purposes: (a) pluralism, sustained by the will of the member countries for integration over the diversity in political and economic which may exist in the region; (b) convergence, which requires progressive multilateralization with partial agreements through regular negotiations among member countries for the establishment of the Latin American common market; (c) flexibility to allow for the conclusion of partial scope agreements and to set standards consistent with progressive future integration. Moreover, differential treatment has to be established for each case. This differential treatment is applicable in both the regional scope mechanisms and in the partial scope agreements. Such differential treatments will be applied in a more favourable manner to less-developed countries. Therefore, the ALADI actions will be open to various forms of agreement between member countries, compatible with the objectives and functions of the integration process, using all possible instruments for the activation and expansion of regional markets.

2.3.1 Specific Objective and Mechanism

The transformation of LAFTA into ALADI gave new impetus to the process of economic integration in Latin America. The new institution adopted a 'flexible' approach to integration, relying mainly on sector-based bilateral or plurilateral negotiation.

ALADI promotes the creation of trade preferences in the region by (1) creating regional tariff preferences, whereby ALADI members grant each other tariff preference on a reciprocal basis; (2) allowing regional scope agreements; and (3) allowing partial scope agreements amongst member countries. Thus, the 1980 Montevideo Treaty is a framework treaty that creates a new legal agenda which could be developed progressively among its member states. It conceived the integration process as being mainly a series of bilateral treaties within a flexible framework of multilateral tariff preferences. Indeed, this promotion of trade agreements works on two levels: (1) an internal level, i.e. among the ALADI member states with two different scopes (regional and partial) and (2) an external level, between ALADI members and third-party Latin American states or associations.

2.3.1.1 Preferential Agreements with Regional Scope

Let us consider the some conceptual elements involved in trade policy. All countries make use of trade barriers or other forms of protection. A preferential trade agreement established between a subset of countries implies preferential tariff reduction between the parties. A free trade area is a complex entity from the conceptual point of view. On the one hand, the lowering of trade barriers generates greater efficiency and social welfare. But on the other hand, it causes distortions by discriminating between goods from different countries. In short, a free trade area is discriminatory, because it involves tariff preferences for member countries; but it also involves a movement towards free trade between its members.[15]

As a specific mechanism to promote trade integration in the ALADI region, Article 2 of the 1980 Montevideo Treaty foresees reciprocal trade among the ALADI members and the development of economic cooperation activities to assist the expansion of markets. Internal exchange of goods is promoted by establishing a system of regional preferences. To achieve this goal the ALADI Treaty promotes an area of trade preference made by a regional tariff preference and allows furthermore regional scope agreements with the participation of all ALADI members and includes schemes that grant non-reciprocal tariff preference to ALADI's 'less-developed countries' (Bolivia, Ecuador and Paraguay), as well as other complementary agreements, within the principles and objectives of the ALADI, to implement the first ones (Article 5 and Resolution 5 of the Council of Ministers).

The legal basis for these regional agreements are Articles 4, 6, 18, 33(f) and 35(a) of the 1980 Montevideo Treaty, as well as Resolution 1 of the Conference on Evaluation and Convergence. Within these kinds of regional agreements, we can find, for instance, trade and agricultural agreements (Articles 15–17), tourism promotion (Articles 8 and 12), cooperation in science and technology and environmental preservation agreements. This open legal framework of the ALADI Treaty has very important consequences: it allows the conclusion of reciprocal trade finance agreements, facilitates the regional movement of capital within the area for the establishment, for instance, of joint ventures, as well as regional agreements to ensure energy supply.

Since the launch of ALADI, members have signed a range of agreements on regional preferences on all types of goods, from agriculture, industrial products, chemicals, beverages (alcoholic and non alcoholic), hides and skins to automobiles and textiles. In each regional agreement each of the preferences that apply to each product is negotiated. States are free to grant other members of ALADI different tariffs, with the exception of the treatment of less developed countries. Consequently, not all States will benefit from the same tariff.

However, the network of regional trade agreements adopted under the framework of ALADI would undermine its effectiveness if its member states do not simultaneously provide a system to ensure their reciprocal credit transactions. Consequently,

---

[15]Meller 2009, p. 91.

in August 1982, the representatives of the Central Banks of Argentina, Bolivia, Brazil, Colombia, Chile Dominican Republic, Ecuador Mexico, Paraguay and Uruguay signed the Association of Latin American Integration, Reciprocal Payments and Credits Agreement. This multilateral treaty governs the flow of funds between the Latin American countries by replacing the international mechanisms that have traditionally been used. Most Latin American central banks now require that, apart from certain specific exceptions, all payments to be made or to be received from signatory countries be channelled through this new mechanism. In a time of economic recession throughout the continent, the provisions of the ALADI Treaty on transactions has demonstrated that trade flow increases by reducing the need for scarce, hard-currency U.S. dollars. Additionally, by reducing the cross-border risk typically faced by banks operating in Latin America and by guaranteeing the convertibility of required local currency payments, the ALADI Treaty encourages an increase in the amount of local bank credit available. This, in turn, should help to stimulate economic recovery in Latin America.[16]

2.3.1.2 Partial Scope Agreements

The ALADI Treaty establishes other specific mechanisms to promote trade preference in the region. It allows partial scope agreements which do not require the participation of all ALADI members, but only with the condition of being open to future, full participation of all its members (Article 6). These partial scope agreements will be held in the framework of the objectives and provisions of the ALADI Treaty, and may relate to matters and depend on the instruments provided for partial agreements set forth in Article 8. Moreover, these partial agreements may be commercial, economic complementation, agriculture, trade promotion or take other forms according to the objectives of the association. Despite this wide range of possible agreements, Article 9 regulates their limitations in detail: they must be open for accession, after negotiation, to the other member countries, and must contain clauses promoting convergence so that their benefits reach all members. They may contain clauses promoting convergence with other Latin American countries, in accordance with the mechanisms established in this Treaty. They must also contain differential treatment according to three categories of countries recognized by the Treaty, whose application forms were determined in each agreement and negotiation procedures for periodic review at the request of any member who is aggrieved. At the same time, partial agreements may contain a deduction for the same type of products or subheadings, but based on a percentage discount on the charges applied to imports originating from countries not participating in ALADI. In addition, partial agreements must have a minimum 1-year period of validity. Finally, such agreements may contain, among others, specific rules on origin, safeguard clauses, non-tariff restrictions, withdrawal of concessions, renegotiation of concessions, reporting, coordination and harmonization of policies.

---

[16]Davison 1985, p. 1308.

Trade agreements with regional scope are intended exclusively to promote trade among ALADI member countries and they are subject to specific rules established for the purpose. Furthermore, Article 11 promotes agricultural agreements among member states in order to be more competitive in the world markets. Such agricultural agreements may have regional scope, but also partial. ALADI changed the goals for integration by recognizing that less developed countries need economic support from more developed countries, and changed the mode of integration by calling for a process of sub-regional integration consistent with the differential treatment of less-developed economies.

Pursuant to Article 13, agreements to promote trade shall refer to non-tariff matters and tend to promote intra-regional trade flows. Particularly, among the actions for the less-developed countries ALADI provides trade-tariff preferences and partial agreements with those and other countries. To ensure the effectiveness of such agreements, member countries will execute negotiated rules concerning preservation of preferences, the elimination of non-tariff barriers and the application of safeguard clauses in justified cases. Over the years, numerous agreements under the ALADI framework have incorporated various safeguard clauses, under which it is possible to recognize a variety of procedures and grounds that can be invoked. But these ALADI safeguard clauses also differ from the scope and other characteristics of the safeguards for trade policy instruments, as the World Trade Organisation (WTO), in each case, adjusted the interest it considered necessary to preserve in each beneficiary country. Today, according to participants of the various agreements, systems coexist with the following guarantees: (1) Regional Safeguard System ALADI Resolution 70 adopted by the Committee of Representatives, (2) the regime of safeguards contained in Chapter IX of the Cartagena Agreement, which applies only among the member countries of the Andean Community, and (3) specific schemes adopted in a number of bilateral agreements, which depend (to a greater or lesser degree) on the normative models of Resolution 70 and Safeguard Agreement of the WTO, whose most important aspects are very similar. Moreover, by express provision of the respective agreements, any safeguard measure shall apply as between states parties to the MERCOSUR Agreement—ACE No. 18, or between Paraguay and Peru No. 20 (Partial Agreement of Renegotiation). Nor will special safeguards apply, after reaching full liberalization of trade, as established in the free trade agreements ACE No. 31 (Bolivia-Mexico), No. 35 (MERCOSUR-Chile), No. 36 (MERCOSR-Bolivia) and No. 41 (Chile-Mexico). Furthermore, safeguards can be implemented only with the consent of the other party.

According to Resolution 16(III) of the Council of Ministers, the Committee of Representatives approved a Resolution concerning the specific regional safeguard regime, on April 1987.[17] Under this Resolution—and unlike the WTO safeguard system—the Regional Safeguard Regime of ALADI, the Andean Community regime and in some bilateral agreements, only two safeguards can be invoked: a clause of 'serious damage' due to imbalance in the balance of payments or to face

---

[17]ALADI/CR/Resolution 70, 27 April 1987.

the serious economic crisis, whose origins are influenced by external factors beyond trade in the products affected. One of the most important issues is that member countries do not apply safeguard clauses to imports originating in the territory of the less-developed countries to correct imbalances in its overall balance of payments. In general terms, safeguards are to be applied for 1 year, except under approved exceptional circumstances.

Taking into account all these considerations, it is worthwhile briefly examining at least few examples of trade agreements under these ALADI provisions. In 1991, under the framework of ALADI, Protocol No. 3 on Mining Integration and Complementation was incorporated into Economic Complementation Agreement No. 16. This Protocol procured the exchange of scientific and technical information between both Argentina and Chile to enable the development of joint projects for the exploration and exploitation of the mineral resources existing along the borders of both countries, in a strip approximately 40 km wide on both sides of the frontier between the respective countries where, historically, legal impediments grounded in security reasons prevented the nationals of Argentina or Chile from the acquisition of property rights. Moreover, both countries agreed to encourage the creation of joint ventures among natural and legal persons of both countries, as well as the participation of foreign investors. (ACE No. 16, Protocol No. 3, Article 3.) The incorporation of an instrument, Protocol No. 3, in 1991, fully demonstrates the cultural and social development of both societies as they began to move towards integration.[18] Not long afterwards, in June 1995, also under the framework of ALADI, an agreement was reached on the need to sign specific protocols for the development of mining projects located throughout the Andean frontier regions of both territories (Argentina and Chile). These Protocols, although ruled by the internal legislation of each State, included provisions dealing with frontier, customs, environmental and other facilities authorizing the competent public bodies of both countries to coordinate actions oriented towards facilitating the performance of mining projects. In 1997, the ACE 16 Additional Protocol XIX ('El Pachón') and the ACE 16 Additional Protocol XX ('Pascua-Lama') were signed, and in March 1998 Additional Protocols XXII and XXIII provided the legal framework for the facilities established for these projects. On the basis of these protocols the Mining Integration and Complementation Treaty between the Republic of Argentina and the Republic of Chile was signed on 29 December 1997, as a stronger cooperation treaty within the ALADI system.

2.3.2 The ALADI Development and Its New Partnerships

2.3.2.1 The New Partial Agreements

Beginning the 1990s, however, the agreements concluded under the 'flexible' approach lost some of their significance when ALADI members entered into more

---

[18]Bauni 2004, p. 67.

comprehensive and far-reaching agreements. As countries in Latin American began embracing broad trade liberalization schemes in the later 1980s and early 1990s, both regional tariff preferences and regional scope agreements, as well as 'selective' partial scope agreements (those negotiated on product-by-product basis or those that cover all products but do not eliminate barriers to trade completely) lost some of their significance. Indeed, with the heightened space of trade liberalization in the hemisphere, these agreements gave way to 'new generation' partial scope agreements, which provide for automatic preferential programmes for the elimination of tariff and non-tariff barriers to trade in all goods, with some exceptions. A large majority of the 26 'selective' partial-scope agreements and all of the new generation partial-scope agreements are registered with ALADI as economic complementary agreements or ACEs (for the Spanish acronym). Most of the exceptions specified in partial scope agreements concluded under the ALADI framework tend to be shared exceptions, that is, they appear in more than one agreement. The majority of these affect the automotive sector, oil and oil-based products, agricultural products, plastic, textiles, clothing and footwear.[19]

In this context, it is important to point out the provision of Article 44 of the Montevideo Treaty. It requires that ALADI members extend any benefit granted to a third State to all members of the Association. In this context, the ALADI Council of Ministers approved the Implementation Protocol of Article 44 of the Treaty in June 1994 according to the Resolution 192 of the Committee of Representatives, and Resolution 43 of the Council of Ministers. Notwithstanding, the Implementation Protocol allows members that have granted preferences to third countries the right not to have to apply the most favoured nation clause embodied in Article 44, provided negotiations are launched to compensate ALADI members. Taking into consideration this Protocol and its implementation, Mexico ratified the Protocol and invoked it in September 1994 in the context of its membership in NAFTA.

The introspective attitude that characterized most of the countries in Latin America in the years preceding and immediately following the creation of ALADI has long faded away. As they turned their backs on the economic theories of the 1970s and early 1980s, which called for the creation of partial trade liberalization agreements among a handful of counties in the hemisphere, ALADI members increasingly sought to engage partners outside the group's boundaries.

This more engaging strategy of ALADI vis-à-vis third countries, as we will see, has led to changes in the group's membership. On 26 August 1999, Cuba became the twelfth member of ALADI. At the time of its entry Cuba had already signed agreements with nine of the eleven ALADI members under the framework of Article 25 of the Montevideo Treaty. Of these agreements, those signed with Bolivia, Colombia, Ecuador and Peru were negotiated in parallel to the Uruguay Round and included provision on service, intellectual property and technical barriers to trade. ALADI members are in the process of updating previous agreements

---

[19]Steinfatt 2001, p. 120.

with Cuba or, in the case of Chile, which had no pre-existing agreements with the Caribbean island, negotiating new arrangements to take into account Cuban membership in the regional organization.

2.3.2.2 New External Relations and Open Agreements

External trade relations in the American region encouraged the proliferation of bilateral or trilateral regional initiatives. The free trade areas established in practice are generally between countries that already have significant and long-standing trading relations. Geography and proximity are important features that have been taken into account, so trade creation ought to dominate trade diversion effects.

The ALADI Treaty, as a framework treaty, creates a legal agreement which could be developed progressively among its member states. Specifically, Article 24 of the ALADI Treaty promotes a multilateral association system with other Latin American trade organizations. Article 25 of the 1980 Montevideo Treaty also foresees the formation of agreements with third parties.

All these circumstances made for a surprising proliferation of bilateral free trade agreements and 'new generation' regional agreements in Latin America generally, and in the Western Hemisphere, specifically during the 1990s. No less than 26 free trade agreements were signed between 1990 and 1994 under the ALADI framework. Of course, trade with close neighbours is relatively easy. There are many advantages to geographic proximity. First, transport and communication costs are relatively lower. Second, there tends to be greater affinity between the personal characteristics of trading partners; there is greater mutual understanding, so it is easier to do business, i.e. transaction costs are lower. Latin American has the great advantage of a common language, but there is still much to do to reduce internal connection costs between countries in terms of better infrastructures (roads, etc.), and harmonization of trade practices. The various trade agreements under the ALADI system are generally established between countries that already have significant and long-standing trade relations. The option of joining a free trade area should be weighed against the decision to stay outside one. In fact, new agreements are being forged between ALADI members and non-ALADI members. The 1990s witnessed the creation of major sub-regional preferential trading areas, such as CARICOM,[20] NAFTA, MERCOSUR and the Group of the Three (Colombia, Mexico and Venezuela). Moreover, a pioneering bilateral trade agreement between Chile and Mexico went into force in January 1992. The agreement, officially called the Economic Complementation Agreements (ECAs), basically cover trade of goods although they give the possibilities of future negotiation of other areas. One year before the Mexico–Chile ECA was ratified, the Argentina–Chile ECA came into force, called ECA 16 of ALADI. These two ECAs as well as many other trade agreements in Latin American were negotiated in the framework of ALADI.

---

[20]See Chap. 8 in this book.

Let us now look briefly at two empirical consequences of the large numbers of trade arrangements that have been established under the ALADI framework:

A. The Agreement on Trade, Economic and Technical Cooperation between the Caribbean Community and the Common Market (CARICOM) and the Government of the Republic of Venezuela, proposed by the Venezuelan President was signed in October 1992 and came into force on 1 January 1993. Almost 2 years later, CARICOM countries and dependent territories signed a similar agreement with Colombia, which became effective on 1 January 1995. Both agreements were concluded under the provision of non-reciprocal partial-scope agreements of the ALADI system, of which Colombia and Venezuela are also members. Consequently, the two preferential schemes are open to accession by other members of the association.

B. Unlike the Andean Group, the Common Market of the South (MERCOSUR) came into being in 1991 as a partial-scope agreement under the framework of ALADI. Argentina and Brazil decided to move towards a mutual integration process by means of a series of sectoral protocols, subsequent to the Declaration of Buenos Aires, signed in 1986, and the Agreement on Argentine-Brazilian Integration. The original goal of MERCOSUR was the creation of a common market between Argentina and Brazil. The broad, general guidelines for the establishment of MERCOSUR were included in the ALADI Economic Complementation Accord No. 14 (ACE No. 14), signed on December 1990. Paraguay and Uruguay's fears that they would be excluded from a common market between two of the largest trading partners caused both countries to ask to be included in the MERCOSUR process. The end-result of this request was the Treaty of Asunción, signed by Argentina, Brazil, Paraguay and Uruguay on March 1991. The Treaty of Asunción was later incorporated into the ALADI framework as ACE No. 18 on November 1991, following the Treaty's almost unanimous ratification in the legislatures of all four signatory States. Many have pointed out that the only reason why the Asunción Treaty was incorporated into the ALADI framework in the first place was to avoid the reporting requirements of Article 24 of the GATT, and that all MERCOSUR countries are members of the GATT.[21] In fact, MERCOSUR reinforced rather than creating new trade relations.[22]

Despite its superiority and the fact that the current MERCOSUR integration project is proceeding pursuant to the multilateral Treaty, it is important to emphasize that the Treaty of Asunción does not supersede ACE No 14. Under Article 8 of the Asunción Treaty the signatory states specifically preserve their obligations under any provision of the ALADI agreement. In the Asunción Treaty there are several provisions that corroborate a very close connection between ALADI and MERCOSUR. Pursuant to Article 1 of the Asunción Treaty, the signatory states propose to allow the free movement of goods, service, and factors of production

---

[21]O'Keefe 1994, p. 445.

[22]Porrata-Doria 2005, pp. 44–45.

(capital and workers) between them by the end of a transition period on 31 December 1994. Such a goal will be accomplished, *inter alia*, through the complete elimination of tariff and non-tariff barriers.

In addition the member states propose to have a common external tariff in place in a specific datum. The Common External Tariff (CET) has been in force since 1995. Then, the free movement of goods, with some exceptions to be discontinued by the years 2001 and 2006, has already been accomplished. Article 15 of the Asunción Treaty sets up an administrative secretariat in Montevideo to coordinate meetings, issue press releases and handle public relations. In this regard, it should be pointed out that, by falling within the ALADI framework, the MERCOSUR process has at its disposal the ALADI administrative and bureaucratic organs, which are also headquartered in Uruguay capital. To date, the MERCOSUR countries have preferred to use their own institutional framework. The one major exception to this avoidance of ALADI institutions is the utilization of the ALADI central clearing-house mechanism. Using this mechanism private sector transactions are channelled through the main clearing agent, Peru's Central Reserve Bank in Lima, and dollar payments are only required to cancel balances remaining at the end of every 4-month period. Daily gaps between credit and debit are financed by bilateral credit lines, also settled at the end of every 4 months. All members of ALADI plus the Dominican Republic participate in this clearing-house mechanism.

2.4 Institutional Structure and Technical Control Power

Logically, the institutional structure that is decided for integration will depend on the objectives, instruments and mechanisms for seeking such an association. At the institutional level, ALADI, unlike LAFTA, has a solid institutional system of an intergovernmental nature. Articles 28 and 29 of the ALADI treaty identify three governing bodies: the Council of Foreign Affairs Ministers, the Conference on Evaluation and Convergence and the Committee of Representatives. The three bodies are intergovernmental. This means that their representatives must always act in accordance with the instructions received.

According to Articles 30–32 and 43 of the ALADI treaty, the Council is ALADI's highest authority, responsible for providing political guidance on the process of integration among the association. Council members are the Ministers of Foreign Affairs of the member states. The Conference on Evaluation and Convergence, made up of plenipotentiaries, examines the functioning of the integration process and seeks to foster convergence between existing agreements (Articles 33 and 34). This Conference on Evaluation and Convergence is quite important because of the principles of the Association as mentioned above, according to Article 3.b) of the ALADI treaty. Thus its main goal is to 'promote actions of broader scope regarding economic integration'. This is an institutional innovation compared to the previous system. By contrast, the Council of Ministers and the Committee of Representatives do not present any innovation.

The Committee of Representatives is a permanent political body and negotiating forum responsible for analysing and agreeing on the initiatives necessary to achieve the objectives sponsored by the ALADI treaty (Articles 35–37). Its resolutions must be adopted by a two-third majority, with each member casting one vote. Although this voting system is quite classic and habitual in many other international organizations, it has important exceptions. A two-thirds majority is needed, but with no negatives votes for the following issues: amendments or additions to the Treaty, establishment and deepening of the regional tariff, the multilateralization, i.e. the conversion of partial trade agreements into general ones; the admissibility of new countries, for the development of the Treaty, together with the adoption of the necessary corrective actions as a result of the periodical evaluation of the integration process.

According to Articles 35(o) and 38(g) of the ALADI treaty, the Committee of Representatives may establish subsidiary organs and working groups, when and if the Secretariat suggests it. Subsidiary organs may be consultative, for advice and technical support (Article 42). Under this provision many auxiliary bodies have been created, for example, the Council on Financial and Economic Affairs,[23] a Budget Committee,[24] a Transport Council for Trade Facilitation,[25] etc. The working groups will consist of members of the Permanent Representatives accredited to the Association, and will be open to participation by all member countries. Each working group will prepare a final report to complete their tasks, which should contain a summary of the work and the conclusions and recommendations adopted. Moreover, working groups may make periodic reports of their activities with specific recommendations.[26]

ALADI also has a Secretariat, based in Montevideo, which is designed to support negotiations between the ALADI members. This technical organ has important new roles: it can make proposals to the other organs of the association and may represent the association before international economic institutions in order to discuss matters of common interest. To strengthen the integration process, the ALADI agreement empowers the Secretariat with two essential competences: (1) to regularly assess the integration process and monitor the ongoing activities of the association and (2) on its own initiative or at the request of the Committee, it can analyse the compliance of the commitments assumed. Moreover, the Secretariat

---

[23]ALADI/CR/Resolution 6, Creación del Consejo para Asuntos Financieros y Monetarios y de la Comisión Asesora para Asuntos Financieros y Monetarios, 17 September 1981; ALADI/CR/Resolution 20, Modificación del Artículo Cuarto de la Resolución 6 del Comité de Representantes, 11 August 1982.

[24]ALADI/CR/Resolution 41, 12 April 1984; ALADI/CR/Agreement 42, 27 March 1985 ALADI/CR/Agreement 203, 10 December 1996.

[25]ALADI/CR/Resolution 57, Creación de un Consejo de Transporte para la Facilitación del Comercio y funcionamiento en los países miembros de organismos nacionales sobre las mismas materias, 27 August 1986.

[26]ALADI/CR/Resolution 262, Reglamento para la creación y funcionamiento de los Grupos de Trabajo del Comité de Representantes, 26 June 2001, dealing with internal regulations.

can evaluate the national regulations that directly or indirectly violate the ALADI arrangements and resolutions. All these technical control powers of the Secretariat may help the Committee of Representatives to achieve its functions, i.e. to propose solutions when contracting parties claim the violation of any Treaty provision or Resolution. At the same time, these technical control powers of the Secretariat may help the Conference on Evaluation and Convergence to do its work and, at least, may help the Council of Ministers to decide on the merits falls the contacting parties claim the breach of treaty. Of course the Secretariat is not a judicial body, but is an alternative dispute resolution 'technical' mechanism and gives an authoritative interpretation of the commitments established under the ALADI framework.

2.5 Final Remarks

As we have seen, there are different approaches to integration in the Americas. LAFTA with ALADI, the Andean Community and MERCOSUR have historical roots, share geographical similarities, economic complexity and difficulties and yet are almost indistinguishable. Since the 1960s, Latin America has mainly used trade agreements as the primary channel for integration. Regional trade agreements can help with this projected economic integration, but only marginally. If the main objective is regional trade integration, then the proper sequencing of the various forms of integration is first to develop integration via the markets before engaging in more formal agreements.

Before making a general balance of the not so far-reaching goals and results obtained under the ALADI system, we ought to bear in mind what trade integration really means. True economic and trade integration requires the political will of the countries concerned to negotiate under the international principle of good faith, according to the Vienna Convention of the Law of Treaties. But trade negotiations are concerned with harmonizing policies and institutions in order to eliminate other elements that cause market segmentation. It is now recognized that trade integration involves far more than trade in goods and services. Trade integration means adopting common rules of conduct among countries, together with certain agreements on policies.

Under this perspective, it is easier to understand that common rules of conduct and agreements on policies are quite difficult within the ALADI framework, that not all the twelve member states of ALADI have the political will to change their national trade relationship, nor the internal existing legal structures to assume legal obligations against their economic interests. Nevertheless, the implementation of a real common market is easier in smaller groups of states, such as the Andean Community and the MERCOSUR, as they are made up of countries with more similar economic and trade policy circumstances.

In 1980, it was problematic to reach such political agreements or some legal obligations to ensure the achievement of a common market gradually. The lack of a sense of community among ALADI at that time and the strong desires to enforce trade regulations blur the objectives of the ALADI integration. That is why a distinguished author rather uncharitably refers in 1991 to ALADI as a 'quasi caricature' of LAFTA since it has no goals or fixed periods, but is rather mostly symbolic.[27] Of course this author could not have been taking into consideration that, thanks to the ALADI, other integration associations (Andean Community and MERCOSUR) could go further in order to achieve a real, but smaller common market. As already mentioned above, from the early 1980s until the 1990s there has been huge regional and partial-scope agreement development. Consequently, the 1990s could well be called the 'free trade area decade' in Latin America.[28]

The goals of MERCOSUR are much more ambitious than the ALADI ones. MERCOSUR member states try to achieve what the ALADI cannot dream of. In this sense, MERCOSUR has achieved the objectives initially proposed more quickly than the larger association ALADI. Moreover, the coordination of an external common trade policy has become a reality ranking both the multilateral system of the WTO and the regional initiative, ALADI in this case. Consequently, as mentioned above, the ALADI treaty aims at trade integration via agreements, which is why the Montevideo Treaty is seen as a kind of 'umbrella', which facilitates the negotiation and realization of a regional tariff preference, regional trade arrangements and partial-scope agreements. Besides, as we have already seen, the ALADI treaty encourages States to establish other integration associations and partnerships between these associations. This 'association of associations' could be significant, since from a strict international law trade perspective, it makes little sense to engage in regional negotiations on matters such as agriculture, investments, intellectual property and dispute resolution, when the WTO sponsors global negotiations on those same items within the multilateral system in the twenty-first century.

Trade integration in Latin America was slower than suspected, although Latin America has comparative advantages in natural resources. In general terms, 17.2 % of Latin American exports were intra-regional in 1995. Ten years later, in 2005, 34.3 % of the Andean[29] exports of manufactured goods were inter-regional too. And 20.2 % of the MERCOSUR exports of goods were shipped to other MERCOSUR members. As for parts and components, the share of ALADI intra-regional exports of components and parts amounted to 14.00 % in 2005.

But if we take a closer look under the ALADI umbrella, and analyse only the Andean Community and MERCOSUR countries, the results are different: 39.5 % of Andean exports of parts and components were shipped to other Andean countries in 2005 and 22.6 % for MERCOSUR. Both the Andean Community and MERCOSUR showed great economic success in their early stages. This success can be attributed to the fact that its member countries have economies that work

---

[27]Chaparro 1989, p. 60.

[28]Meller 2009, p. 91.

[29]Bolivia, Colombia, Ecuador, Perú and Venezuela.

well together.[30] This 'inevitable marriage', combined with the support of businesses and the elite within the region, provided the fuel that drove the relatively rapid creation of a common market within MERCOSUR.

In short, however, if we compare these facts, it can easily be seen that the Latin American economies are less integrated among themselves than East Asian or European economies.[31]

Within the bilateral import and export relation among the ALADI members, the General Secretary is optimistic in its reports for March 2011. Indeed, for instance, Argentina expanded its foreign trade considerably: 32.2 % of its exporters were acquired by Brazil.[32] In contrast, the intra-regional exports of Uruguay contracted slightly (−3.3 %). But it should be noted that in 2010 most of these exports were soyabeans, whose final destination was world trade, to, in particular, Russia (48.4 %), Switzerland (26.5 %) and Turkey (18.19 %). The main destinations of Uruguay exports in June 2011 were Brazil (17.7 %), the Free Zone of Nueva Palmira (14.9 %) and Argentina (7.4 %). At the same time, exports of beef from Uruguay increased by 9.1 %: Russian acquired 28.4 %, Israel 12.9 % and Venezuela 7.2 %.[33] Brazil's foreign trade also grew considerably in 2010: exports increased by 30.6 % and imports by 25.3 %. The expansion of exports was widespread, especially to the European Union (31.2 %), China (48.1 %) and ALADI (28 %).[34]

For these reasons and also because there is some strong resistance to losing state sovereignty, through complete trade liberalization, one can comfortably predict the failure of the Free Trade Area of the Americas. Conversely, we have to recognize the consolidation of MERCOSUR. We must say that MERCOSUR is much more than a regional trade pact, as its scope is distinctly wider, both economically, through the creation of a common market, and politically. To reaffirm this essential point, we only have to corroborate that the MERCOSUR initiative is protected in the constitution of the member states.

References

Aminian N et al (2009) A comparative analysis of trade and economic integration in East Asia and Latin America. Economic Change and Restructuring 42: 105–137

Baquero-Herrera M (2005) Open Regionalism in Latin America: An Appraisal. Law and Business Review of the Americas 11: 139–158

Bauni S E (2004) Argentine-Chilean Mining Integrations and Complementation Treaty: Challenges and Opportunities. Journal of Energy & Natural Resources Law 22(1): 66–79

---

[30]Porrata-Doria 2005, pp. 1–19 stating that MERCOSUR created an imperfect common market in 10 years, and recognizing that while this progress is impressive, there are still tensions and reductions in barriers to be addressed.

[31]Aminian 2009, p. 119.

[32]ALADI/SEC/di 2406.3, 5 May 2011.

[33]ALADI/SEC/di 2406, 26 April 2011.

[34]ALADI/SEC/di 2406.1, 28 April 2011.

Bennet J (2008) The Union of South American Nations: The New(est) Regionalism in Latin America. Suffolk Transnational Law Review 32: 103–133

Chaparro A (1989) Por qué ha fracasado la integración latinoamericana? Monte Ávila, Caracas

Cruz Miramontes R (1995) La cláusula de nación más favorecida y su adecuación al TLC en el marco de ALADI. Anuario Hispano-Luso-Americano de Derecho Internacional 12: 173–186

Davison R H (1985) The ALADI Treaty and Letter of Credit Transaction in Latin America. The International Lawyer 19: 1303–1308

Ferrer Vieyra E (2003) Reflexiones sobre la integración de America Latina (ALADI), Cursos de Derecho Internacional, Comité Jurídico Interamericano, pp. 529–542

Garré Copello B (1995) Compatibilización entre el sistema de la ALADI y otras formas de integración no previstas en su carta constitutiva: el protocolo interpretativo del artículo 44 del Tratado de Montevideo de 1980. In Cristina Vázquez M (ed) Estudios multidisciplinarios sobre el MERCOSUR. Universidad de la República, Montevideo, pp. 305–352

Mace G (1988) Regional Integration in Latin America: A Long and Winding Road. International Journal 43(3): 404–427

Meller P (2009) From Unilateral Liberalization to Regional Free Trade Agreements: A Latin America Perspective, Economic Change and Restructuring. 42(1–2): 85-103

Middlebrook K (1978) Regional Organization and Andean Economic Integration, 1969-75. Journal of Common Market Studies 17(1): 62-82

Niaradi G A (2001) A intergração econômica nas Américas: ALADI e ALALC, MERCOSUR, NAFTA, ALCA. In Estudos de direito internacional, Anais do 2º Congresso Brasileiro de Direito Internacional. Curitiba, Juruá, pp. 419–425

O'Keefe T A (1994) An Analysis of the Mercosur Economic Integration Project from a Legal Perspective. The International Lawyer 28(2): 439–448

Porrata-Doria R A Jr et al (2005) Mercosur: The Common Market of the Southern Cone. Carolina Academic Press, Durham

Radway R (1981) The Next Decade in Latin America: Anticipating the Future From the Past. Case Western Reserve Journal of International Law 13: 3–36

Steinfatt K (2001) Preferential and Partial Scope Trade. In Salazar-Xirinachs J M et al. (eds.) Towards a Free Trade in the Americas, Brookings Institution Press, Washington, D.C., pp. 108–122

Chapter 3
The Union of South American Nations: An Emerging Regional Organization

Mª Ángeles Cano Linares

Abstract The integration process among the 12 countries of the South American region is an important goal. The first foundations of an innovative, progressive and expanded integration process have been established. If the consolidation is achieved, it may be crucial and very useful for the future of the region and its people. Institutionalization is progressing gradually although problems are not inexistent. UNASUR seeks to develop an integrated political, social, cultural, economic, financial, environmental and infrastructural space. This new integration model will include all the goals achieved by MERCOSUR and the Andean Community as well as the experience of Chile, Guyana and Suriname. Its ultimate point is to promote a more equitable, harmonious and integrated development in South America.

Keywords South American Integration · Union of South American Nations (UNASUR) · Integrated integration · Geographical integration · MERCOSUR-CAN · Peace zone

Contents

This chapter has been written as part of a larger research project called "The reform of economic international institutions", project number DER 2010-20414-C02-01 (subprogram JURI), which is funded by the Spanish Ministry of Science and Innovation.

Mª.Á. Cano Linares (✉)
Department of Public International Law and International Relations,
Rey Juan Carlos University, Madrid, Spain
e-mail: angeles.cano.linares@urjc.es

M. Odello and F. Seatzu (eds.), *Latin American and Caribbean International Institutional Law*, DOI 10.1007/978-94-6265-069-5_3

43

3.1 Introduction

The Union of South American Nations (UNASUR)[1] is one of the most recent examples of developing regional integration.[2]

The institutional experience in Latin America[3] throughout the twentieth century brought convincement to the states of the need to find new formulas that could overcome the difficulties they faced to achieve, with effectiveness, the success of their cooperation and integration efforts. They had to avoid obstacles, both economic and political, which so far have prevented the development of most of the integration processes that have been tested in the region.[4] In this context of new regionalism, South American countries have considered that UNASUR may be a useful and, above all, crucial tool for the future of the region and its diverse peoples.[5]

Therefore, the adoption in Brasilia (2008) of the Treaty establishing the Union of South American Nations (UNASUR or Brasilia Treaty)[6] is the end of a process that leads to the establishment, in the international arena, of a framework of cooperation and integration among most South American states. Twelve countries signed the Constitutive Treaty.[7] This process began, as it is known, in the early twenty-first century with the Summits of South American Presidents.

---

[1]Unión de Naciones Suramericanas (UNASUR) is the Spanish official denomination and União de Nações Sul-Americanas (UNASUL) in Portuguese; in English it is Union of South American Nations.

[2]Cano Linares 2010.

[3]In Spain, some authors consider that Iberoamérica is a better denomination for those countries with Spanish and Portuguese languages. See: Díaz Barrado 2010.

[4]Saludjian 2004; González Miranda and Ovando Santana 2008; López 2008.

[5]Serbin 2007: Aldecoa Luzárraga 2007; Álvarez Valdés 2009; Bennet 2008: Cardona 2008.

[6]South American Union of Nations Constitutive Treaty, Third Summit of Heads of State and Government, Brasília, 23 May 2008, at: http://www.comunidadandina.org/unasur/tratado_consti tutivo.htm. Accessed 12 September 2014.

[7]The 12 countries are: Bolivia, Colombia, Ecuador, Peru (members of the Andean Community of Nations-CAN); Argentina, Brazil, Paraguay, Uruguay, Venezuela (members of MERCOSUR); Chile, associate member of MERCOSUR and CAN; Guyana and Surinam (members of CARICOM).

At the same time, the Treaty of Brasilia represents a new beginning.[8] It opens a new phase in the cooperation and integration efforts being made by South American states to achieve some of the objectives for long time desired in the whole Latin American region.[9] It searches a more comprehensive, legal, institutionalized and developed framework.[10] Thus, in May 2011, the entry into force of the Treaty, requiring nine ratifications of this conventional instrument, consolidates a new attempt for the South American countries' integration process.[11] With this, another step is taken in the process for the formation of an instance, which is a strategic goal for South America, that must be built upon solid union pillars.

UNASUR has generated a new and unique initiative in the heterogeneous and diverse reality of integration that has been appearing in the Americas since the decade of 1950. This process of institutionalization is a novel integration scheme, a wide and gradual integration process that also involves two existing customs unions, MERCOSUR/MERCOSUL (Mercado Común del Sur)[12] and the Andean Community of Nations (CAN).[13] It eventually represents a manifestation of the various regional efforts to minimize the effects and consequences of globalization.[14] With UNASUR, another institution joins the already complex web of partnerships in the American continent.

Still, the establishment of UNASUR is due to the need to find particular solutions to many of the political and economic challenges that arise in the South American region. In other words, the creation of a process of integration of this kind is the result, on one hand, of unsatisfying integration processes that have taken place so far in South America. It represents, on the other hand, the will

---

[8]See: Solón 2008.

[9]Since their independence, Latin American countries have attempted to integrate both politically and economically, dreaming with a Bolivarian unification. The first paragraph of the preamble of Brasilia Treaty asserts: 'Based on the shared history and solidarity of our multiethnic, multilingual and multicultural nations, which have fought for the emancipation and unity of South America, honouring the vision of those who forged our independence and freedom in favour of that union and the building of a common future'. See: Díaz Barrado 2005: the first truly modern achievement was in the field of trade, with the Latin America Free Trade Association (LAFTA/ALADI). LAFTA was created in 1960 by the Treaty of Montevideo and sought to eliminate trade restrictions on goods imported from Member States and to improve economic conditions for the people of the region.

[10]Díaz Barrado and Cano Linares 2007, 2009.

[11]The UNASUR Treaty entered into force on 8 May 2011. See Article 26: 'The present Constitutive Treaty of the Union of South American Nations will enter into force thirty days after the date of receipt of the 9th instrument of ratification'. In the following order Bolivia, Ecuador, Guyana, Venezuela, Peru, Argentina, Chile, Suriname, Uruguay and Colombia all ratified the Treaty. As of today, the two countries that have not yet ratified it are Brazil and Paraguay.

[12]See: Chaps. 5 and 6 in this book; Alegrett Salazar 2007; Saccone 2008.

[13]In 2002 the Andean Community and MERCOSUR signed an agreement to create a free trade area between the two trade blocs. Acuerdo de Complementación Económica n° 56, 6 December 2002, http://www.sice.oas.org/trade/Mrcsr/ACMerAns.asp. Accessed 10 October 2014. See also: Salazar 2008.

[14]Díaz Barrado 2005.

of a very significant group of states from Latin America to achieve a level of integration that would ensure the welfare of the peoples of the whole region.

This initiative is, at present, a mechanism with an enormous potential and finds its most immediate antecedents in 2004 with the adoption of the Cusco Declaration (Peru).[15] The Declaration states that the 'The South American Community of Nations is formed bearing in mind: (…) The convergence of their political, economic, social, cultural and security interests as a potential element for strengthening and developing their internal capacity for improving their international trade presence'.

The truth is that in a short period of time, its original name—South American Community of Nations (Comunidad Sudamericana de Naciones; CSN)—has been changed. Since 2007, the organization is named the Union of South American Nations (UNASUR). Article 1 of Brasilia's Treaty expresses the states' decision to 'constitute the Union of South American Nations (UNASUR) as an entity with international juridical character'.

Only time will say if we are witnessing a real and effective process of integration in the Americas and if, lastly, most states of Latin America succeed in achieving their constant efforts and will of cooperation and integration. In any case, some of the topics for a long time understood as the ones that must define cooperation in the Americas, have been gradually crystallized through the configuration of this process and, therefore, should settle the elements for future cooperation.

In this regard, it must be remembered that the change of name was parallel to another decision that should be cherished as a step to institutionalization of the new political space.[16] In fact, at the same meeting, in April 2007, it was decided to abandon the initial mechanism of *pro tempore* Secretariat and to establish a permanent secretariat of UNASUR, based in Quito, Ecuador, where is located the monument known as 'La Mitad del Mundo'.

Finally, with the adoption of the Treaty of Brasilia and its entry into force, an important step was taken defining more precisely the aspects concerning UNASUR's meaning, contents and scope.

3.2 Main Traits: Integration Based on Economy and on Infrastructures

UNASUR represents an attractive and highly relevant initiative, with possibilities for setting up certain areas of cooperation and integration in the South American region in the twenty-first century. It may also trigger far-reaching implications for

---

[15]At the 3rd South American Summit on 8 December 2004, presidents and representatives from 12 South American countries signed the Cusco Declaration, a two-page statement announcing the foundation of the South American Community. Panamá and Mexico attended the signing ceremony as observers, at http://www.comunidadandina.org/documentos/dec_int/cusco_sudamerica.htm. Accessed 1 October 2014.

[16]See: Alegrett Salazar 2008.

the entire American continent and even for the relationship between integration processes at a universal scale.

Also, it cannot be ignored that the creation of a union between South American states opens the debate about 'Latin America' *versus* 'South America'. Most of the more important American states prefer the second option. Hence, this political will directly affects the efforts for Latin American and Caribbean integration as well as the claim of a continental free trade area.[17]

At the same time, the establishment of this organization fulfils some of the aims and objectives that have been marking all integration processes in America. UNASUR also intends to overcome the unification practices based exclusively on the adoption of Free Trade Agreements.

It is therefore not surprising that the proponents of other positions have emerged as the greatest critics of this incipient process of integration and implementation of cooperation mechanisms among the states of South America.[18] Also, one cannot discount the possibility of a lack of political will in the direction of consolidating and projecting UNASUR by some states of the region, which would impact very negatively on its configuration as a process with potential to achieve significant success for South American integration.[19]

In recent years some political drawbacks have been appreciated. If they do not disappear they could not stop, but slow down, the progress in terms of integration needs of South American states.[20] It has been noted that 'There weren't few differences between South American nations in recent months. Paradoxically, they seemed to have occurred when exceptional conditions appeared, objective and subjective, for regional integration'; but 'without ignoring these issues and looking for immediate solutions to them, it is essential to think of integration as a strategic and purposeful state policy, higher than the adverse contingencies that may eventually arise'.[21] The focus on South America, as an integrated whole, is a very suggestive project in itself.

In addition, UNASUR has emerged from the beginning on terms that give it greater interest and potential from both legal and political-economic, as well as in relation to many questions, such as social content or culture. In other words, this integration process addresses different objectives of the states in the region and, above all, the goal that has been stipulated in Article 2 of the Treaty of Brasilia:

> The objective of the Union of South American Nations is to build, in a participatory and consensual manner, an integration and union among its peoples in the cultural, social, economic and political fields, prioritizing political dialogue, social policies, education,

---

[17]Díaz Barrado 2010.

[18]Cardona 2005.

[19]The creation of UNASUR is consistent with Brazil's foreign policy focus of utilizing regional integration as an indispensable platform for the country to project itself more effectively onto the global arena, but also to obtain regional preponderance. See: Wade 2010.

[20]Esparza 2008.

[21]UNASUR, Antecedentes, at http://www.comunidadandina.org/unasur/antecedentes.htm. Accessed 12 October 2014. Also see: Wade 2010.

energy, infrastructure, financing and the environment, among others, with a view to elimi-nating socioeconomic inequality, in order to achieve social inclusion and participation of civil society, to strengthen democracy and reduce asymmetries within the framework of strengthening the sovereignty and independence of the States.

It is possible to highlight some aspects that are present in the political-legal configuration of UNASUR and that, somehow, clarify some of its essential features.

First, a new integration scheme is developed and it may be called 'integration of integration'. Indeed UNASUR, unlike other forms of regional cooperation, does not look forward to a new association of states. UNASUR seeks to link existing processes, trying to unite and join the efforts made so far and the already achieved goals. The two main processes are MERCOSUR and the Andean Community.[22]

Second, the process is not limited to promoting the convergence of Economic Complementation Agreements between the countries of South America. The pro-ponents, in Article 3 UNASUR, have been concerned about establishing values and defining clear principles and specific objectives. They have sought social pro-jection, without neglecting the aspects of economic integration, taking into account both the results obtained so far as the social needs and demands. In this sense, the existence of a vocation that integrates people, not just economies, is considered essential.[23] This explicitly declared purpose[24] could play a crucial role in eliminating, or at least alleviating, some of the serious deficiencies in South America.

Finally, learning from the previous experience, South American countries have assumed that it is not possible to reach certain levels of economic integration if there are no adequate ways of communication among their countries. This led them to prioritize from the beginning the development of appropriate infrastruc-ture as one of the cornerstones of UNASUR. In this context, it is worth noting the establishment of the Initiative for Regional Infrastructure Integration (IIRSA), a

---

[22]The preamble of the Brasilia Treaty affirms the determination to build a South American iden-tity and citizenship and to develop an integrated regional space in the political, economic, social, cultural, environmental, energy and infrastructure dimensions, for the strengthening of Latin America and The Caribbean unity.

[23]UNASUR, Article 3(b): 'The inclusive and equitable social and human development in order to eradicate poverty and overcome inequalities in the region'; 3(j) 'Universal access to social security and health services; (k) Cooperation on issues of migration with an integral approach, based on an unrestricted respect for human and labor rights, for migratory regularization and harmonization of policies'; 3(l) 'Economic and commercial cooperation to achieve progress and consolidation of an innovative, dynamic, transparent, equitable and balanced process focused on an effective access, promoting economic growth and development to overcome asymmetries by means of the complementarities of the economies of the countries of South America, as well as the promotion of the well-being of all sectors of the population and the reduction of poverty'.

[24]UNASUR Treaty, Preamble: 'Convinced that the South American integration and South American unity are necessary to promote the sustainable development and wellbeing of our peo-ples, and to contribute to the solution of the problems which still affect our region, such as per-sistent poverty, social exclusion and inequality'.

forum for dialogue between the authorities responsible of transport infrastructure, energy and telecommunications of those 12 countries.[25] Its main objective is two-fold: first, to promote the development of transport infrastructure, energy and tele-communications with a regional vision, ensuring the physical integration of the 12 states; second, to achieve an equitable and sustainable pattern of local development.[26]

Finally, the stated objective of UNASUR is to develop an integrated South America in the political, social, economic, environmental and infrastructure areas; to strengthen the identity of South America, and to reinforce, in coordination with other regional and sub-regional institutions, its participation in the international arena.

3.3 History of UNASUR: From the Summit of South American Presidents to the Summit of the South American Community of Nations

In the year 2000, the Presidents of Brazil, Colombia, Argentina, Bolivia, Chile, Ecuador, Guyana, Paraguay, Peru, Suriname, Uruguay and Venezuela met in Brasilia and signed the *Brasilia Communiqué* which resumed their agreement to foster international cooperation through the unified treatment of the topics covered in the already mentioned agenda of the Andean Community and the Southern Common Market, with the aim to build shared visions and create solutions for key issues of mutual interest, both at the regional and global stage.[27]

---

[25]In order to achieve the proposed multisectorial objectives, it envisages coordination mechanisms and exchange of information among governments, three of the region's multilateral financial institutions (the Inter-American Development Bank (IDB), the Corporación Andina de Fomento (CAF) and the Financial Fund for the Development of the River Plate Basin (FONPLATA), at http://www.iirsa.org. Accessed 14 October 2014.

[26]UNASUR, Article 3(d): 'Energy integration for the integral and sustainable use of the resources of the region, in a spirit of solidarity'; 3(e) 'The development of an infrastructure for the inter-connection of the region and among our peoples based on sustainable social and economic development criteria'; 3(h): 'The development of concrete and effective mechanisms to overcome asymmetries, thus achieving an equitable integration'.

[27]Another important meeting was held in 2002 at Guayaquil (Ecuador). Some of the essential elements in shaping the integration process were set and discussed in those two Summits. UNASUR considers as a remote precedent the Panama Congress held in July 1826 under Simon Bolivar's initiative. The idea was to form an Iberoamerican Confederation from Mexico to Chile and Argentina. Latin American Free Trade Association (LAFTA) created by Treaty of Montevideo (1960); the Latin American Integration Association (ALADI), an Economic Preferential Zone, created by another Treaty of Montevideo (1980), the Andean Community (1960) and the Treaty of Asuncion (1991) creating MERCOSUR can be considered as part of UNASUR history, at http://www.comunidadandina.org/csn/antecedentes.htm. Accessed 16 October 2014.

The Cusco Declaration was signed on 8 December 2004 at the Third Summit of Presidents of South America, and created the CSN.[28] Four years later, on 23 May 2008 the Presidents of 12 South American countries signed the South American Union of Nations Constitutive Treaty. So, the Treaty of Brasilia can be considered the 'constitutional framework' of the South American integration process and collects some of the most important ideas of previous initiatives. These crucial items, such as democracy, trade, infrastructure integration, illicit drugs and related crimes, information, knowledge and technology were already specifically set in 2000.

It should also be remembered that in 2002 the Declaration on the South American Peace Zone was adopted, declaring South America as a Zone of Peace and Cooperation for the region. The 12 states reiterated their major commitment towards the 'prohibition of the use or threat of use of force between states, the location, development, manufacture, possession, deployment, testing and use of all weapons of mass destruction and their delivery and the commitment to establish a system of gradual elimination of antipersonnel mines'.[29] This Declaration is considered a guiding principle of the integration process, and clearly shows the firm commitment for peace, under the international rule of law, of South American States. To this end, a new Peace, Security and Cooperation Protocol is under discussion.[30]

After the creation of the CSN, the Summit of South American Presidents was transformed with the same composition into the Summit of the South American Community of Nations. Its first meeting took place, once again, in Brasilia in September 2005.[31] The Priority Agenda and Action Program of the Community was defined and incorporated in the Presidential statement.[32] The Declaration specifically gathered up the decision to gradually build up a South American free trade area, and to support the economies of the countries of the region and promote their growth and development, together with the reduction of existing asymmetries.[33]

It was also discussed, in this first Summit, the need to give greater depth to the integration content and institutional forms of the process, learning from positive experiences of sub-regional integration mechanisms.

---

[28]See: Bilbao 2004.

[29]Declaración sobre Zona de Paz Sudamericana, Guayaquil, 27 de julio del 2002.

[30]Declaration of the Council of Heads of State and Government of the Union of South American Nations (UNASUR), Los Cardales, Province of Buenos Aires, Argentina, Tuesday, 4 May 2010, para 7, at: http://alainet.org/active/37964&lang=es. Accessed 11 November 2014.

[31]See: Buenaño 2005; Jaguaribe 2005.

[32]It was also decided to accelerate the implementation of priority projects of integration that constitute 'IIRSA Project Portfolio' and also agreed to boost funding alternatives that take into account the financial realities of South American countries.

[33]This was an objective set up by same studies on the secretariats of MERCOSUR, CAN, and also the Latin American Integration Association (ALADI), with the participation of Chile, Guyana and Suriname.

The Second CNS Summit was held in Cochabamba (2006), with a significant high-level diplomacy. Presidents had an initial document prepared by their personal representatives. The Cochabamba Declaration sought to place the fundamental stone to the South American Union to clearly establish a new model of South American integration for the twenty-first century, laying its guiding principles, the premises for its construction and its main goals.

In April 2007, in Venezuela, the First Summit of Presidents on Energy Integration was held, leading to the adoption of the Declaration of Margarita which addressed one of the sectors that have been considered a priority in the construction and development of UNASUR, and that should become one of the hallmarks of cooperation and integration between South American states.

The statement promotes, among its 17 points, infrastructure investments together with regional energy integration and with the need to work in order to establish a systematic assessment of energy balance in South America. The 12 Presidents pledged to promote the development of renewable energy programmes and activities for energy-saving cooperation, and promote collaboration between their national oil companies, including the industrialization of hydrocarbons. Both the commitment to use the energy integration of the South American Community of Nations as an important tool to promote social and economic development, as well as the intention to eradicate poverty in the region, and the universal access to energy as a civil right deserve special mention. At the same time, a Political Dialogue Decision between the main leaders of the states and governments was also adopted to determine the change of name of the organization and the permanent headquarters of UNASUR.[34]

The year 2008 was crucial in building this integration process with the adoption of its constituent Treaty, and the decision to obtain a greater institutionalization. The necessary conditions were thus given to make possible the successful achievement of the objectives behind such a process. Some of the necessary mechanisms for obtaining practical effects in the South America's regional integration were set. Finally, on 11 May 2008 a new international organization was born.[35]

The initial formation process has already been achieved and, in a very little time, UNASUR has obtained international legal personality and the process of institutionalization has begun.

3.4 Foundations, Principles and Activity

The various statements and documents so far adopted show that UNASUR is founded on the history of the continental integration process, and that South American self-identity as well as shared common values may be able to overcome

---

[34]Bervejillo 2009.

[35]The Declaration of Quito (Ecuador) adopted at the Third Regular Meeting of the Council of State and Government Leaders, held in August 2009, reaffirmed the main objectives.

the undoubted differences or asymmetries between the Latin American states. The principles that govern and build the process have been very broadly formulated. The Treaty of Brasilia, under the expression of specific objectives, collects, in fact, many manifestations of its main areas of activity.

3.4.1 The Principles: Peace, Human Rights and Social and Economic Development

In any case, we can still maintain that UNASUR is founded on the existence of a certain number of main principles that are the following:

(i) Peace. From the beginning, peace has been settled as the first pillar and South America's real and main principle of integration. South American countries have insisted on that not only is peace an essential element of integration, but also that this region must be considered as a peace zone. Establishing such a close relationship between peace and integration, the consolidation of the integration process must be necessarily based on the establishment of peace and security in the region. This fact explains the emphasis placed earlier in the creation of a South American Defence Council.[36] On May 2010,[37] South America's Ministers of Defence met in Guayaquil (Ecuador) and adopted an agreement to develop common mechanisms of transparency in defence policy and spending. The agreement, which also calls for the creation of a multilateral Centre for Strategic Defence Studies, is a recent example of the growing effectiveness of UNASUR as a forum for addressing the most urgent and sensitive issues on the regional agenda.

Therefore, the affirmation of peace and security in the South American region is settled as one of the structural principles of UNASUR, which necessarily leads, through political consultation, the states to develop regional consequences from this principle. It is also worth highlighting the identification of such a process with the values of peace and security, from the assertion of the validity of international law, multilateralism and a firm defence of democracy. UNASUR may, in an effective way, integrate the economic development and social agenda, and set respect for the rule of law in the world, as well as the provisions of the Latin American human rights charter framework for fighting corruption at all levels.

(ii) Human rights. There is no doubt that democracy and respect for human rights have become the principles and foundations of UNASUR. The defence of democracy and respect for human rights constitute essential conditions for

---

[36]The Declaration of Quito, August 2009, expressed satisfaction with the initiatives addressed in the First Meeting of South American Defence Council. A consensus was reached to give operational capacity to the objectives of the American Defence Council so it could strengthen the actions in defence policy, military cooperation, humanitarian matters, peacekeeping operations, training and formation. See: Crisóstomo del Pedregal 2009.

[37]After the United States of America complained about Venezuela's decision to purchase arms from Russia.

the integration of South America. Both aspects have been well reflected in each of the statements that have been emanating from the Summit of South American Presidents, and they also appear in the Treaty of Brasilia.

The Brasilia Declaration of 2000 stated, quite clearly, that 'the determination to respect the values of representative democracy and its procedures, human rights […] constitutes an essential basis of the cooperation process and integration in which South American countries are committed', insisting that 'consolidation of democracy and peace throughout the region is at the root of the historical approach among South American countries […]'.

Beyond this, the Treaty of Brasilia clearly confirms that 'both South American integration and the South American Union are based on the guiding principles of: unlimited respect for sovereignty and territorial integrity and inviolability of states; self-determination of the peoples; solidarity; cooperation; peace; democracy, citizen participation and pluralism; universal, indivisible and interdependent human rights; reduction of asymmetries and harmony with nature for a sustainable development'.[38] And last but not least, it is stated as an objective in Article 2 the importance of 'strengthening democracy'.[39]

With the 2009 Declaration of Quito, South American states have also reaffirmed their 'commitment to democracy as the only system to meet the challenges and provide greater hope and opportunities to our people, with full respect for human rights and fundamental freedoms. In this regard, the institutional framework, democracy and the rule of law through dialogue and negotiation are the only ways to resolve differences, build lasting peace and coexistence'. This has led to the adoption of the 2014 Additional Protocol to the Constitutive Treaty of UNASUR on Commitment to Democracy,[40] which follows other similar documents adopted in the Latin American context.[41] It also foresees a series of sanctions against states which may have suffered unconstitutional changes of government, and the action of all other Member States to restore democracy.

It is important to underline that, within UNASUR, the decision about 'maintaining the rule of law and full respect for the democratic rule in each of the 12 countries of the region provide an objective and a shared commitment, becoming today a condition of participation in South American future meetings' has been

---

[38]UNASUR Treaty, Preamble.

[39]Article 2 states that 'The objective of the Union of South American Nations is to build, in a participatory and consensual manner, an integration and union among its peoples in the cultural, social, economic and political fields, prioritizing political dialogue, social policies, education, energy, infrastructure, financing and the environment, among others, with a view to eliminating socioeconomic inequality, in order to achieve social inclusion and participation of civil society, to strengthen democracy and reduce asymmetries within the framework of strengthening the sovereignty and independence of the States'.

[40]UNASUR, Protocolo Adicional al Tratado Constitutivo de UNASUR sobre Compromiso con la Democracia, Dirección de Comunicación y Relaciones Institucionales, Quito, 2014, entered into force on 19 March 2014.

[41]See: Mercosur, Ushuaia Protocol on the Democratic Commitment in MERCOSUR, 24 July 1998, 2177 UNTS 383.

adopted.[42] Also, as expressed in the Declaration of Quito (2009) this highlights the commitment of the countries of UNASUR in the field of the promotion and protection of human rights, especially in regional initiatives such as the Andean Charter for the Promotion and Protection of Human Rights, and the work being developed in the Meeting of High Authorities on Human Rights and Foreign Ministries of MERCOSUR and associated states (RAADDHH) at regional level. They also recognize the importance of the participation of countries in other multilateral human rights forums, stressing the importance of 'UNASUR in the process of institution building, examining the advisability of creating mechanisms, including the proposal to establish a South American Council of Human Rights, to reflect the existing regional heritage, to strengthen the cooperation between Member States in the matter'.

(iii) Economic development and social settings are also foundations, and basic and essential principles of the South American integration. States in this region have made it clear that one of the foundations and objectives of this process is only achievable through 'integration': the economic and social development in the South American zone. In the Brasilia Declaration of 2000, these points were linked with the elements that define cooperation and integration in this area when declared that 'political stability, economic growth and promoting social justice in each of the 12 South American countries will depend in large measure of the expansion and deepening of cooperation and sense of solidarity in the region, and the strengthening and expansion of networks of reciprocal interests'. This makes clear that UNASUR is configured as a, or may we say *the*, space for social and economic development for the region, and ensures that it will be present in both the economic and social dimensions.

The Treaty of Brasilia insists heavily on this matter. Thus, Article 3, regarding the specific objectives, clearly establishes that: 'The inclusive and equitable social and human development in order to eradicate poverty and overcome inequalities in the region'. Moreover, the Treaty supports the need for:

> Economic and commercial cooperation to achieve progress and consolidation of an innovative, dynamic, transparent, equitable and balanced process focused on an effective access, promoting economic growth and development to overcome asymmetries by means of the complementarities of the economies of the countries of South America, as well as the promotion of the wellbeing of all sectors of the population and the reduction of poverty.[43]

It should be stressed that UNASUR is seeking the convergence of the political, economic, social, cultural and security matters as a path for strengthening and

---

[42]Earlier, in September 2008, UNASUR achieved its first diplomatic challenge, the attempted violent destabilization of Evo Morales' government in Bolivia. An emergency meeting of South American Heads of state in Santiago (Michele Bachelet, President of Chile was the pro tempore President of UNASUR) quickly issued a unanimous statement strongly condemning the attacks against Bolivian democracy and announcing the creation of a commission of "support and assistance" to the Bolivian government. Soon afterwards, Bolivian's opposition groups abandoned their violent tactics and agreed to enter negotiations with Morales government. UNASUR also adopted a position of staunch opposition to the coup in Honduras.

[43]UNASUR Treaty, Article 3(l).

developing the internal capabilities of its members to gain more international participation, not limiting its development to economy-based objectives.[44] Recognizing the
asymmetries in the respective areas must lead to a more just and equitable distribution
of incomes, as well as access to education, social cohesion and inclusion, and the
preservation of the environment and promotion of a sustainable development.

As already mentioned, the development of a new form of regional integration
cannot be based only on trade and commercial relations, especially because the
region has already different structures which operate in those areas: MERCOSUR,
CAN and CARICOM. In their effort to build a balanced integration and regional
consolidation, including the Agenda for Social Integration and Productivity, South
American countries, when working on commercial convergence, should also seek
forms of political, social and cultural development. They should favour a more
equitable, harmonious and integral development of South America.[45]

Maintaining this line or path, we can affirm the common core commitment the
states have expressed in UNASUR, at least formally, including the fight against
poverty, hunger eradication, employment generation and access to decent health
and education, as key tools for the development of their peoples.

Alongside these principles, underlying the state action under UNASUR, the
basic instruments show at least two other dimensions of great interest which are:
the South American assertion of identity and the integration of South American
states. This was explicit in the Cusco Declaration, when South American leaders
expressed their commitment to create a 'politically, socially, economically, envi-
ronmentally and infrastructurally integrated South America area'.

The Brasilia Treaty also makes clear that it required

> The consolidation of a South American identity through the progressive recognition of the
> rights of nationals of a Member State resident in any of the other Member States, with the
> aim of attaining a South American citizenship;

> Convinced that the South American integration and South American unity are necessary to
> promote the sustainable development and wellbeing of our peoples, and to contribute to
> the solution of the problems which still affect out region, such as persistent poverty, social
> exclusion and inequality.[46]

3.4.2 The Pillars: Political Cooperation, Trade Integration, Energy Integration and Regional Development

There are certain pillars on which this South American community building is sustained: political cooperation, commercial integration, energy integration, complementary production and infrastructures, competitiveness and development.[47]

---

[44]See: Contreras Polgati 2009.

[45]http://www.comunidadandina.org/unasur/antecedentes.htm. See: Giacalone 2006; Wade 2010.

[46]UNASUR Treaty, Article 3(i) and Preamble respectively.

[47]Comunidad Andina, Hacia la comunidad sudamericana de naciones: elementos para un plan de
trabajo, Documento de trabajo, SG/dt 288, 9 March 2005.

The first political cooperation begins to open its space thanks to consultation mechanisms, trying to coordinate common positions. However, until this is fully achieved, an intergovernmental relationship is essential, with a preponderant role, if not almost exclusive, of the presidents of South American states with virtually no participation of the respective state administrations. Still, in the international relations field, South America is being consolidated as a new actor, an independent one, positioned against the United States of America and advocating specific strategies with the European Union. This may create conflicts between the governance of UNASUR laws and those of the Organization of American States, which has been the premier supranational organization governing the affairs of South America.[48]

The Treaty of Brasilia points at one of the first specific objectives of this integration process: the strengthening of the political dialogue among Member States to guarantee a space for consultation in order to reinforce South American integration and the participation of UNASUR in the international arena.

Moreover, Article 14 establishes that:

> The political consultation and coordination among the Member States of UNASUR will be based on harmony and mutual respect, strengthening regional stability and supporting the preservation of democratic values and the promotion of human rights.
>   Member States will reinforce the practice of consensus-building on the central themes on the international agenda and will promote initiatives that affirm the identity of the region as a dynamic factor in international relations.

Considering trade integration as the second pillar, the old bilateral trade agreements included in the framework of ALADI started to form the space for gradual convergence, expressed in free trade agreements with which they reached the countries of CAN and MERCOSUR. Nowadays, the challenge is progressively deepening trying to incorporate the necessary elements to consolidate trade integration, such as the free movement of goods and people, infrastructure, common trade policies, industrial complementation and macroeconomic coordination. Only by increasing the South American domestic trade it will be possible, in perspective, to talk about economic integration.

Energy integration, as the third pillar, is based on the enormous potential of the region, and is rightly a key pillar for South American integration. The reserves of oil, gas, hydropower and coal give the South American continent a power production pole position of the utmost importance. This highlights the needed ability to optimize their potential and global position as power providers, and the need to establish viable and efficient energy networks. But it should not just mean the interconnection for the exchange of the final product, but the joining of forces and the establishment of an infrastructure and convergence mechanisms that may allow the potential energy to be used not only commercially, but also and above

---

[48]Nick Allen considers that the OAS has failed to unite South America into a strong, cohesive political unit even such was never the stated goal of the OAS in the first place. Nevertheless, a weakening of the OAS matters because it will not be able to protect the human rights of the peoples of South America as well as they need. See: Allen 2010.

all, to promote the development of the poorest countries and regions. The possibility of building various circuits to interconnect energy around South America is one of the foundations of their future competitiveness in our modern world. This objective is stated in the Treaty of Brasilia in which it is declared that energy integration is indispensable for the integral and sustainable use of the resources of the region, if maintained a spirit of solidarity.

Finally, the development of UNASUR requires much more than free trade, as happened with the process of European integration, it involves enabling conditions for economic complementation, regional development and the physical interconnection between countries and throughout the regions involved in the integration process and that is configured as one of the pillars that supports this integration process. Poor road, port and communications infrastructure in general, are the greatest weaknesses for the economic and social development of South America, and for any integration process undertaken in the region. This makes clear the relevance of IIRSA interconnection projects, which include the building of roads in South America. In order to achieve basic and necessary interconnection between these countries, not only North–South but also East–West, priority has been given to thirty of them.[49] In the Brasilia Treaty this necessary pillar is recognized by highlighting the objective of developing an infrastructure for the interconnection of the region and among our peoples based on sustainable social and economic development criteria.

3.5 The Institutional Framework

The institutional structure is one of the peculiarities that have specially characterized UNASUR as a process of integration. New institutions were initially rejected because of the existence of both CAN and MERCOSUR. The only exception would be the Permanent Secretariat, in Quito (Ecuador).

So, the provisional structure of UNASUR works as follows: The Presidents of each Member State have an annual meeting, and this represents the superior political mandate. The Ministers of Foreign Affairs of each country meet once every 6 months, and formulate concrete proposals of action and of executive decision.[50] Sectorial Ministers' meetings are called upon by the Presidents. The meetings' development is according to MERCOSUR's and CAN's mechanisms.

---

[49]Santa Gadea 2008; Santa Gadea, La iniciativa IIRSA: el reto de integrar el espacio físico de América del Sur, at: http://www.comunidadandina.org/Prensa.aspx?id=1968&accion=detalle &cat=AP&title=la-iniciativa-iirsa-el-reto-de-integrar-el-espacio-fisico-de-america-del-sur. Accessed 20 November 2014.

[50]The President of the MERCOSUR's Permanent Representatives Committee and the Director of the MERCOSUR's Department, the Andean Community's General Secretary, ALADI's General Secretary and the Permanent Secretaries of any institution for regional cooperation and integration, Amazon Cooperation Treaty Organization among others, will also be present at these meetings.

The temporary Presidency is held for a year and rotates among the member countries.

However, the adoption of the Treaty of Brasilia offers a complete institutional coordination for achieving the objectives of the organization. The functions and powers of every member are detailed in a precise manner. So, it is appropriate to present the institutional coordination as detailed in the Treaty.

Article 4 of the Treaty of Brasilia asserts that the Bodies of UNASUR are the Heads of State and Government Council, the Ministers of Foreign Affairs Council, the Delegates Council and the General Secretariat. The Heads of State and Government Council forms the highest organ and establishes policy guidelines while the political leadership of Foreign Ministers operates as an area of executive decisions and coordination.[51] This way, there is a functional structure with at least three levels: strategic decision making, held by the meetings of state leaders; coordination and executive (meetings of Foreign Ministers), and finally a functional operating level (the Delegates Council). The Pro tempore Presidency of UNASUR will be held successively by each of the Member States, in alphabetical order, by annual periods, and will represent the organization in the international arena.

However, a very important role is given to the General Secretariat. It is the body that, under the leadership of the Secretary General, executes the mandates conferred upon it by the organs of UNASUR and represents them accordingly. Former Argentine President, Nestor Kirchner, was elected as the first Secretary General on 4 May 2010. A new Secretary General had to be chosen after his death and since 11 May 2011 Maria Emma Mejia has occupied the Secretary General position, followed by Ali Rodriguez of Venezuela.[52] Only in August 2014 Ernesto Samper, former President of Colombia was appointed as the new Secretary General.

Sectorial Ministerial Meetings, and meetings of the Councils at Ministerial level, Working Groups and other institutional levels, may be convened as required on a permanent or temporary basis, in order to fulfil the mandates and recommendations of the competent bodies. These bodies will report on their activities through the Council of Delegates, which will present its findings to the Heads of State and the Government Council or to the Ministers of the Foreign Affairs Council, as appropriate.

Eight councils have been established so far: Social Development, Education, Culture, Science, Technology and Innovation (COSECCTI), Infrastructure and Planning, Drug Traffic Fighting, Energy Council, Health Council and Defence Council. The last created in June 2012 is the Electoral Council formed by four representatives from each member country. This Council visits countries before

---

[51]See: Serbin 2009.

[52]Former Colombian Foreign Affairs Minister. But due to an unusual arrangement, the new Secretary General will serve only for 1 year before handing over the post to her successor, Ali Rodriguez of Venezuela, who will complete the second year of the two-year term.

elections, engages with candidates, parties, and monitors the election process. In October 2012, the Electoral Council was sent to monitor the presidential election in Venezuela. Two Councils are particularly active and well developed.

One is the Health Council, established by the decision of state leaders of UNASUR in the extraordinary meeting of San Salvador (Brazil, 16 December 2008), with the aim of building a space for health integration, incorporating the efforts and achievements of other regional integration mechanisms promoting common policies and coordinated activities among all Member States. It was launched on 21 April 2009, in Santiago de Chile.

The other council is the South American Defence Council, whose objectives are to consolidate South America as a Peace Zone, and to build an identity on defence and consensus to strengthen regional cooperation. Specifically, it is mainly pointed to advance gradually in the analysis and discussion of common elements of a unified vision on defence, promote the information exchange, contribute to the articulation of common positions of the region in multilateral defence, and strengthen the adoption of measures building confidence and promoting the exchange of military training. Brazil has also launched the proposal to create a Security and Peace Council that can help to ensure peace in the region. In spite of its political objective, the Council would have a more technical role and a limited scope for discussions between governments on the threats regarding peace and security.

Finally, the creation of a South American Parliament is envisaged in Brasilia's Treaty. As it is indicated in Article 17 the creation of a South American Parliament, located in the city of Cochabamba, Bolivia, will be the subject of an Additional Protocol to this Treaty. Therefore, the Quito Declaration (2009) could express the countries renewed commitment to a South American Parliament, highlighting the Parliamentary meeting in October 2008, with a National Representatives Meeting and Sub-UNASUR in Cochabamba, Bolivia, at which is reaffirmed the importance of "South American integration and the need to move towards a South American Parliament". In June 2010, a First Summit of UNASUR Parliamentary Presidents got underway in Quito (Ecuador) and debates began about its establishment.

3.6 The Normative Framework

It is also important to highlight one of the main novelties of the Treaty of Brasilia in the construction of a South American Union. This is the establishment of a framework to regulate the new process, specifying the nature and range of instruments that emanate from each of the bodies of UNASUR. To reach the ultimate and very ambitious objectives established by South American states in the Brasilia Treaty, a legal framework is necessary, as well as the design of standards and instruments through which these objectives can become effective. Although one cannot say that the Treaty of Brasilia provides, in this area, completely satisfactory solutions, at least we note that the states of South America have chosen to establish a policy system for the achievement of the objectives stated in the Constitutive Treaty.

It is worth pointing out some aspects that could be useful in assessing the potential effectiveness of the measures, policies and programmes to be proposed within the institutions of UNASUR. In this sense, we must highlight:

First, Article 11 of the UNASUR Treaty establishes very clearly, that:

> The juridical sources of UNASUR are the following: 1. The Constitutive Treaty of UNASUR and other additional instruments; 2. The Agreements concluded by the Member States of UNASUR as a consequence of the instruments mentioned in the item above; 3. The Decisions of the Heads of State and Government Council; 4. The Resolutions of the Ministers of Foreign Affairs Council; 5. The Provisions of the Delegates Council.

So, this article provides a wide variety of rules based on political agreement. Apart from that another very important question is the approval mechanism of those rules. In that sense, Article 12, relative to the approval of the norms, clearly states that all rules should be adopted by consensus.[53] This means that each of the 12 Member States will have veto power over rules proposals.

Second, we must additionally note that the legal value of each of these standards is very different. At least, a distinction should be made between acts that entail an international agreement and those that emanate as internal rules. In the first case (paras 1 and 2 of Article 11), we are in the presence of international treaties that would be subject to the rules of the Vienna Convention on the Law of Treaties.[54] In essence, they constitute what we might call 'original norms' of UNASUR (at least the instruments referred to in para 1 of Article 11). In the second case (paras 3–5 of Article 11), the set of standards emanating from different bodies of UNASUR would constitute—using European Union terminology—'derivative legislation'. Time and practice will determine precisely the legal effects that, in particular, those acts will have and how they will contribute to the achievement of UNASUR's goals.

Finally, it should be noted that the mandatory rules emanating from this process of integration are dependent on their transposition into Member States' law. The legislative measures emanating from the organs of UNASUR will be binding Member States once they have been incorporated in their national legislation according to their internal procedures.[55]

---

[53]The Decisions of the Heads of State and Government Council, the Resolutions of the Ministers of Foreign Affairs Council and the Provisions of the Delegates Council may be adopted with the presence of at least three quarters of the Member States. The Decisions of the Heads of State and Government Council, the Resolutions of the Ministers of Foreign Affairs Council adopted without the presence of all Member States, shall be forwarded by the Secretary General to the absent States, which shall make known their position within 30 days after receipt of the document in the appropriate language. In the case of the Delegates Council, that deadline shall be 15 days.

[54]United Nations, Vienna Convention on the Law of Treaties, 23 May 1969, UNTS, vol. 1155, p. 331.

[55]UNASUR Treaty, Article 12.

A conclusion could be drawn of all this: the need for the Members to internalize the rules adopted by UNASUR in order to have legal effect in each of them. This way, any notion of supranationality, that would in any way have required the reformation of the constitutions of most of the Members, is surplus.

3.7 Final Considerations

A real integration among the 12 countries of the South American region is still an objective to reach. The covered territory encompasses, as we know, 17.7 million km^2, with a population of 382.4 million persons and a GDP (PPP) of US$ 3.9 trillion.[56] This echoes the enormous potential of South America and the magnitude and ambition of this unifying project.

Such a task cannot be free of obstacles. Some of the difficulties faced by the states for their integration are possible scattering factors inside CAN, and perhaps the special relationship between Colombia and Peru with the US, against the clear confrontation between the United States of America and other South American states (mainly Bolivia, Ecuador and Venezuela). In addition, the traditional competition between Argentina and Brazil produces a moderate scepticism, answering UNASUR essentially to a Brazilian initiative.[57]

Moreover, the need to overcome the challenge of increasing the intra-group trade is an element to take into account. All analysts agree to consider this factor as an immediate difficulty. Furthermore, it should not be ignored the fact that one of the greatest challenges of UNASUR as a real Union is to support the less thriving countries or regions. South America as a whole has key elements for achieving this goal. It has important resources, renewable and non-renewable energies, large mineral reserves and water sources, a huge potential food production and rich biodiversity and an important and diverse industrial park. Unfortunately, up to now all this has not reduced the huge inequality in South America, or the persistent social inequality. Therefore, the new integration process must involve a relative relocation of part of the income of richer regions, and should encourage the productive sectors and the population of these regions to contribute to the economic and political stabilization of each of the other Member States. Motivation is only possible if the productive sectors and the population of the richest regions perceive some progress and receive certain benefits in other fields of community building.

Of course, another transcendent challenge for UNASUR is the development and unification of the infrastructure of South America, a goal that is not exempt from difficulties. No matter the case, a relative consensus has been reached on the

---

[56]CEPAL (2009) UNASUR: un espacio de cooperación por construir. Naciones Unidas, Santiago de Chile, at http://www.cepal.org/pses33/noticias/paginas/2/39172/2009-598-UNASUR-PRESS.pdf. Accessed 30 November 2014. See also: Turienzo Carracedo 2007; Tinker 2009.

[57]Malamud 2009; Pérez Flórez 2009.

impossibility of any further integration processes without substantially improving a physical integration.

It is not easy to predict whether in the coming years this new regional actor will be able to grow and consolidate itself. In any case, it seems desirable for the benefit of all the peoples of the region that the process reaches successfully its internal unity, based on shared values. In this sense, we can consider that UNASUR has the elements, at least theoretically, to advance successfully in the process of integration in the political, economic, trade, defence, health, energy and infrastructure areas. If so, UNASUR will be a main actor in the international system of the twenty-first century. Failing at this attempt, it could, at least, serve to give a considerable boost in order to solve the problem of infrastructure in South America, tending 'bridges' to facilitate the development of the different states. To date, the process remains open.

The success or failure will depend on the political will of the governments of Member States, with Brazil in a starring role, as well as on the support received from their respective populations.

As Simon Bolivar said in a letter dated 31 May 1830, 'the union is certainly what we need to complete the work of our regeneration… It is *union*, obviously; but such union will come about through sensible planning and well-directed actions rather than by divine magic'.[58] Let us hope that UNASUR's former Secretary General, Maria Emma Mejia, was right when she affirmed that by 2020 South America will be 'something different, a united continent, with inter-ocean links, as well as inter-fluvial links helping to bring together the Pacific and the Atlantic oceans, with satellite communications with energy exchanges and obviously a South American continent in peace'.[59]

References

Aldecoa Luzárraga F (2007) La Comunidad Sudamericana de Naciones: algo se mueve en América del Sur. In VV.AA., Nombres Propios 2006. Fundación Carolina, Madrid, pp. 37–41 at http://www.fundacioncarolina.es/es-ES/publicaciones/nombrespropios/Documents/NP2006.pd. Accessed 1 December 2014.

Alegrett Salazar A (2007) La convergencia institucional en Suramérica: el aporte de la Comunidad Andina el proceso de integración suramericano. Revista de la Integración, 1: 106–113.

Alegrett Salazar A (2008) La convergencia institucional en Suramérica", *Revista de la Integración*, 2: 106–114

---

[58]Simón Bolívar, 'Reply of a South American to a Gentleman of This Island [Jamaica]', Kingston, Jamaica, 6 September 1815, translated by L. Bertrand (1951) Selected Writings of Bolivar. The Colonial Press, New York, at: http://faculty.smu.edu/bakewell/BAKEWELL/texts/jamaica-letter.html. Accessed 1 October 2014.

[59]Unasur to achieve a 'South American continent united and in peace by 2020', MercoPress, Wednesday, 11 May 2011, at: http://en.mercopress.com/2011/05/11/unasur-to-achieve-a-south-american-continent-united-and-in-peace-by-2020. Accessed 15 November 2014.

Allen N (2010) The Union of South American Nations, the OAS and Suramérica. ILSA Journal of International & Comparative Law, 1(1): 44–58

Álvarez Valdés R (2009) UNASUR: desde la perspectiva subregional a la regional. Serie Documentos Electrónicos, n. 6. Programa Seguridad y Ciudadanía, FLACSO Chile, at http://www.comunidadandina.org/unasur/unasur_rodrigo_alvarez%28flacso%29.pdf. Accessed 12 December 2014

Bennet J (2008) The Union of South American Nations: The New(est) Regionalism in Latin America. Suffolk Transnational Law Revue, 2(1): 103–133

Bervejillo M (2009) UNASUR: Una nueva experiencia de integración a nivel sudamericano, Programa ICI, Informe Técnico n° 19, 5 March 2009

Bilbao L (2004) Comunidad Suramericana de Naciones. Anuncios de una nueva era en Cusco y Ayacucho. Le Monde Diplomatique, Cono Sur ed., December 2004, at http://www.diariomardeajo.com.ar/eldiplocomunidadsuramericanadenacion.htm. Accessed 11 November 2014

Buenaño G (2005) Hacia la construcción de la Comunidad Suramericana de Naciones. Seminario Regional, los 40 años de creación del INTAL, Escenarios de inserción internacional de la CAN, 23 September 2005, Lima-Perú, at http://www10.iadb.org/intal/intalcdi/PE/2011/07720.pdf. Accessed 10 November 2014

Cano Linares M A (2010) La Unión de Naciones Suramericanas: un ambicioso e innovador proceso de construcción de integración regional. Revista Electrónica Iberoamericana, 4(1): 9–37

Cardona D (2005) ¿Tiene futuro la Comunidad Sudamericana de Naciones?" Foreign Affairs en Español, 5(5): 84–92

Cardona D (2008) El ABC de UNASUR, doce preguntas y doce respuestas. Revista de la Integración, 2: 19–30

Contreras Polgati A (2009) Dialéctica Ideológica Regional por la Integración y la Cooperación para el Desarrollo y la Seguridad. UNISCI Discussion Papers, 21: 28–45

Crisóstomo del Pedregal C (2009) UNASUR y la proyección del Consejo de Seguridad Suramericano. UNISCI Discussion Papers, 21: 62–78.

Díaz Barrado C M (2005) La Comunidad Suramericana de Naciones: propuestas y realizaciones. Revista Española de Derecho Internacional, 57(2): 639–663

Díaz Barrado C M (2010) Latinoamérica, América, Iberoamérica: tres términos, dos realidades, un Proyecto. In AA.VV, Nombres Propios 2010. Fundación Carolina, Madrid, pp. 175–180, at http://www.fundacioncarolina.es/wp-content/uploads/2014/07/NP2010.pdf. Accessed 9 December 2014

Díaz Barrado C M and Cano Linares M A (2007) La Unión de Naciones Suramericanas (UNASUR). Análisis e instrumentos. Cuadernos Iberoamericanos de Integración, n° 1, Gil impresores, Madrid

Díaz Barrado C M and Cano Linares M A (2009) La configuración de un nuevo proceso de integración en América: la Unión de Naciones Suramericanas. Cuadernos Iberoamericanos de Integración n° 11, Plaza y Valdés, Madrid

Esparza M E (2008) Las asimetrías y el proceso de integración suramericano. Revista de la Integración, 2: 86–91

Giacalone R (2006) La Comunidad Sudamericana de Naciones: ¿una alianza entre izquierda y empresarios? Nueva Sociedad, 202: 74–86

González Miranda S and Ovando Santana C (2008) Hacia un nuevo pensamiento integracionista latinoamericano: aproximación a una lectura de segundo orden, Polis: revista académica de la Universidad Bolivariana, 7(21): 265–285, at http://www.scielo.cl/pdf/polis/v7n21/art13.pdf. Acccessed 11 October 2014

Jaguaribe H (2005) El proyecto sudamericano. Foreign Affairs en español, 5(2): 80–83

López A (2008) Las posibilidades de la convergencia de los acuerdos de integración en Suramérica. Revista de la Integración, 2: 78–86

Malamud C (2009) Four Latin American Summits and Brazil's Leadership. Real Instituto Elcano de Estudios Internacionales y Estratégicos, Documento de Trabajo Nº 3/2009, at http://ww w.realinstitutoelcano.org/wps/wcm/connect/a005e7804f018b9dbac8fe3170baead1/WP3-2009_Malamud_Latin_American_Summits_Brazil_Leadership.pdf?MOD=AJPERES&CAC HEID=a005e7804f018b9dbac8fe3170baead1. Accessed 15 November 2014

Pérez Flórez G (2009) UNASUR: la apuesta de Brasil. Política exterior, 23(127): 149–160

Saccone A (2008) UNASUR: visiones desde el MERCOSUR. Revista de la Integración, 2: 31–37

Salazar V (2008) La convergencia entre la CAN, el MERCOSUR, y la naciente UNASUR: ¿Luz al final del camino?. Revista de la Integración, 2:.92–98

Saludjian A (2004) Hacia otra integración sudamericana. Libros del Zorzal, Buenos Aires, 2004

Santa Gadea R (2008) Integración Suramericana y Globalización: el papel de la infraestructura. Revista de la Integración, 2: 45–62

Serbin A (2007) Entre UNASUR y ALBA: ¿otra integración (ciudadana) es posible?. Anuario CEIPAZ (2007-2008). CEIPAZ-Fundación Cultura de Paz, Icaria, 1: 183–288

Serbin A (2009) Multipolaridad, liderazgo e instituciones regionales: Los desafíos de UNASUR ante la prevención de crisis regionales. Anuario CEIPAZ (2009-2010). CEIPAZ-Fundación Cultura de Paz, Icaria, 3: 231–246

Solón P (2008) Reflexiones a mano alzada sobre el Tratado de UNASUR. Revista de la Integración, 2: 12–18

Turienzo Carracedo R (2007) Procesos de Integración en Sudamérica. Un proyecto más ambicioso: La Comunidad Sudamericana de Naciones. Documento de Trabajo, Serie Unión Europea. CEU Publicaciones, Madrid

Tinker M (2009) Commentary: Challenges for the Latin American Left in 2009. Latin American Perspectives, 36(3): 145–160

Wade A E (2010) The Union of South American Nations ("UNASUR"): Challenges and Opportunities for States pursuing Regional Integration, The George Washington University

Chapter 4
Latin American Subregional Development Institutions

Francesco Seatzu

Abstract Sub-regional multilateral organizations are playing a rapidly increasing role in the suppliance of development finance and technical assistance to the countries of the Latin American and Caribbean (LAC) region. However, though surprising, the wide and fast-growing role of sub-regional multilateral institutions in the international financial system has as yet received very little attention from an international legal perspective. The overall goal of this chapter is to fill this gap, and therefore to critically review the experience of LAC countries with international sub-regional development and financial cooperation. Starting from the premise that this experience has been one of the most successful in the developing world (though uneven in terms of country coverage and services provided), this chapter will show that the Andean sub-region has been particularly successful in establishing sub-regional multilateral institutions in the fields of development and finance. Again, this chapter will also indicate that development financing in the LAC region has been wider in scope than cooperation in monetary matters. In doing so, the chapter will stress in particular that the two most successful sub-regional financial institutions, namely the Andean Development Corporation (CAF) and the Central American Bank for Economic Integration (CABEI) have shown the capacity to supply services to member countries in a timely way, with counter-cyclical effects and on a wider scale relative to other types of multilateral financing. Indeed, the genuine sense of ownership of these organizations by member states, preferred creditor status and professional management is reflected in very healthy portfolios, even in the face of default by member countries. This is so even though the services of these institutions could be broadened to support also the growth and integration of the physical infrastructure and macro-economic policy coordination. Concerning its overall structure, this chapter is divided into two main parts. In the first part, it will ascertain and critically discuss and evaluate, from an international legal perspective, the relative position of international

F. Seatzu (✉)
International and European Union Law, University of Cagliari, Cagliari, Italy
e-mail: seatzu@hotmail.com

© T.M.C. ASSER PRESS and the authors 2015
M. Odello and F. Seatzu (eds.), *Latin American and Caribbean International Institutional Law*, DOI 10.1007/978-94-6265-069-5_4

sub-regional financial institutions within the LAC region, focussing both on their financial role and on how they provide a set of tools to channel financial resources, technical assistance and knowledge to countries of this region. In the second part, through a consideration of the structure and functioning of the CABEI and CAF, the chapter will elaborate recommendations and draw some conclusions about the international sub-regional institutions in the fields of development and finance that operate in the LAC region, and how they can better enhance sub-regional cooperation and promote collective action.

Keywords Sub-regional Financial Institutions · Sub-regional Development Banks · Andean Corporation of Finance (CAF) · Central American Bank for Economic Integration (CABEI) · Multilateral Development Institutions

Contents

4.1 Introduction

The starting point of the following analysis is the idea that sub-regional multilateral institutions in the fields of finance and development, in particular sub-regional development banks (SRDBs), have their uses and roles. A discriminating view of these uses and functions is hindered by two essential ingredients of the environment in which such institutions currently operate. First, the growing interdependence of the sovereign states belonging to the same geographical region naturally leads to international cooperation and multilateralism in the running of foreign financial and economic policies to be considered as some sort of intrinsically positive thing.[1] International sub-regional institutions are, as it were, landmarks on the path to an innovation-driven economy, and not only in Latin America.[2] Indeed this is evident if one considers that SRDBs are an innovative institutional tool to channel knowledge and finance to developing countries, as well as to generate knowledge on and supply technical advice and assistance for economic and social growth. Again, this is also clear if one pays attention to the fact that SRDBs are able to spread risk more efficiently compared to risk-averse private sector lenders because they are neutral to risk.[3] Critical assessment of their performance is, therefore, hindered by the necessity not to strike at the principle for which they stand.

Second, SRDBs have generally been created, as their name suggests, as 'banks', i.e. as entities capable of accomplishing certain duties in the exclusive interests of their clients. They were not purported to take on the wider tasks and duties that they have achieved, as instruments for general trends in the running of international financial and economic relations. More specifically, the Latin American system of sub-regional multilateral banks was not conceived as a fully integrated and complex network of international financial organizations, capable of performing what is currently perhaps its main duty; the conduct of financial and economic relations between poor and wealthy countries of the LAC region. Operating in this sector, some SRDBs show, unsurprisingly, a number of documented and recently much known weaknesses such as a proneness to fashion, a proliferating bureaucracy, weak decision-taking capacity and so on.[4] Fully aware of these and other weaknesses, but needing sub-regional multilateral institutions to accomplish certain duties that it is no longer fashionable to accomplish via national foreign policies, LAC states, which are SRDBs' main clients, have major difficulties in setting up clear guidelines and general principles for the optimal distribution of such duties. Efforts are made to concentrate financial resources among the SRDBs that appear to have achieved relatively high efficiency, generally with only rather incomplete attention given to the nature of the duties to be achieved, and the ability of the institution in question to pursue them. Of special significance to this chapter is the political analysts' overall tendency to equate the case for increased internationalism in the transmission of development finance with the case for increasing the resources of a particular set of multilateral development institutions, the financial multilateral institutions belonging to the Inter-American Development Bank (IADB) group.[5]

---

[1]*Amplius* Sampson 2003, p. 3 ff.

[2]For a good account of the role of SDBs in Africa and Asia see, respectively, African Development Bank Group, 'Review of Bank Group Assistance to the Sub-Regional Development Banks—Approach Paper', at: http://www.afdb.org/fileadmin/uploads/afdb/Documents/Evaluation-Reports/18854241-EN-REVIEW-OF-BGA-TO-SUB-REGIONAL-DEV.PDF. Accessed 2 January 2014; Bezanson et al. 2005, p. 12 ff; Tan, Financing for Sustainable Development: The Challenges Ahead for Asian Economies', in F. Bestagno, L. Rubini (eds.), Challenges of Development: Asian Perspectives, (Vita e Pensiero: Milano, 2010), p. 87 ff.

[3]See: Griffith-Jones et al. 2008, p. 4 ff.

[4]See: Ibidem, p. 12 ff.

[5]Further references can be found in Adams 2005.

   This chapter mainly focuses on two sub-regional multilateral institutions which constitute close alternatives to the IADB group as sources of international development finance for the developing countries which are members of them. Both institutions correspond to the IADB in several noteworthy respects and issues. The questions that this chapter tackles, and aims to answer, are as follows. What was the nature of the demand which lead to the creation of these alternative sources of financing? To what extent was the nature of the demand reflected in the physiognomy of the institutions that were created, and what other factors influenced the way in which the demand was formulated? To what extent do the institutions in question have an ability to develop in response to the demand, and what other factors shape or hinder the pattern of this response? What measures are indispensable to strengthen sub-regional multilateral banks as agents towards development in the LAC region? For reasons that shall be clarified here, the last question will only be answered in the final paragraph.

   The chapter makes some attempts to critically assess and evaluate these institutions' efficiency. This is done even though an assumption could be made prima facie that the case for establishing alternatives to the IADB rests on the general perception that the IADB was inefficient, and that relative efficiency might thus be the essential criterion for their appraisal.[6] However, such an assumption would contrast with the circumstance that the developing countries which often played a crucial role in the foundation of sub-regional multilateral banks in the LAC region did not wish to have additional channels for the flow of multilateral finance for the sake of choice.[7] This decision not to do so was made for reasons analogous to those which in the late 1960s and early 1970s led the same countries (which were heavily dependent on a single source of bilateral aid) to diminish this dependence by boosting the interest of other donor countries.[8] On the contrary, as a survey of the evidence clearly shows, the main reason behind the creation of sub-regional multilateral banks in the LAC region was other than that—namely the LAC countries' willingness to accept the prescription of conditionalities (which are generally less strict than in global multilateral institutions) if these are prescribed by international sub-regional development institutions.[9] In this approach, the IADB will only be used as a reference term of comparison where it is indispensable. Implicitly, the chapter will make correlations. It needs to be emphasized here, however, that the goal of this chapter is not to arrive at an assessment of international sub-regional multilateral banks by comparison with the IADB. Implicit conclusions on the institutions of the IADB group are merely incidental. They are relevant only because the existence of the IADB was very much in the minds of the people who created sub-regional multilateral banks in the LAC region, especially the Central

---

[6]On these issues, see among others Culpeper 1990, p. 5 ff; Seatzu (2011–2012), p. 43 ff.

[7]See also Sects. 4.3 and 4.4.

[8]For a good account of these facts see Hira 2007, p. 61 ff.

[9]See Sect. 4.2. See also Griffith-Jones et al. 2003, p. 15 ff.

American Bank for Economic Integration, and of the people who have been responsible for their subsequent growth. What is attempted in this chapter is a narrowly focused analysis of the extent to which sub-regional multilateral development banks have succeeded in enhancing the work of international regional financial institutions by pursuing a complementary role.

4.2 The Demand for Sub-regional Multilateral Development Institutions

The two organizations with which this chapter is mainly—but not exclusively—concerned, namely the Central American Bank for Economic Integration (CABEI)[10] and the Andean Development Corporation (CAF)[11] share at least two aims. These are, first, the mobilization of resources from private capital markets and from official sources to make loans to developing countries on better-than-market terms,[12] and, second, the suppliance of a wide range of complementary services, such as international public goods, to developing countries of the same region and to the international development community.[13] Analogous statutory aims are contained in the articles of other sub-regional financial organizations such as the East African Development Bank (EADB)[14] and the West African Development Bank (WADB),[15] serving African sub-regions.

---

[10]The act that established the CABEI was signed on 13 December 1960, and became effective on 8 May 1961. Constitutive Agreement of the Central American Bank for Economic Integration (CABEI), 32 (1960) (Guatemala, El Salvador, Honduras and Nicaragua). Inaugurated formally on 31 May 1961, the CABEI opened its headquarters in Tegucigalpa, Honduras in September 1961. Central American Bank For Economic Integration (CABEI, 1991/92) XXXI *Annual Report*.

[11]Agreement Establishing the Andean Development Corporation (CAF), 1968, in Venezuela, *Convenio Constitutivo de la CAF,* at: http://www.caf.com/view/index/asp?. Accessed 2 January 2014.

[12]See respectively, Sects. 4.3 and 4.4.

[13]Ibidem.

[14]The East African Development Bank (EADB) was created in 1967 under the constitutive agreement of the then East African Cooperation between Kenya, Tanzania and Uganda. Following the breakup of the first East African Community (EAC) in 1977, the institution was re-founded under its own agreement in 1980. The text of the agreement as well as further information concerning its structure and operation are available on the institution's official website at: http://eadb.org/. Accessed 12 December 2013.

[15]The Bank was established on 14 November 1973 by member states of the West African Monetary Union (WAMU). The original treaty focused on the development of member economies towards balanced development and on preparing economies for future West African economic integration. In 1994 it became the development arm of the West African Economic and Monetary Union (WAEMU/UEMOA). The text of the agreement is available at the bank's official website at: http://www.boad.org/. Accessed 12 December 2014.

Correspondingly, the statutory aims and ways of operation and functioning of the above-mentioned sub-regional multilateral organizations share several features with the statutory purposes and ways of operation of the IADB. Apart from an almost universal tendency to develop a device of closer interaction with client-countries,[16] which represents a contrast in emphasis rather than a difference of fundamental duty, the purposes and ways of functioning that are generally typical of sub-regional multilateral institutions are by and large the purposes and ways of functioning and operating of multilateral regional organizations as a class, rather than of organizations at the sub-regional plane.

These purposes, especially the allocation of financial resources in a timely manner, reflect what has been pointed out above as the functional element of the demand for sub-regional development organizations in the LAC region. The main difference between sub-regional multilateral organizations and other multilateral financial organizations, including regional development organizations, lies in what has been identified as the geographical element of the demand—the peculiar factors which lead to the establishment of such organizations at the sub-regional level. Therefore, the position occupied by a sub-regional development bank is determined by the intersection of two sorts of demand. On the vertical stem, as it were, there is what is essentially an economic demand for institutions which will have certain informational advantages about economic, political and cultural realities of member countries, over global institutions which, by design, accommodate a larger set of countries from different continents. On the horizontal offshoot, there is what is fundamentally a political demand for organizations that will assert the multiplicity and the cultural variety of identities inside the LAC region.

The first of these demands is the main component of the institutional framework of the organization. The second is the main component of what would be usual for an organization with such an institutional framework for the countries which it aims to serve. A bank, to put it in its simplest terms, is a bank. There are various features that it has to possess: capital to make loans to clients on market competitive terms; the organizational structure to provide technical assistance and advice for economic development and so on, if it is to operate as a real bank. SRDBs, like other banks, possess these features.

In the following paragraphs, it will be demonstrated that there was not much of a search for originality in the drafting process of the articles of the Andean Development Corporation (CAF) and the Central American Bank for Economic Integration (CABEI) but rather a search for models and precedents. The originality is not in the creation of a new formula, but in the application of an existing formula at a different level scale. This point should be strongly stressed. SRDBs are not an original type of development institution. They are examples of an existing type of institution, which in the late 1960s was created to meet and address a new and fast-developing demand.[17]

---

[16]See Griffith-Jones et al. 2008, p. 3 ff.

[17]See Sect. 4.3.2.

Since SRDBs have various features which are typical of global financial organizations in general, it is useful to evaluate their utility in practice merely in the functional terms appropriate to institutions belonging to this category. From the perspective of poor countries, the case for sub-regional multilateral banks is sufficiently demonstrated by reference to their need for external financial sources, which in turn suggests that SRDBs should be assessed on the basis of their success in mobilizing resources from private capital markets and from official sources to make loans on better-than-market terms.[18] From the perspective of the developed countries, the case for sub-regional development institutions is well demonstrated by reference to the need for improved technical expertise in the appraisal of socio-economic programmes and projects and to improve informational advantages about the economic, political and cultural realities of member countries. This in turn suggests that SRDBs should be assessed and evaluated by the rate of return on the projects and programmes that they sponsor, that is, by their operational record.[19]

In the following paragraphs, it will be pointed out that the SRDBs that operate in various parts of the LAC region have a very good record as catalysers of financial resources.[20] Indeed SRDBs have been major sources of funding for all the economies of the region, in particular for relatively less developed countries. But the major success obtained in this respect by the Andean Development Corporation (CAF) and the Central American Bank for Economic Integration (CABEI) is due to specific historical and environmental circumstances outside the SRDBs' direct supervision.

Likewise, it is worth stressing that there are sound reasons for speculating that the operational records of the Central American Bank for Economic Integration (CABEI)—focusing mainly on power, infrastructure, energy and water—compare rather favourably with those of the IADB—which concentrate on social services and on support to the public sector and civil society.[21] Meanwhile the CAF, which has placed wider emphasis on the public sector, has guaranteed itself against 'failure' largely by preferentially operating in the same areas of intervention as the IADB, therefore partially undermining the case for its foundation as a distinct organization. But while these criticisms, if substantiated, may have some validity, they do not represent a definite appraisal, because they leave out the geographical element of the demand, namely the case for founding development finance institutions at the sub-regional level in the LAC region. This demand has four basic ingredients, all of which have an essential bearing on the operation and functioning of such institutions. First, the functional element of the demand is to some

---

[18]See, among others, Nelson 2013.

[19]Incidentally, evidence of this approach is found in several documents by the SRBs that are available at the official web pages of the main institutions.

[20]See also: Prada 2012 who stresses that: '*though* both the IDB and SRDBs have expanded their net outstanding loans to the region those of the SRDBs have grown at a faster pace'.

[21]See: Seatzu 2011–2012, p. 45 ff.

extent changed by the level at which it is formulated. Reference has already been made above to the overall tendency of the SRDBs to stress socio-economic integration, and it is argued below that there are other respects in which SRDBs differ inherently from other global financial organizations, including also regional multilateral development banks, irrespective of the peculiar sub-regional contexts in which they work. Second, the geographical component of the demand, the fulfilment of the role which is part of what is expected of all sub-regional development institutions, has to be linked to the specific capabilities and structures which SRDBs have. This tends to be considered initially as the assertion of the exclusive aspects of identity, a demand both for an increased quantity of external financial resources and for wider powers to choose the uses to which such financial resources are put. However this leads, third, to maintenance of the inclusive aspects of identity, the recognition of specific internal features which differentiate the LAC region as an identified entity.[22] The demand for the accomplishment of this task has a feedback consequence, fourth, on the character of the functional demand, in the form of a presumption that the operational policy of the institution will diverge in specific and noteworthy respects from the operational procedures and policies of other multilateral development organizations. As these elements of the demand for sub-regional multilateral organizations in the LAC region commend different criteria for their assessment and evaluation from those that are generally applied to global financial organizations in general, they need to be considered in a little more depth.

SRDBs are in an intermediate position on what has been described here as the vertical axis, or stem, of multilateral financial organizations as a category. Wealthy countries, looking for organizations through which to give technical assistance and direct financial resources to poor countries, are naturally inclined to look first at the universal or regional level, whereas a group they may wield paramount influence over policy elaboration. For example, in the late 1960s and early 1970s the fact that the periodical replenishment of the resources of the IADB was the first to receive the attention of wealthier countries in discussions of the allocation of financial aid to multilateral development organizations is not simply the outcome of chronological accident.[23] This was the obvious point on which to focus their efforts, and it is likely that they would still have had first call even if other multilateral financial organizations had been in operation for longer. Nevertheless, poor countries wishing to keep control over the selection of initiatives and projects to be sponsored are likely to believe first in terms of national organizations, which may

---

[22]On the peculiar features of the LAC region, see among others Centro Latinoamericano para la Competitividad y el Desarrollo Sostenible (CLACDS) del INCAE y el Instituto para el Desarrollo Internacional de la Universidad de Harvard, *Centroamérica en el siglo XXI: una agenda para la competitividad y el desarrollo sostenible: bases para la discusión sobre el futuro de la región,* (Banco Centroamericano de Integración Económica: AVINA, 2000); Pennetta 2013, p. 181 ff; Schelhase 2011, p. 175 ff.

[23]References are found in Alphandery 1993, p. 13 ff.

be required to work in harmony with government policy.[24] However, poor countries are also oriented toward organizations that will allocate external financial resources, so they must move some way towards the level that the rich countries favour.[25] It is the mix of these two requirements, the necessity for external financial resources and the necessity to keep supervision over their distribution, that constitutes the functional demand for the foundation of multilateral sub-regional development organizations at the sub-regional level.[26]

Among SRDBs, the Andean Development Corporation (CAF) and the Central American Bank for Economic Integration (CABEI) are a special category, in that they seem to maximize both the agglomeration of poor countries' interests and the ability to provide financial aid in the service of those interests. This is especially true for the CAF, which has been extremely active and is currently providing support to 'multilatinas',[27] supplying capital to commercial companies to start operations in other countries, and acquiring equities from companies to support their growth.[28] Moreover, the CAF is also currently enlarging its original sub-regional focus and it has started supplying financing to other countries such as Argentina, Brazil, Costa Rica, Panama and Uruguay.[29] Furthermore, the CAF is investing heavily in creating additional capacity to work with new clients and more countries.[30] That is to say, the SRDBs come as close as possible to the resource-mobilizing capacity of universal and regional development organizations without sacrificing, and possibly even strengthening, the poorest countries' ability to supervise how the aid funds are allocated and employed.[31] Even though they may include wealthy countries among their members, so the argument runs, the massive aggregation of poor countries' interests, in an institutional framework in which these interests will be overriding while the interests of wealthy countries will be of secondary importance, is likely to redress the unattractive imbalance of power that is an intrinsic characteristic of relations between wealthy and poor countries in general. The nature of this demand reveals the need for the careful scrutiny of decision-taking procedures in such organizations, together with that of other issues involved in the handling of the relationship between wealthy and poor countries within this peculiar institutional framework.

The assumption that SRDBs at the sub-regional level will always be effective as intermediaries between poor and wealthy countries may be erroneous for at

---

[24]On the issue, see: Little and Clifford 2006, p. 53 ff.

[25]Ibidem.

[26]Accordingly, ses: Titelman 2006, p. 215 who stresses that: '[…]countries eligible to receive resources have more say and decision-making power to influence the policies and instruments of such institutions than of global institutions'.

[27]See also: Santiso 2013, p. 239 ff.

[28]See Sects. 4.3 and 4.4.

[29]See Sect. 4.4.

[30]Ibidem.

[31]See: Prada 2012.

least two reasons. The first is that multilateral development organizations, like the International Bank for Reconstruction and Development (World Bank), are potentially better at providing services, especially when these are linked to their global nature.[32] Second, and finally, this would be false, even though SRDBs have been deeply involved in the sub-regional sphere at various levels. In the following paragraphs, some cases will be illustrated in which SRDBs operating in the LAC region have run into major difficulties in supporting their poorer members' interests.[33] Nevertheless, the existence of this assumption remains compelling as a determinant of the position of SRDBs on the horizontal axis, or offshoot, of subregional economic organizations. As the main task of SRDBs is to structure and finance projects with limited guarantees, the assertion of sub-regional identity in exclusive terms takes the physiognomy of a claim to wider sub-regional autonomy in the supervision of the utilization of financial resources. In other words, the establishment of an SRDB is essentially the achievement of political resistance against the wealthier countries and the IADB and World Bank's leadership in the economy of the LAC region.[34] Evidence is to be found in the history of the CABEI, which is deeply influenced by the history of Latin American opposition to the World Bank's dominance in Latin America.[35] It is also evident in the efforts made by other SRDBs like CAF and the Fondo Financiero para el Desarrollo de los Países de la Cuenca del Plata (FONPLATA) to differentiate themselves, in both the conditionalities and approaches to credit risk measurement,[36] from global and regional multilateral banks operating in the LAC region,[37] and in the enduring competition of these SRDBs with the IADB and World Bank. That this competition/opposition is less evident between the IADB and the FONPLATA is a sign of the latter's narrow scope of intervention,[38] not of its strength and openness, as the IADB stands in this context as a symbol for much of what poor countries resent in

---

[32]See: Griffith-Jones et al. 2008.

[33]On this issue, see also Prada 2012, p. 14 who, after having stressed at the outset that: 'There is enough anecdotal and systematized evidence about how dysfunctional the multilateral development banks (MDB) system in the LAC region can be', concludes by stating that: 'For each example of collaboration between these institutions, there are several examples on how they duplicate efforts, engage in costly and ineffective interventions and support initiatives and projects with politics in mind instead of applying an adequate project evaluation, among other valid concerns'.

[34]Accordingly, Sarwar Lateef 1995, p. 10 ff; Weaver 2008.

[35]On this issue, see Birdsall et al. 2002, p. 60, also for a good resumé of the efforts made by the CABEI to give debt relief to the poorest countries of the region like Honduras and Nicaragua without help from the international community.

[36]See also Krishna Dutt and Ros 2003, p. 419, who stresses that SRDBs generally impose conditionalities which are less strict that in global institutions. See also Bøås 1998, p. 117 ff.

[37]See: Prada 2012, p. 15, who stresses that: 'since SRDBs are neutral to risk, they are able to spread risk more efficiently compared to risk-averse private sector lenders'.

[38]In fact, the primary objectives of FONPLATA include providing financial support for pre-investment studies and technical assistance. More information on the structure and functioning of FONPLATA is available at: http://www.fonplata.org/. Accessed 2 January 2014.

the ordering of international development finance, and SRDBs stand as an emblem of what poor countries occasionally qualify as the fight against neocolonialism.

There are two noteworthy anomalies in the formulation of this demand. The first is that SRDBs, as multilateral development agencies, need financial resources, and the financial resources in question are widely under the wealthy countries' supervision.[39] SRDBs are therefore largely dependent on the wealthy countries' good attitude, if they are to achieve the means with which to accomplish that mission of resistance to the wealthy countries' leadership that is part of what is expected of them. This incongruity is not becoming any weaker. The history of the Caribbean Development Bank (CDB) shows that in certain cases, it may be in the wealthy countries' political interests to give poor countries such a 'channel', even if it clashes with other policy interests, although the dimensions of the 'channel' are likely to be rather meticolously indicated.[40] This seems to be the reason why the CAF has regularly provided, and plans to continue providing, financing for projects to enhance human development and integrate marginalized groups (such as indigenous people).[41]

The second anomaly is more complex to solve. Because the nature of the functional demand for SRDBs needs organizations of a special kind, the poor countries are liable to find themselves taking over an organization structure which was established on different ideological grounds, and even more importantly than that, which often lacks sufficient skills to provide services to them and is unable to establish institutional criteria and guidelines for connecting its mission to its activities at the country and sub-regional level. Therefore, it is far from clear that an SRDB is an appropriate tool for the assertion of sub-regional identity in exclusive terms.[42] Indeed, there is a chance that the biases that an SRDB has acquired from "mission creep" will draw it into struggles to identify itself with organizations on the global plane with which it has deeper affinity and thus wider ability for coordination,[43] rather than into stricter cooperation with other organizations operating at the sub-regional level.[44] If this trend is corroborated, as it appears to be by the circumstances that are set out below, it can be interpreted as evidence that the subregional nature of the organization is sketchily developed, or sidetracked by the provision of an external scheme or vulnerability to extraneous restraints.

The most accessible way of understanding these anomalies is to start with the dispute over the exclusive aspects of identity, as described above, and proceed to the debate over the inclusive aspects of identity. In the following paragraphs,

---

[39]See Sect. 4.3.

[40]See: Ocampo et al. 2007, p. 208 ff, also stressing that: 'CAF at present …. also offers governments and government bodies development bank services for special financing of physical infrastructure and integration projects'.

[41]Ibidem, p. 208 ff.

[42]See Sect. 4.5.

[43]See Sects. 4.2 and 4.4.

[44]Ibidem.

reference will be made to the tensions faced by the SRDBs to find 'sub-regional' solutions, i.e. characteristically Andean, or Caribbean, solutions to sub-regional issues and problems of the LAC region. It is not always evident that such solutions exist, and it is only on very few occasions that the problem that the solution is aimed at is specific to the sub-region in question. However, the explicit need to describe problems in sub-regional terms, and to search for solutions which in some sense express the 'heritage' of the sub-regional identity, is not only evident, but also often essential to the case for creating international organizations operating at the sub-regional level.[45] But this was not deemed necessary for the establishment of the Pacific Alliance that, unlike sub-regional development institutions operating in the LAC region such as MERCOSUR,[46] UNASUR[47] and ALBA,[48] pursues the main (and different) goal of attracting investment and creating export platforms for the global market.[49]

The unique nature of this demand poses a question that is difficult to handle in terms of operational policy. At the macro-economic level at which international multilateral development organizations operate, the striking feature of inter-subregional comparisons is the extent to which they reveal affinities rather than diversities.[50] Some of these affinities, notably the institutional implications of operating in one of the world's largest export markets, are intrinsic to the situation in which poor countries of the LAC region currently find themselves. Other affinities, for instance, in the fields of taxation and monetary policies,[51] arise not from the

---

[45]Accordingly, see: Prada 2012, p. 14 who also maintains that SRDBs: 'need to find comparative advantages and differentiation from other MDBs, other sources of financing (e.g. domestic and international capital markets), and other development institutions (e.g. bilateral donors, private foundations and social responsibility and non-government institutions)'.

[46]Treaty Establishing a Common Market, 26 March 1991, Ar.-Braz.-Para-Uru., UN Doc. A/46/155 (1991) (hereinafter the 'Treaty of Asunción' or the 'Establishing Treaty').

[47]The Constitutive Treaty is available at the official UNASUR website at: http://www.unasursg. org/. Accessed 2 January 2014.

[48]The Bolivarian Alliance for the Peoples of Our America—Peoples' Trade Treaty (ALBA-TCP) is an international cooperation institution based on the idea of the social, political and economic integration of the countries of Latin America and the Caribbean. The denomination 'Bolivarian' refers to the ideology of Simón Bolívar, the nineteenth century South American independence leader born in Caracas who wanted the continent to unite as a single 'Great Nation'. Created originally by Cuba and Venezuela in 2004, it is associated with socialist and social democratic governments seeking to consolidate regional economic integration based on a idea of social welfare, bartering and mutual economic aid. The nine member countries are Antigua and Barbuda, Bolivia, Cuba, Dominica, Ecuador, Nicaragua, Saint Vincent and the Grenadines, Venezuela and Saint Lucia. Suriname was admitted to ALBA-TCP as a guest country at a February 2012 summit. The text of the agreement is available at the ALBA's official website at: http://www.alba-tcp.org/en. Accessed 12 January 2014.

[49]See Ramirez 2013.

[50]See E. Adrian Calcaneo 'Latin American geoeconomics: A Continent Divided', (19 May 2013) at: http://conamp.org/2013/05/latin-american-geoeconomics-a-continental-divide-the-economist/. Accessed 3 December 2013).

[51]Ibidem.

situation in which poor countries find themselves, but from the narrow range of tools available for solving widely divergent problems.[52] It may be pointed out here that sub-regional differences in the type of issues and problems to be solved require alternative instruments for their solution. However, this would paradoxically undermine the case for sub-regional development organizations. If alternative instruments are required, then it would follow that the countries' diversities would be better identified by a multilateral development organization working at the regional or universal level, within an institutional and normative framework of comparative analysis. The reason for this is that the range of tools available is, indeed, very restricted. In selecting from a restricted range of established tools, in a situation in which it is held that there is one tool which is in some objective sense more appropriate than other tools for the specific problem under examination, what is needed is comparative experience as a guideline criterion for selection, and a multilateral universal or regional organization is more likely to have this experience than a sub-regional development organization.[53] Just to make the point clearer, satisfactory validation that the IADB has overall been unsuccessful in developing approaches to project appraisal that have validity in the Latin American context would bolster the case for an allocation of resources in (few) multilateral financial organizations of regional scope such as the IADB, or eventually in multilateral financial institutions of global scope like the World Bank.[54] In practice, nevertheless, it is hard to identify the differences that would give rise to such a claim. Indeed, this is a loose claim, but it is a claim that several political news analysts and business commentators would accept on the grounds of their own acquaintance.[55] Such questions do reappear in analogous forms in other regions of the globe (and especially in Africa), which may indicate that the macroeconomic level of policy elaboration may, in real terms, be an erroneous level at which to draw comparisons.[56]

The fact remains that policy decisions are adopted at the macro-economic level.[57] At this level there is the necessity, if not to ascertain anomalies, at least to create them, so that the suggested solution may gain political consideration in regional or sub-regional terms; hence the frequent references to 'sub-regional' solutions, even by those who are most intransigent in their application of universally established directions.[58] Moreover, although when considered in isolation these problems may be all-encompassing, they appear above all in social and political emergencies that can require special further measures to make the application

---

[52]Ibidem.

[53]On this issue, see also the remarks of Culpeper 1997, p. 107 ff.

[54]Ibidem, p. 114 ff.

[55]For a good resumé of these approaches to multilateral global and regional cooperations in the fields of development and finance, see among others Griffith-Jones et al. 2008.

[56]References can be found in Sims 1990, p. 137 ff.

[57]On the subject, see among others Corden 1978, p. 159 ff.

[58]On this issue, see: Griffith-Jones et al. 2008.

of known techniques attainable. A notable case is that of one of the organizations under consideration in the present chapter, the Andean Development Corporation (CAF), which sees the addition of peculiar Latin-American items to a substantially unmodified institutional framework. If this analysis of the nature of the demand for sub-regional development organizations in general and SRDBs in particular is correct, the troublesome outcome that follows is that there are no guiding criteria for the transformation of such organizations' operational procedures and policies. Confronted with economic issues and problems, they are required to develop a distinctive style for the settlement of these issues and problems, and style is an item that clearly falls outside the scope of economics in which the staff of such organizations are usually trained. Fundamentally, the demand for SRDBs is a cultural demand.[59] Indeed, it is a demand that naturally leads to the elaboration of a substitute to the westernized intellectual world class by which several poor countries of the LAC region are indirectly governed.[60] This is also indirectly confirmed by the history of the CAF and the CABEI. However, their history clarifies neither the meaning nor the content of the alternative that SRDBs are aiming to provide. Through the provision of efficient services in the financial sector and the competition of the RDBs in the profitable lending business that they partly substitute, SRDBs ultimately aim to give their contribution in the development of political self-awareness within the different areas of the LAC region.[61]

Indeed the tools of innovation that a SRDB is given are limited.[62] This is so even though a SRDB is generally able to efficaciously detect sub-regional issues and problems. Such efficacy is well documented by the history of SRDBs such the CAF and the CABEI, which have taken the lead in the LAC region to make financial resources accessible to countries in financial depression; for instance, through the creation of precautionary funding options such as their grant facilities and through interaction with multi-donor funds, such as Haiti's reconstruction fund, as well as via technical cooperation funds under their administration.[63] However, in doing so, an SRDB is expected to find itself working at the cutting edge of the typically socio-economic issues and problems which most poor countries share. The SRDB may ascertain characteristically sub-regional explanations to common problems, but in doing so it is likely to find itself exposed to the allegation that it is applying 'political' parameters, and this will lessen its functional strength as a handler of the mobilization of external financial resources. It can attempt to strengthen the coherence of the region where it operates, in particular through supplying global credits and lines of credit for channeling resources to a variety of

---

[59]See: Ocampo et al. 2007, p. 93, who stress the importance of the SRDBs in supporting regional strategies.

[60]On this issue, see recently Borras et al. 2012, p. 845 ff.

[61]Incidentally, evidence of this is that SRDBs are controlled entirely (or mostly) by developing countries themselves. On the issue, see: Prada 2012, p. 10 ff.

[62]See: Ocampo et al. 2007, p. 94 ff.

[63]See also Sects. 4.3 and 4.4.

projects in the productive sector, but in doing so it will often be hindered by its functional unwillingness to declare its ultimate political mission. The SRDB may submit claims to the wealthier countries' resources on behalf of the region where it works, but the utility of this claim will be compromised by the necessity to keep the wealthier countries' good will. These are the dilemmas an SRDB is faced with in its search for an alternative to compliance with the current international economic order. They are also the dilemmas that all poor countries are faced with when they seek financial resources for the betterment of their own situation.

4.3 The Central American Bank for Economic Integration (CABEI)

4.3.1 The Central American Sub-unit

As already stated above, one of the aims of this chapter is to detect the factors influencing the establishment and development of the two sub-regional multilateral organizations on which it is mainly focused, examining and critically evaluating the effectiveness of their responses to such factors. Both organizations are to a large extent affected by the broader regional environment, namely the LAC environment. Nevertheless, the Andean Corporation of Finance (CAF) and the Caribbean Development Bank (CDB) appear to possess a distinct set of subregional socio-environmental factors. In both organizations, the interplay of these two sets of socio-environmental forces is what makes the organization a driving force of sub-regional aspirations that are channelled or counterbalanced by the constraints of the sub-regional context. In Central America, there is no such single set of social and economical factors.[64] The category of Central American nations is currently merely a nominal one: the term has no proper meaning or content.[65] The organization called the 'Central American Bank for Economic Integration (CABEI)', therefore, lacks the ordinary guidelines by which the development of a sub-regional development bank would be expected to be governed. Indeed, it is doubtful that 'sub-regional' is the most appropriate adjective in this circumstance. The result, as explained below in greater depth, is that the CABEI has found it generally hard to infer any self-evident task from the meaning of its title, as the Andean Corporation of Finance has been prominently able to do. Its situation is such that it is likely mainly to operate as a bank in Central America.[66] To develop

---

[64]On the peculiarities of the Central American sub-regions, see recently Vuskovic 1983, p. 36 ff.

[65]For a fuller discussion of this issue, see Woodward 1999, p. 20 ff, who also stresses the potential of the Central American states for political union.

[66]See XVIIth Ministerial Conference of the San José Dialogue, Guatemala, 26 March 2001, 7363/01 (Presse 121), at: http://www.consilium.europa.eu/uedocs/cms_data/docs/pressdata/en/er/07363.en1-communiqué.doc.html. Accessed on 12 January 2014) also stressing the need of a transformation and modernization of the CABEI.

as a Central American development bank would require it to obtain further specific Central American features, and such features are hard to determine.

In the Andean and Caribbean sub-regions, sub-regional multilateral organizations have developed along similar paths, and there has been a noteworthy level of interaction between the two processes. There has thus been a tendency towards increased cooperation, especially among the Andean countries, and this has led to the rationalization of the structure of the bodies working throughout the sub-region.

In Central America, mainly due to the striking differences among the countries,[67] the 'sub-regional' cooperation followed a different pattern that lacks a clear structure and does not involve long-term strategies. So the CABEI was established not in one environment, but in several. The fundamental issue it had to respond to was not: "How to cater to this socio-economic environment", but: "which of these socio-economic environments should be catered for." For an agency, and more precisely, for a bank that lends money, the allocation of which may be readily quantified, this issue is bristling with difficulties: an organization exclusively involved in research, for example, may allocate its effective resources to its foremost area of interest/concern, while keeping a few side projects ticking over as an allowance for the peculiar interests of its peripheral members. Self-evidently, a bank that 'pursues customer happiness' as its statutory aim can hardly do this. There is no sort of 'quasi-capital' that it may set aside for activities of secondary importance. The choices that lay before the CABEI when it was founded in 1960 by the Republics of Guatemala, El Salvador, Honduras, Nicaragua and Costa Rica were reasonably broad. The area where it started its operations in the early 1960s contained 2.6 million people, at that time approximately a third of the size of the overall Latin American population.[68]

The CABEI area contains seven countries which have gone through different historical stages and political experiences during the twentieth century[69]; it has been characterized by struggles for power that often took the form of revolutionary movements seeking to overthrow authoritarian governments.[70] The substance and hetereogenity of its traditions is mirrored in social structures that may well not be acquiescent to the Western-derived ordinances that overshadow all current development arguments.[71] If this feature makes Central American development rather questionable, the chance that the problem will be solved is also to be found in Central America, in the existence of Costa Rica as at least one country which has developed without acquiring the social implications connected with labour organization, incentive devices and so on of the Western capitalist technological axis.[72]

---

[67]See also Williams 1994, p. 20 ff.

[68]See: Lehoucq 2012, p. 12 ff.

[69]See: Zanatta 2010, p. 121 ff.

[70]Ibidem.

[71]Ibidem.

[72]See: Meléndez Chaverri 1979, p. 15 ff.

In recent years, at least one circumstance has brought Central America to the fore in international relations: several countries of this area, such as Nicaragua and Guatemala, are afflicted by poverty to an extent that is almost unknown elsewhere.[73] So two of the three broad lines of separation in the contemporary world, the economic and the ideological, intersect and interact in a situation where the third fracture, along lines of race, is also present.[74] The tough challenge of economic growth is most powerful in Central America, and that challenge is to be seen in the unstable background of political controversy.

There is one additional broad feature of the Central American context that differentiates it from that of the majority of the other Latin American sub-regions. Not many Latin American sub-units are in a neo-colonial situation, in the general meaning of the term, i.e. in a situation where almost all the strategic sectors of the economy are under direct or indirect foreign supervision. As a result of the Central American Free Trade Agreement (CAFTA),[75] which contains in Chap. 10 (the investment chapter) what has been called a 'legal framework of domination',[76] it appears that international investors do generally have more powerful rights in Central America than, for instance, in South America and the Andean sub-region.[77]

The environment within which the CABEI has to evolve thus lacks definition in one fundamental respect: it lacks a comprehensive set of relations with the developed countries that would supply the framework within which the organization could operate at the sub-regional level as a financial intermediary.[78] In terms of more specific decisions, the heterogeneity of the area is also a stumbling block to operational choices. First, the individual countries of the sub-region are indeed rather different, ranging from well-established countries like that of Costa Rica to weaker and economically much less developed countries like Nicaragua and

---

[73]See: Kinloch Tijerino 2005, pp. 13–40.

[74]On the issue, see: Telles 2007.

[75]The Dominican Republic-Central America-United States Free Trade Agreement (CAFTA/DR) entered into force between the United States and Costa Rica on 1 January 2009, between the United States and the Dominican Republic on 1 March 2007, between the United States and Guatemala on 1 July 2006, between the United States and Honduras and Nicaragua on 1 April 2006, and between El Salvador and the United States on 1 March 2006.

[76]See: Moreno R L, Neocolonialism In Central America: An Analysis (25 February 2009) at: http://www.cispes.org/media/el-salvador-watch-newsletter/neocolonialism-in-central-america-an-analysis-by-raul-moreno/. Accessed 4 November 2014.

[77]Ibid.

[78]But see the CABEI's new development finance strategy which is based on the establishment of two trust funds allowing donor contributions to be combined with CABEI's own commitments to supply: (a) a group of targeted risk mitigation instruments applicable to infrastructure projects and (b) debt and equity financing, as well as targeted risk mitigation for renewable energy projects. On the issue, see S. Sheppard, Reforming the Multilaterals, Project Finance International Yearbook (2009) at: http://www.globalclearinghouse.org/infradev/assets%5C10/documents/Reforming%20the%20Multilaterals%20-%20Sheppard%20(2009).pdf. Accessed on 11 December 2014.

Guatemala. Second, the areas are different in terms of international relations. For some of the smaller countries, such as El Salvador, there is the further problem of isolation. At the other extreme of the sub-region, there is one relatively compact group of countries that is a natural focus for the attentions of any sub-regional organization. Third, levels of development change significantly. In Costa Rica, Central America has a model nation that has a model of substainable development that is concurrent to those of the Western economies like the US. On the opposite side, in Belize and Honduras, there are areas that the development process has hardly touched. And in the middle of the range, Nicaragua dominates, sophisticated in its poverty.

The environment of Central America is, therefore, modelled by its size and divergence, and these features are mirrored in a strangely difficult synergy of economic, political, cultural and social issues. However, it is also an environment which is rapidly shifting, and here too the Central American situation, or situations, should be separated from that of the other sub-regions of the LAC.

From these historical developments, it is possible to detect two issues that were relevant to the constitution and development of the CABEI. First, the pattern of relations between developing and developed countries was in a way more obvious in Central America than elsewhere,[79] since it was not altered by the paralyzing presence of a single or few powerful nations—unlike in other sub-regions of the LAC such as the South American and Andean sub-regions. Therefore, the premise was never challenged that the organization must pursue the broad participation and support of the developed countries, and in this regard it keeps itself different from the Inter-American development bank, with only the United States on the aid-giving side. Second, and finally, the entanglement of the developed countries in Central America had led to an extensive amount of research into the issues and problems towards which the financial assistance was directed,[80] and not merely to some original mechanisms and structures for the transmission of financial assistance and technical aid such as the Ordinary Fund, the Central American Fund for Economic Integration, the Housing Fund and the Social Development Fund. Thus, in the essential mission of a sub-regional development organization, the CABEI had either to accept or to overcome a heavy burden of conventional savoir faire.

In its early years, the CABEI seemed inclined to take the traditional view. Indeed, the first impression was that the representatives of developing countries on both the Board of Governors and the Board of Directors were even more attached to the ideas and projects at that time in fashion—such as the creation of regional highways connecting the major production, distribution, consumption ports and

---

[79]Incidentally, this is the reason why, as pointed out by Bulmer-Thomas 2003, p. 294: 'CABEI channeled funds for regional infrastructure to all countries, with the weaker members (Honduras and Nicaragua) receiving a disproportionately large share of all loans'.

[80]Indirectly, this is confirmed by Cevallos 1996, p. 261 who acknowledged that: '[…] in a short period of time, the CABEI created a solid infrastructure for the integration and development of the region'.

points and the integration of telecommunications throughout the sub-region—than were the representatives of the developed countries.[81] It may be suggested here that the explanation lies in the complexity of establishing a sound identity for such an organization within the hetereogenity of the Central American sub-region. Other reasons are undoubtedly possible. However, it will be seen that the most obvious of these disappear when the physiognomy of the CABEI is considered from a comparative perspective alongside the other sub-regional multilateral organizations of the LAC region in their different environments.

4.3.2 The Origins of the Central American Bank for Economic Integration (CABEI)

Formal discussions of the possibility of establishing a Central American development bank began in the early 1960s, under the aegis of the Central American Common Market (CACM).[82]

The source of those debates was also important. CACM was itself a regional organization,[83] and it was primarily conceived as an economic organization which was formed in response to the demand by member countries to cooperate with each other to attract industrial capital and transform their economies.[84] In other words, the idea to create a Central American development bank arose in an institutional structure,[85] rather than in direct debates among representatives of sovereign countries; moreover, that institutional structure was a structure that gave access to the developed countries from the beginning, which meant that this was an exclusively economic project.[86] In contrast, the proposal to establish a Latin American development bank evolved from a lengthy list of attempts by the Latin American

---

[81]For further references on the CABEI's initiatives in these fields see Ibidem, p. 253, n. 44.

[82]The CACM was founded by Honduras, Guatemala, Nicaragua and El Salvador (and later joined by Costa Rica) with the signing of the General Treaty of Central American Economic Integration ('Tratado General de Integración Económica Centroamericana') in Managua on 15 December 1960. For a thorough examination of the CACM within the context of the historical patterns of development in the Central American sub-region see: Cline et al. 1987; also Tuller 1993, pp. 161–162.

[83]In 1991, the five Central American republics and Panama signed the Protocol of Tegucigalpa to the 1962 Charter of the ODECA establishing the current institutional framework, the Central American Integration System (SICA). On the subject, see: Sánchez Sánchez 2009, p. 138 ff.

[84]See also Peraza 1994, p. 297 ff; Rudolph 1971, p. 37 ff.

[85]The Central American Bank for Economic Integration (CABEI), therefore, was created as an institution of the Central American Common Market (CACM).

[86]On the economic character of the project, see also Article 8 of the Constitutive Agreement which states that: '[…] the bank's operations should be based exclusively on technical, financial and economic criteria; consequently, criteria of a political character relating to any member state should not influence the same'.

countries, and it was finally made possible by the initiative of the Joint Commission which was set up in 1967 to address sub-regional problems and issues.[87] Why the proposal for a Central American development bank emerged in a distinct manner from either of these is thus evident from the preceding observations on the Central American environment.

As such debates proceeded, the talks leading to the establishment of the Central American bank progressed expeditiously. From the initial proposal to the signing of the constitutive agreement of the organization was a period of only just over one year.[88] With the Inter-American bank and the World Bank already in existence and fully in operation, precedents had been set for the structure and aim of such organizations that seem to have been widely accepted by the CABEI's founders. The debate revolved around the main issue, namely the areas where the financing should be concentrated.[89] Accessory issues that arose were for the most part (directly or indirectly) related to the problem of how to counterbalance the necessity for external support (i.e. new capital) against the need to give the new organization, a Central American vocation. In this respect, the position of Costa Rica, as a country that was both developed and Central American, was bound to be essential.

The pattern of membership which finally emerged, with Costa Rica substantially dominant among the sub-regional members, looks natural enough thanks to the decision to create the CABEI as a source of, and mechanism for, financing the integration and growth of the Central America sub-region.[90] Nevertheless, in the chronological account that follows, it will be seen that there were occasions when a rather different membership pattern looked possible in theory, for instance when the CABEI amended its constitutive agreement to include extra-regional partners.[91] This pattern would have resulted in an altogether different organization. While this cannot be said in absolute terms, it is clear that the reason why this alternative was not pursued may be attributed to the acknowledgment of the precedents set in the creation of other multilateral development organizations both at international, universal and regional levels. We have come full circle, although the circle was modelled by precedents that were not always the most appropriate for dealing with the peculiarity and broad heterogenity of the Central American sub-region.

In the 1980s, when Central America experienced heavy indebtedness in Nicaragua and El Salvador, CABEI activities received little attention and assistance from other multilateral development institutions, including the Inter-American

---

[87]See also: Rivera 1979, p. 221 ff.

[88]See: Cevallos 1996, p. 253 ff (providing a detailed history of the origins of the CABEI).

[89]Ibidem.

[90]Article 2 of CABEI's establishing agreement provides that it shall: 'promote the economic integration and the balanced economic development of the Central American countries'.

[91]See Cevallos 1996, p. 257.

development bank and the World Bank.[92] As a result, the CABEI was substantially unable to sponsor the projects that were most indispensable at that time to Central America. This was also because the few resources that the CABEI obtained were generally bound by special conditions that curbed the scope or employment of funds—an issue that heavily hindered the implementation of a sound and coordinated integration action programme.[93] Additionally, intra-regional trade declined and barriers were once more raised by some countries.[94] Moreover, the CABEI was unable to repay the debt granted to it by private and public foreign investors, as its members regularly defaulted or delayed payments as a result of war, critical local economic conditions, and natural disasters such as El Salvador's 1986 earthquake.[95]

However, this situation partially changed during the 1990s when the CABEI made successful efforts to improve its reputation in the international arena by making prompt payments of its obligations[96] and also efforts to transform itself into the financial instrument *par excellence* of the integration and development of the whole Central American sub-unit.[97]

During the 2000s the CABEI confirmed this evolutive trend, in particular by enhancing operations that mainly focused on sovereign borrowers. Naturally enough, this led to several debates in and outside the organization on the borrowing capacity of CABEI clients and the sustainability of the CABEI's business model, including the issue whether the borrowing capacity of CABEI clients would turn out to become a limit for the sustainability of the CABEI's business model. However, these debates did not have many (or any) practical consequences, since the Central American countries were able to increase their absorptive capacity as their internal economies grew significantly during that period.[98] There was therefore room to manoeuver, so much so that the CABEI became able to devote a large quantity of its financial resources to Central American countries on a scale comparable to the IADB and World Bank.

From 2010 to the present, the CABEI has expanded its scope of operation to the private sector in such a manner that investments in this area currently absorb 25 % of the organization's total commitments per year (i.e. US $300 million).[99] Moreover, it has also been actively involved in the sub-regional sphere at several

---

[92]Ibidem.

[93]Ibidem.

[94]Ibidem.

[95]Ibidem.

[96]Ibidem, p. 257, who stresses the CABEI's role as a Credit Guarantee Facility for the Central American sub-region.

[97]Ibidem.

[98]See: Zanatta 2010, p. 233 ff.

[99]References can be found on the CABEI's official webpage at: http://www.bcie.org/?cat=1137 &title=Funds%20and%20Trust%20Management&lang=e. Access on 14 November 2014).

other levels; for instance, on the financial aid front of countries in financial distress through grants and technical cooperation funds[100] as well as in the adoption of the best internationally recognized practices of social responsibility and best environmental practices in order to minimize the direct negative impact of its facilities on the natural environment and its immediate surroundings.[101]

4.3.3 The Structure of the Central American Bank for Economic Integration (CABEI)

The foundation of the CABEI started a trio of corresponding organizations assisting the three sub-territorial units of the LAC region that contain some of the LAC's least developed countries. Its founders seem to have been perfectly aware of this aspect of it as one of a family of organizations. Inasmuch as it was the first of the three to be set up, they might and in fact did draw on several precedents for the settlement of such technical issues as emerged. The allotment of subscriptions among members, for example, was debated at length and discussed wholly in terms of already existing criteria.

The main source of these precedents was IADB, with certain modifications and additional features which had been found attractive in the financial institutions of the World Bank group. In terms of operational policies and principles, the CABEI possesses powers broadly similar to those of the IADB; nevertheless, in its membership and capital structure it is rather different from both the IADB and the World Bank.

The extent to which the articles of the CABEI's constitutive agreement were elicited from precedents has had some bearing on their relevance in the drafting of policy. First, it is significant that the striking features of the articles were subject to fewer discussions before the CABEI was founded, and there was less argument over their interpretation than was the case in the IADB. Second, because most of the features of the CABEI were inferred from existing archetypes, they have not figured distinctly in the organization's public presentation of itself as a Central American organization. Features that were publicized in the IADB as innovations were accepted in the CABEI as tried and reliable solutions to well acknowledged problems. When the staff of the IADB stresses its physiognomy as a Latin American organization, they mean that it is an organization specifically tailored to Latin America's needs. When the staff of the CABEI does so, they mean that it is a family of corresponding organizations—where Central American people are in control. The latter statement is considered below in more detail.

Lastly, the work that led to the drafting of the CABEI's constitutive agreement resulted in a document of noteworthy technical cleverness and high significance that was indeed a sound and feasible model for other multilateral development

---

[100]Ibidem.

[101]Ibidem.

banks working both at regional and sub-regional levels.[102] It may be true that there are not many legal uncertainties concerning the articles, especially those of the IADB. The articles of the CABEI are quite straightfoward and clear, and it seems likely, from such evidence as can be inferred from the organization's relatively long record, that it will further evolve along the lines that its articles indicate. As shown below, the same could also be said about the articles of the Andean development bank and of the Caribbean development bank, the two other sub-regional financial organizations that are currently (and successfully) working in Latin America.[103]

Perhaps this last observation is the most significant of all. Indeed this chapter maintains that it is through the accomplishment of a prescriptive task that the long-term meaning of SRDBs has to be assessed, and that the accomplishment of this task is partially conditioned by the development of a congruous 'tone'. In the following analyses of the Andean development bank and the Caribbean development bank, it is shown that the development of a tone has been a by-product of the search for a mission and character. In the case of the CABEI, the need for such a quest may be hidden by the occasional false transparency with which the organization is described in its articles. To this extent, there is no room for further attempts at innovation.

Moving on to other issues such as membership and voting rights, it is worth observing that, according to Article 4 of the CABEI's constitutive agreement as amended to encompass extra-regional partners, membership is currently open to any country belonging to the Central American Integration System (SICA), to countries of different regions,[104] and also to 'any public international law organization with an international scope of action and having a juridical personality' (i.e. to any international intergovernmental organization).[105] Indeed if sub-regional institutions are defined respectively as those in which membership is open to, and at the same time limited to, states in named sub-continental areas,[106] it would appear that the CABEI should not longer be classified as a truly sub-regional development institution.[107] But this is not so if a sub-regional development bank is qualified as any multilateral development organization that typically includes only borrowing nations, regardless of whether its membership is open to States from outside the territory in which financing activities are allowed.[108]

An analysis of the various groups of member states in terms of voting power generally provides indications of where the real weight of the organization lies.

---

[102]See: Ocampo and Titelman 2009–2010, p. 249 ff.

[103]For a 'positive feedback' of the work and operation of the sub-regional development banks of the LAC region, see among others: Prada 2012, p. 10 ff.

[104]See Article 4, lett. A of the CABEI Constitutive Agreement which states that: 'The non-founding regional members shall be subject to the same legal framework'.

[105]CABEI Constitutive Agreement, Article 4, lett. A.

[106]On the issue, see: Syz 1974, p. 8.

[107]CABEI Constitutive Agreement, Article 35.

[108]See also Article 4, para 3 of the CABEI Constitutive Agreement, in the part which states that: 'The 'A' y 'B' series shares are nominative and shall bear the name of the respective country or international organization that is their holder'. For a fuller discussion of these issues, see: Syz 1974, p. 8.

In the case of the CABEI, the indications are both numerous and clear. Voting rights are undoubtedly biased in favour of the Bank's founding member countries, as suggested in particular by Article 4, section B, lett. (a) which states that: '.... capital with voting rights shall be composed of a series of 'A' shares allocated to founding member countries and a series of 'B' shares allocated to the non-founding members and the non-regional members'.[109] Moreover, this is also confirmed by Article 4, section B, lett. (b) which, after stating that: 'The Bank's authorized capital shall be five billion United States of America dollars (US $ 5,000,000,000.00)', tersely provides that: 'Of the authorized capital, the founding countries shall subscribe to, in equal parts, two billion five hundred and fifty million dollars .... through 'A' series shares, and there will only be two billion four hundred and fifty million dollars .... available to the non-regional members and to the non-founding regional members through 'B' series shares'. Therefore nearly 50 % of voting shares are held by only four countries (namely: the Republics of Guatemala, El Salvador, Honduras and Costa Rica, the four founding member countries),[110] on a flat rate, compared with 11 % in the IBRD, and 3.2 % in the IADB.[111] This figure is a compromise. Especially, Costa Rica and Honduras wanted a figure much higher than that of the IADB. Indeed, this was so in order to have sufficient voting strength to permit them to bring about the adoption of the projects perceived as the most strategic for the implementation of a development programme of the Central American sub-region. The compromise that was finally reached, as will be shown below, guaranteed that the economically weakest countries of the CABEI's founding group (Guatemala and El Salvador) had some increase in voting power, but it left the de facto dominant position of Costa Rica and Honduras in the Central American sub-region substantially unaltered. However, decisions on most issues and topics are taken by simple majority,[112] which means that it would always be possible for the economically weaker countries of the CABEI's founding group to mobilize a blocking coalition.

4.3.4 The Purpose and Functions of the Central American Bank for Economic Integration (CABEI)

The statutory purpose of the CABEI is: 'to promote the economic integration and the balanced economic and social development of the founding countries' in the Central American sub-region'.

---

[109]CABEI Constitutive Agreement, Article 4, (B), para 3.

[110]See also Article 4, (B), lett. (h) of the CABEI Constitutive Agreement which provides that in the event of capital increase, at least 51 % of the subscribed capital shall be held by the founding countries of the bank.

[111]On the issue, see Syz 1974, p. 34.

[112]See e.g. Article 14 of the Constitutive Agreement which embodies the principle that 'each Governor has one vote'.

This definition of the bank's purpose strongly resembles the corresponding definitions in the equivalent articles of the IADB[113] and of the African Development Bank (ADB).[114] Moreover, and of even greater importance, the definition suggests that the founders of the CABEI have a generous view of the development process. In the case of the IADB (and perhaps even more so in the case of the ADB), serious attempts were made to translate this view into the articles of the constitutive agreements by inserting the notions of 'social progress'[115] and 'social development'.[116] Nevertheless, in the peculiar situation of the mid-1960s it was difficult—if not impossible—to translate these notions into a plan of action: this is further confirmed by the history and operation of these multilateral regional institutions.

With the foundation of the CABEI, the broad view was reiterated, though in partially different terms. Economic development was presented in legal statements as economic growth, advancing a more pragmatic and operative approach that would bypass considerations of the values both of tradition and of fairness.[117] As a result of this approach, the far too vague notions of 'social progress' and 'social development', were not included as such in the CABEI's establishing treaty, and they were replaced by the more operative and articulated concepts of 'economic integration' and 'balanced economic and social development'. These were used as catchwords for the comfort of the founding countries that were willing to build up an effective and fully operational organization able to supply financial aid as well as technical assistance to the developing countries of the Central American sub-region. Clearly, the assumption was that this approach would in some way be more feasible. For developed countries, 'feasible' indicates 'not requiring assistance'. For developing countries, among several other things, it indicates being 'in a stronger bargaining position to obtain more assistance'.

In fulfiling its mission, the CABEI is required to attend to only those programmes and projects that are specifically mentioned in Article 2, para 1, lett. (a)–(j) of its Constitutive Agreement. The premise is way too clear and evident: only the programmes and projects indicated may effectively contribute to the balanced growth of the sub-region as a whole. However, it is interesting that no reference is made to a duty upon the governing bodies of the bank to pay special regard to the needs of the less developed member countries of the Central American sub-region.

---

[113]Agreement establishing the Inter-American Development Bank, 8 April 1959, 389 UNTS, 5593, Section 1.

[114]Agreement establishing the African Development Bank (adopted 17 May 1979, entered into force 7 May 1982) 1276 UNTS 501, Article 1.

[115]ADB Constitutive Agreement, above n. 114, Article 1, lett. (a).

[116]IADB Constitutive Agreement, above n. 113, Section 1.

[117]See Article 2 of the CABEI Constitutive Agreement, above n. 10, which, after having stated that: 'The Bank's objective shall be to promote the economic integration and the balanced economic and social development of the founding countries', provides that: 'To achieve its objective, the Bank will attend the following programs and projects: (a) Infrastructure for the completion of existing regional systems or those that compensate for disparities in basic sectors, which hinder the balanced development of Central America'.

There is no mention at all, neither in Article 2, para 1, lett. (a)–(j) nor elsewhere in the constitutive agreement. But perhaps the existence of such a duty can nevertheless be inferred from the purpose definition, as well as from the reference in Article 2, para 1, lett. (a), to a generic duty of the bank to eliminate any disparity that could hinder the balanced growth of the sub-region as a whole. Moreover, the CABEI's tasks also include the promotion of public and private investment, the provision of assistance in the coordination of national policies, especially in foreign trade, and the provision of technical assistance in the preparation of projects and programmes.

Financial resources are clearly indispensable for the CABEI as it is not allowed to be in deficit. Under the CABEI Agreement, the amount of the initially authorized capital ($16 million) is denominated in US dollars, without any reference to the gold value of this currency. This implies in particular that, in the event of a change in the dollar price of gold, the value of the capital of the bank will also vary in relation to gold. The bank's subscribed capital is subject to certain restrictions according to the CABEI Constitutive Agreement. This also suggests that, in principle, the proceeds of bank loans can only be used for procurement in founding member countries.[118] However, this provision is unlikely to prove as unduly restrictive as it might appear at first sight. This is because the Board of Governors is implicitly allowed to make exceptions.[119] The CABEI's ordinary capital resources (OCR) are broadly delineated as the pledged amount of the warranted capital stock achieved through borrowings, funds obtained in reimbursement and revenues arising from guarantees and loans.[120] Unlike what has been established for other international multilateral organizations, such as the IADB and World Bank, the CABEI's capital stock has been divided into a stated number of shares that do not have a stated par value.[121]

4.3.5 The Organization and Management

The highest authority of the organization is the Board of Governors, on which each member is represented by a governor and an alternate governor. The large majority of the governors are, without distinction, the ministers of economic affairs or the Presidents of the Central Banks (or persons acting on their behalf) of their respective countries.[122] The Board of Governors usually meets once a

---

[118]CABEI Constitutive Agreement, Article 7, in the part in which it provides that: 'The capital, capital reserves and other resources of the Bank, or administered by it, shall be used for achieving the objective set forth in Article 2 of this Agreement'.

[119]CABEI Constitutive Agreement, Article 11, lett. (l).

[120]CABEI Constitutive Agreement, Articles 4, (B), lett. (a) and 6.

[121]CABEI Constitutive Agreement, Article 4.

[122]CABEI Constitutive Agreement, Article 19.

year.[123] Certain powers are reserved to it, and may not be delegated.[124] These include questions related to the increment of the authorized capital, the determination of the capital reserves (upon the proposal of the Board of Directors), approbation and modification of the regulations for the Bank's organization and administration, designation of the external auditors of the Bank who are to give an opinion on the annual financial statements, amendments to the constitutive agreement and decisions on the distribution of the Bank's net assets in the event that it terminates operations. One interesting feature of the functions of the Board of Governors is the explicit power to consider and decide on issues raised by the Board of Directors, by a Director, by the Executive President or by the Controller on decisions which, in their judgment, contravene provisions of the Constitutive Agreement or resolutions of the Board of Governors.[125]

The overall functioning of the organization is under the control of the Board of Directors.[126] There are up to nine directors, five of whom are elected at the proposal of the respective founding members and the remaining four are elected by the governors representing non-regional members.[127] The voting procedure contains the usual safeguards to ensure an even distribution of voting power. Any modification of the regulation for the election of the Directors of the Founding States shall require a three-fourths majority of the total votes of the members, including the favourable votes of four Governors of the Founding States.

A remarkable feature of the CABEI is the extent to which the Board of Directors takes an active role in policy drafting. The directors reside in Tegucigalpa (Honduras), where obviously enough their energies are devoted full-time to the bank's business.[128] As a result, the bank is not controlled by the President to the same extent as the IADB, or the World Bank. Confirmation is found in Article 20 of the CABEI's Constitutive Agreement which tersely provides that: '... the President shall conduct the administration of the Bank under the direction of the Board of Directors'. From such evidence as the governors' speeches at the annual meetings, it is clear that the directors most active in policy elaboration are those with the strongest voting power (i.e. the Directors from the founding states).[129] This state of affairs was clearly perceived by the non-founding countries, and they obtained several allowances, such as an increase in the number of directors to curb the strength of the Directors of the founding member states. The executive head of the organization is the President, who is chosen by the

---

[123]Article 13 of the CABEI Constitutive Agreement which also states that: 'In addition, the Board of Governors may hold an extraordinary meeting when it so decides or when convoked by the Board of Directors'.

[124]CABEI Constitutive Agreement, Article 11.

[125]CABEI Constitutive Agreement, Article 11, para 1, lett. (j).

[126]CABEI Constitutive Agreement, Article 15.

[127]CABEI Constitutive Agreement, Article 16.

[128]CABEI Constitutive Agreement, Article 18.

[129]CABEI Constitutive Agreement, Article 19, para 2.

Governors from a list of three candidates, and selected on the basis of a contest. The President is the highest-ranking officer in the administration management of the Bank and the Bank's legal representative,[130] and he has to be a national of a founding member state.[131] His term of office is 5 years.[132] The President is granted relatively broad room for manoeuvre for staffing the organization, and is only required to pay attention to the need to select staff from a wide geographical area within the Central American region. It is most likely that this is the reason why an embryo of staff was built up quickly. The structure of the organization's staff was initially kept light and flexible, and after a few years it was rationalized according to the specific needs of the CABEI's activities as they had arisen through practice. Currently, the core of the organization is the Steering Group which is responsible for the preparation and follow-up of the Annual Meeting and any other business.[133] Research services are provided by Working Groups that are appointed by the Annual Meeting on an ad hoc basis to research and prepare specific topics that currently engage the Club and to develop relevant information and documentation,[134] and technical services are supplied by Sherpas that are appointed by each Member to serve as transmitter contacts between the Secretariat and the Member institutions.[135] Moreover, the organizational structure is complemented by an external body, the Compliance Office, which is responsible for the effective application throughout the organization of the policies and procedures in force concerning the prevention of money laundering and terrorism financing in order to prevent the CABEI from being used as a tool for such aims.[136] Additionally, since its foundation the CABEI has promoted effective communications through its Secretariat.[137]

4.3.6 The Operation and Functioning

While the bank's constitutive articles grant it some margin of manouvre in its spectrum of activities, they provide a fairly terse explanation of the type of operational policy that it is expected to advance. Although the bank's overall aim is to enhance the economic development of the founding member countries, it is not so

---

[130]CABEI Constitutive Agreement, Article 20, para 1.

[131]CABEI Constitutive Agreement, Article 20, para 2.

[132]CABEI Constitutive Agreement, Article 20.

[133]Further references are found in the CABEI's official webpage at: http://www.idfc.org/Who-We-Are/governance.aspx. (Accessed on 29 October 2014).

[134]Ibidem.

[135]Ibidem.

[136]Further information is available at: http://www.bcie.org/?cat=1427&title=Compliance%20Office&lang=en. Accessed 29 October 2014).

[137]Ibidem.

restricted in its current activities, for it may lend to any member, and to any regional or other international organization involved in the Central American region's growth. The bank may lend to any private or public entity established in Central American countries.[138] It may also make direct loans, guarantee loans in which it participates or invest in equity.[139] When the borrower is not a member government, the CABEI may request a government guarantee, but it is not obliged to do so.[140]

Nevertheless, the CABEI's operating rules and principles are set out in some detail. They are summarized in the requirement that the organization 'shall be based only on sound banking practices'.[141] It thus follows that the bank shall finance 'exclusively' those programmes or projects that are technically feasible and economically sound.[142] The bank is required to give precedence to programmes and projects that will advance sub-regional cooperation, and to the smaller Central American countries, although this has not been indicated in the Constitutive Agreement. Guidelines are aimed specifically at guaranteeing that the CABEI does not put its resources at risk. The Constitutive Agreement does not hold the bank to a fixed rate of interest or period of amortization. The conditions of lending shall be linked to the specific circumstances of the loan, but it is not made evident whether this implies an assessment of the project to which the loan is allocated.

Since its earliest times, the organization has relinquished an all-embracing statement on loan policy.[143] However, the document gives a clear enough idea of the bank's main concerns, if not of its overall policy. Paramount among these is what can be described as a belief that in the long term the effectiveness, creditworthiness and accomplishments of the CABEI will essentially depend on the lengths to which it pursues sound development banking rules and principles. Its commitment to 'sound banking principles' would thus appear to give it a more natural inclination towards the manufacturing industry.

4.3.7 Special Funds

The question of special funds has been treated as a matter of primary importance since the bank's establishment. This is because to a significant extent, Article 6 of the CABEI's Constitutive Agreement expressly provides as follows: 'Without

---

[138]CABEI Constitutive Agreement, Article 7, lett. (f).

[139]CABEI Constitutive Agreement, Article 7, lett. (h)–(j).

[140]CABEI Constitutive Agreement, Article 7, lett. (i).

[141]CABEI Constitutive Agreement, Article 8, para 2.

[142]CABEI Constitutive Agreement, Article 8, para 1.

[143]Further references are found in the CABEI's official webpage at: http://www.idfc.org/Who-We-Are/governance.aspx. Accessed 29 October 2014.

prejudice of what has been indicated in the preceding paragraphs, there will exist within the Bank, but as an independent and separate net worth from the general net worth of the Bank, the following funds, *namely* the Social Benefits Fund, the Special Fund for the Social Transformation of Central America and the Technical Cooperation Fund'.

In so far as this attitude is reflected in the CABEI's Constitutive Agreement, what was envisaged were four multilateral funds only available 'for specific purposes' in the bank's operations. Nevertheless, in the deteriorating aid climate of the 1980s[144] the incorporation of such funds in the bank's structure would have required far more forceful pursuit than was deemed appropriate by the CABEI's drafters. In the event, the bank was granted the power to create a special fund, the so-called the CABEI-HIPC Special Fund, for soft lending out of its own resources, and the power to accept from other sources the administration of trust funds, provided that these are aimed at serving the specific purpose and come within the functions of the bank. Thus, from the outset it was assumed that special funds would have limited and specified purposes. The other possibility had been closed off at an early stage: it would have endowed CABEI with a general purpose fund modelled on the International Development Association (IDA) as a key element in the bank's ordinary operations.

Once the CABEI started its operations, the need for special funds was perceived more clearly, and the pursuit of such funds became one of its major concerns. The question was also debated by the Board of Governors and the Board of Directors in several of their meetings. The special fund for social transformation (FETs) was formally constituted at the end of 1999 as part of the CABEI's overall strategy in supporting the social development and productivity of the Central American countries.

More specialized funds, which operate with their own resources, were also established in order to deal with the changing needs of Central America. Such funds include the Central American Fund for the Common Market, the Economic and Social Development Fund for Central America, the Fund for Technical Cooperation, the Regional Fund for Conversion of Foreign Debt, the Microprojects Fund and the Poverty Relief Fund.[145]

Perhaps it is significant that the CABEI was more successful in granting special contributions for technical cooperation.[146] The bank has received contributions for technical assistance from the Inter-American Development Bank (IADB),[147] UNIFEM (part of UN Women) and more recently from MASHAV, Israel's Agency

---

[144]On the issue, see: Sánchez 2009, p. 8 ff.

[145]See: Cevallos 1996, p. 257 ff.

[146]On the subject, see: Gudynas E, 'An Introduction to Regional Financial Institutions in Latin America, Americas Program, 12 August 2008 at: http://www.cipamericas.org/archives/1475. Accessed 3 December 2014, who stresses that: 'In 2006, the bank disbursed $1.647 billion, along three strategic operational lines: integration, globalization, and poverty'.

[147]See: Tussie 1995, p. 19.

for International Development Cooperation in the Ministry of Foreign Affairs, which has signed a technical cooperation treaty with the CABEI.[148] The overall amount available from such sources for technical cooperation was US $ 158.2 thousand according to the CABEI's Annual Report of 2012,[149] but there is no reason to believe that this sum might not be increased whenever this is indispensable. Clearly, therefore, one reason why the bank encountered little difficulty in establishing a technical cooperation fund was that the sums involved were relatively modest. Nevertheless, it is reasonable also to maintain that a further factor was that the rationale for a technical assistance fund was straightforward; whereas, the creation of other special funds raised issues of principle involving the bank's multilateral status and concerning its preferred presentation of itself as primarily a banking organization.

4.3.8 Prospects

Fifty years and more of operations are indeed a sound basis on which to assess the appropriateness of the CABEI for the needs it was created to satisfy. It is thus possible to make an assessment of its performance. Some of the major difficulties encountered by the CABEI have already been considered in detail in the above paragraphs. Here we are concerned with a more general question: to what extent has the ideal type represented by the CABEI demonstrated itself to be effectively tailored to the specific needs of the sub-region where it operates?

The conclusions to be drawn from the above paragraphs can be summarized very succinctly. Undoubtedly the CABEI is a bank, and is not to be condemned for trying to achieve a high standard in being what it is, that is for financing 'exclusively' those programmes or projects which are economically sound and technically feasible.[150] But it is not in any significant sense Central American, and in any case there are some uncertainties as to whether the term 'Central American' in this institutional framework has any true and operative meaning. If it is not Central American, as a development institution is the CABEI at least an institution of the developing countries? The evidence provided above suggests that it is, and that the influence of the developed countries is not so overwhelming that the CABEI's perception of the development process is a limited perception, entirely drawn from the developed countries' experience rather than from the developing countries' perceived needs and ambitions.

---

[148]References are in 'The CABEI and Israel's MASHAV sign a Technical Cooperation General Agreement', CABEI News, 17 October 2013 at: http://www.bcie.org/?art=1533&title=CA BEI%20and%20Israel%B4s%20MASHAV%20sign%20a%20Technical%20Cooperation%20 General%20Agreement&lang=en. Accessed 3 December 2014.

[149]CABEI, Annual Report 2012, at: http://www.bcie.org/uploaded/content/category/1905796452. pdf. Accessed 3 December 2014.

[150]See Sect. 4.3.5.

It would be wrong to attribute these features of the institution to the position adopted by particular countries. Such features are rooted in its capital organization and in its statutory tasks and functions. If the CABEI is an ideal type, by the same token it is not specifically tailored to the Central American situation. To find a particularly Central American role for itself, the CABEI will therefore have to choose the particular features from a range of functions that will give it coherence in a Central American environment. This is in any case the most natural way, due to the diversity and complexity of the Central American sub-region. We shall choose four functions from the list, as suggested by the CABEI's Constitutive Agreement, but it should be pointed out that this list is not a complete one:

(a) financial support of projects which help sub-regional integration and growth;
(b) special focus on the overall position of the smaller Central American countries;
(c) leadership in sub-regional policy issues, such as the development of a telecommunications network;
(d) exploitation of its developed membership as a tool for increasing the flow of aid to the sub-region.

Looking at the projects which enhance sub-regional integration and economic growth in Central America reveals that the CABEI's biggest contribution was to the member countries' infrastructure that connects highways with major ports, cities and airports.[151] These projects helped lower tariffs, advanced socio-economic growth, and brought the Central American countries into stricter connection with each other. The CABEI also financially sponsored the construction of ports that boosted the sub-region's bargaining role vis-a-vis shipping companies which charged extra fees when they considered port conditions to be unsuitable.[152] In this context, the countries most frequently supported by the bank were Honduras and Costa Rica. On wider policy issues, the CABEI has already adopted some initiatives. However, two elements prevent it from integrating those initiatives into a coherent whole. The first is the extent to which the CABEI has placed the main emphasis on project finance and project appraisal. The second is its unwillingness to recognize that discussion of policy issues commits it to a political function.

As far as the smaller countries are concerned, the CABEI has already demonstrated a tendency to direct its projects, and likewise, its technical cooperation, in such countries. Moreover, it has also shown an overall propensity to become involved in macro-economic country programmes and activities which normally lead it into a situation where political considerations are topmost.

That the CABEI will further develop and consolidate as a tool for social and economic change and structural reform in Central American countries seems more natural, due to the circumstance that it is an aid-giving organization. But the

---

[151]See: Cevallos 1996, p. 257.
[152]Ibidem.

struggle between the dogma of assistance and the dogma of sound banking principles makes it uncertain whether the CABEI will always pursue such a course with eagerness. Moreover, from a legal point of view, the bank is potentially subject to influence from its debtors as much as any other international or national lending agency. Furthermore, this is because—over time—CABEI has lost some of its autonomy as a result of its necessity to borrow directly from outside sources.[153]

To develop a functional convergence along these lines would go a long way towards giving the CABEI the innovative role that it requires if it is to evolve as a key point in the strategies of development of Central American countries. In particular, the development of such functions would give the CABEI a specific claim on the developed countries' resources, as distinct from the wider claim of multilateral development institutions in general. However, a more complex question is whether such a role would facilitate the development of a set of characteristically Central American responses to the developmental challenge. Clearly that question cannot be answered in detail here. But to give such a response is precisely that creative act which is the core political mission of a sub-regional development institution. To attempt to clarify, the CABEI's role in advance means to provide a premise as to what should be the conclusion that derives from the sub-regional bank's operational practice and political approach.

Nevertheless, in general terms we can recommend a line of investigation that could suit the purpose, though it is a line of investigation whose realization is almost certainly forbidden by the CABEI's traditional modus operandi and internal structure. In some Central American countries, notably in Guatemala and Honduras, there is growing distrust of the relevance of the US/EU experience to Central American's traditions and present situations.[154] There is the long-term uncertainty that a healthy questioning of established practice may turn into a harsh veto of all that the US/EU still have to offer. If the CABEI could operate as a bridge between the two patterns of approach, applying the questions currently posed by Central American politicians and academics to the evolved experience of US/EU developed societies, then both Central American and the US/Western Europe could gain. The fulfilment of such a role would be very close to the ambitions that the notion of sub-regional development banks sprang from. Nevertheless, it would be distant from the role that comes naturally to the type which has finally evolved. In the broad perspective of what is likely to occur in Central America now and over the coming years, it is difficult to attribute to the CABEI the historical significance attached to it by its drafters and by its current proponents.

---

[153]Ibidem.

[154]On the US influence on Guatemala see *inter alia* Hey 1995, p. 14 who also stresses that: 'US influence in Guatemala decreased at the time that gross human rights violations escalated'.

4.4 The Andean Development Corporation (CAF)

4.4.1 The Andean Sub-unit

Integration is not a new concept to Andeans. The nations of Bolivia, Colombia, Chile, Ecuador and Peru signed the Andean Pact Treaty, the Cartagena Agreement, in 1969. This led to the establishment of the Andean Community (Comunidad Andina or CAN), previously known as the Andean Pact,[155] as soon as they realized the opportunity of a closer sub-regional bloc. While these countries are sometimes generically considered as belonging to the LAC region, they have their own peculiar characteristics that differentiate them from their Latin American neighbours and make the countries in the region less homogenous than they might seem at first sight.[156]

After the agrarian reforms in Ecuador in 1964 and 1973 and the reforms of the 1952 revolution in Bolivia, the Andean countries[157] enjoyed relative stability, though only for a few years, in particular as a result of the external support from the Alliance for Progress.[158] But most of the economic reforms were only partly (or badly) enforced due to the political environment, and this led to the negative economic outcomes that became clear in the late 1970s with excessive borrowing, large budget deficits and inflationary peaks.[159]

Andean economies have traditionally been focused on mining industries, an element that renders the sub-region defenceless against the unstable international commodities markets.[160] Since the late 1980s, when neoliberal programmes and policies indicated mining as a national financial strategy, the Andean countries were not only defenceless towards the increases in the prices of their mining resources, but they were also confronted with more worrying internal issues such as governance and instability problems. In addition, there was the need for socio-economic growth (in particular the multiplication of socio-economic activities), and the absence of democracy, and political participation.[161] Ecuador above all was hit by a severe economic crisis in 1998–1999, and as a result of this it has

---

[155]Andean Sub-regional Integration Agreement, 26 May 1969, 8 ILM, p. 910 ff. See Chap. 5 in this book.

[156]References are found in León Li 2001, p. 10.

[157]By 'Andean Countries' we refer to the countries that are currently members of the CAN (Andean Community of Nations), see Chap. 5 in this book.

[158]Stenman and Follér 2008, p. 6 ff.

[159]Ibidem.

[160]See L. Hinojosa, Mining Economies, Mining Countries: What Mining Delivers for Development in Andean Countries? (University of Manchester, SAS—London, 7 December 2007) at: http://www.sed.manchester.ac.uk/research/andes/publications/conferences/Hinojosa_Presentation_SAS_London.pdf. Accessed 9 December 2014.

[161]Ibidem, p. 6 ff.

suffered currency depreciation and fast-growing inflation that was further aggravated by a serious crisis of the whole banking sector.[162]

These factors contribute towards clarifying the relentless underdevelopment during that period. After being heavily hit by the recession of the 1980s and the worldwide crisis of the mining sector in the 1990s, an attempt was made to expand the sub-region's exports. The main evidence of this is the approximately 3 % recovery in the Gross Domestic Product in the year 2000.[163] Income produced during the 2000s enhanced these economies' ability to import their technology and capital needs, without generating excessive debt.[164] Exports continued to be fundamental to the region's economies. In addition to mining resources, which all of the Andean countries exported, and bananas, exported mostly by Honduras and Costa Rica, the region began exporting cotton, sugar, meat and other products, making these countries less economically vulnerable and less dependent upon a single product. Real GDP growth was on average 1.6 % points higher between 2000 and 2010, compared to the 1990s.[165] There was also some level of experimentation with manufactured products and some level of industrialization was obtained.[166] Indeed industrial development boomed in the 2000s, followed by moderate growth levels since 2010. Furthermore, since 2000 the financial services sector has grown both in the services supplied and in the tools being adopted.

Notwithstanding the relative political stability in the Andes at the establishment of the Andean Community, civil unrest and armed conflicts swept through the region during the late 1990s and early 2000s. Recent economic initiatives cover the hetereogenity of economic initiatives and exports, including the improved employment of natural resources and the modernization of infrastructure.[167] Only in recent times has industrialization achieved the consideration it merits.

---

[162]*Amplius* A Solimano, Governance crises and the Andean region: a political economy analysis, CEPAL, Santiago, Chile, February 2003, at: http://www.cepal.org/publicaciones/xml/2/12092/lcl 1860i.pdf. Accessed 12 December 2014.

[163]Andean Community, Andean Community: Development and Prospects, at: http://www.comunidadandina.org/en/Documents.aspx?id=80&title=andean-community-development-and-prospects&accion=detalle&cat=4&tipo=DOC. Accessed 9 December 2014.

[164]On this issue, see also M Bird, An Andean Hierarchical Market Economy?: Ollanta Humala, New Developmentalism, and an Institutional Turn in Peru, paper presented at the annual meeting of the SASE Annual Conference 2012, M.I.T., Cambridge, MA, 28 June 2012, at: http://citation.allacademic.com/meta/p567627_index.html. Accessed 12 October 2014).

[165]See: Andrian L G, Terms of Trade and Fiscal Sustainability when the Sovereign Exploits a Natural Resource, at: http://www.inesad.edu.bo/bcde2013/papers/BCDE2013-17.pdf. Accessed 9 December 2014.

[166]See also the Andean Community's official website http://www.comunidadandina.org/en/Logros.aspx. sub 'Principal Results of Andean Integration' stressing that: 'About 80 % of intra-Community trade is in manufactured products'.

[167]Andean Community, Regional Indicative Programme 2004–2006, at: http://eeas.europa.eu/andean/rsp/rip_0406_en.pdf. Accessed 9 December 2014.

The first attempt at market integration in the Andes came under the auspices of the Andean Common Market, which is more commonly known as ANCOM.[168] The ANCOM was aimed at structuring the economic development of the sub-region by stimulating the region's growth and intra-regional exports.[169] The ANCOM's main objectives were the establishment of a customs union, internal trade liberalization, the enactment of a Common External Tariff (CET) and the development of sectoral programmes of industrial development (SPIDs). The ANCOM's traditional dispute resolution procedures are considered by some to be the only part of the integration effort that has remained functional for a certain length of time.[170]

The establishment of an Andean Tribunal of Justice (ATJ) and the replacement of the import substitution approach to Andean integration with a policy favouring free trade and economic liberalization—a change reflected in renaming the Pact as the 'Andean Community'—further contributed to the integration process in the Andes. More recently, the judicial activity of the ATJ has also boosted integration among Andean member countries: since these events the ATJ has become the third most active international court, with over 1700 rulings by the end of 2009.[171]

Are these changes effectively beneficial to the sub-region? To understand the possible answers to this question, it is indispensable to consider the economic history of the sub-region and its integration effort in order to assess how these neoliberal ideas affect the Andes and the future role of the CAF.

4.4.2 The Integration Movement: Andean Common Market

4.4.2.1 History and Aims

The ANCOM was the first attempt towards creating sub-regional economic integration in the Andes.[172] The sub-region's integration was officially opened on 26 May 1969, by an international treaty drafting a comprehensive blueprint for integrated growth, the so-called 'The Cartagena Agreement'. The Commission, a decision-making body composed of one plenipotentiary from each member country,[173] and the Junta, an organ composed of three independent members who may be from any Latin American country, were assigned the task of boosting the course of socio-economic integration.[174]

---

[168]Agreement on Subregional Integration (The Cartagena Agreement), signed 26 May 1969, 8 ILM 910 (1969).

[169]*Amplius* O'Leary 1984. See also: Horton 1982, at p. 44.

[170]O'Leary 1984.

[171]References are found in Alter and Helfer 2011.

[172]See: Kearns 1972.

[173]Cartagena Agreement, above n. 168, Article 6.

[174]See O'Leary 1984.

Integration was a slow process which commenced with the early stages of the United Nations Economic Commission for Latin America ('ECLA')'s existence.[175] Since its foundation ECLA has correctly perceived that simply allowing market forces to direct Latin America's development would be unsuccessful. Therefore, it held that the various governments would have to intervene, both at national and sub-regional levels, to direct the progress of their economies. This approach emphasized the 'dynamic' quality of economic growth.[176]

In June 1969 the Cartagena Agreement was ratified by Bolivia, Chile, Colombia, Ecuador and Peru and it gave birth to the CACM. The determination to boost the pace of integration in the Andes was a response to various circumstances, including: the decline in the price of Andean exports outside the subregion, and recent support of the integration process by the United States after its initial distrust.[177] Venezuela joined the Cartagena Agreement in 1973 but withdrew in 2006 after Colombia and Peru concluded free trade agreements ('FTAs') with the United States. Chile withdrew in 1976, affirming the existence of economic incompatibilities. In 1993 four members (except Peru that was temporarily suspended) established a free trade area. In 1995 the members adopted a common trade tariff to be imposed in dealings with non-member countries.[178] In 2006 the Andean Free Trade Area became wholly operational after Peru was fully incorporated.

4.4.2.2 Achievements and Failures of the Andean Common Market

In general, the ANCOM was an attempt to structure the socio-economic growth of the Andes. One of the major achievements of integration was the establishment of a milieu of confidence and an institutional framework among the Andean countries that enhanced intra-regional commerce.[179] Although in ANCOM the share of intra-regional trade is lower than in MERCOSUR,[180] intra-subregional trade in

---

[175]Ibidem.

[176]Ibidem.

[177]See US Direct Investment in South America's Andean Common Market, Department of Commerce: Report to the Congress, US General Accounting Office, New York, 1977.

[178]For further references on these issues see 'Andean Community (CAN)', at: http://mea.gov.in/Portal/ForeignRelation/Andean_Community_February.2013.pdf. Accessed 9 December 2014.

[179]See: Andean Community, 'Andean Community: Development and Prospects', available at: http://www.comunidadandina.org/en/Documents.aspx?id=80&title=andean-community-development-and-prospects&accion=detalle&cat=4&tipo=DO. Accessed 10 December 2014, stressing that: 'Tariff reduction and the prohibition against the application of para-tariff measures to trade within the subregion have boosted trade between Member Countries significantly beyond their worldwide exports, particularly since 1990 when Andean economic opening started'.

[180]See: UNCTAD, Regional Cooperation and Trade Integration Among Developing Countries, at: unctad.org/en/pages/PressReleaseArchive.aspx?. Accessed 3 December 2014.

manufactured goods grew around 20 % per year between 1990 and 1997.[181] Nearly 14 % of the total trade of the countries was intra-regional.[182] In Colombia, for instance, intra-regional commerce represented one fifth of its total trade in the 1990s. However, in the case of the Bolivarian Republic of Venezuela—whose exports are dominated by oil and account for roughly half of total ANCOM exports—less than 5 % of the country's total exports were directed to other Andean countries by 2006.[183] With all that said, other projects, such as trade talks between ANCOM and Mercosur, which culminated in an agreement in 2002, and FTAA negotiations, as well as the implementation of a Social Agenda and of a sustainable-development policy, were indeed much more successful than the increase in intra-regional commerce had been.[184]

The ANCOM also stimulated intra-regional exports and the region's growth. The UNCTAD estimated that between 2000 and 2006, a significant and growing share of ANCOM countries' commerce (about 30 %) has been with other Latin American countries. This suggests that a wider regional treaty (such as the proposed Union of the South involving all South American countries) would already be able to count on considerable trade among the members.[185]

4.4.3 The Structure of the Andean Development Corporation (CAF)

4.4.3.1 History and Development

The CAF was founded in 1969 within the framework of the Andean Community of Nations as a source of, and tool for, financing the integration and development of the sub-region.[186] Its overall purpose was to supply a centralized mechanism to coordinate the goals of the Andean Community, although it was restricted to only the financial aspects of those efforts. Article 3 of its Establishing Agreement provides that it shall: '... foster the sub-regional integration process'. It also states that: 'To this effect, within a sense of rational specialization and an even distribution of investments within the area, taking into consideration the necessity for effective action in favour of the relatively less developed countries and with adequate coordination with the organization in charge of the sub-regional integration,

---

[181]Ibidem.

[182]See: UN 2003, Latin America and the Caribbean in the World Economy, Cepal, New York 2003, p. 165 ff.

[183]See: UNCTAD, above n. 180, p. 9.

[184]See: European Community, Regional Strategy: Andean Community of Nations: 2002–2006, at: http://eeas.europa.eu/andean/rsp/02_06_en.pdf. Accessed 9 October 2014).

[185]See: UNCTAD, above n. 180, p. 9.

[186]Agreement Establishing the Andean Development Corporation, (1969) 8(5) ILM, pp. 940–958.

it shall foster the better use of the opportunities and resources which the area of action offers, through the criterion of production and service enterprises and the expansion, modernization or conversion of the existing ones'. Article 4 highlights areas on which its financing should focus, including the preparation and execution of multinational projects, the attraction and mobilization of external resources, the organization of enterprises, their expansion, modernization and rehabilitation in order to improve their efficiency and competitiveness. Other highlighted areas include the identification of investment opportunities, the acquisition and disposal of movable and immovable property, the promotion of trade inside the sub-region and with non-subregional countries, the promotion of social development and the financing of research and development, the support of the whole spectrum of the business sector and lastly, the enhancement of regional competitive participation in the globalization process.[187]

During the 1970s, the CAF successfully demonstrated that a subregional development organization may operate efficiently even without any industrial-country shareholders and without recourse to concessional funding.[188] In this regard, it is noteworthy that the CAF has done so on a scale comparable to that of the main supranational development organizations like the IADB and the financial institutions belonging to the World Bank Group. Moreover, it is also noteworthy that it has done so notwithstanding the serious economic problems that afflicted some of its main borrowing members.[189]

In the 1980s Andean countries experienced a structural balance of payments deficit, military dictatorship and violent social conflicts especially in Bolivia, Chile and Colombia.[190] During the 'lost decade', the CAF and local governments did not obtain much support from other international financial institutions and, as a consequence, the CAF often lacked the financial resources to support all the projects that the Andean region required.[191] The few financial resources that the CAF could obtain were generally tied to special conditions that restricted the

---

[187]See V Rubio Vega, The Andean Development Corporation (CAF): Continuity, Scope and Role in Regional Long-Term Development Lending, at: http://www.balsillieschool.ca/people/veronica-rubio-vega. Accessed 1 December 2014; AF Reinoso, Regional Financial Cooperation: An Andean Perspective, PECC Finance Forum Conference, Honolulu, 11–13 August 2002 at: http://www.pecc.org/resources/doc_download/449-regional-financial-cooperation-an-andean-perspective. Accessed 2 December 2014.

[188]*Amplius* Ocampo et al. 2007, p. 60 ff. See also AF Reinoso, n. 187, p. 10 who stresses that: 'The CAF is currently the leading source of multilateral financing of the Andean countries, having approved during the last 10 years over 40 % of the total resources approved by multilateral agencies'.

[189]*Amplius* Ocampo et al. 2007, p. 60 ff.

[190]See: Kühnhardt 2010, p. 93 ff; Dabène 2009, p. 182, who also stresses that: 'With a chronic deficit of infrastructure, aggravated since the 1980s by underinvestment, market integration has always been bumping into serious limitations'. See also Suarez Mejias 2006.

[191]See: AF Reinoso, above n. 187, p. 11, who stresses that: 'Although the 1980 s were characterized by the rationing of the international credit and by high interest rates, in the context of external debt, the CAF was the only source of financing in an extremely adverse international context'.

availability or employment of funds—a factor that hindered the implementation of a coherent integration programme in the 1980s and 1990s. Furthermore, internal socio-political issues and problems in each country of the Andean sub-region and conflicts among them further compounded the problem. Intra-regional commerce significantly decreased, and barriers were once more put in place by some countries.

4.4.3.2 Organizational Framework

The CAF is an internationally recognized juridical institution that is governed by its own establishing treaty and by-laws.[192] Its organization is divided into three main bodies: the Shareholders' Assemblies (Regular or Special), the Board of Directors and the Executive President. The Regular Assembly of Shareholders (equivalent to the Board of Governors of the World Bank and IADB), possesses the most authority in the CAF since it can, among other things, increase, reduce or restore corporate capital and dissolve the Corporation.[193] It is comprised of share-holders or their representatives.[194] The Regular Assembly meets at least once a year; the requisite quorum for its meetings is at least four Series 'A' shares and 50 % of the other shares.[195] The Special Assembly can deal exclusively with the issues expressly covered in the Notice calling it.[196]

The Board of Directors is composed of eleven members, five of whom are elected for a period of 3 years by the holders of Series 'A' shares, five by the hold-ers of Series 'B' shares[197] and one (and its Alternate) by banking and financial institutions of the subregional shareholders of the CAF.[198] The Directors are responsible, among other things, for the CAF's ordinary functioning, the definition of its policies including the financial, credit and economic policies of the Corporation, the administration of the CAF structure, the approval of the assets and liability of credit operations, the granting of guarantees for the subscription of shares and securities in general (underwriting) and the setting of its reserves.[199]

---

[192]See: CAF Agreement, n. 11, Article 1 which states that: 'The CAF is a legal entity of public international law and is subject to the provisions contained in the present instrument'.

[193]CAF Agreement, above n. 11, Article 14, lett. (a) and (b).

[194]Ibidem, Article 11.

[195]Ibidem, Article 16.

[196]Ibidem, Article 14, para 2.

[197]Ibidem, Article 24, lett. (b).

[198]Ibidem, Article 24, lett. (c) provides that: 'Director referred in lett. (c) shall be elected pur-suant to internal rules approved by the shareholders of the institutions mentioned above, in which expressly is recognized the principle of alternability, by reason of the nationality of the Directors'.

[199]Ibidem, Article 27, lett. (g).

The Executive President, an international officer, is the legal representative of the Corporation. He/she is elected for a period of 5 years.[200] Designated by the Directors, the Executive President participates in the Board of Directors' meetings without voting, and supervises the CAF's administration and legal representation.[201] Moreover, according to Article 37 of the Establishing Agreement, the Executive President also selects the personnel, and informs the Board of Directors at its next meeting of any action adopted, as well as the powers, obligations and remunerations fixed in accordance with the budget.

4.4.3.3 Finances

The CAF started its operations with two million dollars divided into Series 'A'[202] and Series 'B' shares, in addition to Series 'C'.[203] In 2009, CAF allocated over USD 9.1 billion of new funding, which is a 15 % rise compared to 2008.[204]

At least 50 % of the contributions are made in US dollars, with the exception of the first installment which shall be paid in full in US currency according to the Establishing Agreement.[205] The CAF may participate in overseas capital markets. In the past, the Corporation has placed bonds, certificates of investment and certificates of deposit in U.S. dollars and local currencies in both American and European markets. Currently, the CAF is preparing new issues to increase its presence in the world market.[206]

---

[200]Ibidem, Article 32 also affirmes that: 'The Executive President may be re-elected and shall remain in office until his replacement takes over'.

[201]Ibidem, Articles 31, 35 and 38.

[202]In 2005, shareholders approved a reform to permit any country within Latin America and the Caribbean to become an A shareholder (CAF Establishing Agreement, Article 59).

[203]CAF Agreement, above n. 11 Article 5, authorized capital had increased from $3 million to $5 million by January 2002, see: Declaration of Santa Cruz de la Sierra. Special Meeting of the Andean Presidential Council, at: http://www.comunidadandina.org/en/TreatiesLegislation.asp x?id=54&title=declaration-of-santa-cruz-de-la-sierra-special-meeting-of-the-andeanpresidentialcouncil&accion=detalle&cat=3&tipo=DO. Accessed 13 December 2014.

[204]Further information is available at the CAF's official website at: http://www.caf.com/es. Accessed 13 December 2014.

[205]CAF Agreement, above n. 11, Article 8, paras 2 and 3 which provides that: 'The remaining 50 % of the other installments may be paid in local currency, by the subscribers corresponding to each country, provided that total convertibility and maintenance of the value of the said currency is guaranteed to the satisfaction of the Corporation, and upon prior approval by the Board of Directors, in relation to United States of America dollars in accordance with the weight and the law in force on the date of entry into force of this Agreement'.

[206]Further information is available at the CAF's official website at: http://www.caf.com/es. Accessed 13 December 2014.

On 24 October 2005, CAF amended its Establishing Agreement to include extra-regional partners who shall make contributions in U.S. dollars.[207] More recently, at an extraordinary meeting held in Caracas, Brazil was made a full member of the CAF after signing a treaty to increase its capital in the organization to US $190 million.[208] Andean interests in the CAF still amount to the majority of the CAF's shares, though a percentage of its shares are allowed to be acquired by extra-subregional members.[209]

The CAF made strong efforts to increase its credibility in the international arena by making timely payments of its debts. Additionally, the debt balance has been decreasing moderately, but steadily, in the last few years and at the end of 2013 had decreased by 2.6 % from the previous fiscal year.

4.4.3.4 Operations and Funds

The CAF's establishing agreement, although giving the bank some latitude in its spectrum of activities and operations,[210] provides a terse explanation of the type of operational policies and procedures that CAF was expected to develop.[211] While its overall purpose is to enhance the socio-economic growth of the less developed countries of the Andes,[212] it is not so restricted in its present functioning, for it can lend to any country, and to any sub-regional or other international entity involved in the sub-region's socio-economic growth.[213] It can lend to any private or public company operating in member states. It can make guarantee loans in which it

---

[207]On 24 October 2005, a protocol amending the Agreement was signed; it entered into force on 9 July 2008. Pursuant to that Protocol, the Agreement was opened to accession by other countries. Both for the text of the 2005 Protocol and the list of the other amendments to the CAF Establishing Agreement see the CAF's official website at http://www.caf.com/es.

[208]For further information on this issue see F Sánchez, Brazil becomes full Andean Development Corporation member, at: http://infosurhoy.com/en_GB/articles/saii/features/economy/2009/12/11/feature-01. Accessed 13 December 2014).

[209]See also the CAF Agreement, n. 11 above, Article 3, lett. (i) which provides that: 'The Corporation may transfer the shares, securities, rights, and commitments which it acquires, offering them in the first place to public or private entities of the sub-region and, in the event of lack of interest on their part, to third parties interested in the economic and social development of the same'.

[210]Financial support might be provided in a wider range of manners than other MDBs, including to: 'emit bonds or debentures, act as a guarantor of any type, provide collateral for obligations, and grant guarantees in share issues' (CAF Agreement, Article 4).

[211]CAF Agreement, n. 11 above, Article 5, para 2.

[212]CAF Agreement, n. 11 above, Article 3; also Article 2 which provides that: 'The Corporation may establish … agencies, offices or representation as deemed necessary for the carrying out of its functions in each of the participating countries and thereout'.

[213]CAF Agreement, n. 11 above, Article 4, lett. (i) clarifies that: 'The Corporation may transfer the shares, securities. rights. and commitments which it acquires, offering them in the first place to public or private entities of the Subregion and, in the event of lack of interest in their part, to third parties interested in the economic and social development of the same'.

participates, direct loans, or invest in equity.[214] When the borrower is not a member government, the CAF may ask for a government guarantee, though it is not compelled to do so according to its establishing agreement. Additionally, the CAF boosts funds for activities mainly in the international financial sector.[215]

Nevertheless, the bank's operating principles are set out in some detail. They are summarized in the requirement that the CAF must follow sound banking principles in its activities.[216] Specific projects like infrastructural projects in developing states of the sub-region must be a priority for the Corporation.[217] Indeed the CAF is required to give priority to projects that will enhance sub-regional cooperation, and to the less developed states of the Andes. Guidelines are laid down for ensuring that the CAF does not put its capital resources at risk.[218]

The CAF's establishing agreement does not commit the institution to a fixed rate of interest.[219] The terms and conditions of lending shall always be related to the specific circumstances of the loan as it is evidenced by the fact that full in-country missions during project preparation are indispensable.[220] However, it is not wholly clear whether this leads to an assessment of the project to which the loan is directed. In practice, nevertheless, the CAF adopted a variable amortization period which averages 14 years.[221] Since its early years, the bank's loan approval procedure has turned out to be less formal and much faster than either of the other MDBs, the World Bank and the IADB, which also operate in the Andes as financial intermediaries.[222] Moreover, several officials in borrower governments have affirmed that the Corporation is willing to bypass most formal procedures entirely

---

[214]CAF Constitutive Agreement, n. 11 above, Article 4.

[215]See: V Rubio Vega, above n. 187.

[216]See also Griffith-Jones (2002), Governance of the World Bank, Paper prepared for DFID at: http://stephanygj.net/papers/Governance_of_the_World_Bank._Paper_prepared_for_DFID.pdf. Accessed 12 December 2013, who states that: 'The basic finance co-operative model of the World Bank was also followed in the creation of the CAF'.

[217]CAF Agreement, n. 11 above, Articles 3 and 4.

[218]On the issue, see also V Rubio Vega, n. 187 above, p. 8, who stresses that: 'CAF's business management is divided into two broad functions: client relationship managemetand financial management. Internally the institution is constantly debating within two positions: assuming the "risk" of development—because by definition it is a risk—while trying to get the best credit risk rating possible in the international markets, in order to offer attractive financingterms (CAF Senior Executive, personal interview, 4 October 2012)'.

[219]On the issue, see: Humphrey and Michaelowa 2010 who also stress that: 'By the late 1990s, the CAF had established a clear and widening superiority in annual lending commitments in the Andes'. See: Humphrey and Michaelowa 2013, who also indicate that: 'CAF loans are still usually (but not always) less expensive than private sources for government borrowing'.

[220]See also Humphrey and Michaelowa 2010 who indicate that: 'The World Bank generally requires at least four full in-country missions during project preparation, compared to two or three for the IADB and frequently just one for the CAF (World Bank and IADB operations staff and borrower government interviews)'.

[221]See: Humphrey and Michaelowa 2013, p. 145.

[222]Ibidem.

in cases of urgent need by a government, and that a loan may start being disbursed in as little as a month or 6 weeks if this is indispensable.[223] In terms of sectors, the CAF has shown strong interest in transport, infrastructure,[224] environment and agriculture, as evidenced by the loans it made especially during the 1998/1999 crisis.[225] Its commitment to sound banking rules and principles would appear to indicate that it has a stronger preference for the private productive sector.[226] The way in which this preference has effectively worked out can be better elucidated in terms of a report on the CAF's development.

4.4.3.5 The Role of the CAF in the Andes

The CAF has consistently followed the normative framework under which it was created.[227] Over time, it lost some of its autonomy (but not efficiency) as a result of its necessity to borrow directly from outside sources of financing (i.e. public and private sources of capital in the form of credit lines, bond issues and bank loans).[228] In order to acquire financial resources, the CAF generally had to meet certain lender requirements, such as agreements to support particular industries and to acquire technology and capital goods from certain countries.[229] In an attempt to escape such restrictions, especially conditional agreements, the CAF gradually restrained itself from seeking credit from governmental bodies and public aid agencies. While this approach is commendable in theory, the instability of the sub-region during the last decades caused also private creditors to impose restrictions affecting political decision-making in the sub-region.[230]

---

[223]Ibidem.

[224]See the Andean Development Corporation's $50 million loan for the modernization of Bogota's El Dorado airport. References are found in Peters T, 'Andean Development Corporation approves $50 M loan for Bogota airport' at: http://colombiareports.co/andean-development-corporation-approves-50m-loan-for-bogota-airport/. Accessed 12 December 2014.

[225]See: Humphrey and Michaelowa 2013, p. 145 ff.

[226]The CAF supplies long-term credit to commercial entities for the purchase and construction of assets (such as machinery, civil works and equipment) for the acquisition of goods and services, as well as credit lines for working capital, that can be employed, for instance, to get raw material. References are found in the CAF's official website at: http://www.caf.com/en/areas-of-action/productive-and-financial-sectors/private-sector. Accessed 20 December 2014.

[227]But see: Humphrey 2012, who after having recalled that: 'In a 2009 magazine interview, CAF President Enrique García stated that developed countries would never be allowed to have more than 15 % of shareholding power' stressed that: 'This policy is not in the Constituent Agreement or CAF regulations, but is evidently an unwritten rule followed by the organization's shareholders when considering new members'.

[228]Ibidem, p. 65 ff.

[229]Ibidem, pp. 65 ff, 194 ff.

[230]Ibidem, p. 66 ff.

During its relatively long history, the CAF's Assemblies of Shareholders have experienced negative political influences that have hindered its mission.[231] Representing their different countries, the Assembly of Shareholders frequently forgot the purpose of the CAF and instead often favoured their respective governments.[232] However, the participation of extra-regional partners mitigated political influences in the Assemblies of Shareholders' decision-making.

4.4.3.6 The Current Status of the CAF

During the 1980s, Andean countries felt the adverse consequences of internal conflicts and the international economic conditions of the 1970s. The CAF's negative performance in the 1980s was the result of internal crises, lack of foreign funds to capitalize the Corporation, lenders' conditions in the international market, and the difficulties to access international capital markets.[233]

In the early 1990s, the CAF decided to address these issues by strengthening minimal financial tool innovation as well as supplying services not available to the IADB and World Bank.[234] It started focusing on the main sectors of concern such as the establishment of the loan programmes that help finance local government investment without raising the contingent liabilities of the national government, enhanced corporation efficiency and a reduction of administrative, financial and operative expenses. Currently, the CAF keeps its main focus on enhancing and financing each country's private sector, promoting the strength of local currencies and a more efficient exchange.

The CAF has a newfound optimism that is based on several factors. First, the sub-region has experienced the liberalization of commerce and major changes in the social and political arenas. Second, the CAF has punctually serviced its debt, even during its toughest times. Finally, the CAF's administration is committed to the long-term needs of the sub-region and the need for it to maintain an active role with respect to financing and coordination.[235] Many of the weaknesses identified in the 1980s have been, or are in the process of being, corrected. Extra-regional agreements, especially with the European Union (EU), have provided a positive trend toward the globalization of trade and financial services.

---

[231]Ibidem, p. 65 ff.

[232]Ibidem, p. 64 who also stresses that: 'The voting rules of the bi-annual Shareholders' Meetings as well as the composition and voting rules of the Board of Directors were written to ensure that the A shares of Bolivia and Ecuador gave those countries significant voice, despite their lower contributions. Most notably, either country could veto any changes to the CAF statutes or structure of the Board of Directors'.

[233]Ibidem, p. 64 ff.

[234]Ibidem, p. 185 who also stresses that: 'For example, the MHCP uses the CAF as a deposit-taking institution to manage its liquidity issues'.

[235]Ibidem, p. 196 who stresses that: 'The CAF was always close to the country'.

The CAF is also trying to meet the financial necessities of the private sector through the acceleration of loans at more attractive rates and maturities.[236] Additionally, the CAF has also gained a strong position in the emission of securities. It has participated in European and US capital markets by issuing bonds and certificates of investment. The CAF continually prepares new issues to reaffirm its presence in local and international markets. Aggressive loan recovery programmes have also been enforced. Since the 1990s, the commitment to the collection of past due loans has helped improve the CAF's operations.

Lastly, wider operating efficiency has been achieved. Internal restructuring has taken place by splitting tasks by areas of specialization. New personnel management programmes were enforced to boost the selection and training of employees and to improve their benefit plans. Changes have been introduced to speed up the decision-making process and the execution of plans.

4.4.4 Final Remarks

Torn by natural disasters and conflicts, the Andes is a sub-region that is currently revitalizing its steadfast aim to become integrated. The modernization of infrastructure is underway, new political leaders with a positive view of the future are in charge, and social unrest has significantly diminished.

Much has changed for the Andes. There is general optimism that although the years ahead will be challenging, they will also bring new growth and opportunities. The political leaders of the sub-region wish to develop new economic programmes and policies and depart from the traditional patterns of import substitution and protectionism that previously ended in more damage than benefits to the sub-region. Andean countries want to integrate further and establish a united front. The Andean Community will have the unenviable task of establishing policies that deal with such issues as the movement of labour and capital, and uniting the countries that, at the same time, will be competing for investment capital.

The CAF's role will be essential if it can keep on strengthening its role and status in a way that is autonomous from external leverage. Its monitoring and analysis of the sub-region's economies may help aid these countries to bypass monetary growth that produces inflation and currency overvaluation, and hinders their competitiveness in international capital markets. At a microeconomic level, the CAF can supply financing for sub-regional companies in order to encourage development and socio-economic growth, boost production and reduce expenses. Through its credit policies, it may enhance the transfer of technology, competition and the efficient utilization of resources. The CAF cannot provide regulations on

---

[236]Ibidem, p. 196 who also stresses that the CAF has a credit rating well above that of any of its' members, who are all borrowers, despite serious problems in these borrowing countries.

local economies, but it can stimulate growth and development while operating as a 'watchdog', ever prompt to warn member countries of imminent difficulties and prevent major financial and economic troubles in the Andes.

4.5 Conclusion

A major aspect of this chapter has been the strength of the specific circumstances that have given different features to each of these two major organizations with corresponding institutional frameworks. One conclusion that arises is that it is hard to generalize about them. Conclusions which aim to be of overall validity for the sub-regional development institutions that operate in the LAC region as a category must be viewed with considerable skepticism. The main conclusions of this chapter, both in prescriptive and explanatory terms, are to be ascertained in the substantive sections, and are relevant merely to the specific institutions in question. Yet the demand for the establishment of these organizations, whose expression is illustrated in Sects. 4.1 and 4.2, was analogous in each case. The features of that demand are described in Sect. 4.2. If the demands are analogous and the responses are partially different, the possibility should be explored that sub-regional development institutions are partly failing to meet the demand for which they were founded.

It is worth observing that of the two organizations, the one which seems to come closest to meeting the demand which led to its foundation is the CAF. To a large extent, this impression is the result of the CAF's fast speed and great flexibility in granting loans, an issue that has already been stressed above.[237] But it is also thanks to the CAF's specific ability, whose manner reflects the circumstance that it was itself an innovation when it was established. The CAF added to the well-tested institutional formula of sub-regional identity the original ingredient of *Andean* sub-regional identity. That identity had been shaped by a long succession of historical events.

There are, of course, areas of operation available to all three sub-regional development institutions that operate in Latin America (CABEI, CAF and Fondo Latinoamericano de Reservas) which provide the opportunity for better clarification of sub-regional identity, and therefore a more evident justification for the foundation at the sub-regional level of alternatives to organizations which already operate at the international, universal and regional levels. Such areas of operation are indicated above, but it is useful here to stress a point that has been made frequently in the substantive sections. The precise working out of a more characteristically sub-regional approach is an issue for each individual organization. The formula implicit in the phrase 'sub-regional development bank' is indeed generic. There is no narrower version of that formula which has an intrinsic validity in the Central American or Andean units. The addition of the ingredient of sub-regional

---

[237]See Sect. 4.4.3.4.

identity is fundamentally an issue of subjective appreciation within a wide range of choice. Potential areas of operation are therefore ascertained in Sects. 4.2–4.4, but the appropriate tool of operation within those areas is not.

Although in theory there is a broad range of choice, in practice it is partially reduced by the restraints within which some sub-regional development institutions like the CABEI operate in Latin America. These restraints arise from conflicts of interest between the developing member countries, which formulate the demand, and developed member countries, which supply the financial and technical aid through which the demand may be met. Sub-regional development institutions like the CABEI often tend to maintain that they may only work in the thin area over which these two sets of interests are the same. If both developed and developing states have an interest in the defence and growth of sub-regional development institutions, there are two courses action accessible to them. Either they may try to enlarge the area over which their interests are the same, or they may identify selected interests which may be prejudiced in the pursuance of the common goal.

It is most doubtful that the first course will be enacted. Developing countries consider sub-regional development institutions as a means of having wider control over the allocation of financial and technical aid to themselves. Developed countries generally consider sub-regional development institutions as a tool for making their own supervision of resources less evident, while maintaining some power over how the resources are used and over the pattern of economic and financial relations which developed countries provide. More simply, developed countries often consider sub-regional development institutions as a tool for making their own position as aid-givers less evident, while developing countries consider sub-regional development institutions as a tool for puzzling the aid-givers more effectively. It is hard to see how these two interests can be adjusted.

The second course of action is therefore the one to be examined. Both categories of countries uphold the usefulness of establishing financial institutions at the sub-regional level, even though there may be some uncertainties as to how reliable such statements may be on the grounds of the evidence given here. Each category of countries has one specific resource that it may yield in the interest of strengthening such institutions. Developed countries have financial resources, and developing countries have sovereignty. It is in these two areas that sacrifices can be made. Sacrifices in these two areas are likely to merge, since in practice both types of sacrifice involve a diversion of resources from one path to another. From the developed countries' perspective, allocation of increased resources to sub-regional development institutions is hindered by the conviction that there are other multilateral paths that are much more 'efficient', which respond more adequately to the developed countries' demands. So for the developed countries, it comes down to a choice between sub-regional development banks and the IADB and the World Bank. From the perspective of developing countries, allocation of increased decision-taking responsibility to sub-regional development institutions is hindered by the fear that this would affect their special relationships with specific bilateral donors, and possibly result in a decrease in the absolute amount of aid. So for the developing countries it comes down to a choice between sub-regional institutions and their current bilateral programmes. Putting these two views together, questions may be raised about the institutional device of the transmittal of financial resources from developed to developing countries.

If there is some sort of limitation on the overall amount of financial resources, how should resources be allocated between sub-regional institutions, regional development banks and the IBRD? And what should the relation be between sub-regional development institutions and bilateral aid programmes? The answer to the first question is in the hands of the developed countries. The answer to the second is in the hands of the developing countries. The CAF has succeeded in persuading the developed countries of the Andes of its practical utility as an alternative to the IADB. Once established, as the result of a particular set of historical events, it quickly consolidated such a role for itself. An accelerating force behind its foundation was the idea that sub-regional institutions as a category had an overall utility.

There are two grounds for which developed countries could try to support sub-regional development institutions. They might consider that the tasks performed by the IBRD could be more usefully achieved on the sub-regional plane, on the assertion that at this level there will be a better perception of local necessities and obstacles; or they might consider that there are certain further tasks, apart from those performed by the IBDR, for which sub-regional institutions are better suited, such as the enhancement of sub-regional integration. Even if the latter perspective is held, and this is the view that is more commonly expressed in developed countries' official declarations, the fact is that developed countries must deal with structurally rather analogous organizations at the universal and the regional levels. Thus what is at stake is merely the proportional allocation of the developed countries' financial resources between the universal, the regional and sub-regional levels.

References

Adams F (2005) External Financing for Development: The Role of the Inter-American Development Bank. International Studies/Etudes Internationales 36 (3): 301–316

Alphandery E (1993) Introduction. In Turnham D, Foy C, Larraín C (eds), Social Tensions, Job Creation and Economic Policy in Latin America, OECD, Paris

Alter K J and Helfer L R (2011) Legal Integration in the Andes: Law-Making by the Andean Tribunal of Justice. European Law Journal 17: 701–715

Bezanson K, Sagasti F, Prada F (2005) The Future of Development Financing: Challenges, Scenarios and Strategic Choices. Palgrave, Oxford

Birdsall N, Williamson J, Deese B (2002) Delivering on Debt Relief: From IMF Gold to a New Aid Architecture. Peterson Institute, Washington, DC

Bøås M (1998) Governance as Multilateral Development Bank Policy: The Cases of the African Development Bank and the Asian Development Bank. The European Journal of Development Research 10(2): 117–134

Borras S M Jr., Franco J C, Gómez S, Kay C, Spoor M (2012) Land Grabbing in Latin America and the Caribbean. The Journal of Peasant Studies, 39(3–4): 845-872

Bulmer-Thomas V (2003) The Economic History of Latin America Since Independence. Cambridge University Press, Cambridge

Cevallos R (1996) The Central American Bank for Economic Integration. Tulane Journal of International and Comparative Law 4(2): 245–274

Cline W R, Delgado E, Bulmer-Thomas V (1987) The Political Economy of Central America since 1920, Cambridge University Press, Cambridge

Corden W M (1978) Keynes and the Others: Wage and Price Rigidities in Macro-Economic Models. Oxford Economic Papers, 30 (2): 159–180

Culpeper R (1990) Crossroads or cross-purposes: Inter-American Development Bank at 31. North-South Institute - Institut Nord-Sud, Ottawa 1990

Culpeper R (1997) The Multilateral Development Banks: Titans Or Behemoths? Lynne Rienner Publishers, Boulder

Dabène O (2009) The Politics of Regional Integration in Latin America: Theoretical and Comparative Explorations. Palgrave Macmillan, New York

Griffith-Jones S, Bhattacharya A, Antoniou A (2003) Enhancing Private Capital Flows to Developing Countries. Commonwealth Secretariat, London

Griffith-Jones S, Griffith-Jones D, Hertova D (2008) Enhancing the Role of Regional Development Banks. United Nations, New York

Hey H (1995) Gross Human Rights Violations: A Search for Causes. A Study of Guatemala and Costa Rica. Kluwer Law International, The Hague

Hira A (2007) An East Asian Model for Latin American Success: The New Path. Ashgate, Aldershot

Horton S (1982) Peru and ANCOM: A Study in the Disintegration of a Common Market. Texas International Law Journal 17 (1): 39–61

Humphrey C and Michaelowa K (2010) The Business of Development: Trends in Lending by Multilateral Development Banks to Latin America, 1980–2009, (November 16). CIS Working Paper No. 65, at http://dx.doi.org/10.2139/ssrn.1709988. Accessed 13 December 2013

Humphrey C (2012) The business of development: borrowers, shareholders, and the reshaping of multilateral development lending. PhD thesis, London School of Economics and Political Science, London

Humphrey C and Michaelowa K (2013) Shopping for Development: Multilateral Lending, Shareholder Composition and Borrower Preferences. World Development 44: 142–155

Kearns K C (1972) The Andean Common Market: A New Thrust at Economic Integration in Latin America. Journal of Interamerican Studies and World Affairs 14(2): 225–249

Kinloch Tijerino F (2005) Historia de Nicaragua. Instituto de Historia de Nicaragua y Centroamérica, Universidad Centroamericana, Managua

Krishna Dutt A and Ros J (2003) Development Economics And Structuralist Macroeconomics: Essays in Honor of Lance Taylor. Edward Elgar Publishing, Cheltenham

Kühnhardt L (2010) The Global Proliferation of Regional Integration. Berghan Books, New York

Lehoucq F (2012) The Politics of Modern Central America: Civil War, Democratization, and Underdevelopment. Cambridge University Press, Cambridge

León Li J M (2001) Regional Integration Process in South America: Analysis of Institutions and Policies under the EU Framework. Diplomica Verlag, Hamburg

Little I M D and Clifford J M (2006) International Aid: The Flow of Public Resources from Rich to Poor Countries. Transnational Publisher, New Jersey

Meléndez Chaverri C (1979) Historia de Costa Rica. Editorial Universidad Estatal a Distancia, San José

Nelson R M (2013), Multilateral Development Banks: Overview and Issues for Congress, Congressional Research Service, Washington DC, at: http://fas.org/sgp/crs/row/R41170.pdf. Accessed on 2 December 2014

Ocampo J A, Kregel J, Griffith-Jones S (2007) International Finance and Development. Zed Books, London

Ocampo J A and Titelman D (2009–2010) Subregional Financial Cooperation: The South American Experience. Journal of Post Keynesian Economics 32(2): 249–268

O'Leary T F (1984) The Andean Common Market and the Importance of Effective Dispute Resolution Procedures. International Tax & Business Lawyer 2: 101–128, at: http://scholarship.law.berkeley.edu/bjil/vol2/iss1/5. Accessed 9 December 2014

Pennetta P (2013) Consideraciones sobre los procesos de integracion regional en Europea y América Latina. Cultura Latino Americana: Annali 15: 181–206

Peraza G (1994) The Central American Common Market. In: Lacasse N., Perret L (eds) Le libre-échange dans les Amériques: une perspective continentale. Wilson & Lafleur, Montréal

Prada F (2012) World Bank, Inter-American Development Bank, and Subregional Development Banks in Latin America: Dynamics of a System of Multilateral Development Banks, (ADBI Working Paper Series No. 380, September 2012), at: http://www.iadb.org/intal/intalcdi/PE/2012/12263.pdf. Accessed 3 December 2014

Ramirez S (2013) Regionalism: The Pacific Alliance. Americas Quarterly (Special Issue: Latin America Goes Global) at: http://www.americasquarterly.org/content/regionalism-pacific-alliance. Accessed 3 January 2014

Rivera J (1979) Latin America: A Socio-cultural Interpretation. Irvington Publisher, New York

Rudolph J P (1971-1972) Investment Possibilities in the Central American Common Market. Case Western Reserve Journal of International Law 4:37-60

Sánchez Sánchez R A (2009) The Politics of Central American Integration. Routledge, Abingdon

Sampson G P (2003) Introduction. In: Sampson GP, Woolcock S(eds), Regionalism, Multilateralism, and Economic Integration: The Recent Experience. United Nations University Press, Tokyo, pp. 3–17

Santiso J (2013) The Decade of the Multilatinas. Cambridge University Press, Cambridge

Sarwar Lateef K (1995) The Evolving Role of the World Bank: Helping Meet the Challenge of Development. World Bank, Washington DC

Schelhase M (2011) The Changing Context of Regionalism and Regionalization in the Americas: Mercosur and Beyond. In: Shaw T M, Grant J A, Cornelissen S (eds), The Ashgate Research Companion to Regionalisms, Ashgate, Farnham, pp. 175–192

Seatzu F (2011-2012), Civil Society Participation in the Inter American Development Bank's Activities and Operations: Enhancing Democratic Accountability?. Spanish Yearbook of International Law, XVII: 43–72

Sims C A (1990) Macroeconomics and Reality. Oxford University Press, Oxford

Stenman Å and Follér M L (2008) Alternative Developments in the Andean Region 2018-2028. University of Gothenburg, Göteborg

Suarez Mejias J L (2006) Integración y supracionalidad en la Comunidad andina proceso decisorio, sistema jurisdiccional y relación con los derechos nacionales. PhD thesis, Universidad Complutense, Madrid

Syz J (1974) International Development Banks. Oceana Publications, Leiden

Tan C (2010) Financing for Sustainable Development: The Challenges Ahead for Asian Economies. In: Bestagno F, Rubini L (eds), Challenges of Development: Asian Perspectives. Vita e Pensiero, Milano, pp. 87–114

Telles, E E (2007) Race, Ethnicity and the UN's Millenium Development Goals in Latin America. Latin American and Caribbean Ethnic Studies 2(2): 185–200

Titelman D (2006) Subregional Financial Cooperation: The Experiences of Latin America and the Caribbean. In: Ocampo J A (ed), Regional Financial Cooperation. Brookings Institution Press, Baltimore, pp. 200–226

Tuller L W (1993) Doing Business in Latin America and The Caribbean. AMACOM, American Management Association, New York

Tussie D (1995) The Inter-American Development Bank. Lynne Rienner Publishers, Boulder, CO

Vuskovic P (1983) Economic Factors in the Evolution of Central American Societies. In: Fagen R R, Pellicer de Brody O, Aguilar Zinser A (eds), The Future of Central America: Policy Choices for the U.S. and Mexico. Stanford University Press, Stanford

Weaver C (2008) Hypocrisy Trap: The World Bank and the Poverty of Reform. Princeton University Press, Princeton

Williams R G (1994) States and Social Evolution: Coffee and the Rise of National Governments in Central America. University of North Carolina Press, Chapel Hill

Woodward R L (1999) Central America, A Nation Divided. Oxford University Press, Oxford

Zanatta L (2010) Storia dell'America Latina contemporanea. Laterza editore, Bari

Chapter 5
The Andean Community of Nations

Marco Odello

Abstract This chapter provides a detailed account of the institutional and legal structures of the Andean Community, one of the oldest sub-regional organisations in Latin America. The structures and the legal system developed by the organisation resemble and take into account the structures and functions of the European Union. However, the legal system developed by the Andean Community does not reach the same level of sophistication as the European model. The chapter also considers some of the emerging issues that are linked to the evolution of the integration process in the Andean region, and that show some similarities with the European Union model. There are also some reforms and processes that are taken into consideration at the end, in light of the emerging integration processes which affect most Latin American countries.

Keywords Comunidad Andina de Naciones · Andean Pact · Andean Community of Nations · Andean Parliament · Arbitration · Court of Justice of the Andean Community · Andean Community legal order

Contents

M. Odello (✉)
Department of Law and Criminology, Aberystwyth University, Wales, UK
e-mail: mmo@aber.ac.uk

© T.M.C. ASSER PRESS and the authors 2015
M. Odello and F. Seatzu (eds.), *Latin American and Caribbean International Institutional Law*, DOI 10.1007/978-94-6265-069-5_5

5.1 Introduction

The Andean Community of Nations[1] (in Spanish: *Comunidad Andina de Naciones* or CAN) is one of the oldest integration structures among the Latin American states.[2] It started as a trade bloc comprising the South American countries of Bolivia, Colombia, Ecuador and Peru and has recently developed in a more integration-type organisation with new objectives and purposes, which tend to go beyond the integration of markets in the sub-region.

The historical and ideological precedents of this cooperation are based on the post-colonial attempts to maintain a macro-region in Latin America based on the 'Andean' culture, which was linked to the Inca territories and the subsequent Spanish Viceroy of Peru. Some of these processes were initiated with Simon Bolivar in the early nineteenth century, and soon afterwards. The basis of this cooperation is based on the geographical and cultural links among peoples in the region, which are often linked to the so-called project of Gran Colombia,[3] which emerged at the time when the independence of Spanish colonies took place in the first half of the nineteenth century. However, the integration process was not particularly successful and several new independent states were established at the time. With the development of new regional structures within the American continent, the idea of a trading block in the Andean region was retaken, and the Andean Pact was supposed to strengthen the economic links among states within this sub-region. The main model for this initiative was the emerging European Communities structure, with a specific focus on the market economy and evolving trade cooperation among member states. Actually, the subsequent evolution of the Andean Pact into the Andean Community, including the establishment of a dispute settlement body, in the form of a community court, and later the creation of an Andean passport, has clearly followed, in part, the evolution of the European Union (EU) experience.

---

[1]Previously known as the Andean Pact or Andean Common Market.

[2]See, among others, Xenias 2006; Quindimil López 2006; Adkisson 2003; Rodríquez et al. 1999; O'Keefe 1996; Garcia 2011, pp. 132–137.

[3]Bushnell 1993, Chap. 3.

The Andean Pact was signed in Bogota in 1969 under the name of Cartagena Agreement[4] with the objective of creating a customs union and a common market, with the purpose of reversing the stagnation of the Latin American Free Trade Association,[5] in line with the purposes of the Latin American Economic Integration,[6] and addressing the integration and development needs of the main Andean countries (Venezuela, Colombia, Chile, Ecuador, Peru and Bolivia).[7] The document was later amended by the Additional Instrument for the accession of Venezuela (1973); the Protocol of Lima (1976)[8]; the Protocol of Arequipa (1978); the Protocol of Quito (1987),[9] the Protocol of Trujillo (1996),[10] the Protocol of Sucre (1997)[11] and the Additional Protocol to the Cartagena Agreement.[12] Presently, the Cartagena Agreement is governed by the amended and consolidated text of the Andean Subregional Integration Agreement, which was adopted by the Commission of the Andean Community in 2003.[13]

In 1979 the Andean Council of Foreign Ministers established the Court of Justice of the Cartagena Agreement[14] and the Andean Parliament in Bogotá.[15] In 1985 the Andean Parliament created the Andean University Simon Bolivar located in Sucre, former capital of Bolivia. In 1993 the free trade area was established and in 1995 the Andean countries adopted a Common External Tariff.

---

[4]Andean Subregional Integration Agreement (Cartagena Agreement), Bogotá, 26 May 1969, entry into force on 16 October 1969, 8 ILM (1969) p. 910 http://www.wipo.int/wipolex/en/other_treaties/details.jsp?treaty_id=393. Accessed 9 March 2015.

[5]Latin American Free Trade Association (LAFTA) created with the Treaty of Montevideo of 1960, which included, besides the Andean countries, Argentina, Brazil, Paraguay and Uruguay, was later transformed with the Treaty of Montevideo of 1980 into the Latin American Integration Association or *Asociación Latinoamericana de Integración* (ALADI). See Chap. 2 in this book.

[6]Middlebrook 1978, pp. 64–65. See also Avery and Cochrane 1972, p. 89.

[7]In 1995, Colombia and Venezuela (the main economic partners within the AC) formed with Mexico the Group of Three (G-3) with the purpose of establishing a FTA fully functioning by mid-2004.

[8]Lima Protocol Amending the Cartagena Agreement on Andean Subregional Integration, Lima, 30 October 1976, 16 ILM (1977) p. 235.

[9]Quito Protocol to the Cartagena Agreement Creating the Andean Common Market, concluded in Quito, 12 May 1987, 28 ILM (1989), p. 1165.

[10]Trujillo Act, concluded in Trujillo, 10 March 1996, *Gaceta Oficial del Tratado de Cartagena*, Year XIII, N° 273, July 1997; UN, GA, *Trujillo Act and the Protocol Amending the Cartagena Agreement*, UN Doc. A/51/87, 25 March 1996. In addition, the Protocol of Trujillo authorises the necessary adjustments to the numbering of the articles, therefore the numbering of the previous Codified Text (Decision 236) does not necessarily coincide with the present numbering (Decision 406).

[11]Sucre Protocol Establishing the Andean Parliament, Quito, 25 June 1997.

[12]Additional Protocol to the Cartagena Agreement 'Andean Community Commitment to Democracy', 10 June 2000.

[13]CAN, Commission, Decision 563, Official Codified Text of the Andean Subregional Integration Agreement (Cartagena Agreement), 25 June 2003.

[14]Andean Group: Treaty Creating the Court of Justice of the Cartagena Agreement, Cartagena, 28 May 1978, 18 ILM (1979), pp. 1203–1210.

[15]See Sect. 5.4.1.

The organisation was called the Andean Pact (*Pacto Andino*) until 1996, when the Protocol of Trujillo, signed by the Andean Presidents during the Eighth Presidential Council that was held in the city of Trujillo, Peru, in March of 1996, amended the original institutional structure with the establishment of the Andean Community. The Protocol created the Andean Council of Presidents and the Advisory Council of Foreign Ministers. The Board of the Cartagena Agreement became the General Secretariat based in Lima, Peru, which encompassed not only technical but also political functions, and gave a new political direction to the integration process.

The evolution of the process at sub-regional level clearly took as a model the EU example. For instance, the Andean Passport[16] was introduced in June 2001[17] and since January 2005 citizens of the member countries can enter the other Andean Community member states without the requirement of visa. The passport is effective in Bolivia, Ecuador and Peru, because Venezuela left the CAN in 2006 and joined the Mercosur. This means that by December 2015, all passports held by Member Country nationals will be Andean passports. However, the passport is valid only for tourist purposes for a period of 90 days that can be renewed for another 90 days. Other types of travellers, such as students, business people and workers would be subject to other conditions connected to immigration regulations. This document clearly is not comparable to the European passport, as the conditions are not comparable at all, particularly in relation to the freedom of movement and settlement of citizens of European Union countries.

In 2005 the integration of Latin American and Caribbean regions gained priority in the agenda of CAN with a series of initiative that led to stronger cooperation among different sub-regional institutions in the continent. They are also included in more structured plan which is foreseen by the development of the Union of South American Nations or UNASUR.[18]

An interesting development in the evolution of Latin American institutional integration is the process that involves the Andean Community and Mercosur[19] (Argentina, Brazil, Uruguay and Paraguay) which represent the two main trading blocs within South America. In 1999, these organisations began negotiating a merger with the aim of creating a South America Free Trade Area (SAFTA). In December 2004 the representatives of 12 Latina American States signed the Cuzco Declaration,[20] a cooperation agreement, and published a joint letter of intention for

---

[16]The Andean passport is based on a standard model containing harmonised features of nomenclature and security based on the recommendations of the International Civil Aviation Organization (ICAO).

[17]CAN Decision 504, Creation of the Andean Passport, 22 June 2001; CAN Decision 524, Minimum specific technical characteristics of Andean Passport nomenclature and security, 7 July 2002.

[18]See Chap. 3 in this book.

[19]See Chap. 6 in this book.

[20]The Third Summit of South American Presidents, *Declaration*, Cusco, 8 December 2004, at: http://www.iirsa.org/admin_iirsa_web/Uploads/Documents/oe_cusco05_declaracion_del_cusco_eng.pdf. Accessed 30 September 2014.

future negotiations with the purpose of integrating all South American States following the example of the European Union. The Cusco Declaration created the South American Community of Nations (SACN) which included Argentina, Bolivia, Brazil, Chile, Colombia, Ecuador, Guyana, Paraguay, Peru, Suriname, Uruguay and Venezuela. This regional body was intended to be a combination of the Andean Community and Mercosur plus other states in the region which were not party to other sub-regional bodies. The SACN only lasted for 2 years, and at the South American Energy Summit, in April 2007, the organisation was renamed as the Union of South American Nations (UNASUR).[21] The twelve heads of state of South American countries including those of Chile, Venezuela, Guyana and Suriname signed the UNASUR treaty[22] on 23 May 2008 at the third South American Summit held in Brasilia.[23] The purpose of the new organisation was to strengthen the cooperation among the two major sub-regional organisations (CAN and Mercosur) and other states within the region. However, the process did not foresee a gradual replacement, or merging route, of the existing institutions and structures, which makes somehow difficult to foresee the creation of a new international organisation which would be independent from the existing ones, or a different form of sub-regional organisation. This is a recurring aspect of Latin American integration processes that need some attention and creates sometimes excessive expectations, which are not supported by adequate institutional and legal structures.[24]

Since 1996 the CAN has also developed links with the EU in the form of a political dialogue with the Declaration of Rome (1996),[25] later replaced by the Political Dialogue and Cooperation Agreement of 2003,[26] which will constitute the framework for their reciprocal relations, as will be discussed later in this chapter.

---

[21]See Chap. 3 in this book.

[22]South American Union of Nations Constitutive Treaty, signed on 23 May 2008, at: http://www.unasursg.org/uploads/0c/c7/0cc721468628d65c3c510a577e54519d/Tratado-constitutivo-english-version.pdf. Accessed 30 September 2014.

[23]Its members are the following South American countries: Bolivia, Colombia, Ecuador and Peru (countries that are also members of the Andean Community of Nations, or CAN), plus Argentina, Brazil, Paraguay and Uruguay (countries that are also members of Mercosur), plus Chile, Guyana, Suriname and Venezuela. UNASUR's constitutive treaty was signed on 23 May 2008, and entered into force on 11 March 2011.

[24]See, Malamud 2013.

[25]Joint Declaration political dialogue between the European Union and the Andean Community (Declaration of Rome) Rome, 30 June 1996—DN:PRES/96/191, 1 July 1996 http://eeas.europa.eu/andean/docs/decl_rome_en.pdf. Accessed 11 November 2014.

[26]EC Commission, *Proposal for a COUNCIL DECISION on the signature of a Political Dialogue and Cooperation Agreement between the European Community and its Member States, of the one part, and the Andean Community and its member countries, the Republics of Bolivia, Colombia, Ecuador, Peru and the Bolivarian Republic of Venezuela, of the other part*, Brussels, 14 November 2003, COM(2003) 695 final, 2003/0268 (CNS) at:
http://eur-lex.europa.eu/LexUriServ/LexUriServ.do?uri=COM:2003:0695:FIN:EN:PDF. Accessed 15 November 2014.

The Andean Community has various organs and institutions that are coordinated by the Andean Integration System, known as the AIS. According to Article 48 (Cartagena Agreement) the CAN is a sub-regional organisation with international legal personality or status. The Andean Community headquarters are located in Lima, Peru.

5.2 Membership

Presently, member states of the CAN are: Bolivia, Colombia, Ecuador and Peru. This membership has changed slightly over time as Chile, an original founding member of the Andean Pact, withdrew in 1976, during the Pinochet regime for alleged incompatibility with the liberal economic system.[27] Venezuela acceded in 1979,[28] but later withdrew in 2006 (with official cessation in 2011) due to disagreements in relation to the negotiations between Colombia and Peru with the US for the establishment of a Free Trade Area. However, in 2006 Venezuela joined the Mercosur.

According to Article 133, the Cartagena Agreement 'may not be signed with reservations and shall remain open to the adherence of the rest of the Latin American countries'. It also provides some specific conditions for states that are less economically developed as they can be entitled to a treatment similar to that agreed for Bolivia and Ecuador (under the conditions agreed in Chapter XV of the Cartagena Agreement).

Under Article 134, the Cartagena Agreement shall have an indefinite duration. However, it foresees the possibility of denunciation and withdrawal, under Article 135. In this case, the member state shall inform the Commission. From the date of denunciation, the country 'shall cease to enjoy the rights and have the obligations deriving from its status as a Member, with the exception of the benefits received and granted in accordance with the Subregional Liberalization Program, which shall remain effective for a period of 5 years after the date of the denouncement'. This provision was applied when Venezuela withdrew from the CAN in 2001, and a separate Memorandum of Understanding (MoU) was adopted among the member states of CAN and Venezuela.[29]

Article 136 Cartagena Agreement foresees also the possibility of Associate Membership[30] for states which 'entered into a free trade agreement with the

---

[27]Vargas-Hidalgo 1979.

[28]Andean Commission-Venezuela, *Final Act of the Negotiations of the Entry of Venezuela into the Cartagena Agreement*, 13 February 1973, 12 ILM 344 (1973).

[29]CAN, Commission, Decision 641, *Approval of the Memorandum of Understanding signed by the Member Countries of the Andean Community and the Bolivarian Republic of Venezuela*, 9 August 2006, at: http://www.comunidadandina.org/ingles/normativa/D641e.htm. Accessed 9 October 2014.

[30]Associate Membership was introduced by the Sucre Protocol (1997) which added Chapter XVIII to the Cartagena Agreement.

Andean Community Member Countries'. Presently, they include: Argentina, Brazil, Chile, Paraguay and Uruguay which joined in July 2005.[31] According to Article 137 Cartagena Agreement the conditions of participation of Associated Members are defined by the Andean Council of Foreign Ministers and the Andean Community Commission which shall adopt a decision in relation to the following issues:

a. The bodies and institutions of the Andean Integration System to which the Associate Country shall belong, together with the terms for its participation;
b. The mechanisms and measures of the Cartagena Agreement in which the Associate Member Country shall participate; and
c. The provisions that shall be applied to the relations between the Associate Member Country and the rest of the Member Countries, as well as the way those relations shall be administered.

According to Article 3 of CAN Decision 613, the Associate Members are also parties to the Andean Community Commitment to Democracy,[32] and to the Andean Charter for the Promotion and Protection of Human Rights.[33] In September 2006, Chile became an Associated Member through ratification of the Council of Foreign Ministers and the Andean Commission with Decision 645,[34] while its specific legal relationship between Chile and the CAN is defined in Decision 666 of 2007.[35] Also other states in the region: Argentina, Brazil, Paraguay and Uruguay were admitted as Associate Members in 2005 due to the entry into force of the Mercosur free trade agreement with Colombia, Ecuador and Venezuela.[36] However, the precise relationship with these other countries is not specified as in the case of Chile. It is only mentioned that the CAN institutional bodies would meet twice, once only with the members, and a second session, when required, with both the CAN and Mercosur members.[37] It is also required that Associate

---

[31]CAN, Andean Council of Foreign Ministers, Decision 613, Lima, 7 July 2005.

[32]CAN, Additional Protocol to the Cartagena Agreement, Andean Community Commitment to Democracy, signed by the Andean Foreign Ministers on 10 June 2000, at: http://www.comunidad andina.org/ingles/normativa/democracy.htm. Accessed 30 September 2014.

[33]CAN, Andean Charter for the Promotion and Protection of Human Rights, 26 July 2002, at: http://www.refworld.org/docid/3de4f94a4.htmlAccessed 30 September 2014.

[34]CAN, Andean Council of Foreign Ministers meeting in Enlarged Session with the Representatives to the Andean Community Commission, Decision 645 Granting of the status of Associate Member Country of the Andean Community to the Republic of Chile, New York, 20 September 2006.

[35]CAN, Decision 666, Participation of the Republic of Chile, as an Associate Member Country, in Andean Community bodies, mechanisms and measures, Lima, 8 June 2007.

[36]CAN, Andean Council of Foreign Ministers Meeting in Enlarged Session with the Titular Representatives to the Andean Community Commission, Decision 613, Association of the Republic of Argentina, the Federative Republic of Brazil, the Republic of Paraguay and the Eastern Republic of Uruguay, States Parties of Mercosur, with the Andean Community, Lima, 7 July 2005.

[37]Ibid., Article 2.

Members shall accede to the Additional Protocol to the Cartagena Agreement "Andean Community Commitment to Democracy" and to the Andean Charter for the Promotion and Protection of Human Rights.[38] This expansion of associated members is also part of the policy in the region to develop a common market in South America, the UNASUR.

There are also four states with observer status: Mexico, Panama, the Sahrawi Arab Democratic Republic and Spain. The observer status has been defined in Decision 741[39] and provides the opportunity for states and international organisations to take part to activities of the CAN without the right to vote.

A member state can withdraw, as mentioned before, or can be suspended. A sort of 'in between' option occurred in April 1992, when Peru withdrew its membership after facing strong criticism from the other member states[40] due to the fact that its President, Alberto Fujimori, abrogated the country's constitution and closed the Courts and Congress. Similar types of sanctions can be carried out by the Council of Foreign Ministers in application of Article 4 of the Additional Protocol to the Cartagena Agreement[41] which foresees the following measures, depending on the gravity of the situation in one of the member states:

a. Suspension of the Member Country's participation in any of the bodies of the Andean Integration System;
b. Suspension of its participation in the international cooperation projects carried out by the Member Countries;
c. Extension of the suspension to other System bodies, including its disqualification by Andean financial institutions from obtaining access to facilities or loans;
d. Suspension of rights to which it is entitled under the Cartagena Agreement and of the right to coordinate external action in other spheres; and
e. Other measures and actions that are deemed pertinent under International Law.

In part, the various sanctions are linked to the adoption of several documents in the American continent which support democratic governments as a way to promote human rights. In particular, the 1998 Ushuaia Protocol among the Mercosur States and Bolivia and Chile,[42] and the Inter-American Democratic Charter adopted by the Organisation of American States in 2001.[43] Both documents require some conditions of democratic governments for admission of states to the

---

[38]Ibid., Article 3.

[39]CAN, Andean Council of Foreign Ministers, Decision 741, Lima, 22 July 2010.

[40]CAN, Commission, Decision 321, Lima, 25 August 1992.

[41]CAN, Additional Protocol to the Cartagena Agreement, 'Andean Community Commitment to Democracy', note 32 above.

[42]Ushuaia Protocol on the Democratic Commitment in the Southern Common Market, the Republic of Bolivia and the Republic of Chile, open for signature on 24 July 1998, 2177 UNTS 383, entered into force 28 January 2002, in particular Articles 1, 3 and 5.

[43]OAS, General Assembly, Inter-American Democratic Charter, Lima 11 September 2001, XXVIII Extraordinary Session, AG/doc.8 (XXVIII-E/01), 6 September 2001.

organisation and also possible sanctions and suspension of a member state in case of democratic deficit, often linked to undemocratic changes of government.

5.3 Structure

The CAN is an international organisation which is constituted by several organs and institutions which are coordinated by the Andean Integration System (AIS), which was defined in the New Strategic Design adopted in Quito in 1995[44] and then incorporated in the Trujillo Protocol of 1996.[45] This institutional reform abolished the Andean Pact and replaced it with the CAN and the AIS, with a renewed General Secretariat. The coordination of the various components is ensured by the Chairman of the Andean Council of Foreign Ministers who convenes and chairs the Meeting of Representatives of the System's component institutions. The meeting is held regularly at least once a year, but special meetings may take place whenever requested by any of the member institutions. The Andean Community General Secretariat acts as Meeting Secretary. The main reasons for these meetings are:

(a) Exchange of information on the activities carried out by the respective institutions in complying with the Directives issued by the Andean Presidential Council;
(b) Examine the possibility and convenience of having all the institutions, or some of them, make decisions on the undertaking of coordinated actions with the purpose of contributing to the achievement of the Andean Integration System objectives; and,
(c) Submit to the Andean Council of Foreign Affairs Ministers, in an extended meeting, reports concerning the activities conducted in pursuit of the Directives received.

Each organ and institution has its own functions, which range from regulatory and policy making to legal, executive, deliberating, social, financial and educational. The institutional structure has been very much inspired by the Treaty of Rome that created the European Economic Community, since it revolved around two organs: the Commission (similar to the EEC Council) and the Agreement Board (similar to the EEC Commission). Later on, new organs were created with separate agreements: the Court of Justice (1979),[46] the Andean Parliament (1979), and the

---

[44]See Taccone and Nogueira 2002, pp. 2–3.

[45]Later the Cartagena Agreement of 1997 was amended by the Sucre Protocol of 2003 and the consolidated text was adopted by CAN, Commission, Decision 563, *Official Codified Text of the Andean Subregional Integration Agreement (Cartagena Agreement)*, Quirama, Colombia, 25 June 2003, Articles 6–9.

[46]See Sect. 5.4.3.

Andean Presidential Council (1990). This institutional structure was finally reorganised and altered by the Protocol of Trujillo (9th and 10th March 1996)[47] which created the Andean Community and Andean Integration System under the Cartagena Agreement (CA).

The main organs and institutions are divided into different types according to the powers and functions which are given to them by the constitutive documents. The structure includes intergovernmental institutions, which are working on the basis of traditional international organisations, there are also community bodies, which are part of a more integrated process, and a series of advisory bodies which specialise on several policy issues and provide specific support to the organisation and to member states in relation to identified policies within the system. The structure of the AIS is presently as follows:

Intergovernmental organisations

- Andean Presidential Council
- Andean Council of Foreign Ministers
- Andean Community Commission

Community organisations

- Court of Justice of the Andean Community
- Andean Parliament
- General Secretariat
- Corporación Andina de Fomento
- Latin American Reserve Fund
- Andean Health Organization
- Universidad Andina Simón Bolívar

Instances of civil society participation

- Business Advisory Council
- Labour Advisory Council
- Advisory Council of Indigenous Peoples[48]
- Working Committee for the Defense of Consumer Rights.[49]

In the following subsections the different bodies and institutions shall be described in light of their internal structure, taking also into consideration the policies and activities that they develop as institutions. Particular attention will be given to the dispute resolution mechanisms which allow the application of Andean community law within the member states and have reached a quite sophisticated procedure

---

[47]The Commission of the Andean Community, in its Eighty-seventh Special Term held in Quito, Ecuador, on 25 June 1997, approved the Decision 406: *Codification of the Andean Subregional Integration Agreement (Cartagena Agreement)*.

[48]Decision 524, 7 July 2002.

[49]Decision 539: Andean Working Group on the Participation of Civil Society for the Defense of Consumer Rights, Bogota, Colombia, 11 March 2003.

compared to other existing sub-regional organisations within the American continent.

5.3.1 Intergovernmental Organs

The three main intergovernmental organs are the Andean Presidential Council, the Andean Council of Foreign Ministers and the Andean Community Commission. The three organs constitute the Andean Integration System (AIS), and all have competence as entities with powers of political direction and decision-making within the system. They are intergovernmental structures as their individual members are official representatives of member states, and they bring into the negotiation process and decision-making the interests of their respective governments, rather than the 'community' interests as such.

5.3.1.1 Andean Presidential Council

The Andean Presidential Council (APC), made up of the Presidents of Bolivia, Colombia, Ecuador and Peru, is responsible for defining the political course of the CAN, and is considered the highest level body of the Community. The Andean Council of Foreign Ministers formulates the foreign policy of the Andean countries on all matters relating to the integration process and, if necessary, coordinates joint stands to be taken in international forums or negotiations. The Commission, comprised of plenipotentiary delegates—with full powers—takes charge of formulating, executing and evaluating integration policies in the areas of trade and investment and adopts laws and regulations that are binding for the four member states. The APC developed as a body in the period between May 1989 and December 1991,[50] when the Presidents of the Andean countries met on nine occasions trying to revitalise the integration process after the stagnation period. However, with the suspension of Peru's membership in 1992, the Andean Presidential meetings resumed 3 years afterwards in Quito, on 5 September 1995, when new strategies of integration were adopted.[51]

The APC was officially established on 23 May 1990[52] and its chair is allocated on a rota basis each year, in alphabetical order among the member states. It

---

[50]Caracas, 3 February 1989; Cartagena, 25 and 26 May 1989; Galapagos, 17 and 18 December 1989; Machu Picchu, 22 and 23 May 1990; Lima, 28 July 1990; Bogota, 7 August 1990; La Paz, 29 and 30 November 1990; Caracas, 17 and 18 May ; and Cartagena, 3 and 5 December 1991.

[51]See Sect. 5.3.

[52]Acta de Machu Picchu, Instrument for the Creation of the ACP, Machu Picchu, Peru, 23 May 1990, CAN, Secretaría General, Documentos de las Reuniones del Consejo Presidencial Andino 1989–2002, at: http://www.comunidadandina.org/cumbreSC/Presidentes.pdf. Accessed 12 December 2014.

regularly meets at least once a year, usually in the country which holds the presidency, but extra meetings can be called if the members of the APC agree.[53]

One of the main functions of the Presidential Council is the revision of the activities of the AIS and the adoption of guidelines, which were introduced since the Sucre IX Summit in 1997. The guidelines are adopted and passed to the other organs and institutions of the AIS. However, the guidelines do not have legally binding force, as the exclusive legislative capacity is given to the Commission under Articles 6 and 7 of the 1987 Quito Protocol. It is assumed that the guidelines bind the organs of the CAN, therefore they are internally binding documents at institutional level, based on Chapter II of the Cartagena Agreement. The APC's main function is to develop the integration process and identify the areas of integration for the sub-region. However, the results very much depend on the political will of individual Heads of State in the region and their leadership. Therefore, in some cases, when the collaboration is good, a short time is needed to implement new areas of integration, as in the case of the establishment of the FTA between 1990 and 1993 (despite the suspension of Peru), and the creation of the Andean Common External Policy which led to the Sucre Protocol in 1997, included in Chapter III of the Cartagena Agreement. However, on several occasions, due to the internal troubles of individual States, and tensions among them, as in the conflict between Ecuador and Peru,[54] the cooperation and integration process has been difficult and not always sustained.

5.3.1.2 Council of Foreign Ministers

The Council of Foreign Ministers (the Council) consists of the Ministers of Foreign Affairs of the member states and is the CAN policy-making body. It was established in 1979 and in 1996 it was incorporated in the legal framework of the Cartagena Agreement under the Trujillo Protocol. The subsequent 1997 Sucre Protocol included a chapter on foreign relations. Its relevance has increased with the development of external relations of the organisation, for instance in negotiations with the Latin American Integration Association, with the General Agreement on Tariffs and Trade first and the World Trade Organisation later, and also with the negotiation with the United States, the EU and other sub-regional organisations, like the Mercosur. The functioning of the Council is based on its internal regulations which were adopted in 1997 during its first official meeting.[55]

According to Article 16 Protocol of Trujillo, the Council is responsible for formulating the Member Countries' foreign policy in matters of sub-regional interest as well as for coordinating the external relations of the organs of the AIS. The

---

[53]CA, Articles 11–13.

[54]Simmons 2005.

[55]CAN, Decision 407, Reglamento del Consejo Andino de Ministros de Relaciones Exteriores, Quito, 25 June 1997.

Council has the main task of implementing the guidelines which are issued by the Presidential Council and to develop the general policy to strengthen the integration process in the sub-region. It is responsible also for the implementation of the obligations that are defined in the Cartagena Agreement[56] and in the 1980 Treaty of Montevideo.[57] It also has a general competence to deal with all disputes that fit within its areas of competence.[58] The Council meets twice a year and the chairmanship rotates every year in accordance with the chairmanship of the Presidential Council.[59] It meets at least once a year in an enlarged composition with the members of the Commission when it has to discuss matters that are relevant to both organs,[60] for instance for the preparation of the meetings of the Presidential Council, the appointment and removal of the Secretary General of the CAN, and to propose amendments to the Cartagena Agreement.[61]

The Council may adopt two types of documents, Declarations and Decisions, only by consensus. According to the statute of the Andean Court of Justice, and to Article 17 CA, only Decisions are legally binding and become part of the 'Community Law'.

Within the Common Foreign Policy, the Council is particularly important in relation to the coordination of joint positions of the CAN states in international forums and negotiations. Such activities have gained momentum since the adoption of 'Common Foreign Policy Guidelines' by the Council in 1999,[62] which were later confirmed and supported in the year 2000, when the Commission adopted two Common Foreign Policy documents.[63] The General Secretariat unified the texts of Decisions 475 and 499[64] on the Common Foreign Policy by issuing Resolution 528 of 13 July 2001.

The CFP is implemented by three main organs of the CAN, the Presidential Council, the Council of Foreign Ministers and the Meeting of Vice Ministers of Foreign Affairs or High-Level Officials. The Andean Commission contributes to the CFP in the areas of its competence and in coordination with the Council of Foreign Ministers.[65]

---

[56]CA, Article 16(h).

[57]Instrument Establishing the Latin American Integration Association (ALADI), Montevideo, 12 August 1980. See also Chap. 2 in this book

[58]CA, Article 16(k).

[59]Protocol of Trujillo, Article 18.

[60]CAN, Decision 407, n 55 above, Article 3.

[61]CAN, Decision 407, n 55 above, Article 7.

[62]CAN, Council of Foreign Ministers, Decision 458, Common Foreign Policy Guidelines, Cartagena de Indias, 25 May 1999.

[63]CAN, Council of Foreign Ministers, Decision 475, Directive No. 1 on Common Foreign Policy; Decision 476, Common Foreign Policy Follow-up, Lima, 27 April 2000.

[64]CAN, Decision 499, updating Directive 1 on the formulation and execution of the Common Foreign Policy, Valencia, 22 June 2001.

[65]CAN, Decision 458, n. 62 above, Section IV.

5.3.1.3 Andean Community Commission

The Andean Community Commission (the Commission) is the main policy-making body within the AIS. The law-making bodies within the AIS are the Andean Council of Foreign Ministers and the Andean Community Commission. The Commission has a Chairman, who holds the office for one calendar year, and that office is taken by the representative of the country that is chairing the Andean Presidential Council.[66] The Commission meets regularly three times a year, but it can be convened 'in special session whenever such a meeting is called by its Chairman at the request of any of the Member Countries or the General Secretariat'.[67] The Commission meets with the presence of an absolute majority of the member states representatives and failure to attend is considered an abstention.[68] The members of the Commission include one plenipotentiary, and an alternate representative, for each member state of the CAN.[69] However, according to Article 25 CA, if a member state, or the Secretary General so requests, the Commission's Chairman may call for a meeting of an Enlarged Commission, in order to address sectorial issues, consider provisions for coordinating the development plans and harmonising the economic policies of the member states, and address other matters of common interest. In this case, meetings are presided over by the Commission Chairman, and shall include representatives to the Commission and the Ministers or Secretaries of State of the respective area. Each country is entitled to cast one vote when approving Decisions that will become part of Andean Community Law.

Decisions are adopted by affirmative vote of the absolute majority of the member states. However, there are some exceptions to this rule, under Article 26 CA. In case of matters included in Annex I to the Cartagena Agreement,[70] the Commission shall adopt its Decisions by the affirmative vote of the member states with no

---

[66]CA, Article 23.

[67]CA, Article 24.

[68]CA, Article 24.

[69]CA, Article 21.

[70]The matters included in Annex I are: 1. To delegate to the General Secretariat the attributions it deems advisable. 2. To approve the draft amendments to this Agreement. 3. To amend the General Secretariat's proposals. 4. To approve the provisions that are needed to make it possible to coordinate the development plans and harmonise the economic policies of the Member Countries. 5. To approve the provisions and define the time frames for gradually harmonising the Member Countries´ instruments to regulate foreign trade. 6. To approve the physical integration programmes. 7. To accelerate the Liberalization Program, by products or product groups. 8. To approve the joint agricultural and agro-industrial development programmes, by products or product groups. 9. To approve and modify the list of agricultural products to which Article 92 refers. 10. To approve the measures for joint cooperation established in Article 96. 11. To approve, not approve, or amend Member Country proposals. 12. To reduce the number of subject matters included in this Annex. 13. To establish the terms for adherence to this Agreement. 14. To approve the Common External Tariff in accordance with the modes provided for in Chapter VIII, establish the terms for its application and modify the common tariff levels. 15. To approve the measures referred to in the last para of Article 91.

negative votes being cast. The Commission may also add new matters to that Annex through the affirmative vote of the absolute majority of the Member Countries.

For the cases listed in Annex II, which are

1. To approve the terms for the incorporation for non-participant Member Countries in the Industrial Integration Programmes;
2. To approve the list of products that are not produced in any country of the sub-region;
3. To approve the special rules of origin;

the General Secretariat's proposals shall be approved with the affirmative vote of the absolute majority of the member states, provided that no negative vote is cast. Any proposal that receives the affirmative votes of the absolute majority of the member states, but also a negative vote, shall be returned to the General Secretariat for consideration of the grounds for that negative vote. Within a period of no less than two months or more than six, the General Secretariat shall present the proposal once again for consideration by the Commission, including any modifications it deems appropriate. The amended proposal shall be considered approved if it receives the affirmative vote of the absolute majority of the member states, with no negative vote. In this case, the vote of the country that had dissented previously shall not be counted as a negative vote.

Similar exceptions apply in the case of Industrial Development Programs and Projects that shall be approved with the affirmative vote of the absolute majority of the member states, provided that no negative vote is cast.

The Commission has a variety of functions which are defined in Article 22 CA. In particular, it develops, implements, and evaluates Andean sub-regional integration policies in the areas of trade and investment; adopts the necessary measures for achieving the objectives of the Cartagena Agreement and for implementing the Guidelines of the Andean Presidential Council. Regarding foreign relations activities, the Commission coordinates the joint position of the member states in international institutions, meetings and negotiations within its area of responsibility.

Both Declarations and Decisions must be adopted by consensus.[71]

The decisions adopted by the two law-making bodies and resolutions adopted by the General Secretariat are binding upon member states. According to Article 3 of the Treaty creating the CJAC these documents are binding from the date of their publication in the Cartagena Agreement Official Gazette (*Gazeta Oficial del Acuerdo de Cartagena*, GOAC) 'unless they indicate a later date' or '[w]hen their text so stipulates, Decisions must be incorporated into national law through an express act stipulating the date they will enter into effect in each Member Country'.[72]

---

[71]Decision 406, Codification of the Andean Subregional Integration Agreement, Presentation, 25 June 1997, Article 17.

[72]On the concept of direct applicability see Sect. 5.6.

5.4 Community Organisations

5.4.1 Andean Parliament

The Andean Parliament was established in 1979,[73] and it is also foreseen in Article 6 of the Cartagena Agreement. Its permanent headquarters are in Bogotá (Colombia). The reason for its creation was to establish a forum for discussion on integration issues, as a 'common deliberative body'[74] different from the other Andean bodies, which had stronger governmental influence, due to their composition. However, the Andean Parliament was not foreseen since the beginning of the integration process, probably due to the fact that three countries of the region (Bolivia, Peru and Ecuador) were for long periods of time ruled by military dictatorship regimes, which were not particularly interested in promoting democratic institutions of governance within the region.[75] The Andean Parliament is partly involved in the law-making process through proposals that are then passed to the organs of the Andean Integration System.[76] Subsequently, the Sucre Protocol[77] was adopted in 1997, and entered into force in 2003, to further enhance the powers and functions of the Andean Parliament.

The Andean Parliament meets only 1 week a year, and its composition is still based on national representation, rather than on citizens' mandate. According to the Trujillo Protocol, between 1984 and 1996, the Members of Andean Parliament (MAPs) were delegated by individual States' parliaments.[78] With the Sucre Additional Protocol of 1997, that amended the original treaty, it was foreseen that MAPs would be elected by direct and universal vote,[79] for a period of 5 years.

Until the 2003 reform, the Andean Parliament included five national MPs of each member state elected according to their own national regulations. So there were 25 MPs from 1979 to 2003 and 20 since Venezuela left the Community in 2006. In 1997, the Andean countries decided that the Andean Parliament will be elected, from 2001, through direct and universal elections. In three countries, Peru, Ecuador and Colombia, general elections have already taken place. In the case of Bolivia, direct elections are planned for the near future subject to a previous

---

[73]Treaty Establishing the Andean Parliament, adopted on 25 October 1979 at La Paz, entered into force on 17 December 1979, *International Legal Materials*, Vol. 19, No. 2 (March 1980), pp. 269–272.

[74]Treaty Establishing the Andean Parliament 1979, Article 1.

[75]See Londoño Sánchez 1989.

[76]CA, Article 43(e).

[77]Additional Protocol to the Treaty Establishing the Andean Parliament, Sucre, 23 April 1997, at http://www.wipo.int/wipolex/en/treaties/text.jsp?file_id=224740. Accessed 10 October 2014.

[78]According to the provision of Article 3 of La Paz Treaty the Members of Parliament were elected in an indirect way.

[79]Sucre Additional Protocol 1997, Article 1.

constitutional reform. According to Article 5 of the Sucre Protocol, 'representatives to the Andean Parliament shall be elected in each Member Country on the date of the legislative or other general election, including special elections, in accordance with its own national laws'.

The rules related to the functioning of the Andean Parliament were adopted in 1984.[80] Articles 12 and 13 of the 1979 La Paz Treaty, Articles 11 and 12 of the Additional Protocol of 1997, and Articles 42 and 43 of the Cartagena Agreement define the objectives and functions of the Parliament.

The Parliament is a deliberative organ, it can examine strategies and policies, for instance in relation to the progress of integration,[81] promote action of cooperation and suggest actions. According to Article 12(c) it can also express recommendations on the draft annual budgets of the bodies and institutions of the Andean Integration System that are financed through the direct contributions of the member states. The Rules of Procedure of the Parliament provide for sanctions against those organs of the Andean System that refuse to present reports or information. Article 118 of the Rules of Procedure allows the Parliament to file a complaint before the Andean Presidential Council or to resort to the diplomatic or legal actions that it deems adequate. In the case of legislative initiative, the Parliament has a quite marginal role as it does not share this power of initiative with the Commission or the Secretariat.

Even if in some cases, and since the 1996 reform, Parliament decisions may be adopted by a simple majority of votes, in the great part of cases the Parliament's decisions require the absolute majority to be approved. However, the binding force of these decisions is considerably limited by the fact that they are only 'recommendations'.

Finally, it is worth noting that in the process of reform of the Andean Integration System, which is addressed below, the Andean Parliament is supposed to leave the Andean System, and integrate into the new structure that should be developed under the UNASUR.

5.4.2 General Secretariat

As any international organisation, the CAN has a General Secretariat[82] which deals with the performance of the organisation and acts on a daily basis for the accomplishment of the tasks that are given to the organisation and its different organs and institutions. Therefore it is the executive body of the organisation, and

---

[80]Rules of Procedure, Cartagena (Colombia), 17 December 1984.

[81]Additional Protocol to the Treaty Establishing the Andean Parliament, Article 12(b).

[82]It was created on 10 March 1996 by the Trujillo Protocol and started its activities on 1 August 1997.

it works for the exclusive interest of the sub-region.[83] The powers of the Secretariat are mainly defined under Articles 29–39 of the Cartagena Agreement. The structure and functioning are defined in the by-laws of the Secretariat adopted in 1996 at the time of its creation,[84] while the internal organisation of the Secretariat is defined in Resolution 1075,[85] which was adopted by the Secretary General following the approval of the Commission.[86] The administrative acts of the Secretariat are regulated by Decision 425.[87] The General Secretariat expresses itself through resolutions, which do not require ratification by national government bodies and enter into force on the date of their publication in the Official Gazette. Resolutions have legal value when they do not have an individual specific addressee and when are applicable within the Andean Community as a whole.

The head of this organ is the Secretary General, who is supported by several directors in the performance of his duties. The Secretary General is elected by the Council of Foreign Ministers and the Commission by consensus for a period of 5 years and the mandate can be renewed only once.[88] The Secretary General can be removed, also by consensus, at the request of a Member Country, only in the case of gross negligence foreseen in the General Secretariat Regulations.[89] In a couple of cases, the Secretary General has resigned.[90] In these cases, the *ad interim* position is taken by the more senior director general in the Secretariat,[91] until the election of the new Secretary General. The headquarters of the Secretariat are based in Lima, Peru. The Secretariat has the power to make legislative proposals to the Andean Council of Foreign Ministers and to the Commission.[92]

The General Secretariat is the executive body of the Andean Community, which, starting on 1 August 1997, took on, among other things, the functions of the Board of the Cartagena Agreement. Its main functions, defined in Article 30 of the Cartagena Agreement and in the by-laws,[93] are:

---

[83]CA, Article 29.

[84]CAN, Reglamento de la Secretaría General de la Comunidad Andina (Decisiones 409 and 426), Quito, 25 June 1996.

[85]CAN, Texto Único Ordenado del Reglamento Interno de la Secretaría General (Resolución 1075), 15 December 2006, which replaced previous documents concerning the internal organisation of the Secretariat.

[86]CAN, Reglamento de la Secretaría General de la Comunidad Andina, n. 84 above, Article 11(c).

[87]CAN, Andean Council of Foreign Ministers meeting in Enlarged Session with the Representatives to the Andean Community Commission, Decision 425, Reglamento de Procedimientos Administrativos de la Secretaría General de la Comunidad Andina, Montevideo, 14 December 1997.

[88]CAN, Reglamento de la Secretaría General de la Comunidad Andina, n. 84 above, Article 5.

[89]CAN, Reglamento de la Secretaría General de la Comunidad Andina, n. 84 above, Articles 15 and 32.

[90]In 2003, Guillermo Fernández de Soto of Colombia; and in 2010, Freddy Ehlers of Ecuador.

[91]See Andean Council of Foreign Ministers, Decision 567, Resignation of the Andean Community Secretary General, Lima, 31 October 2003.

[92]CA, Article 27.

[93]CAN, Reglamento de la Secretaría General de la Comunidad Andina, n. 84 above, Article 3.

(1) To ensure respect for the community legal order governing the issues provided for in the Cartagena Agreement, such as specific requirements relating to origin, determination of restrictions and duties, tariff deferrals, safeguards, dumping, subsidies and trade competition in accordance with the provisions of Decision 425[94];

(2) To use its dispute-settling power in matters delegated to it by the Commission of the Andean Community or the Andean Council of Foreign Ministers, which may be of a normative or administrative character;

(3) To apply the Rules relating to the prejudicial phase of actions for non-compliance, in accordance with Decision 623.[95]

The Secretariat has a broad competence due to the fact that the Andean Presidential Council has given to it the task of supporting both the Council of Foreign Ministers and the Andean Commission. This means that the Secretariat not only provides the administrative support for the two main executive bodies of the AIS, but also undertakes studies and analysis that may be required in relation to the drafting of proposals and regulations.

In the 2014 administrative elections in Ecuador, the Secretariat also acted as an observer to monitor the electoral process.

The General Secretariat is also competent to settle by administrative arbitration disputes which are submitted to it by individuals concerning the application or interpretation of specific points contained in private contracts governed by the legal regime of the Andean Community.[96] The award is decided in equity according to criteria of fairness and technical elements that conform to the Andean Community's legal system.

Unless otherwise agreed by the parties, the award is binding and, in principle, not subject to appeal, and provides sufficient grounds for requesting its execution, in accordance with the domestic provisions of each member country.

5.4.3 Court of Justice of the Andean Community

For the first 14 years, the CAN did not have a judicial body supervising the application of its legal provisions. The Court of Justice of the Andean Community (CJAC)[97]

---

[94]See n. 87 above.

[95]CAN, Council of Foreign Ministers, Decision 623, Rules of the Pre-judicial Phase of the Action for Non-Compliance, Lima 16 July 2005.

[96]Treaty Creating the Court of Justice, n. 98 below. Article 39.

[97]The *Tribunal de Justicia de la Comunidad Andina* (TJCA) was initially established as the Court of Justice of the Cartagena Agreement and later named Court of Justice of the Andean Community (1996 Trujillo Protocol, Article 6).

was established with the Treaty of Cartagena in 1979,[98] which was later modified by the Treaty of Cochabamba in 1996[99] (hereinafter Treaty Creating the Court of Justice, TCCJ), and officially started operating on 2 January 1984. Other relevant documents that concern the functioning of the CJAC are the Statute[100] and the bylaws of the Court.[101] Changes to the Statute of the Court must be adopted by the Council of Foreign Ministers on a proposal by the Commission and in consultation with the CJAC.[102] The Court adopts its own internal regulations.[103]

Before the establishment of the CJAC, the Andean Commission could apply its procedures of negotiation, good offices, mediation and conciliation which were necessary to solve disputes in relation to the interpretation and application of the Cartagena Agreement and its own decisions. If the Commission could not solve the dispute, member states could use the procedures which were foreseen under the Protocol for the settlement of disputes, signed in Asunción in 1967,[104] by the Ministers of Foreign Affairs of states parties to the Treaty of Montevideo. However, this dispute resolution system was never used and, as a replacement, the new judicial body was established. Some discussions on this issue shall be provided later when dealing with the Andean Community legal order.

The Court of Justice of the Andean Community (*Tribunal de Justicia de la Comunidad Andina*—TJCA) settles disputes between CAN member states that arise under Community law and also deals with individual complaints in relation to the application of community law. Its jurisdiction and powers are structured on the basis of the Court of Justice of the European Union (CJEU)[105] and some of the principles, such as the principle of direct applicability of community law, are clearly derived from the practice of the CJEU. The CJAC is based in Quito, Ecuador, and serves the Community's four member states.

---

[98]Treaty Creating the Court of Justice of the Cartagena Agreement, Cartagena, 28 May 1979, entered into force 19 May 1983, International Legal Materials, Vol. 18, No. 5, 1979, pp. 1203–1210, and modified by the Cochabamba (Protocol Modifying the Treaty Creating the Court of Justice of the Cartagena Agreement, Cochabamba, 28 May 1996).

[99]The Protocol of Modification of the Treaty Establishing the Court of Justice of the Andean Community, approved in May 1996, and which came into force in August 1999, assigns new spheres of competence to this institution of the Andean Integration System (AIS), including Appeals for Omission or Inaction, Arbitration and Labour Jurisdiction. Its new Bylaws, which update and define the procedures applied by the CJAC, were approved on 22 June 2001 by the Andean Council of Foreign Ministers, at: http://www.comunidadandina.org/ingles/normativa/d184e.htm. Accessed 10 October 2014.

[100]CAN, Decision 500, Estatuto del Tribunal de Justicia de la Comunidad Andina, 22 June 2001.

[101]CAN, Decision 184, Bylaws of the Court of Justice of the Cartagena Agreement, 19 August 1983.

[102]TCCJ, Article 13.

[103]TCCJ, Article 13.

[104]Latin American Free Trade Association, Protocol for the Settlement of Disputes, Asunción, 2 September 1967, 7 I.L.M. 747 (1968).

[105]Alter et al. 2012.

5.4.3.1 Structure and Jurisdiction

The structure of the CJAC is defined in the Treaty Creating the CJAC (TCCJ).[106] The CJAC includes one judge for each member state,[107] who is appointed for 6-year periods,[108] with a maximum of two mandates. The figure of the Advocate General, which is based on the similar institution within the Court of Justice of the European Union, is outlined in the Statute of the Court, but is not yet implemented in practice.[109] The judges enjoy a special status based on the diplomatic immunities defined in the 1961 Vienna Convention on Diplomatic Relations,[110] equivalent to Head of Mission, particularly 'with respect to the immunity of their records and their official correspondence and in all matters concerning civil and criminal jurisdiction'. The Secretariat of the Court and its international personnel have diplomatic status according to the agreement between the Court and the host state.[111] However, 'the Court may lift the immunity granted to magistrates by virtue of Article 13 of the Treaty'.[112] Article 10 of the TCCJ allows judges to be removed from their position in accordance to the by-laws, which foresee the following reasons:

a. Notorious bad behaviour;
b. Any activity that is incompatible with the nature of the post;
c. Repeated failure to fulfil the duties inherent to the role;
d. Involvement in professional activities, raid or otherwise, except those of a teaching or academic nature; and
e. Breach of the oath in accordance to Article 4 of the same document.[113]

The procedure before the Court is in Spanish. For documents in another language the simple translations could be used unless the Court requires official ones. Dialects and indigenous languages can be used, but the documents must be accompanied by a Spanish translation.[114]

According to Article 4 of its Statute, the CJAC is a supranational and communitarian institution, whose main functions include the clarification of Andean

---

[106]TCCJ, Articles 5–16.

[107]TCCJ, Article 6.

[108]TCCJ, Article 8.

[109]TCCJ, Article 6, para 3.

[110]UN, 1961 Vienna Convention on Diplomatic Relations, 18 April 1961, 500 UNTS 95; (1961) 55 *American Journal of International Law*, p. 1064.

[111]TCCJ, Article 12.

[112]CJAC, Bylaws, Article 5.

[113]CJAC, by-laws, Article 4 foresees that judges who take their position in the Court swear 'to carry out their job conscientiously and completely impartially, to keep the Court discussions secret and to fulfil all the duties inherent to their role'.

[114]CJAC, Statute, Article 34.

community law and ensuring its uniform application and interpretation in all member states.[115] Its relevance is stressed by the fact that Member Countries may not submit trade disputes that arise in connection with the application of the rules of the legal regime of the Andean Community to any other court, arbitration system or procedure other than those contemplated in the Treaty Creating the Court of Justice of the Andean Community (Article 42).

The decisions of the Court are published in the Official Gazette of the Community[116] and, because those decisions may clarify some important points of Community law, the interpretation provided by the CJAC is binding for national judges of member states.[117]

Article 1 of the TCCJ and Article 2 of the Statute of the Court define the content of community law which includes the Cartagena Agreement and its protocols, the Treaty Creating the Court of Justice, the decisions of the Andean Council of Foreign Ministers and the Commission of the Andean Community, resolutions of the General Secretariat, and agreements entered into by member states in the context of Andean integration. Most of these documents and decisions deal with regional trade and competition law. However, some of them deal with the rights of workers, labour migrants and consumers, public health and intellectual property, among other topics. Therefore, despite the fact that the CJAC does not have competence to hear individual complaints concerning alleged fundamental rights violations, individuals may bring claims to determine whether member states are in compliance with trade-related obligations to respect the rights of certain groups. This issue has raised some possible legal problems in relation to the competence of the CJAC and the CAN in the field of human rights. For instance, the Constitutional Court of Colombia has addressed the issue by affirming that the CAN regulates economic, financial, monetary and technical matters and is not an agreement concerning human rights, therefore, in these areas, under Article 93 of the Colombian constitution, international human right obligations would prevail in the national legal order.[118]

The jurisdiction of the CJAC is defined in the TCCJ and further clarified in its Statute (Decision 500). There are several types of actions and functions that the CJAC can exercise: (1) nullity actions; (2) actions to declare non-compliance; in addition, the CJAC can adopt binding interpretations of Community law, as (3) prejudgment interpretation actions; it can decide on (4) inactivity or omission actions; and with the Cochabamba Protocol its (5) arbitration function and (6) labour jurisdiction were later added.

---

[115]CJAC, Statute, Article 4.

[116]CJAC, Statute, Article 94.

[117]TCCJ, Article 35.

[118]Colombian Constitutional Court, Sentencia C-988/04, 12 October 2004, Section VII, paras 4–7.

These powers have made the CJAC the third world most active international court,[119] after the European Court of Human Rights and the Court of Justice of the European Union. So far, the most widely used jurisdiction has been the preliminary reference. It is also worth noting that most of the decisions of the CJAC are related to intellectual property law, while the arbitration and labour jurisdictions have been used in very limited circumstances. In the following section the different competences of the CJAC are going to be discussed.

5.4.3.2 Nullity Actions

The main scope of nullity actions[120] is the control of legality of Community law. Nullity actions are available to member states, individuals and companies which may challenge the validity of Decisions and Resolutions issued by the Andean Community Commission, the General Secretariat and the Andean Council of Foreign Affairs that allegedly are not in conformity with Community law, or may amount to a misuse of power.[121] The same type of action is applicable against 'Industrial Complementarity Agreements and any such other agreements as the Member Countries may adopt among themselves within the context of the Andean subregional integration process'.[122]

The same organs mentioned before are also those entitled to be the applicants in these types of actions. States may only file such actions if they did not vote in favour of the challenged document.[123] Individuals and companies may challenge Community law that applies to them and affects their subjective rights or legitimate interests.[124]

According to Article 20 TCCJ, a nullity action 'must be brought before the Court within a period of 2 years following the date of the Decision of the Andean Council of Foreign Ministers or of the Andean Community Commission, the General Secretariat's Resolution, or the Agreement in question becomes effective'. However, in case of individual applications, one of the parties can invoke the nullity of the act in front of a national tribunal even beyond the 2 years limit, as far as their rights or legitimate interests would be affected by the application of the Decision, Resolution or Agreement in the specific case.

---

[119]According to the Court website, by 31st December 2013, the Court has adopted 2444 preliminary rulings which were requested by national courts, 119 non-compliance actions against member states, 54 nullity actions, 17 labour trials and 6 inactivity or omission actions involving community organs.

[120]TCCJ, Articles 17–22; CJAC, Statute, Articles 101–106.

[121]TCCJ, Article 17.

[122]TCCJ, Article 1(e).

[123]TCCJ, Article 18.

[124]TCCJ, Article 19.

Once the nullity action has been filed by one of the parties, the national judge shall consult the Court in relation to the validity of the act and 'shall then suspend the process until receipt of the Court's decision' which shall be binding on the national judge for the decision of the case.[125]

The filing of a nullity action will not affect the efficacy or validity of the rule or agreement which is challenged. The Court may, however, order the provisional suspension of the measure challenged or establish other precautionary measures, if it ascertains that the application of the specific document could cause irreparable harm or harm that is difficult to redress.[126]

Once the CJAC declares the total or partial nullity of the act, it has also to define the effects of this decision over time. Furthermore, the organ or institution of the CAN which adopted the document which was later annulled shall have to act in accordance with the decision of the Court in order to make sure that the judgment is fulfilled within the period of time defined by the Court.[127]

5.4.3.3 Non-compliance Actions

In actions of non-compliance,[128] the CJAC decides whether a member state has failed to fulfil its obligations under Community law. This consists in a claim in which it is alleged that a member state is in breach of its obligations arising from the rules that make up the Andean legal regime. The failure to comply with an obligation can be positive, that is issuing norms or acts that hinder Community law, or negative, that is, by failing to act (omission) or by issuing norms or acts opposed to the specific obligation(s).

This procedure foresees two phases: (1) a preliminary phase which entails bringing an action before the General Secretariat, and (2) a judicial action before the CJAC.

It is possible to notice that this power is very similar to the powers of the EU Commission in relation to non-compliance by EU member states.[129] It is also an exception in the context of American sub-regional organisations, as this is the only case where these powers have been granted to a supranational institution within the continent. However, this action may be activated only after the General Secretariat has made a written finding regarding the suspected non-compliance, followed by a request to the CJAC by the General Secretariat to rule on this issue.

For this action to be operative there is first an administrative procedure before the General Secretariat. In this first phase, the General Secretariat, by its own

---

[125]TCCJ, Article 20(3).

[126]TCCJ, Article 21.

[127]TCCJ, Article 22.

[128]TCCJ, Articles 23–31; CJAC, Statute, Articles 107–120.

[129]Treaty on the Functioning of the European Union, Article 258, Consolidated version of the Treaty on the Functioning of the European Union, *OJ C 115*, 9 May 2008, p. 160.

initiative, or upon the initiative of a member state, or a natural or legal person with affected interests, will formulate the observations in writing to the member state and give it a term to answer, which cannot exceed 60 days. When the General Secretariat receives the answer, or the 60 days term expires, the General Secretariat will issue a final motivated decision in the form of an opinion (administrative ruling),[130] which must be issued within the next 15 days.[131] The final decision concludes the compliance or non-compliance of the obligations of the member state. Also, there is no appeal against the opinion with statement of grounds.

Therefore, member states, natural and legal persons may raise complaints of non-compliance with the General Secretariat, and they may bring the case directly to the CJAC after the General Secretariat:

- Has issued a finding of non-compliance, but does not bring the case to the Court within 60 days;
- Has issued a finding of compliance; or
- Has failed to issue a finding regarding the alleged non-compliance within 75 days of receiving the complaint.

The natural or legal persons affected can invoke the action either directly before the Court or before a national court, but this second option would preclude the procedure before the CJAC.[132]

At this point the second phase may take place in front of the CJAC. Irrespective of the opinion handed down, once it has been issued (or in the absence of such an opinion), the complainant country, the natural and legal person has the option of resorting to the Court.

If the final decision of the General Secretariat concludes a non-compliance and the member state persists in its behaviour, the General Secretariat must bring the action before the CJAC. In that case, the member state affected by the non-compliance can join the procedure.

If the Court rules that there is non-compliance, the member state has to take all necessary measures (and especially those mentioned in the decision) within 90 days after notification of the decision.[133] It is the responsibility of the Court to follow the compliance with its decision. If the member state does not comply, the CJAC, after having heard the opinion of the General Secretariat, can take other measures, which it considers convenient and which can comprehend the suspension or restriction of the benefits granted under the Cartagena Agreement.[134]

---

[130]This is statement of grounds in which the General Secretariat presents its view on the status of non-compliance with community obligations, and, if appropriate, sets a deadline for the member country to remedy the situation.

[131]TCCJ, Article 23; CAN, Council of Foreign Ministers, Decision 623, Rules of the Prejudicial Phase of the Action for Non-Compliance, Lima 16 July 2005.

[132]TCCJ, Article 31.

[133]TCCJ, Article 27.

[134]CJAC, Statute, Articles 112–120.

The ruling of non-compliance handed down by the Court in the disputes initiated by natural or legal persons whose rights have been infringed by non-compliance by a member country constitute legal and sufficient grounds for that person to request from the national judge compensation for the losses and harm resulting therefrom (Article 30 TCCJ).

These rulings are not reviewable except by the Court itself, on the request of one of the parties, if it is appraised of some fact that could have had a decisive influence on the outcome of the process and if this fact was unknown at the date of issue of the ruling by the party requesting the review. The request for review must be presented within 90 days of the date when the fact was discovered and, in any case, within one year from the date of the ruling. The temporary suspension of Community law operates in this action as well.

5.4.3.4 Prejudgment Interpretation Actions

The main objective of the prejudgment interpretation procedure is to give the CJAC the power to ensure the uniform application of Community law in all member states.[135] This procedure is very much structured on the model of the so-called 'preliminary ruling' within the EU.[136] In this type of procedure, the Court gives an interpretation of community law, which is binding for national judges.

The procedure is initiated by national judges if Community law is applicable or disputed in cases brought before them. Similar to the same procedure from the Court of Justice of the European Union, there are two options: the mandatory request for interpretation, and the optional request for interpretation. The mandatory request for interpretation is applied *ex officio* by the judge, or if one of the parties requests it, when the case is in front of a court or tribunal of unique or last instance and without any possibility or appeal or revision under national law. In this case, the procedure must be suspended until the interpretation of the CJAC is received.

However, in cases which can be appealed in domestic law the optional request for interpretation is possible and the national judge may request an interpretation of the CJAC, but the trial is not suspended. This means that if the national judge is ready to reach a decision, but the interpretation of the CJAC has not been provided, the judge can decide on the case. However, if the interpretation is received on time, the judge is bound to decide accordingly.

The CJAC has 30 days after the admission of the request by the national judge to issue a decision or interpretation on the points of community law raised. In this decision the Court will only be able to refer to the content and scope of the Community law in the context of the case, and will not be allowed to refer to the scope or content of national law, neither to judge on the facts of the case.

---

[135]TCCJ, Articles 32–36; see Helfer and Alter 2009.

[136]Treaty on the Functioning of the EU, Article 267.

However, it shall refer to the facts when they are relevant to provide the requested interpretation.[137]

The national judges that requested interpretations must send a copy of the final decision adopted by the national court to the CJAC, in order to ensure the fulfilment of the obligations. Furthermore, Article 36 of the TCCJ emphasises that the member states shall supervise the application of decision of the CJAC by national judges in this specific procedure. If the national judges do not comply with the obligation to adopt the interpretation in the final decision or to request the interpretation, the member state, or the legal or natural person affected, can still exercise the action of non-compliance before the CJAC to solve the dispute.

5.4.3.5 Inactivity or Omission Actions

The Council of Foreign Ministers, the Commission, the General Secretariat, the member states any natural or legal person whose rights or legitimate interests are affected may request the judgment of the Court when any of the community bodies abstain from accomplishing certain activities that they are obliged to perform according to the Community law.[138]

First, the party concerned must directly request the competent body to fulfil the specific obligation. If within the 30 following days there is no answer, or the answer provided by the relevant body is not satisfactory, the petitioner can appeal to the CJAC to rule on the issue. Once the case has been admitted, the Court will ask for an explanation from the representative of the entity which allegedly has failed to act on the basis of its obligations. The Court has 30 days to issue the corresponding ruling, based 'on the existing technical documentation, background of the case, and explanations by the body whose behaviour is subject matter of the action' (Article 37 TCCJ). The decision should specify the way, form and period of time by which the obligation should be fulfilled, and shall be published in the Official Gazette of the CAN.

5.4.3.6 Arbitration Function

The Court has the jurisdiction to settle through arbitration those disputes that arise as a result of the application or interpretation of contracts or agreements concluded between the bodies and institutions of the AIS or between these and third parties, when the parties so agree.[139] Individuals may, however, also agree to submit to arbitration through the Court any disputes arising from the application or interpretation of specific points contained in private contracts governed by the legal

---

[137]TCCJ, Article 34.

[138]TCCJ, Article 37; CJAC, Statute, Articles 129–134.

[139]TCCJ, Article 38.

regime of the Andean Community. The Court may decide the case either in law or in equity, as the parties choose.

Once the award is issued, it is binding and cannot be appealed and constitutes legal and sufficient grounds for requesting its execution in accordance with the domestic provisions of each member state. It is worth noting that the solution of disputes by arbitration can be also provided by the General Secretariat of the CAN.[140]

5.4.3.7 Labour Jurisdiction

The Court is competent to hear labour disputes that may arise within the bodies and institutions of the AIS.[141] This jurisdiction gives the Court the power to solve the controversies that may arise between institutions of the Andean Community and their employees related to labour matters or labour relationships. In doing so, the Court will have to take into account the applicable law in order to solve such kind of controversies which include the general principles of labour law recognised by the International Labour Organisation, the common legal principles of member states of the CAN,[142] and the Headquarters agreements which may be applicable.

To invoke this action, it is a fundamental prerequisite that the employee notifies the institution the claim in relation to a possible violation of labour rights. The institution has 30 days to provide an answer. If the institution does not answer within that period, or if the answer is totally not or partially in favour of the petitioner, it is possible to bring the action before the CJAC. In this action, a conciliation procedure can be exercised at any moment. The possibility to undertake the action will expire 3 years after the occurrence of the fact or act which originated the petition.

5.5 The Aims and Purposes of the CAN

The main purpose of the original Andean Pact was the establishment of Customs Union (CU) with a Common External Tariff (CET) by the end of 1980. However, the Andean Group never came close to achieving its objectives. The process was very slow and a series of crises in the sub-region had further limited the integration process. Among them were, the closing of the Peruvian Congress by President Fujimori in 1992, an old border dispute between Ecuador and Peru in the Amazonia which resurfaced in 1995; a political crisis in Ecuador which forced

---

[140]See Sect. 5.4.2.

[141]TCCJ, Article 40; CJAC, Statute, Articles 135–139.

[142]CJAC, Statute, Article 135.

President Abdalá Bucaram out of office in 1997.[143] In 1995, with the Quito New Strategic Design,[144] the Andean Pact, which was a mainly inward looking structure focusing on the internal marked, was replaced by the Andean Community with a revised institutional structure, that should strengthen the Andean subregional integration, promote the external relation and increase the integration process of the organisation.

The Andean Community' purpose is defined in Article 1 of the Cartagena Agreement whose main objective is 'to promote the balanced and harmonious development of the Member Countries under equitable conditions, through integration and economic and social cooperation'. In the same provision it is affirmed that the ultimate purpose of CAN is 'the gradual formation of a Latin American Common Market'.

A free trade area—with no goods exempted—went into effect in 1993 between Bolivia, Colombia, Ecuador and Venezuela. Peru did not join the free trade area, but negotiated bilateral trade arrangements with each of its Andean counterparts.

The Sucre policy reforms, based on the 1997 Sucre Protocol, extended the scope of integration beyond pure trade and economic issues to include social and environmental issues.

The Presidential Council Meeting in June 2000 adopted the 'Act of Lima'[145] which stressed the enhancement of the integration process in various policy areas. In particular, the Council repeated its determination to create an Andean Common Market by the year 2005, with the purposes of developing the free circulation of goods, services, capital and persons. It also launched a Common Foreign Policy of the Andean Community and the implementation of a Social Agenda.

In May 1999, the Council issued Decision 458 containing the Common Foreign Policy Guidelines of the CAN.[146] According to these guidelines, the Common Foreign Policy is broadly understood as aiming at 'defending and promoting the common identity, values, rights and interests'. More specifically, the Common Foreign Policy aims at strengthening peace and security and enhancing the negotiating position of the member countries in order to accelerate sub-regional integration. Three main fields of cooperation are included in this policy: political, economic, social and cultural areas. In addition, the consolidation of democracy and the rule of law, the promotion and respect of human rights, sustainable development and the fight against drugs, corruption and terrorism are mentioned. The Common Foreign Policy is implemented through the adoption of common positions and joint actions.

---

[143]Rodríguez Mendoza 1998.

[144]See text accompanying note 44 above.

[145]Twelfth Andean Presidential Council, Act of Lima, Lima, 10 June 2000, at: http://www.sice.oas.org/Trade/Junac/XIIacta_e.asp. Accessed 20 October 2014.

[146]CAN, Andean Council of Foreign Ministers, Decision 458, Common Foreign Policy Guidelines, Cartagena de Indias, 25 May 1999.

It is also worth noting that the CAN adopted, in the year 2000, an additional protocol to the Cartagena Agreement which deals with the promotion and rein-forcement of democratic governments within the region.[147] Article 4 of the Andean Community Commitment to Democracy[148] foresees that, in case of undemocratic government in one of the member states of the CAN the following measures can be taken:

a. Suspension of the member country's participation in any of the bodies of the Andean Integration System;
b. Suspension of its participation in the international cooperation projects carried out by the member countries;
c. Extension of the suspension to other System bodies, including its disquali-fication by Andean financial institutions from obtaining access to facilities or loans;
d. Suspension of rights to which it is entitled under the Cartagena Agreement and of the right to coordinate external action in other spheres; and
e. Other measures and actions that are deemed pertinent under International Law.

Also, the purpose of the CAN is to promote democracy beyond its member states, and Article 8 affirms that the 'Andean Community shall seek to incorporate a dem-ocratic clause in the agreements it signs with third parties'. As a further support for this engagement towards democratic governance in the region, it is relevant to note that the Presidents of the Andean Community and the Mercosur countries approved, on 1 September 2000 in Brasilia,[149] the so-called 'democratic clause', included in para 23 of the Communiqué, which states that 'Maintenance of the rule of law and full respect for the democratic system in each of the twelve coun-tries of the region constitute an objective and a shared commitment, which as of today is a prerequisite for participation in future South American meetings'. In the same document the Heads of State affirmed that 'Respecting the existing regional mechanisms, they agreed, in that connection, to hold political consultations if a disruption of the democratic order in South America is threatened'.

In 2002, the Andean Charter for the Promotion and Protection of Human Rights[150] further stressed the commitment of the member states towards the pro-tection of fundamental rights. Article 96 of the Charter provides an interesting clause, as it instructs the Ministers of Foreign Affairs, 'given the dynamics of the

---

[147]See Dabène 2009, pp. 78–81.

[148]CAN, Andean Foreign Ministers, Additional Protocol to the Cartagena Agreement 'Andean Community Commitment to Democracy', Oporto, 10 June 2000; Andean Presidential Council, Declaration about Democracy and Integration, Santafé de Bogotá, 7 August 1998.

[149]Reunião de Presidentes da América do Sul, Comunicado de Brasília, 1 September 2000, at: http://www.oei.es/oeivirt/cimeira1.htm. Accessed 23 November 2014.

[150]See note 33 above; see also: Declaración de Machu Picchu sobre la Democracia, los Derechos de los Pueblos Indígenas y la Lucha contra la Pobreza. Lima—Machu Picchu, 28–29 July 2001; Act of Carabobo, 24 June 2001; Declaration of the Andean Council of Presidents on Democracy and Integration, Bogotá, 7 August 1998.

evolution of international law on human rights, to review every 4 years the contents of this Charter to the effect of updating and improving it'. The same article also includes a quite unusual statement in relation to the legal effect of the Charter, as it affirms that the 'Andean Council of Ministers of Foreign Affairs shall decide in due time upon the binding nature of this Charter'. It also foresees that the text of the Charter should be translated 'into the main ancestral languages of indigenous peoples in the Andean countries', showing a special interest for the protection and promotion of human rights in relation to indigenous peoples in the region.

5.5.1   Instances of Civil Society Participation

As part of the integration process, the CAN has also tried to develop some instances for the direct participation of the civil society in the integration process. A Business Advisory Council and a Labour Advisory Council have been established since 1983 and operational since 1998. They are foreseen by Article 44 of the Cartagena Agreement and are regulated by specific decisions of the Andean Commission.[151] In 2002 the Andean Indigenous Board was inaugurated, followed in 2007 by the Andean Indigenous Advisory Council with representatives of Andean indigenous community organisations, governmental organisations, ombudsmen and a group of experts. The scope of this body is to provide opinions and recommendations on matters of relevance to the Andean indigenous communities, particularly in relation to the reduction of poverty, development with social equity, and recognition of the role of the indigenous communities in the Andean countries. In 2003, the Andean Council of Foreign Affairs Ministers passed Decision 539, which establishes another consultative body, the Andean Consumer Defense Board, responsible for ensuring fair market and commercial practices for the citizens of the CAN Member Countries.

Finally, the Andean Council of Municipal Authorities was established in 2004[152] with the aim of including local authorities in the integration process. It includes three representatives for each member state, one representative of the capital city of each State, and two other members of local governments elected among the representatives of cities which are part of an Andean network (*Red Andina de Ciudades*).[153]

In addition to the aforementioned forums for institutional representation of civil society, the Andean Community has other participatory instruments for social policy, such as the Simón Rodríguez Agreement adopted in 1973 and modified in

---

[151]CAN, Andean Commission, Decisions 442 and 464 (25 May 1999) for the Business Advisory Council; and Decisions 441 (26 July 1998), 464, and 494 (30 March 2001) for the Labour Advisory Council.

[152]CAN, Andean Council of Foreign Ministers, Decision 585, 7 May 2004.

[153]The network was established in Quito, Ecuador, on 8 September 2003.

2001 by the Protocol of Substitution of the Simón Rodríguez Convention[154] (one of the so-called "Social Agreements"),[155] which consists of a tripartite forum for debate, participation and coordination between labour ministers, employers and workers, in order to address socio-occupational policies at regional level.

The scope of these bodies is to provide consultative opinions to the main institutions of the AIS, usually in the form of recommendations to the Council of Foreign Ministers, the Commission or the General Secretariat. They can also attend the meetings of the main institutions with the right to express their opinions but without a vote.

It is also foreseen that these instances should be involved in the negotiations with external actors, and contribute to the social dimension in the negotiation of institutional agreements, as in the case of the EU.[156] However, this opportunity has not been considered particularly successful due to some limitations linked to the limitations that some social actors and organisations face in relation to their relationship with the national governments in the Latin American context.[157]

5.5.2 Human Rights Protection

It is also worth noting that in relation to the protection of human rights, the CJAC has no jurisdiction to hear cases and individual complaints. Although the Andean Community has adopted the Andean Charter for the Promotion and Protection of Human Rights,[158] this document is considered a statement of Community values, rather than a binding source of Community law and is therefore not necessary interpreted or applied by the CJAC.[159] The Andean Charter 'reiterate[s] the will of the Andean Community Member States to accept the decisions of the Inter-American Human Rights Court' and affirms that they will 'cooperate actively with the United Nations and Inter-American systems for the protection and promotion of human rights' (Article 82), but does not mention the same type of obligations in relation to the CJAC. However, Article 86 of the Charter provides that cooperation with those mechanisms does not preclude 'the future incorporation of other follow-up ways and means through the pertinent Community channels'. It is however

---

[154]Adopted by the Andean Presidential Council on 24 June 2001.

[155]Other agreements include the Andrés Bello Agreement, which tackles education policy in the Andean Region, and the Hipólito Unanue Agreement, which addresses health policy.

[156]See IV EU-LAC Summit, Vienna, 11–13 May 2006, Declaration of Vienna, 12 May 2006, para 36.

[157]See Huybrechts and Peels 2009, pp. 218–225.

[158]See note 33 above.

[159]See: TCCJ, Article 1; Statute of the CJAC, Article 2; CAN, Council of Foreign Ministers, Decision 586, Working Program for the Dissemination and Execution of the Andean Charter for the Promotion and Protection of Human Rights, Guayaquil, 7 May 2004, Section II, 2.2.

possible to consider that the CJAC could refer to the Charter for the Promotion and Protection of Human Rights in its own decisions, as it may constitute a set of principles that are part of the legal values of the individual countries of the region.

5.6 The Andean Community Legal Order

The CAN represents an interesting example of integration and cooperation in the Latin American context. It has developed, particularly over the past 20 years, an Andean Community Law,[160] that has become common to the member states, and which is creating a specific legal order quite similar to the EU, even if in more restricted areas of cooperation. In particular, due to the establishment of the CJAC, the integration system has allowed the development of a community legal system which is similar to the EU. The legal order of the CAN is both vertically and horizontally applicable in member states.[161] Decisions adopted by the Council of Foreign Ministers and by the Commission are binding from the date of their adoption and have direct effect in the national legal systems without the need of further ratification by the member states.[162] Decisions and Regulations approved by the General Secretariat are directly applicable from the date of their publication in the GOAC. These provisions establish the direct applicability of community law in national a legal system, which has been confirmed by the case law of the CJAC.[163] Article 3 TCCJ expressly recognises the direct applicability of decisions of the Andean Council of Foreign Ministers and of the Commission and the resolutions of the General Secretariat.

The principle of supremacy is included in Article 4 TCCJ which states:

> Member Countries are under the obligation to take such measures as may be necessary to ensure compliance with the provisions comprising the legal system of the Andean Community.
> They further agree to refrain from adopting or employing any such measure as may be contrary to those provisions or that may in any way restrict their application.

The principle has been clarified by the CJAC in its first preliminary ruling in 1987,[164] when it took the opportunity to explain the operation of the Andean legal system, and has been reaffirmed in the case law of the CJAC,[165] using the concept

---

[160]Salmón Gárate et al 2003.

[161]Jiménez 2013.

[162]TCCJ, Article 2.

[163]CJAC, Proceso 02-AN-86, Gaceta Oficial N° 21, de 15 de julio de 1987; Proceso 34-AI-2001. publicado en la GOAC N° 839, de 25 de septiembre de 2002

[164]CJAC, Proceso 1-IP-87, GOAC. N° 28, de 15 febrero de 1988, p. 3.

[165]CJAC, Proceso 02-IP-88, GOAC N° 33, 26 June 1988; Proceso 1-IP-96, GOAC N° 257, 14 April 1997; Proceso 1-AI-2001, GOAC N° 818, 23 July 2002, *Secretaría General c. República Bolivariana de Venezuela*, case: Patentes de segundo uso, which cites Proceso 2-IP-90, GOAC N° 69, 11 October 1990.

of direct applicability included in Article 3 TCCJ. The CJAC has applied a similar reasoning of the CJEU, even if it has elaborated the concept in a less sophisticated way, as it made reference to the provisions of the TCCJ. It is also true that the concept had been clarified in the TCCJ in a clearer way, compared to the original Treaties of the European Community, where the direct applicability and direct effect were not explicitly defined, and therefore, the arguments and reasoning of the—at the time—European Court of Justice needed a much higher level of legal arguments to justify the establishment of those principles which later become embedded in the EU legal system.

The powers and decisions of the CJAC are in part framed on the experience and legal reasoning that have been developed by the CJEU. In this context, it is possible to say that the CJAC contributes to the development of the Andean Community legal system.[166] However, there are quite significant differences between the two systems. Some authors have pointed out that the creation of the CJAC has received relatively little consideration despite the fact that is a unique example in the American continent. In particular, among legal scholars the development of the CJAC is generally accepted as a positive factor, and there is little manifestation of critical analysis of this phenomenon that might question why the CAN needed a special court to deal with the application of its legal rules.[167]

5.7 Relationship with the European Union

The European Union (EU) political dialogue with the CAN began in 1983, with the establishment of a Joint Committee set up by the Cooperation Agreement which also created three subcommittees on science and technology, industrial cooperation and trade cooperation.[168] In 1993 the representatives of both organisations signed a framework agreement of cooperation based on the respect for human rights and democracy and including several areas with a clause that allowed further implementation.[169] The development of relationships between the CAN and the EU has been one of the main external activities of the organisation. The development of this dialogue is based on the 1996 Trujillo Protocol which defined a common foreign policy of Andean countries. Four months later this type of external dialogue was formalised for the first time with the Declaration of Rome (1996). It is in 2003 that the CAN and the European Community, with their

---

[166]Alter and Helfer 2011.

[167]In particular, see: Saldías 2014.

[168]See: Molano Cruz 2007.

[169]EEC-Andean Community Cooperation Agreement, between the EEC and the member states of the Cartagena Agreement signed on 23 April 1993 in Copenhagen, entered into force on 1 May 1998, EEC *Official Journal* L 127 of 29 April 1998; CAN, Decision 329, Acuerdo Marco de Cooperación entre la Comunidad Económica Europea y el Acuerdo de Cartagena y sus Países Miembros: Bolivia, Colombia, Ecuador, Perú y Venezuela, Bogotá 22 October 1992.

respective member states, signed a political dialogue and cooperation agreement,[170] which governs the relationship between the two organisations till now.

During the XIII Ministerial Meeting of the Rio Group, held in Santo Domingo (Dominican Republic) in April 2007, the EU's and the CAN's ministers of foreign affairs announced their intention to start negotiations on an Association Agreement in May 2007, and actually started only after the adoption of a general framework for the negotiation agreement adopted in June 2007 by the CAN.[171] The Association Agreement was envisaged as a comprehensive agreement, embracing the whole array of the multifaceted relations of the EU with the Andean Community. The objectives of the Association Agreement were:

- Enhance the political dialogue between both regions;
- Intensify and improve their cooperation in a variety of areas; and
- Enhance and facilitate bi-regional trade and investments.

However, the member countries of the CAN were allowed to take into account the existence of different levels of development and economic approaches among them and 'the right to express the differences and to negotiate different levels of coverage and depth, as the case may be, of the subjects and commitments of that Agreement'.[172]

As a consequence, on 17 May 2008, during the V Latin America and Caribbean-European Union Summit, the Andean Community and the EU agreed to a flexible framework agreement for the association of both blocs. The agreement would cover three aspects: trade, political and cooperation. Each country of the Andean Community (Bolivia, Colombia, Ecuador and Peru) would be able enter into any one of the aspects of the agreement according to the country's possibilities, ambitions, deadlines and pace. The fourth round of negotiations took place in Brussels in July 2008.[173] Following a series of rounds of negotiations, on 19 May 2010, in Madrid, during the VI European Union-Latin America and the Caribbean Summit of Heads of State and Government, Colombia and Peru concluded their respective free trade negotiations with the EU.

---

[170]EC-CAN, Political dialogue and Cooperation Agreement between the European Community and its Member States, of the one part, and the Andean Community and its Member Countries (Bolivia, Colombia, Ecuador, Peru and Venezuela), of the other part, Rome 15 December 2003; CAN, Extended Meeting of the Andean Council of Ministers of Foreign Affairs with the Principal Representatives before the Andean Community Commission, Decision 595, Political Dialog and Cooperation Agreement between the European Community and its Member States and the Andean Community and its Member States, Bolivia, Colombia, Ecuador, Peru and Venezuela, Quito, 11 July 2004.

[171]CAN, Enlarged Meeting of the Andean Council of Foreign Ministers and the Commission of the Andean Community, Decision 667, General framework for the negotiation of the Association Agreement between the Andean Community and the European Union, Lima, 8 June 2007.

[172]Ibid., Article 1.

[173]The first round of negotiations was held in Bogotá on 17 September 2007. The second round took place in Brussels, Belgium on 14 December 2007. The third round of negotiations was concluded in Quito, Ecuador on 25 April 2008.

In June 2012 the EU signed an ambitious and comprehensive Trade Agreement with Colombia and Peru.[174] The agreement was provisionally applied with Peru since 1 March 2013 and with Colombia since 1 August 2013. Contacts are maintained to explore a possibility to integrate Ecuador and Bolivia into the trade deal with the EU. This type of agreement is possible within the CAN because Decision 598 of the Andean Council of Foreign Ministers allows member states to negotiate commercial agreements in individual, combined or communitarian form, whilst for individual EU countries this is not possible any more.

The Agreement focuses on tariffs among the countries and the EU and the liberalisation of trade in goods. At the end of the transition period, there will be no customs duties at all on industrial and fisheries products and trade in agricultural products will become considerably more open. The Agreement has established a Trade Committee (Article 12 Agreement), with representatives of the EU and the Andean countries that have ratified the treaty, which would supervise its application. The Trade Committee can also adopt binding decisions (Article 14 Agreement) by consensus. Several subcommittees on specialised areas, such as market access, agriculture, intellectual property (Article 15 Agreement) are established.

The Agreement also includes provisions on sustainable development, the respect of human rights, the rule of law and effective implementation of international conventions on labour rights and environmental protection. Civil society organisations will be systematically involved to monitor the implementation of these commitments. For instance, there is a EU-Colombia Human Rights Dialogue, which was established in 2009, and a high-level group from the Colombian government, the EU Delegation and Member States Embassies in Bogota meet twice a year to discuss both parties' activities in promoting and protecting human rights. This mechanism has promoted human rights protection in Colombia, including the development of new legal instruments concerning government intelligence activity,[175] the restitution of lands to victims of the Colombian internal conflict,[176] and the reform of several laws in relation to the protection of citizens' rights and access to justice.[177] The Andean region is also cooperating in the fight against drugs. In 1995 it was the first regional organisation to institute a

---

[174]EU, Council Decision of 31 May 2012 on the signing, on behalf of the Union, and provisional application of the Trade Agreement between the European Union and its Member States, of the one part, and Colombia and Peru, of the other part, *Official Journal of the European Union*, L 354. Vol. 55, 21 December 2012, p. 1.

[175]Colombia, Ley n. 1621 'Por medio de la cual se expiden normas para fortalecer el marco jurídico que permite a los organismos que llevan a cabo actividades de Inteligencia y contrainteligencia cumplir con su misión constitucional y legal, y se dictan otras disposiciones', 17 April 2013.

[176]Colombia, Ley de Víctimas y Restitución de Tierras, n. 1448, 10 June 2011.

[177]Colombia, Ley de Seguridad Ciudadana, n. 1453, 24 June 2011.

specialised dialogue on drugs, consisting of periodic meetings of high-level technical experts on the subject with the EU.[178] This dialogue has produced positive developments in the Andean region which has adopted new legal instruments dealing with anti-narcotics,[179] and more generally with issues of development, poverty reduction and social cohesion related to drugs.[180]

For the Andean Community, the EU is the second largest trading partner after the US, as trade with the EU was worth 14.3 % of the total trade of the Andean Community in 2010, while for the EU the Andean Group ranks place 29 among the EU's main trade partners. In 2008, EU- Andean trade was US\$ 17.92 billion. EU's imports from CAN (US\$ 11 billion in 2008) are raw materials, concentrating on some key sectors notably agriculture and mining. The only exception is Venezuela, which sells primarily oil and four related products to the EU. EU exports to CAN (US\$ 6.92 billion in 2008) are mainly manufactured goods, especially machinery and chemical products. The EU grants Andean countries a preferential access to its market under the EU's Generalised System of Preferences Plus (GSP+).[181] The EU is the leading investor in the CAN, accounting for more than a quarter of total foreign direct investment in the region. EU direct investment in the Andean Community has significantly increased in the last few years, with EU companies taking part in privatisation processes of services, in the financial system, manufacturing, mining and oil activities.

However, the negotiations and dialogue between the EU and the CAN go beyond the pure economic and commercial dimension. They also include social, political and governance forms of cooperation that are considered to be an essential dimension of integration policies. The EU has stressed this element in a series of meetings not only with the CAN but also with other partners in Latin America,[182] as part of its approach to external relations in the region.[183]

---

[178]EU drugs strategy for the period 2005–2012 was endorsed by the European Council of 16–17 December 2004, and for the period 2013–2020 on 7 December 2012, *Official Journal of the European Union* C402/1, 29 December 2012.

[179]CAN, Andean Council of Foreign Ministers enlarged by the Titular Representatives to the Andean Community Commission, Decision 602 "Andean Regulations for the Control of Chemical Substances used in the Illegal Manufacture of Narcotic Drugs and Psychotropic Substances", Cuzco, 6–7 December 2004.

[180]CAN, Andean Council of Foreign Ministers, Decision 614 'Andean Integral and Sustainable Alternative Development Strategy', 15 July 2005.

[181]The "GSP+" enhanced preference means full removal of tariffs on the same product categories as those covered by the general arrangement. These are granted to countries which ratify and implement international conventions relating to human and labour rights, environment and good governance. On 1 January 2014, the new GSP preferences under EU Regulation 978/2012 started to apply.

[182]Santander 2005.

[183]Grugel 2004.

5.8 Reform of the Andean Community

The structure of the CAN has sometimes been criticised for its bureaucratic nature and heavy dependence on the will of Heads of State of the member countries. This has led very recently to proposals for the reform of the AIS structure and functions.

The initiative started as a proposal of the APC discussed in two meetings held in 2011.[184] In 2012 the plan was discussed by the Andean Council of Foreign Ministers jointly with the Andean Community Commission which adopted a specific decision[185] for the purpose of restructuring the Andean System and led to the establishment of a joint study group for the reform entrusted to the Economic Commission for America and Caribbean (CEPAL) to evaluate the thematic aspects and to the Getúlio Vargas Foundation[186] to evaluate the institutional aspects of the reform. The results of this study were officially presented during the XXXVI meeting of the Andean Council of Foreign Ministers jointly with the Andean Community Commission on 15 June 2013, which established also an ad hoc Working Group.[187] In September 2013 the same two organs discussed the suggested reforms and the comments made by an ad hoc Working Group, and adopted a decision[188] concerning priority areas of reform and the creation of a High Level Group[189] of the CAN to elaborate proposals for the specific implementation of the reform. The main ideas included the reduction of existing Committees which often replicate other work and are mainly bureaucratic structures with limited decisional powers[190]; the abolition, through a new protocol,[191] of the Andean Parliament, as it is an organ without any specific power and decision-making authority.

According to the initial proposal, the Parliament should be integrated into the existing South American Parliament, within the UNASUR, but it is not yet specified in which way. At the same time, it is stressed that the reform should increase the powers and functions of other institutions created by the CAN. In particular,

---

[184]The meetings were held in Lima on 28 July and in Bogotá on 8 November 2011.

[185]CAN, Consejo Andino de Ministros de Relaciones Exteriores en Reunión Ampliada con la Comisión de la Comunidad Andina, Decisión 773, Reingeniería del Sistema Andino de Integración, Lima, 31 July 2012, GOAC, N. 2077.

[186]The Getúlio Vargas Foundation is a Brazilian higher education and think tank, see http://portal.fgv.br/en (11 October 2014).

[187]CAN, Consejo Andino de Ministros de Relaciones Exteriores en Reunión Ampliada con la Comisión de la Comunidad Andina, Decisión 791, Lima, 15 June 2013.

[188]CAN, Consejo Andino de Ministros de Relaciones Exteriores en Reunión Ampliada con la Comisión de la Comunidad Andina, Decisión 792, Lima, 19 September 2013. The Annex to this document also contains the proposals formulated by the ad hoc Working Group.

[189]Idem., Article 1.

[190]Idem., Article 3.

[191]Idem., Article 2.

the Development Bank of Latin America (*Corporación Andina de Fomento*, CAF) which was established in 1969 as a CAN institution.[192] Now it has grown to include eighteen member states from Latin America, the Caribbean and Europe and private banks,[193] which make it the main sources of multilateral financing in the region. Other institutions that may need some reform include the *Fondo Latinoamericano de Reservas* (Latin American Reserves Fund), which supports the balance of payments of member countries by granting loans or guaranteeing third-party loans, the *Organismo Andino de Salud* (Andean Health Agency— Hipólito Unanue Agreement),[194] and the Andean University Simón Bolívar.[195]

More relevant, from the legal institutional point of view, there is a request to strengthen the dispute resolution mechanisms in the region and the possible reform of the Court of Justice of the Andean Community.[196] The reform also tries to reinforce the mechanisms that may be needed to promote the institutional cooperation with UNASUR and Mercosur.[197]

5.9 Conclusion

It is possible to affirm that in the American continent, the Andean Community represents the most developed system of integration at sub-regional level. Compared to other existing examples, the process and the aims of the organisation go beyond the economic and commercial integration, and include a variety of other areas, such as political, cultural and social cooperation and development. There is a well-established institutional structure with organs and mechanisms which have operated for more than 30 years. The legal system also foresees a legal order that is showing its effects directly into the legal orders of member states and an international court which is in charge of the application of legal obligations within the

---

[192]CAF, Agreement Establishing: *Corporación Andina de Fomento*, Bogotá, 7 February 1968, at http://www.caf.com/media/3610/ConvenioConstitutivoingles.pdf. Accessed 18 October 2014.

[193]Its shareholders are: Bolivia, Colombia, Ecuador, Peru,Venezuela, Argentina, Brazil, Chile, Costa Rica, Spain, Jamaica, Mexico, Panama, Paraguay, Dominican Republic, Trinidad & Tobago, Uruguay and 16 private banks of the region.

[194]Hipólito Unanue Agreement on Cooperation on Health in the Andean Area Countries, Lima, 18 December 1971, at: http://www.orasconhu.org/documentos/REMSAA-I-1.pdf. Accessed 11 November 2014. The incorporation of the Hipólito Unanue Agreement into the CAN institutional structure was realised by Decision 445, approved by the Andean Council of Foreign Affairs Ministers on 10 August 1998. The Andean Council of Foreign Minister, with Decions 528 (7 July 2002), changed the name of the Hipólito Unanue Convention on Cooperation on Health in the Andean Area Countries into Andean Health Body—Hipólito Unanue Convention.

[195]CAN, Decisión 792, note 188 above, Article 5.

[196]CAF, Articles of Agreement, Bogota, 7 February, 1968 at: http://www.caf.com/media/1412720/agreement-establishment-caf-march-2012.pdf. Accessed 22 October 2014.

[197]CAN, Decisión 792, note 188 above, Article 6.

member states. These are relevant developments in the region which may provide further processes of integration and enhance the existing institutions in the region.

The CAN is also actively involved, as an international organisation with legal personality, in the negotiations with other States and organisations within the American continent and beyond, as in the case of the EU.

However, if compared to the EU the integration and supranational character of the CAN is quite different. On paper the organisation tries to express the supranational character of its purpose, but the institutional structure and the decision-making processes show a much more intergovernmental nature. The only two allegedly supranational institutions, the Secretariat and the Andean Parliament, have limited powers in relation to legislative action. The Secretary General is elected by unanimity by the Ministers of Foreign Affairs and the Commission. The legislative initiatives of the Secretary General must be sent to the two previous organs which are controlled by member states.[198] The Andean Parliament, despite the reform and its direct election since 2003, has no autonomous or shared law-making powers and therefore it does not directly intervene in the law-making process.[199]

Apart from the institutional weakness of the supranational structures, the political background, as in any integration policy and institution, is an essential element that would determine the effective success of this organisation. The past experience has shown that changes of governments in one or more of the member states have determined periods of crisis and stagnation in the process of integration. Nationalistic approaches by certain governments have limited the expansion of the institutional structures in the region and in the rest of Latin America.

There are still problems in relation to adequate levels of participation of the civil society in the institutional framework, mainly due to the experience of authoritarian regimes in the region which did not facilitate a gradual development of different types of civil society organisations. The adoption of human rights standards and the commitment to democratic governance which has been stressed in the American continent in the last few years will need specific incorporation in the working structures and processes that are established in the CAN and other sub-regional mechanisms. These developments would certainly contribute to a wider support of national institutions and individuals for the development of community structures at regional level.

References

Adkisson R V (2003) The Andean Group: Institutional Evolution, Intraregional Trade, and Economic Development. Journal of Economic Issues 37(2): 371–379
Alter K J and Helfer L R (2011) Legal Integration in the Andes: Law-Making by the Andean Tribunal of Justice. European Law Journal 17(5): 701–715

---

[198]CA, Article 30(c).

[199]Ibid., Article 43(d).

Alter K J, Helfer L R, Saldías O (2012) Transplanting the European Court of Justice: The Experience of the Andean Tribunal of Justice. American Journal of Comparative Law 60(3): 629–664

Avery W P and Cochrane J D (1972) Subregional Integration in Latin America: the Andean Common Market. *Journal of Common Market Studies* XI(1): 85–102

Bushnell D (1993) The Making of Modern Colombia: A Nation in Spite of Itself. University of California Press, Berkeley and Los Angeles

Dabène O (2009) The Politics of Regional Integration in Latin America: Theoretical and Comparative Explorations. Palgrave Macmillan, New York

Garcia B (2011) The Amazon from an International Law Perspective. Cambridge University Press, New York

Grugel J B (2004) New Regionalism and Modes of Governance—Comparing US and EU Strategies in Latin America. European Journal of International Relations 10(4): 603–626

Helfer L R and Alter K J (2009) The Andean Tribunal of Justice and Its Interlocutors: Understanding Preliminary Reference Patterns in the Andean Community. New York University Journal of International Law & Politics 41: 871–930

Huybrechts H and Peels R (2009) Civil Society and EU Development Policies in Africa and Latin America. In Orbie J and Tortell L (eds) The European Union and the Social Dimension of Globalization. Routledge, Abingdon 2009, pp. 207–227

Jiménez W G (2013) Papel de la jurisprudencia del Tribunal de Justicia de la Comunidad Andina en decisiones judiciales de los países miembros. International Law: Revista Colombiana de Derecho Internacional 23: 87–118

Londoño Sánchez J O (1989) Las elecciones directas en los Parlamentos regionales: el caso del Parlamento Andino. Integración Latinoamericana 146-147: 28–39

Middlebrook K J (1978) Regional Organizations and Andean Economic Integration. Journal of Common Market Studies XVII(1): 62–82

Malamud A (2013) Overlapping Regionalism, No Integration: Conceptual Issues and the Latin American Experiences. EUI Working Paper, RSCAS – 2013/20, European University Institute, San Domenico di Fiesole

Molano Cruz G (2007) Actores y estructuras del interregionalismo Unión Europea-Comunidad Andina. Revista Mexicana de Sociología 69(4): 571–591

O'Keefe T A (1996) How the Andean Pact transformed itself into a friend of Foreign Enterprise. Int'l Lawyer 30: 811–824

Quindimil López J A (2006) Instituciones y Derecho de la Comunidad Andina. Tirant Lo Blanch/IUEE Universidad de La Coruña, Valencia

Rodríguez Mendoza M (1998) The Andean Community in Motion: A progress Report. II Annual Conference Trade and Investment in the Americas, Washington, DC

Rodríquez. Mendoza M and Kotschwar B, Low P (eds) (1999) Trade Rules in the Making: Challenges in Regional and Multilateral Negotiations. Organization of American States and Brookings Institution Press, Washington, DC pp. 89–105

Saldías O (2014) The Judicial Politics of Economic Integration: The Andean Court as an Engine of Development. Routledge, Abingdon

Salmón Gárate E et al (2003) Derecho Comunitario Andino. Pontificia Universidad Católica del Perú, Lima

Santander S (2005) The European Partnership with Mercosur: a Relationship Based on Strategic and Neo–liberal Principles. Journal of European Integration 27(3): 285–306

Simmons B A (2005) Forward-Looking Dispute Resolution: Ecuador, Peru, and the Border Issue. In Zartman I W and Kremenyuk V (eds), Peace Versus Justice: Negotiating Forward- and Backward-looking Outcomes. Rowman & Littlefield, Lanham, MD, pp. 243–263

Taccone J J and Nogueira U (eds) (2002) Andean Report, vol 1, IDB-INTAL, Buenos Aires

Vargas-Hidalgo R (1979) The crisis of the Andean Pact: lessons for Integration among Developing Countries. Journal of Common Market Studies XVII(3): 213–226

Xenias A (2006) Andean Community. In: Vaidya A K (ed), Globalization: Encyclopedia of Trade, Labor, and Politics, vol. 1. ABC-CLIO, Santa Barbara (US), pp. 453–459

Chapter 6
The Southern Common Market (Mercosur)

Francesco Seatzu

Abstract This chapter looks at various issues related to Mercosur. It evaluates some of its key characteristics and provides an outline of its historical background, internal structure and functioning. It takes the EU and NAFTA as points of reference where indispensable, since a conceptual comparison between a Mercosur-type free trade area and a NAFTA-type free trade area or an EU-model customs union may demonstrate the relative uniformity of these types of trading conglomerates but also their functional and taxonomic diversities. The second part of the chapter (Sects. 6.5–6.8) assesses Mercosur's main achievements and shortcomings in the areas of socio-economic cooperation and sub-regional integration. It also endeavours to assess Mercosur's effectiveness in the achievement of its objectives and, where possible, will discuss, from an international legal perspective, the latest developments in Mercosur. Finally, it concludes with a summary and thesis of the chapter.

Keywords Common market of the southern cone · Latin American cooperation · NAFTA · Treaty of Ouro Preto · Protocol of Olivos

Contents

F. Seatzu (✉)
International and European Union Law, University of Cagliari, Cagliari, Italy
e-mail: seatzu@hotmail.com

© T.M.C. ASSER PRESS and the authors 2015
M. Odello and F. Seatzu (eds.), *Latin American and Caribbean International Institutional Law*, DOI 10.1007/978-94-6265-069-5_6

6.1 Introduction

When one starts to describe the Common Market of the Southern Cone, commonly known as Mercosur,[1] one is immediately confronted with several contradictory aspects that give an interesting picture of this institution within the framework of Latin American cooperation and the integration process.[2] For many years now, an increasing number of people have voiced doubts about the future of the Mercosur, the main arguments used being, respectively: (a) the inability of this relatively small institution that only has four member states to compete with the other world's largest trade areas and main international economic institutions (NAFTA, EU and Japan)[3]; (b) the economic asymmetries among the members of Mercosur (two strong countries and two not so strong ones)[4]; (c) the protectionism practices imposed by its members[5]; and last but not least the continuing disputes between Argentina and Brazil.[6] Without subscribing to or denying the foundation of these arguments, it is clear that the same could be said 'mutatis mutandis' about the Community of Latin American and Caribbean States (CELAC)[7] and the Caribbean Community and Common Market (CARICOM).[8] Instead the contrary is true, and the activities of Mercosur

---

[1]Treaty Establishing a Common Market, Asunción, 26 March 1991, entered into force 1 January 1995, Argentina, Brazil, Paraguay and Uruguay, UN Doc. A/46/155 (1991); 30 ILM 1041 (hereinafter the 'Treaty of Asunción' or the 'Establishing Treaty').

[2]On the Latin American cooperation and integration process, see among others Barbosa 1991, p. 200 ff; Haines-Ferrari 1993, p. 413 ff.

[3]See: Hummel and Lohaus 2011, p. 71 ff; Giordano 2002, p. 20 ff.

[4]See: Hijazi 2012, p. 30 ff, also stressing that the smaller countries have a greater dependence that the bigger partners on neighbouring countries' markets.

[5]See: Bouga 2013, p. 15 ff. See also Bouzas et al. 2002 who stress that: 'The worsening macroeconomic environment during 2001 led the Argentine government to implement additional restrictions and discriminatory practices (including a two-tiered foreign exchange system and sector "competitiveness agreements" based on tax-breaks and other incentives)'.

[6]See: Carranza 2003, p. 67 ff.

[7]See: Santulli 2012.

[8]See: O'Brien 2008.

have been so successful in the first 15 years of its existence[9] that its seems justified to describe this institution in the present volume, which is dedicated to the understanding and functioning of the American sub-regional organizations. Indeed, Mercosur has generated many great achievements since 1990, more than any other economic integration organization in Latin America.[10] It has formalized and expanded cooperation and trading relationships among Brazil, Argentina, Paraguay and Uruguay, and has developed these relationships into a viable and vibrant economic integration framework.[11] For a substantial period of time, its members enjoyed unprecedented expanded trade and greater prosperity.[12] As discussed below, it has agreed on a common external tariff encompassing 85 % of the items currently being traded by its members and has reached consensus on a significant number of trade issues.[13] Moreover, Mercosur has enacted several measures to remove barriers to free trade and to harmonize the legal and regulatory systems of the member states[14]; it has persuaded the elites of its member states that the idea of economic integration is both feasible and desirable[15]; it has an agenda for the future and is working towards its enforcement[16]; it has created an awareness in the private sectors of the member states of new regional export markets; and it has enhanced diversification and new investments.[17]

The way Mercosur operates makes it more an organization, rather than an economic agreement. It has a financial character, a legal personality of international law, it can negotiate and sign treaties with third countries, groups of countries and international organizations, according to its establishing agreement as revised by the 1994 Treaty of Ouro Preto.[18] But when we look at the circumstances that Mercosur lacks 'rules for rule-making', influence regarding

---

[9]See Schelhase 2011, p. 175 ff; Malamud 2005.

[10]See: Pang and Jarnagin 2009, p. 99 ff.

[11]See: Toscano et al. 2010, Introduction, p. 1 ff.

[12]See: Grimoldi 2005.

[13]See: Fuders 2010.

[14]*Amplius* Devlin 2000, p. 6 ff.

[15]See, among others, Foders 1996, p. 4 ff.

[16]See: Porrata-Doria 2005, p. 80 ff.

[17]See: Guira 2003, p. 114 ff.

[18]Additional Protocol to the Treaty of Asunción on the Institutional Structure of Mercosur. 17 December 1994, (1994) 34 ILM, 1244 (hereinafter Protocol of Ouro Preto). Article 34 of the 1994 Treaty of Ouro Preto reads as follows: 'Mercosur shall possess legal personality of international law'. Article 35, sets out the limits of that personality, and Article 36 allows Mercosur to establish headquarters agreements.

Mercosur's instruments,[19] independence from its member states,[20] and a method for the political handling of national diversity,[21] it becomes evident that Mercosur is not a proper organization either: like other economic treaties such as AFTA,[22] NAFTA,[23] EFTA[24] and CAFTA,[25] the first and main objective of Mercosur is trade liberalization, more precisely the creation of a free trade area between its members (Argentina, Brazil, Venezuela, Urugay and Paraguay) and the implementation of a sui generis common market.[26]

This chapter seeks to examine in brief a selected number of the basic issues of Mercosur. It evaluates some of its key characteristics and provides a short outline of its historical background, internal structure and functioning. It takes the EU and NAFTA as points of reference where indispensable, since a conceptual comparison between a Mercosur-type free trade area and a NAFTA-type free trade area or an EU-model customs union may demonstrate the relative uniformity of these types of trading conglomerates but also their functional and taxonomic diversities. The second part of the chapter (Sects. 6.5–6.8) assesses Mercosur's main achievements and shortcomings in the areas of socio-economic cooperation and sub-regional integration. It also endeavours to assess Mercosur's effectiveness in the achievement of its objectives and, where possible, will discuss, from an international legal perspective, the latest developments in Mercosur. Finally, it concludes with a summary and thesis of the chapter.

---

[19]See, among others, Bouzas 2003, p. 40 ff; Kaltenthaler and Mora 2002.

[20]As describes below in Sect. 6.4, Mercosur's institutions, with the exception of a very small Administrative Secretariat, are all member-state based. The members of the various institutions and their staff are representatives of the governments of the member states and are subject to their government's authority and direction. Member states have not delegated a substantial amount of power to the organization's institutions. Furthermore, no institution equivalent to the EU Commission or its extensive bureaucracy is in charge of identifying, implementing or enforcing the Mercosur rules and agenda.

[21]See Sect. 6.4.

[22]Agreement Establishing the ASEAN-Australia New Zealand Free Trade Area, at: http://asean.fta. govt.nz/assets/Agreement-Establishing-the-ASEAN-Australia-New-Zealand-Free-Trade-Area.pdf. Accessed 3 June 2014.

[23]North American Free Trade Between the Government of Canada, the Government of Mexico and the Government of the United States, 17 December 1992, CTS 1994-No. 2; (1992) 32 ILM, 605 (entered into force 1 January 1994).

[24]Agreement of the European Economic Area, OJ No L 1, 3 January 1994, p. 3.

[25]The full text of the Agreement may be found on the website of the United States Representatives, http://www.ustr.gov. Accessed 10 June 2014.

[26]Article 1, para 1 of the Treaty of Asunción states that: 'The States Parties hereby decide to establish a common market, which shall be in place by 31 December 1994 and shall be called the "Common Market of the Southern Cone" (MERCOSUR)'.

6.2 The History of Mercosur

The negotiations for Mercosur started in Paraguay in March 1991.[27] An integration scheme which involves the economic might of Argentina, along with the vast resources of Brazil, is of special importance in the first place, but it was the incorporation of three other Latin American states, Uruguay, Paraguay[28] in this equation that added a further dimension to the issue: it made it possible to create an ambitious project, both in terms of the level of integration (a potential market of over 200 million people and with an added GDP of about 1 trillion dollars)[29] and the scope of integration (a geographical area of about 12 million km).[30] If successful, the agreement promised to make Mercosur 'the Common Market of the Twenty-First Century',[31] as well as a mechanism of democratic consolidation in the sub-region and it might even set a precedent for trade and economic cooperation between the Latin American and Caribbean states.

Mercosur took effect on 1 January 1995. It provided a new set of regulations to cover foreign direct investments and trade among the regional partners and consequently it drastically diminished the cost of thousands of imported services and products.[32] It not only gradually removed all trade barriers but also committed member states to the coordination of policies on agriculture, industry, transport, finance, and monetary affairs.[33] The intention of all member countries was to conclude a trade agreement that would lead to an integrated market for goods as well as most services and factors of production, and provide for greater mobility for professional and business travelers.[34] In order to achieve this, they decided to establish a Common External Tariff (CET) and the undertaking of a common trade policy, including the coordination of macroeconomic policies among member countries in different areas such as foreign trade, agriculture, industry, fiscal and monetary issues, foreign exchange and capital, services, customs, transport and communications. After the Treaty of Asunción, usually referred as the 'Treaty Framework', the next step in the integration process occurred when the Protocol of Ouro Preto was signed on December 16, 1994.[35] This Protocol amended the Treaty of Asunción with regard to the institutional structures of the economic bloc, transforming Mercosur from a free trade area to a customs union.[36]

---

[27]However, Brazil and Argentina started conversations for greater regional cooperation that were formalized in the *Declaração de Iguaçu* in 1985. On this issue, see: Gardini 2010. See also Alterini and Favier Dubois 1996, p. 320 ff.

[28]Paraguay was suspended from Mercosur in July 2012, following a decision from Argentina, Brazil, Uruguay and Venezuela. Venezuela officially joined the Mercosur in July 2006.

[29]See: Mye and Palagonia 1996, pp. 17–18.

[30]Ibidem, p. 17.

[31]See: Porrata-Doria 2004.

[32]See: Busse et al. 2004.

[33]See: Fuders 2010, p. 87 ff.

[34]See: Mansueti 2010.

[35]Protocol of Ouro Preto, Ouro Preto, Brazil, 17 December 1994, (1995) 34 ILM 1245.

[36]See: Pérez Otermin 1995, p. 15 ff; Teubal Alhadeff 1995, p. 1244 ff.

Finally, in 1996, after extensive, lengthy (and often complex) negotiations, Mercosur entered into economic complementation agreements,[37] first with Chile[38] and then with Bolivia.[39] According to these agreements, Chile and Bolivia[40] are not full but only 'associate members' of Mercosur.[41] One could thus distinguish, theoretically, member states in the following categories: member states having ratified the Treaty of Asunción and the Protocols of Ouro Preto, Brasilia[42] and Olivos[43]; member states not having ratified them; founding members; non-founding members; and, finally, 'associate members'. With the exception of the associated states, although these distinctions may be important from a legal point of view they are fortunately almost purely theoretical and have no real practical bearing.

Besides that, Mercosur has had some relationships with the European Community/EU almost since the beginning of its existence.[44] An interinstitutional cooperation agreement was entered into between Mercosur and the EU in May 1992 and the EU has provided substantial economic and technical assistance to Mercosur since then.[45] This relationship was substantially formalized and expanded by an interregional framework agreement on cooperation, which was signed in December 1995.[46]

---

[37]These agreements establish relationships which have as primary goals the establishment of a free trade area with Chile and Bolivia within a period of 10 years, the creation of judicial institutional frameworks for economic integration and cooperation, the promotion of economic, scientific, technological and energy cooperation and complementation, the promotion of reciprocal investment, and the promotion of the development of physical infrastructure facilities. See Rafael A. Porrata-Doria 2005, p. 124 also stressing that: 'These relationships are very carefully enumerated and described in the agreements, and are administered and implemented by a separate Administrative Committee for each, and not by any of the Mercosur institutions'.

[38]*Acuerdo de Complementación Económica Mercosur—Chile* (ACE No 35) signed in Potrero de los Funes, 25 June 1996, reproduced in Santos Belandro 2001.

[39]*Acuerdo de complementación Económica Mercosur—Bolivia* (ACE No 36) done in Fortaleza, 17 December 1996, reproduced in Santos Belandro, 2001.

[40]On December 2012 Bolivian President Evo Morales subscribed the Mercosur incorporation protocol which makes it the sixth member of the regional group.

[41]For a criticism of the qualification of Chile and Bolivia as 'associate members' of Mercosur, see Borba Casella 2000, p. 120 ff.

[42]Protocol of Brasilia for the Settlement of Disputes. 17 December 1991, (1991) 36 ILM 691 [hereinafter Protocol of Brasilia].

[43]Olivos Protocol for the Settlement of Disputes in Mercosur. 18 February 2002, (2002) 42 ILM 2 [hereinafter Protocol of Olivos].

[44]See Arnaud 1996, p. 22 ff.

[45]Memorandum of Understanding between the European Community and Mercosur Concerning the Multiannual Guidelines for the Implementation of Community Cooperation (Annex to the Mercosur-European Community Regional Strategy Paper (2002–2006) issued by the European Commission (External Relations Directorate General) 10 September 2002.

[46]Interregional Framework Cooperation Agreement between the European Community and its Member States, of the one part, and the Southern Common Market and its Party States, of the other part—Joint Declaration on political dialogue between the European Union and Mercosur, OJ L 69, 19 March 1996, pp. 4–22.

6.3 The Aims of Mercosur

The rationale behind the creation of the Mercosur is indicated in Article 1 of the Treaty of Asunción and is not without legal significance,[47] as is clear from a number of Mercosur arbitral awards which have stressed its importance with respect to the scope of the new institution,[48] its status as successor to the Latin American Free Trade Association (LAFTA)[49] and as an aid to interpretation in construing certain substantive provisions in the various additional protocols to the Treaty of Asunción.[50] The ultimate objectives of the Mercosur are threefold: the creation of a free trade area, of a customs union and of a common market for goods and services between the participants, showing that economic development is the number one regional priority.[51] In seeking to achieve these objectives, Mercosur should take into account the environment and the needs of the different sectors of the economy, based on the principles of gradualism, flexibility and balance.[52]

The means for achieving these objectives are reminiscent of those set out in the LAFTA[53] and the 1960 Treaty of Montevideo that establishes the organization that followed LAFTA, the Latin American Integration Association (ALADI),[54] on which they are substantially based, thereby reinforcing Mercosur as the successor

---

[47]The Treaty of Asunción includes five annexes that established: (a) an automatic, linear and generalized program of elimination of intra-zone tariffs, (b) a system of rules of origin, (c) a transitory system of intra-zone safeguards, (d) a timeframe for the setting up of a dispute settlement mechanism and (e) ten working groups to promote the coordination of specific economic and sector policies. Annex I had to be fully incremented by 1994 (1995 for Paraguay and Uruguay) and the other Annexes were envisaged only for the transitory period until December 31st, 1994. For a fuller discussion of these issues, see: Bouzas et al. 2002.

[48]See Mercosur, Tribunal ad hoc, Laudo sobre Aplicación de Medidas Apropiadas para Prevenir y/o Hacer Cesar los Impedimentos a la Libre Circulación Derivados de los Cortes en Territorio Argentino de vías de Acceso a los Puentes Internacionales Gral. San Martín y Gral. Artigas (Uruguay v. Argentina), 6 September 2006, at: http://www.sice.oas.org/dispute/mercosur/laudo%20 librecirculacion_006_s.pdf. Accessed 10 June 2013.

[49]Comunicados No. 37 del 17 de diciembre de 1997 y No. 7 del 20 de febrero de 1998 del Departamento de Operaciones de Comercio Exterior (DECEX) de la Secretaría de Comercio Exterior ('SECEX') [Case Concerning Import Licenses imposed by Brazil (Communications DECEX 37/97 and 7/98)] (Arg.-Braz.). 9 B.O. del Mercosur 227, 248 (Tribunal Ad Hoc del Mercosur 1999).

[50]See e.g. Aplicación de Medidas de Salvaguardia Sobre Productos Textiles [Application of Safeguard Measures to Textile Products] (Braz. v. Arg.), 13 B.O. del Mercosur 117. 118 (Tribunal Ad Hoc del Mercosur 2000); 29. Obstáculos al Ingreso de Productos Fitosanitarios Argentinos en el Mercado Brasileño [Obstacles to the Import of Argentine Phytosanitary Products into the Brazilian Market] (Arg. v. Braz.), 21 B.O. del Mercosur 221, 223 (Tribunal Ad Hoc del Mercosur 2002).

[51]See, amongst others, Domínguez and Guedes de Oliveira 2004, p. 142 ff.

[52]Preamble to the Treaty of Asunción (fourth recital), available at: http://idatd.eclac.cl/controvers ias/Normativas/MERCOSUR/Ingles/Treaty_of_Asuncion.pdf. Accessed 3 May 2014.

[53]For a clear exposition of these objectives see: León Li 2011, 8 ff.

[54]On the ALADI see Opertti Badán 2006.

to the former LAFTA treaty regime.[55] The legal instruments that are to be employed in achieving the Mercosur objectives may be summarized as the continued agreement among members on substantial reduction of tariffs and other obstacles to trade[56] and the reduction of discriminatory barriers, in particular to services trade.[57] While both these aims endorse the practice of the Contracting Parties with respect to substantive and procedural provisions under the former LAFTA treaty regime, thereby ensuring a certain continuity of practice and principles in Mercosur, there is no reference in the overall aims to institutional continuity and that is since there simply was none, at least in the formal sense of the term.

Instead, the institutional rationale for the organization is set out for the first time in the Preamble of the Treaty of Asunción where it is stated that Mercosur: 'shall *provide the institutional framework for the promotion of* the scientific and technological development of the States Parties and to modernize their economies in order to expand the supply and improve the quality of available goods and services, with a view to enhancing the living conditions of their populations' (emphasis added).[58] However, a reading of the Treaty of Asunción shows that the initial organic structure of Mercosur was far too modest to achieve this. Indeed, the Treaty of Asunción created only a Common Market Council and a Common Market Group.[59] Based on Article 18 of the Treaty of Asunción, the institutional structure of Mercosur was further elaborated in the 1994 Protocol of Ouro Preto.[60]

---

[55]This is so even though Article 8, para 1 of the Treaty of Asunción provides that: 'The States Parties undertake to abide by commitments made prior to the date of signing of this Treaty, including agreements signed in the framework of the Latin American Integration Association (ALADI), and to coordinate their positions in any external trade negotiations they may undertake during the transitional period'.

[56]See e.g. Article 5 of the Treaty of Asunción which provides that: 'During the transition period, which shall last from the entry into force of this Treaty until 31 December 1994, the main instruments for putting in place the common market shall be:

(a) A trade liberalization programme, which shall consist of progressive, linear and automatic tariff reductions accompanied by the elimination of non-tariff restrictions or equivalent measures, as well as any other restrictions on trade between the States Parties, with a view to arriving at a zero tariff and no non- tariff restrictions for the entire tariff area by 31 December 1994 (Annex I);

(b) The coordination of macroeconomic policies, which shall be carried out gradually and in parallel with the programmes for the reduction of tariffs and the elimination of non-tariff restrictions referred to in the preceding paragraph;

(c) A common external tariff which encourages the foreign competitiveness of the States Parties;

(d) The adoption of sectoral agreements in order to optimize the use and mobility of factors of production and to achieve efficient scales of operation' (emphasis added).

[57]See: Stephenson S M and Contreras P (1999), An asymmetric approach to services liberalization: the European Union-Mercosur case (Paper produced in the framework of the Working Group on EU-Mercosur negotiations of the Mercosur Chair of Sciences Po., Paris), p. 20, available at: at: http://www.sedi.oas.org/DTTC/TRADE/PUB/STAFF_ARTICLE/steph01_asym.asp. Accessed 3 March 2014.

[58]Treaty of Asunción, Preamble, eight recital, n. 52 above.

[59]See: Domínguez and Guedes de Oliveira 2004, p. 151.

[60]See Sect. 6.4.

The approach taken in the Treaty of Asunción of describing the organization's mandate in terms of its functions follows the approach taken by the drafters of the LAFTA in 1960.[61] The Mercosur has five functions that are explicitly laid down in Article 1 of the Treaty of Asunción.

The first function is set out in para 1 of Article 1, where it is stated that Mercosur shall aims to: 'promote the free movement of goods, services and factors of production between countries through, inter alia, the elimination of customs duties and non-tariff restrictions on the movement of goods, and any other equivalent measures'. Implicit in the wording of this provision is the idea of Mercosur as a deep integration project that would evolve.[62] Confirmation is in Article 18 of the Treaty of Asunción which provides that: 'Prior to the establishment of the common market on 31 December 1994, the States Parties shall convene a special meeting to determine the final institutional structure of the administrative organs of the common market, as well as the specific powers of each organ and its decision-making procedures'. Indeed, under the Protocols of Ouro Preto and Olivos, seven institutions were charged with enforcing Mercosur's principles and objectives. As indicated below, they include the Council of the Common Market (Council), the Common Market Group (Group), the Mercosur Commerce Commission (MCC), the Joint Parliamentary Commission, the Economic and Social Consultative Forum (Forum), the Administrative Secretariat (Secretariat), and the Permanent Appellate Tribunal ('Tribunal').[63]

The second function of Mercosur is to operate as a customs union, through the introduction of a 'common external tariff' that: 'encourages the foreign competitiveness of the States Parties'.[64] The wording 'common external tariff' in Article 1 of the Treaty of Asunción clearly matches well with the other functions of the institution that are summarized therein and in particular with the promotion of the free movement of goods, services and factors of production. Indeed, a 'customs shock treatment'[65] that is a reduction in current tariff and non-tariff import controls is essential to enhance and liberalize trade in goods and services between member countries.[66] This is since tariffs normally reduce the international demand for the import-good and service.[67] However, the idea of introducing a 'common

---

[61]For further details concerning the aims and structure of the LAFTA see: O'Keefe 2009, p. 5 ff.

[62]*Amplius* Lorenzo and Vaillant, 2005, p. 2 ff.

[63]See Sect. 6.4.

[64]Treaty of Asunción, Article 5, para 1(c).

[65]See: F Peña, El MERCOSUR y sus perspectivas: una opción por la inserción competitiva mundial, (Paper delivered at the seminar on the outlook for sub-regional integration processes in Latin America and South America, held in Brussels, 4–5 November 1991), as quoted by Luiz Olavo Baptista, *Mercosur, its Institutions and Juridical Structure*, at: http://ctrc.sice.oas.org/geograph/south/mstit2_e.pdf. Accessed 17 June 2014.

[66]Ibidem.

[67]See: Olarreaga et al. 1999, p. 3; Estrella Faria 1993, p. 190.

external tariff' structure[68] looks a bit surprising if one considers that Mercosur is small in terms of world GDP and that the larger members of Mercosur (Argentina, Brazil and Venezuela) are sufficiently large trading countries per se to influence world prices,[69] at least in some markets.[70]

The third function of Mercosur is: 'the adoption of a common trade policy in relation to third States or groups of States'.[71] Since 'Mercosur may be summarized as first of all a customs union with a common trade policy' to use Finn Laursen's same words,[72] trade policy for goods and services is a core competence of this institution. Indeed, this is why since its adoption in 1995, Mercosur's trade policy has become one of its more important instruments. The reasons behind the enactment of a common trade policy are both clear and straightforward. Given the objective of a completed internal market in the Treaty of Asunción, with undistorted competition, a comprehensive common policy is a logical tool.[73] Moreover, a common trade policy may eliminate negative externalities, produced by disparate national trade policies in a Mercosur with free movement.[74] Furthermore, it may also help to introduce bargaining power and legal uniformity throughout the whole Mercosur area. However, it is also true that the trade policy of Mercosur members has been primarily driven by non-economic considerations rather than commercial pragmatism.

The fourth function, not less important than the previous ones, is the: 'co-ordination of positions in regional and international economic and commercial forums'.[75] A teleological reading of this expression hints at the conclusion that Mercosur's coordination role can be exercised in a variety of manners, including through participation as a permanent observer in the work of international organizations such as the WTO, ILO and UN. However, to date this status has not been accorded to Mercosur by any international economic organization.

The fifth function, which the Mercosur is said to fulfil, is the: 'co-ordination of macroeconomic and sectoral policies between the States Parties in the areas of foreign trade, agriculture, industry, fiscal and monetary matters, foreign exchange and capital, services, customs, transport and communications and any other areas

---

[68]A common external tariff structure was introduced in 1995, ranging from zero to 20 %. Capital goods and many electronic goods were not included in the common external tariff schedule, although tariffs were expected to converge by 2006 for some goods and some countries. See: Palva and Gazel 2013.

[69]Although Mercosur has successfully increased trade among its members, part of the trade flows within Mercosur were achieved by the economic policies of Brazil and Argentina, which were not primarily directed to trade integration but rather to macroeconomic stability. For a fuller discussion of these issues, see: Baer et al. 2002, p. 273.

[70]Ibidem, p. 5.

[71]Treaty of Asunción, Article 8(1).

[72]See: Laursen 2010, p. 251 ff.

[73]See: Harrison 2002, p. 26 ff.

[74]Ibidem.

[75]Treaty of Asunción, Article 1(1).

that may be agreed upon, in order to ensure proper competition between the States Parties'. It is clear that also this is an essential function for the institution. Conclusive evidence can be derived from the absence of macroeconomic and exchange rate coordination policies in Mercosur, since these have both been serious impediments to bringing the full potential trade benefits of a common market to the region.[76]

The sixth and last function of Mercosur is the goal to harmonize legislation: 'in the relevant areas, in order to complete the integration process'.[77] As seen below, the adoption of uniform laws or the harmonization of legislation, which the Treaty of Asunción's signatories committed themselves to apply and respect occurred in different ways, such as through cooperative treaties, of which a good example is the Protocol of Colonia on judicial cooperation where harmonized norms of procedure were adopted in order to simplify judicial proceedings.[78] If regarded in abstracto, such a duty to harmonize legislation is indeed not surprising or new, since the organization of a common market naturally implies the harmonization of the domestic legislation of the States parties.[79] But things radically change if consideration is given to the fact that: 'the laws of Mercosur countries are generally speaking harmonious, since they differ only in certain details, even though their norms are formally different'.[80]

6.4 The Functioning of Mercosur

Mercosur has a hierarchical structure at the apex of which stands the Consejo del Mercado Común (CMC), the highest political organ according to both Article 3 of the Protocol of Ouro Preto (POP) and Article 9 of the Treaty of Asunción.[81] At the

---

[76]Indeed it has caused substantial amounts of price and exchange rate fluctuations. For a fuller discussion of this issue, see: Arbuet-Vignali 2004, pp. 20–40.

[77]Treaty of Asunción, Article 1(1) also stresses the existence of a 'commitment by States Parties to harmonize their legislation in the relevant areas in order to strengthen the integration process'.

[78]See: Vervaele 2005a, who stresses that: '*Although* judicial cooperation is not expressly included in the Treaty, either as an objective or as an instrument [...] judicial cooperation within Mercosur, both in the private law and the criminal law sense, has been an important priority from the start' (emphasis added).

[79]In fact, 'an integration process means that certain domestic rules in each country will have to be set aside in favour of common norms of integration law, relating to the free circulation of goods. Therefore, a common customs zone implies the free circulation of goods and the absence of tariff and non-tariff barriers, and this requires legislative harmonization' (Palva and Gazel 2013).

[80]See: Palva and Gazel 2013, who also stress that: '[...] the norms governing contracts, for example, are no doubt harmonious, and it is difficult to pinpoint any aspects that differ significantly, since they all flow from the same root stock, which was Roman law'.

[81]See also Article 9 of the Treaty of Asunción that qualifies the CMC as: 'the highest organ of the Common Market, responsible for conducting its policy and for taking decisions to ensure fulfilment of the objectives and timetables established for constituting the common market'.

second level there are: the Grupo del Mercado Común (GMC), the executive branch of Mercosur that runs working groups and specialized meetings concerning the harmonization of technical product norms, the environment, agricultural matters, financial services, border control, tourism, etc.; the Comisión del Commercio del Mercosur (CCM) that has competence in specialized economic issues such as competition, procurement, customs, consumer protection, etc.; and also Mercosur's quasi-judicial institution, the Appellate Tribunal (charged with the administration of the dispute settlement system).[82] The third level consists of the institutions with purely advisory powers, such as the Comisión Parlamentaria Conjunta (CPC) and the Foro Consultivo Economico Social (FCES). Finally, at the fourth level is the administrative secretariat (SAM) which is a supporting secretariat that organizes meetings and handles documentation[83] and thus only has weak powers.[84]

Altogether, Mercosur comprises some 16 institutions that are charged with implementing Mercosur's aims and principles, of which five are standing bodies, whereas the remaining 11 or so bodies are ad hoc and include such bodies as the Work Subgroups or the Joint Parliamentary Committee.[85] With a few exceptions all the aforementioned bodies are bodies of the whole, in which there is equality of voting power among the members but where decisions are generally taken on the basis of consensus (unanimity can occur only if a vote is taken and if no negative vote is cast during the process).[86]

The institutional apparatus of the various Mercosur bodies and the separation of powers between them[87] clearly reflects a more general observation in international institutional law that the underlying relationship between several international organizations and their members is generally complex, even chaotic.[88] A fatal tension arises between states, as primary subjects of the international legal order, and as members of an international institution, that can lead to states aiming to control the ability of an international institution to act on the international level, at times showing how legal acts of the institutions can become identical to the acts of

---

[82]Article 10 of the POP.

[83]Article 31 et seq. of the POP.

[84]In 2002 it was decided to expand the Administrative Secretariat and turn it into a Technical Secretariat.

[85]A complete overview of the Mercosur institutional structure is available at: http://www.mercosur.int/t_generic.jsp?contentid=492&site=1&channel=secretaria&seccion=3. Accessed 15 September 2014.

[86]For a fuller discussion of this issue, see: Palva and Gazel 2013. On the subject, see also Olavo Baptista 1998, p. 10 ff; Kotabe 1997, p. 20 ff.

[87]See: Palva and Gazel 2013, who stresses the absence in Mercosur's organization of: '… the conventional tripartite division of functions such as we find in modern democratic states, and in many international organizations'.

[88]See: Klabbers 2001, p. 227. Accordingly see also Footer 2006, p. 41 ff.

individual participating members. Professor Klabbers has eloquently suggested that: '[T]his constant oscillation between the organization and its members has given rise to a rather volatile set of legal rules and principles' governing international organizations.[89]

Clearly inherent in this assertion is the reference to the internal legal order of an international institution that, according to Article 1, lett. j) of the 1986 Vienna Convention on the Law of Treaties between States and International Organisations or between International Organisations,[90] consists of 'constituent instruments, decisions and resolutions, adopted in accordance with them, and established practice of the organisation', that has been characterized by the International Law Commission (ILC) in its work on the law of international responsibility between States and International Organisations or between International Organisations as the internal law of international organisations.[91] In the case of Mercosur, the situation is volatile precisely since this institution *is* the members and does not always properly exist as an autonomous legal entity.[92] This is though, as indicated above, the Protocol of Ouro Preto explicitly establishes the legal personality of Mercosur.[93] Moreover, this is notwithstanding the fact that this institution has spent (and keeps on spending) large amounts of money, time and human assets to elaborate its legal system.[94] The efficacy of its internal law may only be determined against the practice of the members[95] and this will be recalled when examining in the subsequent paragraphs the competences of the institution exercised by various Mercosur bodies.[96]

Keeping this limitation in mind, we turn briefly to an examination of the main Mercosur bodies and analysis of their powers, including such issues as the foundation of those powers and the legal character of those powers, i.e. whether such powers are expressly attributed by means of treaty or are implied, and whether their conferral is by means of delegation or attribution.

---

[89]See: Klabbers 2001, p. 227.

[90]United Nations Conference on the Law of Treaties between States and International Organisations or between International Organisations A/CONF.129/16 (adopted 18 February–21 March 1986, not yet in force).

[91]See International Law Commission (ILC) 'Report of the International Law Commission on the Work of its 55th Session (5 May–6 June and 7 July–August 2003), UN Doc. A/58/10, 37 (note 33) and 48 (para 10).

[92]Incidentally, supporting evidence of this statement may be found in that the right of legislative initiative is exclusively in the hands of the States parties, which may submit proposals in the CMC, GMC, or CCM.

[93]See above.

[94]See: Duina 2006, p. 187, who also stresses that: 'overseeing the implementation of *its* legal system has also taken enormous quantities of resources'.

[95]See below Sects. 6.6 and 6.7.

[96]See: Footer 2006, p. 41 for similar remarks on the WTO.

6.4.1 The Consejo Del Mercado Común

The CMC is the main plenary body in the Mercosur and it meets at least twice a year. It engages in deliberations exclusively when all of its members are present, failing which such deliberations will be without effect.[97] Its composition and functions are set out in Articles 10–12 of the Treaty of Asunción, and these are substantially repeated in Articles 3–7 of the Protocol of Ouro Preto. The importance of the CMC in the overall Mercosur institutional structure flows from the circumstance that it is the highest decision-making authority, as explicitly indicated in the Treaty of Asunción.[98] Its primary task is to: '[…] conduct the policy of the integration process and to take decisions in order to ensure compliance with the objectives set forth in the Treaty of Asunción and for achieving the final constitution of the common market' on the basis of Article 3 the Protocol of Ouro Preto.[99] On the decision-making power of this body, the Protocol of Ouro Preto is explicit since it states that:

> The decisions adopted by the Mercosur organs provided for in Article 2 of this Protocol shall be binding and, when necessary, must be incorporated in the domestic legal systems in accordance with the procedures provided for in each country's legislation.[100]

The broad decision-making powers of the CMC have led to the adoption of various decisions in a wide range of fields, including judicial cooperation in private and criminal matters—though this was not expressly included in the Treaty of Asunción either as an objective or as a tool.[101]

There have been some questions as to whether on the basis of very broad, general powers the CMC is in a position to take decisions which are legally binding on Mercosur member states. This is since, as the Protocol of Ouro Preto states, the decisions of the CMC must be executed by the respective competent national bodies.[102] Indeed, the legal acts of Mercosur have neither immediate applicability nor direct effects.[103] Further confusion has arisen for member states with respect to the effective meaning and scope of the duty of enforcement, due to the fact that: 'the practical meaning of 'binding' in each member state differs according to the domestic constitutional background'.[104]

While the desirability of the CMC's exercise of broad, general powers is open to question, it may be explained on historical grounds. Under the original, unamended version of the Treaty of Asunción, the mandate granted to the—at that

---

[97]See: Palva and Gazel 2013.

[98]Treaty of Asunción, Article 9.

[99]Article 3 of the POP.

[100]Article 42 of the POP.

[101]See: Tiburcio 2010, p. 211 ff.

[102]Article 42 of the POP.

[103]See Laursen 2010, p. 254.

[104]Ibidem.

time permanent—conference of ministers on the basis of Articles 9 and 10 was very broad indeed. The number and range of actions that the representatives of the member states were allowed to take collectively permeated the administration and execution of the Treaty and of the specific agreements and decisions that were enacted within the legal framework established during the transition period of the Mercosur,[105] and while individual representants were free to seek limitations on this wide and generic mandate, they never did so. It is therefore unsurprising that the member states, acting through the CMC, have not taken any action to re-allocate powers, previously granted to this body under the original version of the Treaty of Asunción (Articles 9 and 10), to different Mercosur organs. A simple explanation for this failure to act by the CMC might be that representants of the member states were reluctant to relinquish the broad powers they enjoyed under the unamended version of the Treaty of Asunción in favour of other bodies such as the Common Market Group (CMG) that function within a larger and less elevated ranking setting in which a greater number of bureaucrats representing member governments exercise those powers through a range of Mercosur bodies.[106] However, things partially changed in 1994 with the approval of the Protocol of Ouro Preto that amended and supplemented the Treaty of Asunción, delineating the institutional framework and conferring international legal personality on the organization. As a result of the signature of the Protocol of Ouro Preto, an international organization was created, CMC functions changed, and others were added to them,[107] thus altering the juridical nature of this organ.[108]

Alongside broad and generic decision-making powers, the CMC is allocated a number of specific powers that are explicitly set out in various provisions in the Treaty of Asunción and Protocol of Ouro Preto. The specific powers of the CMC include: (a) the power to negotiate and sign agreements on behalf of Mercosur with third countries, groups of countries and international organizations;[109] (b) the power to guarantee the observance of the Treaty of Asunción; (c) the power to create, amend and abolish organs, such as working subgroups and specialized meetings; (d) the power to propose draft decisions to the CMG; (e) the power to draw up programmes of work to ensure progress towards the establishment of the

---

[105]Treaty of Asunción, Article 9.

[106]Incidentally, this emerges clearly from a comparison of Article 11 of the Treaty of Asunción which states that: 'The council shall consist of the Ministers for Foreign Affairs and the Ministers of the Economy of the States Parties' with Article 14 of the same Treaty which reads differently and provides that: 'The Common Market Group shall consist of four members and four alternates for each country, representing the following public bodies: Ministry of Foreign Affairs; Ministry of Economy or its equivalent (areas of industry, foreign trade and/or economic co-ordination); Central Bank.'.

[107]Article 3 of the POP.

[108]See: Palva and Gazel 2013, also stressing that: 'The differences between it and the GMC are more clearly stated than under the Treaty of Asuncion, in particular with respect to its prescriptive activity'.

[109]Article 8, para 4 of the POP.

common market; (f) the power to approve the budget and the annual statement of accounts presented by the Mercosur Administrative Secretariat; (g) the power to adopt financial and budgetary Resolutions based on the guidelines laid down by the Council; (h) the power to organize the meetings of the Council of the Common Market and to prepare the reports and studies requested by the latter; (i) the power to choose the Director of the Mercosur Administrative Secretariat; (j) the power to supervise the activities of the Mercosur Administrative Secretariat and (k) the power to approve the rules of procedure of the Trade Commission and the Economic-Social Consultative Forum.

Thus far during the first 20 years and more of Mercosur (1991–2012), the most important of the ten aforementioned powers have not been exercised by the CMC. Clearly, there are several possible explanations for this trend. One is that the number of meetings of this political body that meets only from time to time and normally not more than twice per semester is against the exercise of the aforementioned powers, in particular: (a) of the power to negotiate and sign agreements on behalf of Mercosur with third countries, groups of countries and international organizations; (b) of the power[110] regarding the observance of the Treaty of Asunción and of its additional Protocols.[111] In other words, more generally speaking, that the CMC normally meets not more than twice per semester has certainly contributed to the current stalling of the integration process in the LAC.

6.4.2 The Common Market Group

The Common Market Group (GMC) meets at the second level and consists of all Mercosur members, represented by government or diplomatic representatives (normally at ambassadorial level) rather than ministers.[112] On the basis of Article 14 of the Protocol of Ouro Preto, it is primarily responsible for the continuing day-to-day management of the institution in between the two-yearly sessions of the CMC and involves the exercise of the full (general and special) powers of the

---

[110]Incidentally, this is well demonstrated by the fact that concluding two free trade agreements with Chile and Bolivia, Mercosur has failed to reach a deal with Mexico and the Andean Community.

[111]On this issue, see also Bouzas et al. 2002, p. 177, who claim that: 'CMC should meet, at the very least, once per month in order to provide adequate political guidance to MERCOSUR and to have enough time to deepen the debate and find adequate solutions on legislative issues'.

[112]See Article 11 of the Protocol of Ouro which, after having stated that: 'The Common Market Group shall consist of four members and four alternates for each country, appointed by their respective governments', goes on by providing that: '*it* ... must include representatives of the Ministries of Foreign Affairs, the Ministries of the Economy (or their equivalents) and the Central Banks'.

latter body.[113] In essence, the GMC provides the vehicle for the membership's exercise of an executive function,[114] because it is specifically charged with: 'taking the steps necessary to carry out decisions taken by the Council', as well as: 'ensuring compliance with the Treaty'.[115]

Institutionally speaking, the GMC exercises its 'executive' functions on three different planes by means of: (1) general decision-making powers (these powers revert to the CMC when it is in session); (2) specific powers attributed to it on the basis of the establishing treaty, the Treaty of Asunción and (3) an additional general power that is one of surveillance, since the GMC has overall supervision over lower Mercosur bodies, like the Mercosur Trade Commission, which reports to the GMC within the hierarchical structure of the institution.[116] Under its general decision-making powers, the CMC conducts the functions of the CMC between the twice-yearly sessions meeting 'as often as necessary'[117] but on a regular basis, in practice this is usually once a month.[118]

Additionally, and somewhat confusingly, the GMC has not only been attributed the explicit power to prepare CMC decisions but also the power to adopt legal acts that are binding on the States parties, 'resoluciones', without referring them to the CMC though this is an organ hierarchically over it.[119] Clearly this is a type of structure prone to create overlapping and even inconsistent decisions that indeed may have serious negative consequences on the integration process between Mercosur member states, since GMC resolutions share the same legal nature as the CMC decisions and Trade Commission directives.[120]

The GMC has also been assigned a number of specific powers, i.e. it should carry out the functions assigned to it by the Treaty of Asunción and Protocol of Ouro Preto, as explicitly set out in these instruments. They include: deciding work programs for moving towards establishment of the common market and creating, amending or abolishing organs, such as 'working subgroups' and specialized meetings to assist it in its activities.[121] It also may, if authorized by the CMC, negotiate agreements with non-member countries, groups of countries, or

---

[113]See: Bouzas et al. 2002, who also stress that: 'The reason behind the creation in 1994 of the CCM was the need to manage day-to-day problems related to intra-zone trade and to implement common trade policy instruments'.

[114]Incidentally, this explains why The GMC, according to the wording of the Treaty *of Asunción*, is: 'the executive organ of the Common Market'.

[115]Article 14 of the POP.

[116]See: Olavo Baptista 1998, p. 30 ff.

[117]Article 13 of the POP.

[118]See: Bouzas et al. 2002, p. 117.

[119]Ibidem, p. 117.

[120]Articles 41 and 42 of the POP. For a fuller discussion on binding secondary Mercosur law, see amongst others Pustorino 2001, p. 117 ff. Bouzas et al. 2002, p. 117, who also stress that: 'There have been two attempts to clarify and re-organize this structure (one in 1995 and the other in 2000—CMC Decision 59/00), but with very little success'.

[121]Article 14 of the POP.

international organizations on behalf of Mercosur, and administer the international organization and supervise its activities.[122]

Finally, the GMC approves the Mercosur budget, the Secretariat's annual expenditures and supervises the Secretariat staff and Council meetings.

6.4.3 The Mercosur Trade Commission

The Mercosur Trade Commission (CCM) was created by Decision 9/94, and was consolidated by Articles 16 to 21 of the Protocol of Ouro Preto that define it as an intergovernmental decision-making organ.[123] The CCM operates at the third level, directly below the GMC.[124] Just like most other Mercosur bodies, it has a quadri-partite composition and like the GMC is composed of national sections.[125]

Apart from its administrative powers, the CCM exercises representative powers that, as with the GMC, are of a delegated nature.

The CCM has also been assigned a decision-making power, i.e. the power to issue directives, which is restricted to issues within its jurisdiction,[126] namely issues relating to the exercise of its powers and attributes.[127] Moreover, the CCM has been assigned the power of initiative, and is then allowed to propose customs and commercial provisions, or amendments thereof, to the GMC.[128] Furthermore, the CCM is also responsible for establishing its own internal regulations (which should be approved by the GMC), and such technical committees as it considers indispensable to carry out its powers-attributes. Again, the CCM considers claims submitted by the National Sections of the Mercosur Trade Commission, or

---

[122]Ibidem.

[123]See: Pérez Otermin 1995, p. 152, who criticizes the institution of the CCM by the CMC: '[…] on the basis that the CMC had no power to do so, because the Treaty of Asuncion had estab-lished a structure without stating that it could be modified or expanded, except by means of a new Treaty (article 18) and, finally, because the Annex to Decision 4/94, Articles 3(B), 4(A) and 5, gave the CCM the power to issue decisions that were binding on the States Parties, whereas such delegation of powers had not been authorized by the Treaty'. But see also Olavo Baptista 1998, p. 79 who stresses that: 'This question has lost its importance, because the Protocol of Ouro Preto not only created the CCM, but authorized the creation of new organs and the defini-tion of their respective competencies, except for those of a prescriptive character, a power that was reserved to the CMC, the GMC and the CCM'.

[124]Because it is hierarchically subordinate to the GMC, it reports to the latter on all questions for which it is responsible. It must also perform any functions that the senior body may assign to it.

[125]See: Olavo Baptista 1998, p. 79.

[126]Article 20 of the POP.

[127]Articles 19 and 20 of the POP.

[128]The Protocol of Ouro Preto, however, does not clarify whether these initiatives relate to the rules of Mercosur or to the internal rules of the Member States. In the latter case, they will merely constitute suggestions to be routed through the GMC to the senior authorities. For a fuller discussion of this issue, see: Pérez Otermin 1995.

originating with the States Parties or in complaints brought by private persons, individuals or corporations, relating to the situations envisaged in Articles 1 or 25 of the Protocol of Brasilia, where these fall within its area of competence. Examination of these claims within the Mercosur Trade Commission is without prejudice to the right of the state party bringing the claim pursuant to the Protocol of Brasilia to have recourse to the dispute settlement procedure.[129]

Finally, the CCM can adopt measures with respect to application of the single external tariff, with a view to its uniform application and administration. In this case, as well, its power is restricted by the intergovernmental character of Mercosur.

6.4.4 The Joint Parliamentary Commission

The Joint Parliamentary Commission (JPC), was formally established by Article 24 of the Treaty of Asunción. However, it was only through the Protocol of Ouro Preto that reference to it as an official organ of the Mercosur was included.[130] Just like the CCM, JPC operates at the third level, directly below the CMC and GMC.

Apart from representing the legislatures of the member states, JPC pursues the most ambitious task of planning and setting the stage for the establishment of a future Mercosur parliamentary assembly. The JPC has also been charged with the duty to assist Mercosur in the implementation of its policies and, to the extent that the integration process so requires, in the harmonization of domestic legislation therewith.[131] Additionally, on a strict reading of Articles 8 to 13 of the JPC rules of procedure, it might appear that JPC also enjoys an advisory function to the CMC and GMC.[132]

6.4.5 The Administrative Secretariat

The Mercosur Administrative Secretariat (Mercosur Secretariat)[133] of around 26 people is located in the city of Montevideo, taking advantage of the circumstance that the Secretariat of ALADI was already located there.[134] As originally conceived

---

[129]Article 21 of the POP. On this issue see, amongst others, Olavo Baptista 1998, p. 83.

[130]Articles 1 and 2 of the POP.

[131]Incidentally, it is worth noting that the initiative for legislative harmonization measures often come from the Common Market Commission (See Article 3 of the JPC Rules of Procedure).

[132]See also Article 26 of the Protocol of Ouro Preto which provides that the CPC is to communicate by means of recommendations, addressed to the Common Market Council, through the intermediary of the Common Market Group.

[133]According to Decision 30/02 of the Common Market Council, the current denomination of the Administrative Secretariat is Mercosur Secretariat.

[134]Article 31 of the POP.

by the Treaty of Asuncion, it consisted of a documents registry and a tool to facilitate the activities of Mercosur bodies. The same principles as those governing all other bodies of Mercosur apply to its management and organization.[135]

Unlike the JPC, the Mercosur Secretariat was conceived by the Treaty of Asunción as an official body of the institution.[136] Since it was initially modelled on the GATT Secretariat, which still existed at the time of the Treaty of Asunción, the Mercosur Secretariat was initially characterized as a non permanent organ, but it was transformed into a permanent body by the Protocol of Ouro Preto which did not otherwise substantially alter the functions of the Mercosur Secretariat.[137] More recently, by the Decision 30/02 of the CMC, the Mercosur Secretariat was finally converted from an Administrative Secretariat into a Technical Secretariat with some changes in its organization.[138] The rationale behind this decision was clear: a Technical Secretariat was considered more appropriate to overcome a shortcoming in the initial Mercosur structure where no one was allowed to give objective inputs on Mercosur developments from a wider, regional perspective that went above national interests.[139] Not unlike some permanent secretariats that assist the member states of free trade agreements or FTAs, the Mercosur Secretariat and its Director are considered as merely fulfilling a supportive role for the members, which is supposed to be of a strictly professional nature.[140] The Director is elected by the Common Market Group and appointed by the Council. It is interesting to note that the election and appointment of the Director are separated. As far as we know, this separation was at the insistence of Uruguay during the negotiations. That country wished to enhance the standing of the Director and the Secretariat, by having the former designated by the Council. Other delegations, on the other hand, insisted that since the administrative body of Mercosur was the Common Market Group, it should be responsible for naming the Director. The solution adopted represented a consensus, and appears to have satisfied all parties.[141] Similarly, like those secretariats to FTAs, neither the Director-General nor the staff of the Mercosur Secretariat exercises any independent decision-making powers, including any right of initiative, although they do occasionally act informally in launching initiatives and submitting proposals for the membership to examine, as well as advising members on trade issues.[142]

---

[135]Article 34 of the POP.

[136]See: Olavo Baptista 1998, p. 23.

[137]For a fuller discussion of this issue, see: Pérez Otermin 1995, p. 152 ff.

[138]Secretaría del Mercosur, CMC Decision 30/02, at: http://www.mercosur.int/msweb/portal%20 intermediario/es/arquivos/Dec_030_002.pdf. Accessed 15 October 2014.

[139]Accordingly, see: O'Keefe 2009, p. 143.

[140]The Mercosur Secretariat was qualified by Articles 31 and 32 of the POP as a body of operational support, responsible for supplying services to the other bodies of Mercosur, including those of file-keeping, dissemination and the issuance of the Official Bulletin of the Mercosur.

[141]For a full examination of this issue, see: Olavo Baptista 1998, p. 84.

[142]On this issue, see: Leathley 2007, p. 158 ff.

6.4.6 Economic and Social Advisory Forum

As established by Article 28 of the Protocol of Ouro Preto, the Economic and Social Advisory Forum (FCES) is an organ representing the social and economic sectors. Its operation is governed by rules of procedure that are approved by the CMG, as is the case with other bodies of Mercosur, for instance the CCM.

On the basis of Article 28 of the Protocol of Ouro Preto, FCES is committed with advisory functions that are exercised through the form of "Recommendations" to the CMG and other Mercosur bodies and the formulation of proposals. In essence, it provides the vehicle for making the activities of Mercosur more transparent and democratic, since it is specifically charged with the task of opening up channels of communication through which society at large might voice its ambitions to Mercosur. In so doing, FCES analyzes and evaluates the social and economic impact of the various integration policies and their enforcement, suggests the adoption of economic and social policies and provisions concerning the integration process and performs research and studies on economic and social issues relevant to the Mercosur member countries.

6.4.7 Mercosur Dispute Settlement Mechanism at Glance

Just like the World Trade Organization, Mercosur has a dispute settlement mechanism of an arbitrary character. Currently, its main regulation is found in the 2002 Protocol of Olivos, in force since 2004, which has replaced the Brasilia Protocol for dispute settlement.

Of all the changes introduced by the Protocol of Olivos, the Permanent Tribunal of Revision ('TPR') is indeed the most important one.[143] On the basis of Article 18 of this Protocol, the TPR is composed of five members with expertise in law or international trade, who are permanently available to resolve disputes during the term of their mandate (2 or 3 years depending on the circumstances).[144] Although the goal pursued with the creation of the TPR was to guarantee greater consistency in the interpretation and application of Mercosur laws, the Olivos Protocol keeps on enhancing dispute resolution via arbitration and direct negotiation ('diplomatic phase').[145]

---

[143]Incidentally, it is worth noting that the creation of a Mercosur Tribunal along the lines of the European Court or the Andean Tribunal runs into a constitutional obstacle in Brazil, as noted in a speech some years ago by Minister Moreira Alves. According to him, article 92 of the Federal Constitution stipulates what are the bodies of the Judiciary Power, and lists them expressly, which means that we are faced with a 'numerus clausus' (closed number).

[144]See Olivos Protocol for the Settlement of Disputes, Chapter VII, Article 18, (2003) 42 ILM. See also Welbel Barral, 'Introductory Note to Mercosur: the Olivos Protocol', (2003) 42 ILM, p. 1 ff.

[145]See: Bouzas and Soltz 2001.

More generally, the Olivos Protocol establishes two procedures for dispute settlement, depending on who submits a complaint—a state member or a private litigant. With regard to State to State dispute resolution, the Olivos Protocol establishes an expedited State to State negotiation procedure and a facultative provision for referral to the CMG, the executive body of Mercosur.[146] In the event that a dispute is not settled through this initial procedure, the Olivos Protocol provides a mechanism for ad hoc State to State arbitration closely modelled on the Dispute Settlement Understanding of the WTO.[147] In fact, Mercosur's ad hoc State to State arbitration system currently allows member states to refer disputes arising under the Treaty of Asunción and its additional Protocols to the WTO.[148] On the basis of Article 1 of the Olivos Protocol, as soon as a procedure of dispute settlement has commenced neither party will be allowed to appeal to mechanisms envisaged in other forums for the same subject matter. In the event that a member state wishes to reverse the interpretation given by an ad hoc tribunal created pursuant to this system, it may apply to the TPR that has the power to issue decisions which are final and binding on the states involved in the controversy. The Olivos Protocol makes it clear that whichever party might demand an appeal of revision against the decision of the Ad Hoc Tribunal to the TPR.[149] The TPR will review the issue, restricting itself to the legal issues involved. In this case, the ruling of the TPR will be final and will prevail over the decision of ad hoc Arbitration Tribunal.

With regard to the dispute settlement mechanism initiated by private individuals (individuals or corporations), the Olivos Protocol grants private litigants, the 'private parties', the power to address a claim to the National Section of the Common Market Group of residence that decides if the claim can be accepted or not. Prima facie at least, the claim looks like it is largely—if not totally—dependent on the political will of the member states and consequently it may be postponed by them. Indeed, confirmation of this is that only very few claims by private litigants have been settled in front of a Mercosur ad hoc tribunal up to the present.[150] However, things are different, in the sense that the claim does not look dependent on the political will of the member states, if one considers that the National Section must only determine the truth of the violation and the existence or threat of injury according to Article 41 of the Olivos Protocol.

---

[146]See Chapters IV and V of the Olivos Protocol. On this issue, see: Giorgetti 2012, p. 493.

[147]On the Dispute Settlement Understanding of the WTO, see among others Feldstein de Cárdenas 2004; Olivera Garcia 2002.

[148]See: ASEAN Studies Center, Report n. 5, MERCOSUR Economic Integration: Lessons for ASEAN, ISEAS Publishing, Singapore, p. 61.

[149]Article 17 of the Olivos Protocol.

[150]References can be found in Laursen 2010, p. 185 ff.

6.5 Achievements of Mercosur

The institutional weaknesses of Mercosur, in particular the absence of a clear and objective division of powers and functions between its main internal bodies, have not wholly compromised its achievements. Even the strong economic asymmetries and trade tensions among its founding members have not hindered it from achieving success, especially during the first 15 years of its existence.[151]

In general, Mercosur has achieved several noteworthy results since 1990, more than any other economic integration organization in the LAC.[152] Indeed it has built and enhanced intra-regional cooperation and trading relationships among Argentina, Brazil, Paraguay and Uruguay, and has enhanced these relationships into a feasible economic integration institution.[153] For a substantial period of time its members have benefited from unprecedented expanded commerce and wider prosperity.[154]

In particular, Mercosur has agreed on a common external tariff encompassing 85 percent of the items currently being traded by its members and has reached agreement on a significant number of economic issues.[155]

Not less importantly, Mercosur has created a structural convergence fund, Focem, that aims to help gradually eradicate structural asymmetries especially for Mercosur junior members Paraguay and Uruguay. Again, Mercosur has enacted several measures to uniformize the normative systems of the member countries in various fields including judicial cooperation, both in the private law and the criminal law sense, and to eradicate barriers to free commerce.[156] Indeed Mercosur law has grown fast and the tentative outlines of, for instance, Mercosur consumer and environmental laws are now fairly evident and clear.[157] The same is true of the harmonization of trademark law, competition law, etc.[158] Furthermore, an identical conclusion applies, mutatis mutandis, to the field of customs cooperation that has also seen significant progress. In that regard, it is sufficient to recall that an assistance treaty was concluded in 1997 regarding the prevention and repression of customs breaches.[159] The assistance may be used in the framework of both

---

[151]Accordingly, see: Franko 2007, p. 263, who stresses that: 'the achievements of Mercosur over the past 15 years are important, particularly in locking in progress toward free trade in the region'.

[152]See also Lizardo 1995, p. 123, who states that: 'Most achievements of MERCOSUR to data have been in the political realm'.

[153]See: Laciar 2003, p. 6 ff.

[154]See: Tosi 1999, p. 10 ff.

[155]See Sect. 6.2.

[156]For a full discussion of these issues see, among others, Olivar Jiménez 2010, p. 191 ff.

[157]See: Lima Marques 2010; Franca 2010.

[158]See: Diz (2010).

[159]*Convencion de Cooperación y Asistencia Recíproca entre las Administraciones de Aduanas del Mercosure Relativo a la Prevención y Lucha Contra Ilícitos Aduaneros.* Mercosur/CMC/Dec. No 1/97, reproduced in Santos Belandro 2001, p. 318 ff.

administrative law and criminal law enforcement procedures and the information achieved can circulate and be transmitted on between the judicial and administrative authorities. The member states are also fully aware of the 'acquis' that has been developed within the institutional framework of Mercosur and are not willing to see it threatened, for instance, by a subsequent international treaty.[160] Similarly, member states are aware that an 'acquis' is being built within Mercosur in the sectors of intelligence police cooperation.[161] Moreover, Mercosur has persuaded the elites of its member countries that the project of economic integration is both feasible and convenient.

Finally, Mercosur has also enhanced foreign investments ('FDI'), and diversification.[162] Indeed, evidence of this progress are the free trade agreements concluded with Bolivia and Chile[163] as well as the agreement with Mexico to liberalize trade in the automotive sector in 2002.[164]

6.6 Prospects for the Future of Mercosur

If combined with the modest progresses in the fields of free movement of workers, persons, services and capital,[165] the enduring gaps in the common market regulations in sectors of strategic relevance from an economic perspective—such as public procurement, agriculture and intellectual property—20 years and more after the inception of Mercosur show that this is more of an intra-commerce agreement rather than the Common Market of the Southern Cone. This is notwithstanding what has been solemnly proclaimed by the Treaty of Asunción, in its Preamble, that conceives Mercosur as a deep integration project which would evolve, though it lacks 'rules for rule-making'. Thus far, the Mercosur has kept its common market agenda to a minimum. Mercosur member states consider the free movement of goods, rather than the other internal market freedoms, as more relevant to its activities and identity.

Nevertheless, despite its age Mercosur is still—if not in its 'infancy'—at a relatively early stage of evolution. Indirect confirmation can be found in the references to human rights—as guaranteed by the Inter-American Convention of Human

---

[160]Accordingly, see: Vervaele J A E 2005b, p. 405.

[161]Ibidem, p. 405 ff who stresses the similarity in many respects to the Schengen acquis and the cooperation within the third pillar of the EU, although in this case not with the scope of compensating for the elimination of internal barriers.

[162]See: Lerner 2010.

[163]See notes 38 and 39 above.

[164]However, so far it has failed its most ambitious goal—to sign a free trade agreement with the EU which has long been under consideration, see: EU-Mercosur FTA vs Trade-Willing 'Pacific Alliance' at: http://ipezone.blogspot.it/2013/02/eu-mercosur-fta-vs-trade-willing.html. Accessed 10 October 2014.

[165]See: Porrata-Doria 2005, p. 124 ff.

Rights (IACHR)—or to citizenship that are still far from being realized[166] Therefore, it is clear that only time will indicate the direction in which it may progress. Considering these possible scenarios in the evolution and development of Mercosur is thus both useful and appropriate.

Logically speaking, the first possible scenario is the maintenance of the existing status quo. In other words, Mercosur member states will continue to enhance their cooperative socio-economic programs and initiatives, and to integrate their economies, largely through their own internal acts and initiatives but partly as a result of the Mercosur process, activities and acts. Socio-economic integration amongst its members are likely to be the final result of market and political driving forces rather than Mercosur internal acts and decisions that, when they are legally binding, are not generally enforced at the domestic level. Indeed the maintenance of the existing state of affairs will probably require some level of harmonization of national enforcement laws, including the harmonization of punitive sanctions. In other words, it will be likely to require the creation of a sort of effective enforcement mechanism to guarantee that Mercosur provisions are effectively incorporated in a uniform fashion and that those members who fail to do so are sanctioned.

Thus, while holding its commitment to the current cooperative programs and initiatives, Mercosur may need to partially modify its agenda and establishing treaty.[167] Clearly, one way of achieving this is to move towards a more comprehensive, but also clear and rational, harmonization process.[168] Mercosur might develop toward the models of the Andean Community and European Union that put the principle of the primacy of their laws over the legal systems of the member states at the very core of their internal legal orders. This idea has already been suggested by others and it has also been enhanced in legal writings recently.[169]

Nonetheless, this scenario is unlikely to develop since it goes against to Mercosur's general modus operandi, which is the promotion of harmonization through the development of international agreements to be ratified by member states. Moreover, this is so also for political reasons, namely the enduring asymmetrical interdependence among its members and the absence of a method for the political handling of national diversity, unlike the EU and NAFTA. However, Mercosur seems to have been unable to find a political solution for this kind of

---

[166]See: Pierini 2000.

[167]See: Machinea 2003, who states that the problems of implementation stem in large part from the formal rule of implementing rules, as laid down in Article 40 of the Protocol of Ouro Preto. Indeed providing that, for Mercosur's legal measures to enter into force, these rules must be transposed by the four members and communicated to the Administrative Secretariat, this Article has made the effectiveness of the decisions taken by Mercosur's political bodies dependent on domestic mechanisms and interests, which often use this circumstance as an informal tools for hindering measures. Accordingly, see also Bouzas et al. 2005, p. 14, affirming that: 'having been adopted by the Mercosur bodies, the norms enter into a sort of limbo where they can remain indefinitely, awaiting the end of the transposition process'.

[168]On the scope of the harmonization in Mercosur see, among others, Malamud 2010, pp. 9–28.

[169]See: Cajarville Peluffo 1998.

dilemma, combining managed trade measures with an institutional rivalry that lacks implicit rules and does not enjoy legitimacy among the member countries. It might be suggested, of course, that this situation partially reflects the contradictions in the revision of national development models, which amounts to a review of paradigms and policy preferences.[170] Nonetheless, it should be acknowledged that the inability to find a political solution to the matter of regulatory and institutional diversity heightens uncertainty about (and the unpredictability of) the rules of the game in the integration process:[171] a Mercosur that has the primacy of its law over the laws of its members would be infeasible. First, this is because it presupposes the existence of a real community of nations and peoples amongst its members that it is hard to envisage at present. Second, and finally, because it presupposes a new and clear-cut division of competences and powers between the internal bodies of the institution and thus a far too complex and time-consuming revision of the Treaty of Asunción and its accompanying Protocols, including the Protocol of Olivos for disputes settlement.

Understandably, the third and final option might be stagnation and disintegration. Mercosur could stagnate as a result of the disagreement among its member states as to the pace and scope of economic and political integration between its members. In the absence of any meaningful momentum on at least some of the areas of Mercosur's agenda, it may prove difficult to keep the attention of political leaders.

Mercosur could also fall apart and rapidly change if a recession in the community of members leads Mercosur member states' interests to become so-far detached as to destruct consensus and complementarity,[172] or if a recession leads members to redirect their consensus to a competing institution such as the newly established Pacific Alliance.[173]

6.7 Approaches to the Future Progress of Mercosur

Unsurprisingly, because of the coexistence of five to six member states in Mercosur that have differences of size and economic structure, at least two distinct approaches to Mercosur's possible progress exist: the 'Brazilian-Argentinan and Venezuelan' approach, and the 'Uruguayan-Paraguayan' approach.

The traditional approach of Brazil to Mercosur, which has also been followed by Argentina and Venezuela, clearly shows: 'the perception that the limits to the integration-related cession of sovereignty must be defined by national aims which

---

[170]See: Arnaud 1996, p. 12 ff.

[171]See: da Motta Veiga 2004, p. 5.

[172]See: Ruiz Díaz Labrano 1998, p. 3 ff who stresses that the dramatic economic distress that the MERCOSUR member states are currently undergoing is distracting them from the MERCOSUR agenda.

[173]See: Ramirez 2013.

take primacy (in terms of political priorities) over the aims of the sub-regional project, and that those national aims must not be affected by Mercosur'.[174] In the application of this approach, Brazil's natural industry development project was kept intact in the hegemonic matrix of foreign policy at the Mercosur level, and it was not even combined with issues of a sub-regional industrial project.[175] Indeed, in the negotiations with Brazil's Mercosur partners, the national development project was systematically illustrated as a project of competition and conflict, and hardly ever as an issue of cooperation.[176] Hence, in Brazil, 'the great obstacle … to a real 'investment' in the Mercosur project is the ambiguity with which, apart from the rhetoric of the pro-integration discourse, the various sectors of civil society and government regard Mercosur', as Botofogo Goncalves has rightly observed.[177] While the process is admittedly slower, defendants of this approach argue that it is the only one that can foster confidence and voluntary concession-making, considering the level of development and the interests of Mercosur member countries of such diversity. Adherents of the 'Brazilian and Argentinan' approach enhance it as the only way by which Mercosur, like other international regional institutions in the LAC, may survive and grow. The rationale behind this approach is straightforward and clear: the idea that the main problems of Mercosur arose when the process moved beyond its most cooperative level from the institutional perspective, and its least contentious phase from the standpoint of the member countries' internal politics.

On the other hand,[178] the traditional approach of the smaller members of the institution, Uruguay[179] and Paraguay,[180] enacts an institutional view that stresses the importance of the harmonization process as well as of the competences and powers of the main internal bodies of Mercosur, and operates under bigger

---

[174]See Vervaele 2005b, p. 387 ff who stresses that: 'Since 1999, when major economic difficulties created substantial distress, […] Argentina and Brazil found themselves unable to agree on further norms and seeking (or talking about seeking) to repeal or ignore norms previously agreed to.

[175]See Machinea 2003.

[176]Ibidem.

[177]See: Botafogo Gonçalves 2002, p. 25, who stresses that much of the Brazilian elite, viewing Mercosur as a 'political contingency, one option among others', not only avoids thinking of the bloc as 'part of the Brazilian project' but also hampers 'the as-yet incomplete assimilation in the four member countries of a truly regional approach'.

[178]Paraguay has been suspended from Mercosur over the impeachment of President Fernando Lugo on 22 June 2012, adducing a "rupture of democratic order" opposed to the commitment of democracy and integration agreed by the trade bloc. Further information is to be found at: http://www.voxxi.com/mercosur-paraguay-francochavez/#ixzz2YBJ2d9B3Paraguay. Accessed 7 July 2014.

[179]See S Abreu, Una visión oriental (uruguayana) de la realidad regional. Analisis del Centro Uruguayo de Relaciones Iinternacionales, Análisis n. 01/11, 16 February 2011 at: http://curi.org.uy/archivos/analisis/Hasta2011/analisis01del11abreu.pdf. Accessed 15 October 2014; Magariños 1991, p. 10 ff.

[180]See: Gustafson 2003; Ryan-Collins 2009.

expectations.[181] Emblematic of such an approach are the continuous references by Mercosur official components and main bodies to political and economic integration between the members as the ultimate goal of the Treaty of Asunción. Moreover, equally emblematic of this approach is the invocation of a social (alias a non-trade) agenda for Mercosur.[182] Adopting the approach of Uruguay and Paraguay,[183] the Andean Community and the EU would clearly become feasible models to be used for relaunching Mercosur, in the sense of expediting the integration process and making it more effective and efficient.

To achieve a reasonable compromise between these two conflicting views, a combination of the two approaches should be tried. Without rules for making and implementing powers in the CMC and GMC, no one in Mercosur can mandate the enactment of either approach. Nevertheless, in the interests of cooperation between its members, member states must reach an agreement concerning the reconciliation of both views.

6.8 Final Remarks

The Mercosur results are clearly an important achievement, warranting the large amount of resources and time utilized in its negotiation.[184] If this approach may be repeated with a new Mercosur Summit or Round, or whether we will now need to restructure the procedures for ongoing evolution of its institutions and rules,[185] is still uncertain and open to debate. Mercosur would seem to have enough institutional adaptability to address a number of the issues and concerns which have been raised in the paragraphs above. However, it still remains to be seen whether Mercosur can mediate on such a large landscape of policy objectives, including non-economic ones as indicated in the previous paragraphs, or whether Mercosur

---

[181]See: Gustafson 2003, who stresses that: 'Although intra-Mercosur trade liberalization was not a minor matter for Brazil's Mercosur partners, from the domestic political viewpoint all the countries of the sub-region were then in the process of opening up to the world'.

[182]The problems involved in tackling matters not directly related to trade are neither exclusive to not typical of Mercosur. See: Machinea 2003, who recalls that: 'the non-trade agenda, by definition, imposes greater institutional demands: domestic politics are more sensitive to it, since much of its focus comprises regulations and laws that are deemed fundamentally internal, that are to be preserved as such, and that are managed by public, private or mixed institutions that conceive of their accountability (when they do so at all) only in highly domestic terms'.).

[183]Since 2010, Paraguay has been suspended as a member of Mercosur.

[184]See: Pérez Otermin 1995, p. 10 ff.

[185]For this opinion, see among others Porrata-Doria 2005, p. 162 who, after having stressed that: 'relaunching MERCOSUR, in the sense of expediting the integration process and making it more effective and efficient, will require a paradigm change', concludes in the sense that: 'The supranational integration process, by now very successful, needs to be managed by a supranational actor with adequate resources and authority'.

will be fundamentally a somewhat less ambitious and narrower inter-trade agreement. Can it happily accommodate several different policy approaches in such different areas as developing members' necessities, judicial cooperation in civil and criminal matters, harmonization of competition and consumer laws, economy in transition, and so on? And do we wish to have an institution that exercises a relative monopoly on any matters that are essential to political and economic integration in the sub-region? Rather, do member states currently prefer to have their aims taking primacy (in terms of political priorities) over the aims of Mercosur so the latter can be kept comparatively weaker?

Lastly, we can note that members of international institutions often have tensions between them.[186] These tensions constitute components of a process of dialetic between member states that frequently have differences of size and economic structure.[187] This process is generally very untidy, but arguably leads to a more adequate governing structure, meeting some of the problems that have been indicated above. Smaller and less economically powerful member states normally tend to regard the implementation and development of communitarian policies as the ultimate aim of the institution.[188] Bigger and economically more powerful members, on the contrary, tend to have a more internally oriented view of matters.[189] Indeed, these tensions are a true dilemma for supranational institutions. We see them in the United Nations, and we see them also in the international financial institutions that are affiliated to the World Bank Group. Therefore, we may wonder whether there will inevitably be some parallels that will necessarily develop at the international regional level. This leads us to two final quotations that we can terminate with: one is Christoph Schreuer's statement that: 'Regional and universal efforts have both been severely obstructed by nationalism and inward-looking politics of States'.[190] The other is by Miles Kahler in his Introduction to a recent book titled 'International Institutions and the Political Economy of Integration', which states that: 'Regional institutions reveal even more dramatically the tension between national desires to maintain policy autonomy and, at the same time, benefit from intensified economic exchange'.[191] This is a tension which we face in Mercosur, as well as in the World Trading System.

---

[186]See: Klabbers 2002, p. 40.

[187]See Sect. 6.1.

[188]In fact, as a result of the asymmetrical interdependence among member countries, the smaller countries have a greater dependence than the bigger partners on neighbouring countries' markets; they are much more affected by the economic decisions of the larger countries than the other way round. Hence, each country has substantially different incentives to include certain issues on the agenda: in principle, the bigger countries have fewer incentives to include issues that reduce national autonomy in economic policy making, while the smaller countries tend to support such proposals. For a full discussion of this issue, see: da Motta Veiga 2004, p. 5.

[189]See: da Motta Veiga 2004, p. 5.

[190]See C. Schreuer, 'Regionalism v. Universalism', (1995) 6 *EJIL*, p. 499 (emphasis added).

[191]See Miles Kahler, *International Institutions and the Political Economy of Integration*, (Washington DC, 1995), vii.

References

Alterini A A, Favier Dubois E M (1996) Negocio Internacionales y Mercosur. Ad Hoc, Buenos Aires

Arbuet-Vignali H (2004) Claves Jurídicas de la Integración. Rubinzal-Culzoni, Buenos Aires

Arnaud V G (1996) Mercosur, Unión Europea, NAFTA y los Procesos de Integración Regional. Abeledo-Perrot, Buenos Aires

Baer W, Silva P A, Cavalcanti T (2002) Economic integration without policy coordination: the case of Mercosur. Emerging Markets Review 3(3): 269–291

Barbosa R A (1991) América Latina em Perspectiva: A integração regional, da retórica á realidade. Aduaneiras, São Paulo

Borba Casella P (ed) (2000) Mercosul: Integração Regional e Globalização. Renovar, Rio de Janeiro

Botafogo Gonçalves J (2002) Mercosul após 2002: propostas a partir de um testemunho pessoal. In Hugueney Filho C and Cardim C H (org), Grupo de Reflexão Prospectiva sobre o Mercosul. IPRI, Brasilia

Bouga P (2013), Latin-American Integration: MERCOSUR, CELAC and EU-CELAC partnership as a new form of inter-regionalism. Institute of International Economic Relations, Athens, at: http://www.idec.gr/iier/new/bouga_latin_america.pdf. Accessed 15 December 2014.

Bouzas R (2003) Economic Integration in the Southern Cone: Can Mercosur Survive? In: Margheritis A (ed), Latin American Democracies in the New Global Economy. North South Center Press, Miami, pp. 63–81

Bouzas R and Soltz H (2001) Institutions and Regional Integration: The Case of Mercosur. In: Bulmer-Thomas V (ed) Regional Integration in Latin American and the Caribbean. Institute of Latin American Studies, London, pp. 95–118

Bouzas R, da Motta Veiga P, Torrent R (2002) In-Depth Analysis Mercosur Integration, Its Prospectives and The Effects Thereof on The Market Access of EU Goods, Services and Investment. Observatory of Globalisation, Barcelona

Busse M, Hefeker C, Koopmann G (2004) Between Two Poles: Matching Trade and Exchange Rate Regimes in Mercosur. HWWA Discussion Paper n. 301. Hamburg Institute of International Economics, Hamburg at: http://ageconsearch.umn.edu/bitstream/26327/1/dp040301.pdf. Accessed 11 November 2014

Cajarville Peluffo J P (1998) Garantías constitucionales del procedimiento administrativo en los países del Mercosur. Actualidad en el Derecho Público 8: 25–47

Carranza M E (2003) Can Mercosur Survive? Domestic and International Constraints on Mercosur. Latin American Politics and Society 45(2): 67–103

da Motta Veiga P (2004) Mercosur in Search of a New Agenda. Mercosur's Institutionalization Agenda: The Challenges of a Project in Crisis. Working Paper. Intal–Itd, Buenos Aires

Devlin R (2000) The Free Trade Area of the Americas and MERCOSUR-European Union Free Trade Processes: Can they Learn Something from Each Other? Occasional Paper n. 6. Intal-Itd, Buenos Aires

Diz J B M (2010) International Taxation in MERCOSUR. In: Toscano M, Filho F, Lixinski L, Olmos Giupponi M B (eds) The Law of MERCOSUR. Hart publishing, Oxford, pp 259–276

Domínguez F and Guedes de Oliveira M (eds) (2004) Mercosur: Between Integration and Democracy. Peter Lang, Oxford, Bern, Berlin, Bruxelles, Frankfurt/M., New York, Wien, 2004

Duina F G (2006) The Social Construction of Free Trade: The European Union, Nafta, And Mercosur. Princeton University Press, Princeton

Estrella Faria J A (1993) O Mercosul: princípios finalidade e alcance do Tratado de Assunção. Ministerio das Relaçoes Exteriores, Brasilia

Feldstein de Cárdenas S (2004) Sistema de Solución de Disputas en el Mercosur. Revista del Colegio Público de Abogados de la Capital Federal 75: 1–18

Foders F (1996) MERCOSUR: a new approach to regional integration? Kiel Working Papers, No. 746. Universität Kiel, Institut für Weltwirtschaft

Footer M E (2006) An Institutional And Normative Analysis of the World Trade Organization. Martinus Nijhoff, Leiden

Franca, A C L M (2010) MERCOSUR and Environmental Law. In: Toscano M, Filho F, Lixinski L, Olmos Giupponi M B (eds) The Law of MERCOSUR. Hart publishing, Oxford, pp. 225–239

Franko P M (2007) The Puzzle of Latin American Economic Development. Rowman & Littlefield Publishers, Lanham

Fuders F (2010) Economic Freedoms in MERCOSUR. In: Toscano M, Filho F, Lixinski L, Olmos Giupponi M B (eds) The Law of MERCOSUR. Hart publishing, Oxford, pp. 87–130

Gardini G L (2010) The Origins of Mercosur: Democracy and Regionalization in South America. Palgrave Macmillan, New York

Giordano P (2002) An Integrated Approach to the European Union-Mercosur Association. Chaire Mercosur de Sciences Po, Paris

Giorgetti C (ed.) (2012) The Rules, Practice, and Jurisprudence of International Courts and Tribunals. Martinus Nijhoff Publishers, Leiden

Glenn W. Harrison G W (2002) Políticas comerciais regionais, multilaterais e unilaterais do Mercosul para o crescimento econômico e redução da pobreza no Brasil. IPEA-Instituto de Pesquisa Econômica Aplicada, Rio de Janeiro

Grimoldi G (2005) La teoría de la Integración Económica y su aplicación a la experiencia del Mercosur. Working Paper n. 7. Centro Argentino de Estudios Internacionales CAEI, Buenos Aires

Guira J (2003) Mercosur: Trade and Investment Amid Financial Crisis. Kluwer Law International, The Hague

Gustafson K (2003) Uruguay and Mercosur: A Study on Integration and Trade. Department of Economics, Minor field study series no. 140, University of Lund

Haines-Ferrari M (1993). MERCOSUR: A New Model of Latin American Economic Integration. Case W. Res. J. Int'l L. 25: 413–48

Hijazi H (2012) Asymmetries Among the Members of Mercosur. *Open Access Theses.* Paper 327, University of Miami, at: http://scholarlyrepository.miami.edu/oa_theses/327. Accessed 2 December 2014

Hummel F and Lohaus M (2011) MERCOSUR: Integration through Presidents and Paymasters. In: Tanja A. Börzel, Goltermann L, Lohaus M (eds) Roads to Regionalism: Genesis, Design, and Effects of Regional Organizations. Ashgate, Farnham, pp. 59–78

Kaltenthaler K and Mora F O (2002) Explaining Latin American Economic Integration: The Case of Mercosur. Review of International Political Economy 9(1): 72–97

Klabbers J (2001) The Changing Image of International Organizations. In: Coicaud J M and Heiskanen V (eds) The Legitimacy of International Organzations. United Nations University Press, Tokyo, pp. 221–255

Klabbers J (2002) An Introduction to International Institutional Law. Cambridge University Press, Cambridge

Kotabe M (1997) Mercosur and Beyond: The Imminent Emergence of the South American Markets. Center for International Business Education and Research, University of Texas, Austin

Laciar M E (2003) Medio Ambiente y Desarrollo Sustentable: Los Desafíos del Mercosur. Editorial Ciudad Argentina, Buenos Aires

Laursen F (2010) Requirements for Regional Integration: A Comparative Perspective on the EU, the Americas and East Asia. In: Laursen F (ed.) Comparative Regional Integration: Europe and Beyond. Ashgate, Abingdon

Leathley C (2007) International Dispute Resolution in Latin America: An Institutional Overview. Kluwer Law International, The Hague

León Li J M (2011) Regional Integration Process in South America: Analysis of Institutions and Policies of Regional Integration under the EU Framework. Verlag GmbH, Hamburg

Lerner D F (2010) The Protection of Foreign Direct Investment in MERCOSUR. In: Toscano M, Filho F, Lixinski L, Olmos Giupponi M B (eds) The Law of MERCOSUR. Hart publishing, Oxford, pp. 277–290

Lima Marques C, (2010) Consumer Protection Policy in MERCOSUR. In: Toscano M, Filho F, Lixinski L, Olmos Giupponi M B (eds) The Law of MERCOSUR. Hart publishing, Oxford, pp. 331–350

Lizardo S M (1995) Latin American Trading Blocs and the Western Hemisphere Free Trading Area (WHFTA): An Impact Assessment of CACM, ANPACT, and MERCOSUR. PhD Thesis, University of Pittsburgh

Lorenzo F and Vaillant M (2005) The MERCOSUR and the Creation of the Free Trade Area of the Americas. In: Lorenzo F and Vaillant M (eds), Mercosur and the Creation of the Free Trade Area of the Americas. Woodrow Wilson International Center for Scholars, Washington DC, pp. 1–28

Machinea J L (2003) La inestabilidad cambiaria en el MERCOSUR: causas, problemas y posibles soluciones. INTAL-ITD, Buenos Aires

Magariños G (1991) Uruguay en el Mercosur. Fundación de Cultura Universitaria, Montevideo

Malamud A (2005) Mercosur Turns 15: Between Rhetoric and Declining Achievements. Cambridge Review of International Affairs 18(3): 421–436

Mansueti H R (2010) Circulation of Workers in the Law of MERCOSUR. In: Toscano M, Filho F, Lixinski L, Olmos Giupponi M B (eds) (2010) The Law of MERCOSUR. Hart publishing, Oxford, pp. 241–258

Mye R and Palagonia L (1996) MERCOSUR's Potential Market is Now Over 200 Million People with a Combined Economy of Nearly \$1 Trillion. Business America 118(8): 17–18

O'Brien D (2008) CARICOM and Its Court of Justice. Common Law World Review 37: 334–355

O'Keefe T A (2009) Latin American and Caribbean Trade Agreements: Keys to a Prosperous Community of the Americas. Martinus Nijhoff Publishers, Leiden

Olarreaga M, Soloaga I, Winters L A (1999) What's Behind Mercosur's Common External Tariff? The World Bank Development Research Group Trade, Washington DC

Olavo Baptista L (1998) O Mercosul, Suas Institutuições e Ordenamento Jurídico. LTr, São Paulo

Olivar Jiménez M L (2010) The Law of MERCOSUR and International Law: The Struggle for Independence. In: Toscano M, Filho F, Lixinski L, Olmos Giupponi M B (eds) (2010) The Law of MERCOSUR. Hart Publishing, Oxford, pp. 191–208

Olivera Garcia R (2002) Dispute Resolution Regulation and Experiences in MERCOSUR: The Recent Olivos Protocol. Law & Bus. Rev. Am. 8: 535–550

Opertti Badán D (2006) Globalización e integración: presente de la Asociación Latinoamericana de Derecho Internacional (Aladi). In: AA.VV. XXXII Curso de Derecho Internacional: organizado por el Comité Juridico Interamericano y la Secretaría General de la OEA en agosto de 2005. OEA, Washington, DC, pp. 213–256

Palva P and Gazel R (2013) MERCOSUR Economic Issues: Successes, Failures and Unfinished Business. CLAS Working Papers, Center for Latin American Studies, UC Berkeley, at: http://www.escholarship.org/uc/item/3zd0h0z0. Accessed 3 May 2014

Pang E S and Jarngin L (2009) The Elusive Quest for Regional Integration. In: ASEAN Study Centre (ed) MERCOSUR Economic Integration: Lessons for ASEAN. Institute of Southeast Asian Studies, Singapore, pp. 87–130

Pérez Otermin J (1995) El Mercado Común del Sur: Desde Asunción a Ouro Preto. Fundación de Cultura Universitaria, Montevideo

Pierini A (2000) Derechos Humanos en el Mercosur. Archivos del Presente: Revista Latinoamericana de temas internacionales 2: 145–152

Porrata-Doria R A (2004) MERCOSUR: The Common Market of the Twenty-First Century? Ga. J. Int'l & Comp. L. 32(1) 1–72

Porrata-Doria R A (2005) MERCOSUR: The Common Market of the Southern Cone. Carolina Accademic Press, Durham, NC

Pustorino P (2001) Sull'adattamento ed il rango degli atti del MERCOSUR negli ordinamenti degli Stati membri. In: Del Vecchio A (ed), Aspetti dell'integrazione latinoamericana. Giuffrè, Milano, pp. 117–126

Ramírez S (2013) Regionalism: The Pacific Alliance, special issue: Latin America Goes Global. Americas Quarterly, at: http://www.americasquarterly.org/content/regionalism-pacific-alliance. Accessed 22 march 2014

Ruiz Diaz Labrano R (1998) Mercosur. Integración y derecho. Intercontinental Editora, Buenos Aires

Ryan-Collins L (2009) Power and Choice in International Trade: How Power Imbalances Constrain the South's Choices on Free Trade Agreements, With a Case Study of Uruguay, (London School of Economics, Working Papers Series, London, at: www.lse.ac.uk/depts/destin. Accessed 7 July 2014

Santos Belandro R B (2001) Bases Fundamentales del Derecho de la Integración y Mercosur. Asociación de Escribanos del Uruguay, Montevideo

Santulli C (2012) Retour à la théorie de l'organe commun: réflexions sur la nature juridique des organisations internationales à partir du cas de l'Alba et de la Celac, comparées notamment à l'Union européenne et à l'O.N.U. Revue générale de droit international public 116: 565–578

Schelhase M (2011) The Changing Context of Regionalism and Regionalization in the Americas: Mercosur and Beyond. In: Shaw T M, Grant J A, Cornelissen S (eds), The Ashgate Research Companion to Regionalisms, Ashgate, Farnham, pp. 175–192

Teubal Alhadeff E (1995) Argentina-Brasil-Paraguay-Uruguay Additional Protocol to the Treaty of Asunción on the Institutional Structure of Mercosur (Protocol of Ouro Preto). ILM 34: 1244–1259

Tiburcio C (2010) Cooperation in Civil Judicial Matters. In: Toscano M, Filho F, Lixinski L, Olmos Giupponi M B (eds) (2010) The Law of MERCOSUR. Hart publishing, Oxford, pp. 211–224

Toscano M, Filho F, Lixinski L, Olmos Giupponi M B (eds) (2010) The Law of MERCOSUR. Hart publishing, Oxford

Tosi J L (1999) Comercio internacional y Mercosur. Ediciones La Rocca, Buenos Aires

Vervaele J A E (2005a) Mutual trust and Mercosur integration in South America, Igitur Archief-Utrecht Publishing and Archiving Service, Open Educational Resources (OER) Portal at: http://igitur-archive.library.uu.nl/law/2006-0203-200119/mercosur.southafrica..rtf. Accessed 12 July 2014

Vervaele J A E (2005b) Mercosur and Regional Integration in Latin America. The International and Comparative Law Quarterly 54(2): 387–409.

Chapter 7
The Alliance of the Pacific: A New Instrument of Latin American and Caribbean Economic Integration?

Francesco Seatzu

Abstract This chapter considers a selected number of the structure and aims of the Alliance of the Pacific (the Alliance). It evaluates some of its key features and provides an outline of its background, internal structure and functioning. It takes the MERCOSUR as a point of reference where appropriate, since a conceptual comparison between a MERCOSUR-type free trade area and an Alliance-type free trade area can show the relative uniformity of these types of trading conglomerates but also their functional diversities. The second part of the chapter endeavours to assess the Alliance's effectiveness in the achievement of its statutory aims and, where possible, will discuss some proposals for reformulating the structure and functioning of the Alliance's agreement.

Keywords Latin America and the Caribbean · Alliance of the Pacific · Summit of Paranal · Latin American Integration Association (LAIA) · Trans-Pacific partnership · Framework agreement · Free trade area · Economic integration

Contents

F. Seatzu (✉)
International and European Union Law, University of Cagliari, Cagliari, Italy
e-mail: seatzu@hotmail.com

© T.M.C. ASSER PRESS and the authors 2015
M. Odello and F. Seatzu (eds.), *Latin American and Caribbean International Institutional Law*, DOI 10.1007/978-94-6265-069-5_7

7.1 Introduction

The so-called 'Framework Agreement' (*Acuerdo Marco de la Alianza del Pacífico*)[1] was signed on the occasion of the Summit of Paranal, and it led to the creation of the Alliance of the Pacific (Alliance) between Argentina, Chile, Colombia, Mexico and Peru on 6 June 2012.[2] As drafted, the 'Framework Agreement' indicates a cautious approach by the member states toward economic integration in Latin America and the Caribbean (LAC).[3] The Alliance's caution is due to various factors, especially the circumstance that this organization 'reinforces' but does not substitute the other integration processes in the LAC region.[4] Manifestly, this approach is strictly linked to the member states' refusal to accept a supranational legal scheme consistent with the advanced instruments of integration pursued. Instead, the LAC region has once again chosen the traditional tools of international law for the same reason as before: to authorize member states to be the ultimate controllers of the integration process. Regardless of the circumstance that establishing arrangements are normally incapable of realizing their thrust towards integration, this excessively timid attitude noticeably mirrors the LAC countries' conflicting inclinations. For example, while these countries aim to achieve in-depth integration in the economic and social fields, they have refused to entrust the community institutions of their area with the decisional powers they need for international amalgamation, which is unlike what occurs in the European Union.

This incongruity between the indicated socio-economic aims and the legal institutional framework has been the real *leitmotif* of the Latin American and Caribbean experiences of integration since 1980 when the Latin American

---

[1]The text (in Spanish) of the Framework Agreement is available at: http://alianzapacifico.net/doc uments/2014/Acuerdo_Comercial.pdf. Accessed 10 November 2014).

[2]Costa Rica and Panama—which currently are 'candidate observers' (*observadores candidatos*) to the Alliance—are expected to join as full members once free trade agreements with all the four current member states have entered into force.

[3]See Ramírez 2013; Saltamacchia Ziccardi 2014.

[4]According to Article 8 of the Framework Agreement, the decisions of the Council of Ministers and any other agreements adopted shall not modify or replace the bilateral, regional or multilateral economic, trade and integration agreements in force among the parties.

Integration Association (LAIA),[5] the first 'real' experience of integration in Latin America, was established under the Treaty of Montevideo.[6] This trend was confirmed by the Treaty of Asunción, which created the Southern Common Market (MERCOSUR), and it was further confirmed by the 2012 Framework Agreement which establishes the Alliance. All these agreements were aimed at establishing areas of regional economic integration in Latin America. However, this incompatibility is more evident in the Framework Agreement because there is more emphasis on the economic commitment for creating a common space for the movement of goods, services, capital and people than on former occasions.[7] Looking at the way the Alliance was formed, the incompatibility between aims and instruments is understandable as the group could become the deepest and perhaps most ambitious economic and trade bloc of Latin America and the Caribbean.[8] Yet, while the foundation of the Alliance was the main commitment under the Framework Agreement, any normative super-organization to implement this all-encompassing economic and social task is currently absent.

On the other hand, the Alliance does achieve a shift of focus in the economic strategy of integration compared to that applied, for instance, by MERCOSUR which was grounded on the establishment of an outward-looking Common Market.[9] New scenarios in the world economy have led three of the four founding members of the Alliance (Chile, Mexico and Peru) to be part of the ongoing negotiations to establish the Trans-Pacific Partnership (TPP)[10] that would connect this area of the Latin American Pacific with Asia Pacific, North America and also the European space, and in 2012 these negotiations made it difficult to replicate the more traditional model of integration as such without any changes. The objectives laid down in the Framework Agreement are broad and ambitious, and together with the expression of 'deep integration' that implies the idea of going beyond the simple free trade treaties, the Alliance was conceived as a space for the

---

[5]*Amplius* Oelsner 2005, p. 97 ff.

[6]It is worth noting that an earlier attempt of integration was made in Latin America in 1960 under the Treaty of Montevideo, which established the Latin American Free Trade Association (LAFTA). See Sect. 7.2.1 and Chap. 2 of this book. On the subject, see also Milensky 1973, p. 289.

[7]See Sect. 7.3.1.

[8]See M Naím, The Most Important Alliance You've Never Heard Of, *The Atlantic,* 17 February 2014, at: http://www.theatlantic.com/international/archive/2014/02/the-most-important-alliance-youve-never-heard-of/283877/. Accessed 11 November 2014.

[9]As observed by the majority of commentators, the main purpose of MERCOSUR is to bridge the gap between member states' economies and the world economy by seeking international competitiveness of domestic products through technological advancement. See also Chap. 6 in this book.

[10]The Trans-Pacific Partnership Agreement (TPP) is a FTA currently being negotiated by nine countries: United States, Australia, Brunei Darussalam, Chile, Malaysia, New Zealand, Peru, Singapore and Vietnam. For a commentary of the TPP draft of November 2013, see: Polanco 2013, p. 231 ff; Vincent 2013.

development of productive chains aimed above all at making the most of the mega-preferential interregional trade agreements.

A critical assessment of the Framework Agreement indicates that the failure of the Alliance member states to foresee a supranational normative structure caused them to be unprepared at the time of the agreement to consent to any transfer of those decisional powers that are indispensable for making the Alliance a tool for realizing reciprocal trade liberalization, i.e. the main purpose of the Alliance according to the Preamble of its Framework Agreement.[11] Perhaps the member states chose to keep the opportunity to unilaterally maintain connections with third states and other economic areas or, alternatively, to strengthen the integrative process.[12] This final result appears to be conditioned by the chances the Alliance gives to member states to reach wider international integration on joint grounds rather than on individual grounds.[13] The analysis will therefore maintain that this result will establish the Alliance's definitive normative model.

7.2 Building a Viable Tool of Integration

7.2.1 From Regionalism to Sub-regionalization

Pursuing economic integration through a supranational normative scheme has always been complex for Latin American and Caribbean countries. Clearly, the juridical feature of normative schemes contained in agreements pursuing economic integration, such as the Treaty on European Union (TEU)[14] and the Treaty on the Functioning of the European Union (TFEU),[15] shows the underlying political determination of their member states to achieve such an outcome. However, examples like the European Union, where member states agreed to a definitive

---

[11]The Preamble includes the commitment to create: 'a predictable legal framework for trade in goods and services, and investment'.

[12]See the Preamble of the Framework Agreement which stresses that: 'that regional economic integration is one of the instruments for Latin American countries to make progress towards their sustainable economic and social development'.

[13]See also F Peña, El MERCOSUR y sus perspectivas: una opción por la inserción competitiva mundial, paper delivered at the seminar on the outlook for subregional integration processes in Latin America and South America, Brussels, 4–5 November 1991, at: http://ctrc.sice.oas.org/ge ograph/south/mstit2_e.pdf. Accessed 11 November 2014, who stresses that: 'More than enforceable legal commitments, this agreement (the 'Framework Agreement') proposes objectives and expresses the willingness to work together, setting the institutional framework for doing so'.

[14]Treaty on the European Union (TEU), Consolidated version, C 115 (2008), available at: http:// eur-lex.europa.eu/JOHtml.do?uri=OJ:C:2008:115:SOM:EN:HTML. Accessed 12 November 2014.

[15]Treaty on the Functioning of the European Union (TFEU), Consolidated version, C 83/49, *Official Journal of the European Union*, 30 March 2010.

transfer of decisional powers to a superstructure in order to achieve socio-economic integration in the EU area,[16] are in sharp contrast to those where such a transfer is conditioned by the positive outcomes of a (usually lengthy) step-by-step inter-country negotiation. As such, it is intuitive that a sound interest in a wider and integrated market project among the largest industrial groups would be of help, since it would work as an incentive. When the EEC (the predecessor of the TFEU) and the Latin American Free Trade Association (LAFTA) treaties were respectively drafted, such interest was present among EEC (now EU) member states, but not among all the Latin American and Caribbean countries. Yet in that period (1960s), LAFTA was not accepted with great enthusiasm by some states, such as Colombia and Chile, which held that LAFTA mainly helped the LAC region's 'Big Three' (Mexico, Argentina and Brazil).[17] This perception was also aggravated by the economic and political instability of the region that worked as a deterrent against a possible regional cooperation in Latin America. The pre-existing democratic gap was strengthened by the rise of military dictatorships throughout the continent during the 1970s, and this did not favour the enhancement of regional integration, especially in light of the conflicting interests of the LAC countries.[18]

Since the mid-1970s, the failure of LAFTA has led most leaders in Latin America (especially in Brazil and Argentina) to start pushing for a reformulation of their regional integration strategies.[19] This led to the negotiation of a new Treaty of Montevideo in 1980. The outcome was the creation of the Latin American Integration Agreement (LAIA), which was believed to be more flexible and pragmatic in terms of regional integration tools. In fact the common market established by this agreement was aimed at absorbing external commerce and fostering a network of economic interdependence between LAC countries through two separate types of trade liberalization instruments (respectively, an overall tariff reduction scheme for all member states and a framework in which the signing partners might commit themselves to additional commerce liberalization schemes or increased economic cooperation).[20] LAIA was therefore set up with the

---

[16]This is also true after the entry in force of the Treaty of Lisbon which allows member states to withdraw from the EU. Under Article 50 of the TEU, a member state would notify the European Council of its intention to secede from the Union and a withdrawal agreement shall be negotiated between the EU and that state. *Amplius* Nicolaides 2013.

[17]Valvis 2008.

[18]*Amplius* Williamson 2003, Chap. 10.

[19]Ibidem.

[20]See: Valvis 2008, stressing that LAIA embodied an innovative technique to by-pass the unconditional application of the most-favoured nation clause (MFNC). Two or more member states were enabled to build bilateral or multilateral discriminatory economic blocks, framed as Partial Scope Agreements (PSA), freezing the operation of the MFNC and curtailing its automatic application. Multilateralization would then take place not automatically but through unilateral negotiations with remaining LAIA member states. On the history of this organization, see: Reinalda 2009, p. 475 ff.

essential task of redirecting international commerce towards the common market. Countries were asked to liberalize reciprocal commerce and promote sustained development. Accordingly, under the LAIA Treaty, the establishment of a common market for Latin American was agreed upon with the initial basis of this market being a Free Trade Area—an Economic Preferential Zone—among member states.

Nevertheless, notwithstanding the liberal methodological proposals the LAIA did not work. A possible reason is that, like LAFTA, LAIA applied import-substitution policies regionally, whereas its members kept favouring world market connections. Therefore, no supranational devices were forecast in LAIA. Consensus was missing for normative integration devices working without States' specific control so integration did not progress beyond the initial stages. Again, political eagerness did not succeed in supporting the development of an area of economic preference. In other words, the constant rivalry between individual states with analogous inward-looking growth strategies led the LAIA agreement to disaster. Internal markets did not open and, as a result, the objective of diverting third party imports to intra-regional manufacture and export did not actually occur.

A further experiment of integration was made in the early 1990s with the Treaty of Asunción establishing the MERCOSUR,[21] not at the regional but at subregional level. The rationale behind the creation of the MERCOSUR is indicated in Article 1 of the Treaty of Asunción and is not without legal significance.[22] This is clear from a number of MERCOSUR arbitral awards which have stressed its importance with respect to the scope of the new institution, its status as successor to the LAFTA and as an aid to interpretation in construing certain substantive provisions in the various additional protocols to the Treaty of Asunción.[23] The ultimate objectives of the MERCOSUR are threefold: the creation of a free trade area, of a customs union and of a common market for goods and services between the participants, showing that economic development is the number one regional priority.[24] In seeking to achieve these objectives, MERCOSUR should take into account the environment and the needs of the different sectors of the economy, based on the principles of gradualism, flexibility and balance.

---

[21]Treaty of Asunción, Treaty Establishing a Common Market, Asunción, 26 March 1991, entered into force 1 January 1995, Argentina, Brazil, Paraguay and Uruguay, UN Doc. A/46/155 (1991); 30 ILM 1041; see Chap. 6 in this book.

[22]The Treaty of Asunción includes five annexes that established: (a) an automatic, linear and generalized programme of elimination of intra-zone tariffs, (b) a system of rules of origin, (c) a transitory system of intra-zone safeguards, (d) a time frame for the setting up of a dispute settlement mechanism and (e) ten working groups to promote the coordination of specific economic and sector policies. Annex I had to be fully incremented by 1994 (1995 for Paraguay and Uruguay) and the other Annexes were envisaged only for the transitory period until 31 December 1994. See: Alonso García 1997.

[23]See Mercosur, Tribunal ad hoc, Laudo sobre Aplicación de Medidas Apropiadas para Prevenir y/o Hacer Cesar los Impedimentos a la Libre Circulación Derivados de los Cortes en Territorio Argentino de vías de Acceso a los Puentes Internacionales Gral. San Martín y Gral. Artigas (Uruguay v. Argentina), 6 September 2006, at: http://www.sice.oas.org/dispute/mercosur/laudo%20librecirculacion_006_s.pdf. Accessed 10 June 2013.

[24]*Amplius* Lorenzo and Vaillant 2005, p. 2 ff.

The means for achieving these objectives are reminiscent of those set out in the LAFTA[25] and the 1980 Treaty of Montevideo that established the organization that followed LAFTA, the Latin American Integration Association (ALADI),[26] on which they are substantially based, thereby reinforcing MERCOSUR as the successor to the former LAFTA treaty regime. The legal instruments that are to be employed in achieving the MERCOSUR objectives may be summarized as the continued agreement among members on the substantial reduction of tariffs and other obstacles to trade and the reduction of discriminatory barriers, in particular to services trade. While both these aims endorse the practice of the Contracting Parties with respect to substantive and procedural provisions under the former LAFTA treaty regime, thereby ensuring a certain continuity of practice and principles in MERCOSUR, there is no reference in the overall aims to institutional continuity. The reason for this is that there simply were none, at least in the formal sense of the term.

7.2.2 A New Institution for Integration in Latin America

The Lima Declaration calling for the creation of a Pacific Alliance in April 2011 dramatically shifted the focus of the Peru–Chile–Colombia and Mexico economic relationship. Its distinctive characteristics were to enhance cooperation among members with the explicit purpose of forging closer relations with the Asia-Pacific region that has become the most important trade partner of LAC countries.[27] Thus, unlike other recent agreements that tend to be regionally focused, such as the Union of South American Nations (*Unión de Naciones Suramericanas*, UNASUR),[28] the Bolivarian Alliance for the Peoples of Our America (*Alianza Bolivariana para los Pueblos de Nuestra América*, ALBA)[29] and the Community of Latin American and Caribbean States (*Comunidad de Estados Latinoamericanos y Caribeños*, CELAC),[30] the Alliance operates as a scheme of integration that is open to the participation of other countries (including even Canada which does not belong to the LAC region) that share the readiness to

---

[25]See Chap. 2 in this book; for further details concerning the aims and structure of the LAFTA, see: O'Keefe 2009, p. 5 ff.

[26]On the ALADI, see Chap. 2 in this book; Opertti Badán 2006, pp. 213–256; Ferrer Vieyra 2003, pp. 529–542.

[27]Ramírez 2013.

[28]The text of the 2008 Union of South American Nations (UNASUR) Treaty can be found at: http://www.comunidadandina.org/ingles/csn/treaty.htm. On the subject, see Chap. 3 in this book; Amoroso Botelho 2013; Manzolillo 2011, p. 203 ff.

[29]See: Lamrani 2012; Santulli 2012.

[30]See: Fernández 2012.

achieve the Alliance's objectives and comply with the essential requirements on democracy and rule of law.

In June 2012 the 'Framework Agreement', which incorporated most of the 1990 Lima Declaration statements, was concluded by Peru, Chile, Colombia and Mexico with the aim of setting up a model of economic and political integration primarily aimed at attracting investment and creating export platforms for the global market.[31] On 10 February 2014, Colombia, Chile, Mexico and Peru signed the Additional Protocol to the Framework Agreement which liberalizes 92 % of their commerce, with the remaining 8 % over the coming years.[32] All four founding countries of the Alliance are also members of the ALADI; therefore, they are participating in two distinct overlapping integration schemes.[33]

7.2.3 A Preliminary Appraisal

A trend rejecting regionalism and in-depth integration seems discernible in Latin America. This is manifest from various circumstances. In the first place, it arises from the fact that sub-regional multilateral institutions are rapidly becoming substitutes of the Inter-American Development Bank (IADB) and the World Bank in the suppliance of development finance and technical assistance to the countries of the LAC region.[34] Second, this is suggested by the more general fact that expectations generated with the launch of an integration agreement, at least among Latin American countries, have often resulted in frustration. Accordingly, countries would not be willing to consent to legal integration models operating without their full individual control. This unwillingness appears to have permeated the Framework Agreement establishing the Alliance. Under this agreement, the member states, while expressly agreeing to go beyond the simple free trade agreements (FTAs), have not yet consented to a normative framework capable of developing relentless progression toward such a goal.

In reality, as it also appears from the fact that the member countries of the Alliance are already linked with each other by preferential agreements concluded

---

[31]See SELA, The Pacific Alliance in Latin American and Caribbean Integration, Permanent Secretariat. Caracas, Venezuela, May 2013 (SP/Di N° 1–13) at: http://www.sela.org/attach/2 58/EDOCS/SRed/2013/07/T023600005209-0-SP-DI_N_1-13_ALIANZA_PACIFICO_EN_ LA_INTEGRACION_LA_Y_CARIBENA-INGLES.pdf. Accessed 15 September 2014, stressing that the Alliance provides a new integration space aimed at shaping up a process of convergence of existing agreements among member states. See also Rivarola Puntigliano and Briceño-Ruiz 2013, p. 2 ff.

[32]Additional Protocol to the Framework Agreement of the Pacific Alliance, Cartagena de Indias, 10 February 2014 at: http://www.sice.oas.org/Trade/PAC_ALL/Index_PDF_s.asp. Accessed 11 November 2014.

[33]Incidentally, it is worth stressing that Colombia and Peru are also part of the Andean Community (CAN).

[34]*Amplius* Seatzu 2014, p. 165 ff.

in the framework of the LAIA, the Alliance shall be understood as a sub-system operating within LAIA's global framework. More exactly, it has to be considered as a Partial Scope Agreement. It may be recalled that, within each such subsystem, concessions granted between its Parties are not automatically extended to remaining LAIA members. In fact, the Alliance member states participate in a wide network of overlapping independent agreements.

Against the above background, an analysis of the Framework Agreement will be proposed. After a general discussion of the approach adopted for the development of the Framework Agreement signed in 2012, it will be held that this Agreement, far from embodying a single agreement to establish the deepest and most ambitious economic and trade bloc of Latin America and the Caribbean, contains two distinct overlapping agreements. On one hand, there is an agreement concluded under a compulsory normative framework leading to the creation of a Free Trade Area alone, which does not hinder member states from maintaining integration links with other countries. On the other hand, there is an agreement for member states to carry out negotiations leading to the setting up of a convergence process of existing agreements among member states and organizing a new institutional environment for the enactment of initiatives to deepen or complement such agreements. In other words, this is an agreement that would be consolidated, provided there is enough political consensus to support the structure on which to build the independent trade relations necessarily involved in the implementation of such a market system.

The following analysis of the Framework Agreement has been organized into two parts. First, the Agreement's textual contents will be examined, having regard to its ability to achieve its statutory aims. Subsequently, an attempt will be made to discuss the rationale underlying its model in the light of the viability of translating into juridical terms the actual political decision of member states to establish a Free Trade Area system.

7.3   The Model of the Framework Agreement

7.3.1   Describing the Framework Agreement: Is This Agreement (and Its Additional Protocol) a Viable Tool for Achieving Economic Integration?

With the Framework Agreement, Peru, Chile, Colombia and Mexico agreed to the establishment of the Alliance by June 2012.

The Framework Agreement marked a drastic methodological and conceptual departure from the model adopted by the Treaty of Asunción establishing the Southern Common Market (MERCOSUR). In methodological terms, the diffuse definition envisaged by the Treaty of Asunción was reformulated to facilitate entry into the Asian market and, particularly, to create wider bargaining power than any of the individual countries of the Alliance could muster separately when approaching China.[35]

On the other hand, the Framework Agreement adopted the principle of not imposing any obligations for the members of the Alliance in matters related to the trade of goods and services, investments, the movement of people, government procurement and dispute settlement. In this way, since all these issues are issues that shall be negotiated through the relevant technical groups created for this purpose under the guidance of the High Level Group (HLG) formed by the Vice Ministers of Trade and Foreign Affairs of the four founding countries, the Framework Agreement abandoned the concept of comprehensiveness of regulation applied by a large number of Free Trade Agreements (FTAs).

Through a brief text containing 17 Articles, the Framework Agreement organized the legal machinery grounding the creation of the Alliance.

Adopting a conceptual framework of a common market system founded upon the 'four freedoms' as set forth in the TFEU and Treaty of Asunción: free movement of goods, services, persons and capital, Article 3 of the Framework Agreement categorically mandated by June 2012 the creation of the Alliance for the Pacific. This system involved, amongst other things:

(a) The free movement of capital, goods, services and other factors of production between member states by means of, among others, the elimination of customs duties and of non-tariff restrictions and of measures of equivalent effect to the circulation of goods;
(b) The progressive integration of member states through new mechanisms of cooperation;
(c) A support to the strengthening of the legal framework to combat and prevent organized crime;
(d) The promotion of the 2001 Pacific Cooperation Platform.

From the combination of Articles 2 and 16 of the Framework Agreement it appears that the free trade area on which the Alliance is to be identified is 'permanent' (i.e. no date/period restrictions). However, and curiously, neither these articles nor any other articles of the Framework Agreement specify whether this free trade area is based on the reciprocity of rights and of obligations among member states or not.[36]

These provisions enshrined the focus of the Framework Agreement of setting up a fully-fledged trade area within the span of a single and remarkably brief stage. It is worth noting that this happened without giving differential treatment to Peru and Colombia, consistent with relatively lower economic development levels.

It is against this overall backdrop that an attempt will be made in this chapter to examine the practical validity of the Framework Agreement's normative system to

---

[35]*Amplius* Perry 2014.

[36]On the contrary, Article 5 of the Framework Agreement suggests that the principle of reciprocity is not a core principle of the Alliance.

accomplish the Article 3 obligational framework, through a compatibility assessment of the mechanisms imposed to enforce its component freedoms.

It will be maintained that the normative system inherent in the Framework Agreement is unfeasible, per se, to ground such a common trade area throughout the territories of the member states as of 2 June 2012.

This evaluation will be made against the simple allegation that the legal implications are quite considerable and thus require the creation of a sound common juridical framework for the ensemble of economic operators within a space such as that of the Alliance, since a common area of free trade is: 'an area which allows the agreeing nations to focus on their competitive advantage and to freely trade for the goods they lack the experience in making, thus increasing the efficiency and profitability of each country'.

Establishing agreements creating deep integration systems, like the TFEU and TEU, provide for such a framework either directly through provisions or by entrusting enactment to community bodies and institutions. Remarkably, in this regard, the normative corpus of the Framework Agreement is inadequately developed at both the institutional and instrumental levels.

In other words, the Alliance's founding agreement not only does not contain a comprehensive normative framework, but it also does not provide a coherent institutional framework capable of reshaping internal legislation in order to guarantee (throughout the Alliance area) free movement of production factors and non-discriminatory access to the growth of economic activities by nationals of any member state. It follows then that their integration would be comparable to economic activities within a single country.

In reality, in contrast to its Article 3, the Framework Agreement's instrumental mechanisms and institutional tasks are aimed at the establishment of a common external tariff towards third countries and the liberalization of goods and services circulation among member states. This is to the clear detriment of the other core freedoms, which the Framework Agreement in combination with its 2014 Additional Protocol[37] regulated in a rather generic manner. On one hand, the achievement of free circulation of interstate services and goods was organized via a clear-cut regulation in the above named Additional Protocol and its administration was attributed to Alliance bodies. Nevertheless, the free interstate circulation of capital and people between the Alliance's member states, agreed to be attained together with the liberalization of services and goods by Article 3 of the Framework Agreement, failed to enjoy equivalent institutional support. No clear timetables and mechanisms were indicated, nor was their enactment overtly entrusted to Alliance bodies, which gave further prominence to the dichotomy.

Admittedly, the generic abolition of obstacles for access to a member state's internal economy by other members' nationals tends to be strongly resisted because it clearly impinges on the true content of state sovereignty. Such a dual attitude was also evident in the EU.

---

[37]Additional Protocol to the Framework Agreement of the Pacific Alliance, n. 32 above.

Nevertheless, the incapacity of the Framework Agreement's normative scheme is demonstrated by the misshaped treatment given to liberalization measures regarding the movement of capital and people—measures that cannot work as feature-modelling of market integration. Clearly, these were also sensitive issues in the Andean Community and EU cases. Despite these and other issues, the creation of a common market system in Europe was clearly grounded on specific treaty provisions and procedures containing the global liberalization of factors of production together with the re-writing of competition rules. Therefore, while the Treaty of the EC (currently the TFEU) initially created a customs union, it went much further than that, establishing a single common market.

From this perspective, it is evident that the member states approached the Alliance for the Pacific in a contradictory and cautious manner. Nevertheless, while their caution may be justified (see, among others, the Treaty of Asunción establishing MERCOSUR), the fixed approach that they adopted in rejecting, respectively, the 1969 Andean Pact[38] and its subsequent modifying acts, is surely not.

Remarkably, after adopting a commitment to create a common free trade area within a short timeframe, unlike the Andean Community and EU member countries the Alliance member states omitted to provide such a commitment with an autonomous normative system to achieve it. In other words, the Alliance was not built up within a self-sufficient normative system autonomous from and above the member states, in contrast to the Andean Community and EU members that operate by means of supranational laws that are legally mandatory for their members.[39] To follow the Andean and EU legal models would have imposed on the parties to the Alliance the duty to agree on a legal order transcending the national systems governing economic issues like for the Andean Community and EU countries. This would have been achieved by including supranational provisions in the Framework Agreement and by granting Alliance bodies' decisional powers to make their acts superior to national laws.

In contrast, the transfer of sovereignty always inherent in this type of international agreement was rejected by the Alliance parties. In other words, Alliance members zealously maintained their governance over their economies, subordinating the enhancement of market integration to direct supervision and negotiation.[40] Nevertheless, the Alliance's members decided to pursue integration through the classical tools of international law. In so acting, the legal effectiveness of the Framework Agreement and of its Additional Protocol was entirely different from

---

[38]Andean Sub-regional Integration Agreement, May 26, 1969, (1969) 8 ILM 910. On the subject, see: Avery and Cochraine 1973, pp. 198–199.

[39]This is confirmed in Article 8 of the Framework Agreement which states that the acts of the Alliance (Council of Ministers) do not affect the legal validity of any other (bilateral, regional or multilateral) agreements already in force between the member states.

[40]See e.g. Article 5 of the Framework Agreement, n. 32 above.

what it would have been if a supranational normative order had been enacted. Briefly speaking, the accomplishment of integration was to leave member states' sovereignty unaltered. As for its competence and tasks, the formation of the Alliance was not to involve a normative corpus possessing its own sovereign power upon domestic jurisdictions. In other words, in drafting the Framework Agreement and its Additional Protocol, member states did not transfer any sovereignty to Alliance bodies. Instead they remained the exclusive holders of decisional powers, consistent with the classical concept of sovereignty.

Against this backdrop, the viability of the normative framework provided by the Framework Agreement to set up the Alliance will be examined from a three-fold perspective:

(1) The legal character of the Alliance institutional framework established to administer the setting up of the common free trade area was of an intergovernmental nature with no community bodies foreseen. This institutional and normative framework functioned under classical international law, leaving no space for supranational features. Thus, the core issues of the common free trade area will be negotiated by the member states because, arguably, such a task was not assigned to the Alliance bodies.

(2) The tools provided by the Framework Agreement were primarily aimed at the liberalization of goods circulation amongst member countries, but omitted to deal regularly with the enforcement of the common trade area established by Article 1. Specifically, the liberalization of services, persons and capital circulation was not dealt with consistently.

(3) Framework Agreement rules applicable to inter-member states relations during the transitional period permitted their enduring participation in pre-existing international treaties and their future participation in new ones.

7.3.2 The Framework Agreement and Its Additional Protocol at Work

7.3.2.1 Enforcing Tools

The Framework Agreement, read in combination with the Additional Protocol of 2014, mandates the global establishment of a common area of free trade between the four founding members of the Alliance. Accordingly, core mechanisms were stipulated by Chap. 3 (Articles 3.1–3.14) of the 2014 Additional Protocol, complemented by other Protocol provisions. From these provisions it appears that the main tools to set up the common free trade area are:

(a) the coordination of macro-economic policies to be carried out gradually and in convergence with the tariff dismantlement and non-tariff abolition programmes;

(b) programmes for the liberalization of trade in goods and services including financial services, consisting of progressive tariff reductions, accompanied by the abolition of non-tariff barriers or measures of equivalent effect, as well as of other restrictions to interstate trade;

(c) the conclusion of sectorial treaties to optimize production factors, employment and mobility, and thus achieve an efficient operative scale.

Additionally, Article 3.3 of the Additional Protocol stated the principle of national treatment for goods. It held that products originating from any member state were to enjoy the same treatment as one's own nationals with respect to taxes, tariffs and other internal charges. Article 12 of the Framework Agreement stipulated that to help the establishment and subsequent operation of a common free trade area between the Alliance members, a settlement of disputes mechanism and safeguard provisions were thereby enacted by the member states.

7.3.2.2 Liberalization of Trade in Goods and Services

With the future enforcement of the Additional Protocol, a legal regime for the liberalization of inter-country commerce in goods and services will become compulsory. Its core instrument, the commercial liberalization programme envisaged in Articles 3.3–3.12 of the Protocol, will operate together with a system for the settlement of disputes and rules of origin.

As a result of the above named liberalization programme, a process of tariff reduction will therefore start to take place throughout the Alliance members' territories.[41] The programme will operate in a linear manner, encompassing the entire range of goods and services. Its aim is to abolish all restrictions to reciprocal commerce by the entry in force of the Protocol, when zero duty will be achieved. A rigid scheme of safeguard provisions (Chapter 18 of the Protocol) will also allow goods and services to be temporarily removed from the program. Clear 'Rules of Origin' guarantee that products will benefit from preferential treatment.

Similarly, when the Protocol is in force it will abolish non-tariff obstacles. In fact, the removal of tariffs will be accompanied by measures to boost international commerce and suppress non-tariff commerce and technical obstacles, including by enacting common standards and provisions on government procurement to guarantee national treatment, transparency in procurement processes and clear rules for all the Alliance members.[42]

---

[41]See Malthouse E, Pacific Alliance eliminates 92 % of tariffs between members, *Santiago Times*, 11 February 2014 at: http://santiagotimes.cl/pacific-alliance-eliminates-92-percent-tariffs-members/. Accessed 12 November 2014 (stressing that the Alliance has agreed to abolish tariffs immediately on 92 % of the goods traded between the member states, with the remaining tariffs to be dismantled in the following years).

[42]See: European Parliament-Policy Department, The Pacific Alliance: Regional Integration or Fragmentation? 10 January 2014 at: http://www.europarl.europa.eu/RegData/etudes/briefing_note/join/2014/522318/EXPO-AFET_SP(2014)522318_EN.pdf. Accessed 12 November 2014).

**... Institution of a Common External Tariff
... of Free Movement of Factors of Production**

... of Article 4

... to the liberalization of interstate commerce in goods and services, ... Framework Agreement nor its Additional Protocol provides a spe-... ment for the establishment of a Single External Tariff and/or a Single ... Commercial Policy toward third countries. In reality, the recognition of ... national mechanisms was not grounded on an obligatory instrumental ... was its later enclosure imperatively envisaged, whether by the ordinary ... activity of the Alliance or by provisions otherwise prescribed by the Agreement.

Nevertheless, if the Framework Agreement meant to supply an all-covering instrumental outline to set up the Alliance consistently with the Article 1 model—as would have been predictable from its all-encompassing wording stating: '[...] an area of regional integration'—it omitted to do so. In practical terms, Article 3, para 2(a) of the Framework Agreement contains two distinct instruments to enforce the Alliance, both of which are principally dedicated to the liberalization of goods, services and capital: on one hand, the cooperation platform for the Pacific (Article 3, para 2(f)); on the other hand, the coordination of national secto-rial and macroeconomic policies (Article 3, para 2(f)). Although the former was specially formulated for the circulation of free services, capital and goods, the lat-ter—after being articulated in global terms—was narrowed down to facilitate the interchange of goods and services, and substantially neglected to refer to the free movement of people. This is despite the fact that Article 3, para 2, let. (d) of the Agreement explicitly refers to the cooperation between consular and migration national authorities as a tool for enhancing the free movement of persons within the Alliance region. Moreover, this is also regardless of the elimination, from November 2012, of visa requirements for business travellers and people not exer-cising paid activities for stays up to 180 days.[43]

In a nutshell, the five aims containing the integrated market's foundational free-doms and the single external tariff enclosing the single customs territory, plus the devices provided for their satisfaction, substantially boiled down to three opera-tional instruments sufficient to realize the free circulation of goods, capital and services.

Beyond Article 4 of the Framework Agreement

Having exhausted the means indicated in Article 4 of the Framework Agreement, it is found that throughout the Agreement no other provisions explicitly deal with

---

[43]Ibidem.

tools aimed at allowing natural and juridical persons from any member state to supply services work and invest within any other member state.

Questionably, these complex issues were substantially left in a normative vacuum, and member states decided to enact all of them within their national jurisdictions in order to facilitate the realization of the Alliance as from 2012. Thus, authority for their achievement may only be established by going back to the general duty assumed by member states in Article 3 of the Framework Agreement itself: to liberalize inter-country commerce in goods and services for consolidating the free trade area amongst Alliance countries.

Against such a general duty, it may be argued that an alternative approach is provided for the liberalization of goods and services it is contended in this article that an alternative approach to that applied for liberalization of trade in goods and services is deceptive here; instead of supplying a mandatory comprehensive set of general provisions, of guiding rules and common schedules in accordance with the peculiarity of each of the three remaining market freedoms, the Agreement organizes a framework for member states to negotiate for themselves the advancement towards Alliance—beyond its commercial features.

The process of this negotiation framework is almost entirely left to the pledge of member states. The Agreement gives no timetables or mandatory rules and principles to be observed. It merely organizes its procedural substructure within the Alliance institutional framework through the establishment of several 'Working Groups' at whose level inter-country negotiations for coordination of national macroeconomic and sectorial policies, under Articles 4 and 5, are to be commenced.

Possibly, as will be argued in Part II, the systematic and progressive development of these tools was not envisaged in the Framework Agreement as an ordinary course of action and was not included among the ordinary tasks of the Alliance's bodies. On the other hand, the Framework's actual normative corpus fell short of the Alliance's extra-commercial aims. Thus, member states seem to have decided to examine and negotiate the enforcement of all of the remaining constituent issues of the Alliance rather than to include such policy decision-making among the Alliance bodies' regular tasks.

This would clarify why no theoretical guidelines and general principles governing coordination actions under Articles 4 and 5 are stipulated and why tariff abolition is the sole tool of automatic application.

Admittedly, the Framework Agreement does not prevent the employment of further tools as its text is envisaged as the stipulation of the main tools. Nevertheless, the silence concerning the common external tariff is at odds with the necessities of the common free trade area proclaimed by Article 3. It is equally indicative that the most substantive provisions in the Framework Agreement and its Additional Protocol are openly devoted to regulating inter-country commerce, whereas the residual freedoms receive less attention. There is no doubt that closer interlocking would have been expected to efficaciously coordinate the achievement of the four freedoms within the single-phased structure positively indicated in Article 3 but dismally fulfilled thereafter.

Additionally, the Framework Agreement omits to impose the principle of non-discrimination. Remarkably, such a foundational frame to market integration has been overlooked, contrasting with Article 18 of the TFEU that prohibits discrimination on the grounds of nationality. In the latter, in addition to being generally indicated, the principle is developed throughout the TFEU in the spheres of people and capital, as well as being reaffirmed by Article 21 of the EU Charter of Fundamental Rights and being included in primary EU law by Article 6 TEU.

From this viewpoint, the EU's supranational dynamics are clearly identifiable, especially in its institutional and normative interaction. Unquestionably, through the joined operation of the principles of integration and non-discrimination contained in Articles 11 and 18 of the TFEU, and of their enforcement by the normative activities of the EU bodies, the general integrative thrust may be projected beyond domestic normative limitations. This interaction takes place on the ground of the TFEU providing a pattern of demanding the gradual abolition of limitations on free circulation, the elimination of discrimination in the application of domestic provisions, and abstention from inserting further restrictions on free circulation, combined with the Court of Justice of the European Union (CJEU)'s direct action.[44]

A striking contradistinction is manifest in the method actually taken by Alliance member states. As we progress through the Framework Agreement, we find it promptly loses strictness and fast displays purely declamatory content, since the few tangible obligatory provisions become progressively weakened by non-enforceable rules. Evidence of this is:

(a) with respect to non-tariff abolition, member states agree to the compulsory nature of enforcement via policies management, though no rigid rules are imposed other than a general commitment to establish 'a predictable legal framework for trade in goods and services, and investment';

(b) with respect to the enforcement of the Common External Tariff, a complete absence of compulsion exists. Such vital components of market integration had not yet been negotiated by member states at the time of the Agreement establishing the Alliance.

Thus, no real commitments to devise these issues were reached. Indeed, the consciousness that the core of any market integration unavoidably impacts on internal sovereignty clarifies the choice of a largely non-binding negotiational framework, lumped within the general scheme of macroeconomic management and harmonization of internal legislation under Article 4.

What is perhaps even more curious is that such far-reaching coordination to eliminate tariff barriers is so stymied by its inoperativeness. This defeats the object of the exercise to achieve zero duty among LAC members, threatening the core target of the free circulation of goods and services.

---

[44]See e.g. Oliver 2010, p. 239 ff.

From the instrumental viewpoint, member states also accepted a cautious approach to the institutional framework. Accordingly, the Alliance was established as a cooperative institution, described as being characterized by its respect for the internal sovereignty of its members and with a limited authority of its own. In contrast, integration institutions are characterized both by their being capable of exercising certain competencies belonging to the states and by the prominence of their powers, including decisional powers, the performing of compulsory community provisions, the supremacy of such community provisions, their direct applicability and majority procedural practices.[45]

The Framework Agreement did not include any of the latter formulations. Two main bodies were set up: The Council of Ministers (Council) and the High Level Group (*Grupo de Alto Nivel*). The Council is comprised of member states' Ministers of Foreign Relations and the Ministers responsible for Foreign Trade, and was conceived as the supreme organ of the Alliance, empowered with policy-making and deliberative tasks leading to the enforcement of the purposes and timetables imposed for the creation of the single area of economic integration. It meets at least once per year, but can meet extraordinarily if one of the members so demands.[46] Perfectly in accordance with its inter-governmental character, the decisions of the Council are adopted by unanimity. The High Level Group, which includes the member states' Vice Ministers of Foreign Affairs and Trade, was conceived as the executive body, commended to oversee the fulfilment of the Framework Agreement and the functioning of the technical working groups in five key areas: trade and integration, services and capital, movement of persons, cooperation and institutional matters.

In addition to these bodies, a Business Council (*Consejo Empresarial*) has been established to submit proposals for the integration process and enhance joint actions on third markets.[47] Encouraging direct dialogue between government and business, the Alliance's first Business Forum (*Encuentro Empresarial*) took place on 23 May 2013 during the summit in Cali and brought together some 50 businessmen and representatives of the Alliance's member and observer countries.[48]

A system of solving disputes with compulsory ad hoc arbitration was decided upon by the 2014 Additional Protocol (not yet in force) in compliance with the Framework Agreement's directives. Additionally, an Alliance Parliamentary Committee (*Comisón de Seguimiento Parlamentario al Acuerdo de la Alianza del Pacífico*) was set up in July 2013 in Chile with members designated for a period of 4 years according to the rules of the national parliaments.

---

[45]See e.g. Klabbers 2009, p. 24.

[46]*Amplius* European Parliament-Policy Department, n. 42 (stressing that the meetings of the ministers have been very frequent: the most recent one, held in Mexico on 9 January 2014, was the tenth since the launch of the Alliance).

[47]European Parliament-Policy Department, n. 42 above.

[48]Ibidem.

7.4 Institutions in Action

Insti tional powers have mainly been circumscribed to the management and impl nentation of commerce liberalization issues, while activities regarding the exe on of residual components of the Alliance were largely left to the initia- tive the single member states. In reality, Alliance bodies do not have the law- ma ability to endorse legislation leading to fully realizing the area of regional in on. Since all decisions require unanimity according to the Framework A nt, only the member states themselves might supply valid contents to the g ucture envisaged by Article 1 of the Agreement.

er words, there were no supranational effects ascribed to the Alliance al and normative framework, either at the decision-making or at the tation stage of integrative actions; neither were there bodies whose tasks al definitive independent powers. Instead, bodies were mainly repre- of the member states. Therefore, as already noticed above, the latter's indispensable to endorse both the enactment and the implementation of gislation. As regards implementation, unlike EU Law, Alliance legis- tirely dependent upon the intermediation of member states' normative erein each order indicates the rank, the technique of insertion, and the ity upon its natural and juridical persons. This results from the interna- utline enacted by Alliance members.

relationship of Member States

escribes that the Framework Agreement does not prejudice commit- ed at the date of its entry in force, including existing regional and trade agreements between member states. Accordingly:

- states shall refrain from damaging one another's interests in com- gotiations concluded *inter se;*
- states shall refrain from damaging the interests of remaining member d the area of regional integration's objectives in future treaties con- ith third countries;
- states will automatically extend to other member states any advan- ur, concession or privilege granted upon products from or to third member countries.

this provision, the Framework Agreement establishes a relatively work for the relationship of Alliance Parties. In particular, member banned from concurrently participating in other economic blocks, or extra-Alliance. However, the reference in Article 3.3 of the

Additional Protocol to Article 3.3 of the 1994 GATT containing the so-called Most Favoured Nation Clause (MFN)[49] suggests that the participation of Alliance members in discriminatory economic blocks is not allowed.

7.6 The Model of the Framework Agreement

7.6.1 Debating the Model of the Framework Agreement

In the previous part of this chapter it was argued that, in practical terms, the Framework Agreement has explicitly governed only a few (though crucial) issues of the regional integration system envisaged in Article 1: the free circulation of goods, services and capital between member states. It was also pointed out that regulations for the enforcement of the residual modules of Alliance—the single external tariff and the free movement of persons—are lacking or have obtained insufficient legal treatment while enactment by the Alliance bodies is not indicated in detail. An attempt will now be made to put forward some justification for the Agreement's scheme so as to understand the core reasons of the Agreement's stark omissions.

It has been recognized that the Framework Agreement was not perceived as a foundational frame for the Alliance, and that the main aim of the Agreement was only to supply a basic normative outline for its existence and functioning.[50] This contention is based on the lack of a permanent secretariat or administrative body to support decision-making. It is also supported by the wording of the Preamble that explicitly refers to the establishment of a regional area of integration between Colombia, Mexico, Peru and Chile.

This may be easily contrasted with the EEC Treaty (now the TFEU) that adopted progressiveness as a universal principle encompassing the entire range of market integration. Yet, since its inception, the creation of the single market, now internal market has been at the core of the EU's action. As the European Court of Justice (ECJ) duly explained in *Commission* v. *UK*, 'The EEC Treaty, by establishing a single market and progressively approximating the economic policies of the member states seeks to unite national markets in a single market having the features of an internal market'. [51]

Accordingly, the EEC Treaty displayed a pattern of introducing a duty to eradicate constraints during the transitional period, so that a specific outcome was to be achieved by the end of it, coupled with a 'standstill' rule that displayed its effect from the entry into force of the Treaty. Instead, the Framework Agreement omits resorting to such a progressive application in global market terms.

---

[49]On the subject, see the classical work of Fisher 1967, p. 841 ff.

[50]*Amplius* European Parliament-Policy Department, n. 42 above.

[51]ECJ, Case 207/83 *Commission* v. *UK* [1985] ECR, p. 1202.

A thorough investigation gives another conceivable justification for the incompleteness of the Framework Agreement, as there is enough evidence to contend that it embodies two distinct, though strictly interrelated, agreements. On one hand, there is a conclusive tangible agreement by member states to liberalize the reciprocal circulation of services and goods, therefore leading to the foundation of a single free commerce area. On the other hand, there is a general and latent agreement to create a single market alongside, but not subsequent to, the liberalization of reciprocal commerce. Consequently, concerning the free trade agreement, the Framework Agreement,[52] in combination with its Additional Protocol, provides a compulsory normative outline through a clear institutional and legal system. With respect to the single market agreement, the Framework Agreement provides a general normative scheme for member states themselves to pursue negotiations that lead to the enforcement of the single market. Agreements reached on these latter issues would integrate the Framework Agreement, but would obviously fall outside the original outline of the Framework Agreement and therefore demand national parliamentary endorsement to bestow them with legal meaning. This is because, unlike EU bodies, Alliance bodies have not been created with real powers to accomplish independently such tasks within the context of the Framework Agreement itself, therefore overriding internal parliamentary involvement.

This contradiction explains why, between Alliance member states, the Framework Agreement firmly discards the model of regulating implementation of two progressive phases pertaining to a single conceptual treaty, namely, the creation of a single market based on the prior establishment of a free trade agreement (FTA). Yet, this would have imposed a completely different arrangement between member states from the one in reality contained in the Framework Agreement.

More surprisingly, commerce liberalization is not foreseen as a mere constituent element intertwined with all the other corresponding constituent elements of a single compact unit to be established, i.e. a comprehensive single market. In effect, commerce liberalization is treated as an overlying issue of two distinct agreements.

This conclusion seems unavoidable. Generally observed, under the Framework Agreement there is but a single aim, namely the creation of a fully comprehensive area of regional integration, and there is but a single phase during which to achieve this aim. Indeed, the Framework Agreement does not explicitly regulate between member states the two progressive phases pertaining to a single agreement, which is the establishment of a single market to be grounded on the prior establishment of an FTA. Instead, it implicitly regulates the implementation of two separate agreements whose common aspect, trade liberalization, is not envisaged to perform a liaison between each distinct system embodied in each separate agreement, but is simply left as an overlapping component.

This deduction seems unavoidable. Roughly observed, under the Framework Agreement there is a single goal to be accomplished: the creation of a totally

---

[52]Framework Agreement, n. 1 above, Article 3, para 1(a).

all-inclusive single market. In describing this single market, commerce liberalization is considered as an element of a coherent whole. In organizing the enactment of the whole, real normative rules are contradictorily focused on commerce liberalization in such a universal manner that this fundamental phase seems severable from the whole. The Framework Agreement contains no explicit mention whatsoever of a free trade agreement as the first step of an evolutionary process; it merely desists from precisely regulating the enactment of the residual constituents of the single market, other than falling back on individual member states' negotiations. Going a step further, it can be claimed that such negotiations are ineludibly connected to the Framework Agreement's apparatus.

Accordingly, liberalization of trade in goods and services shall not be assumed as an expression of an arranged technique leading to the ongoing enactment of the single market. Apparently, member states decide to develop the single market through specific agreements negotiated and concluded among them as and when they see fit to do so. Therefore, a 'wait and see' approach seems to have been adopted.

On the other hand, it is in the nature of things that the accomplishment of tariff abolition can eventually accomplish the task of eliciting the final integrative thrust. In this case, the single market agreement would turn feasible due to one element enabling inter-country entrepreneurial economic networks and establishing a more favourable setting for member states consultations.

7.6.2 Reformulating the Machinery of the Framework Agreement

7.6.2.1 Realizing the Free Commerce Area

Free circulation in services and goods among member states has merited thorough and stringent regulation by the Framework Agreement and is provided with a compatible normative and institutional framework to guarantee its operation. Institutions accomplish executive tasks related to domestic economic policies coordination for the eradication of non-tariff obstacles. In this setting, measures enjoy an obligatory character, suggesting member states' duties under international law to regulate internal legislation and see to its implementation.

Relations among member states have been systematized in a manner consistent with a free trade area arrangement; as a result, countries reserve full control over commerce links with third states. As explicitly indicated by the Framework Agreement, member states keep their capacity to conclude commerce agreements with one another and with third countries.[53] In practical terms, the lack of a single external tariff would mean the establishment of a free commerce area.

---

[53]Framework Agreement, n. 1 above, Article 8.

7.6.2.2 Realizing the Common Market

In contrast to trade liberalization, the Framework Agreement does not empower Alliance bodies to endorse rules leading to the enactment of mechanisms useful to shaping a real single market, i.e. the principles of supremacy of community provisions, of their direct applicability and the external single tariff as well as free movement of persons. The approach of the Framework Agreement is to establish a pattern for member states to negotiate the achievement of some but not all of these issues, a pattern framed under the general duties member states assumed under Article 3 to coordinate and harmonize domestic economic policies and relevant regulation.

It might be held that coordination devices regarding the establishment of the area of regional integration under Article 3, para 1(a) carries a different normative character from harmonization acts under Article 3, para 2(a) regarding the eradication of non-tariff obstacles to trade in services and goods. Under Article 3, para 2(a) coordination was intended as a foundational instrumental tool of an obligatory nature. Instead, in the latter, coordination was considered not as an instrumental device to be employed by Alliance bodies in a direct way, but as a prior approach to allow member states to negotiate among themselves. In other words, coordination is not an activity for the bodies themselves to accomplish, but an activity for member states to realize within the outline of the Framework Agreement. Alliance bodies only give the organization for negotiations through Working Groups. Nonetheless, such activities help to integrate the Agreement itself and provide it with specific devices and guidelines so far lacking express stipulation.

Alongside this background the institutional organization of the Alliance reveals a dual nature: at times, it supplies an organized apparatus of bodies aimed at carrying out tasks related to the enactment of inter-country services, capital and goods liberalization. At other times, it introduces a setting to host the development of direct consultations among the member states themselves and the conclusion of arrangements that are indispensable for supplying the foundational agreement for the establishment of the area of regional integration. Although the liberalization of factors of production corresponds with the Alliance's main aim, the community bodies themselves only provide the outline for conferences held by member states' delegates at Ministers Council Summit Meetings.

7.7 Concluding Remarks

With the exceptions of the Andean Community and MERCOSUR, marked diversity among Latin American and Caribbean countries in the socio-economic field has undermined multilateral integration attempts to go a lot further than embryonic levels, as under LAIA. In-depth integration at bilateral and multilateral stages appears to be heavily influenced by countries' different economic tendencies and policy orientations to retain individual connections with developed marketplaces.

The Framework Agreement strives to enact integration, but it omits to establish a harmonious normative framework to bring it about. Dissimilarly, widespread leniency concerning member states' relations with third states and a stringently planned intra-Alliance commerce liberalization discipline are the foremost features of the Framework Agreement. Thus, in the final remarks it cannot be too audacious to conclude that perhaps, as Colombia and Peru are also part of the CAN, they can proceed to enjoy the benefits deriving from their membership of the new area of regional integration based on the Alliance without compromising their relations with non-Alliance countries. Undeniably, these countries have been left with the chance to become partners in—and yet to go no further than—an area of free commerce without abandoning current and prospective commercial connections with third states and with economic organizations and blocs other than the Pacific Alliance.

References

Alonso García R (1997) Tratado de Libre Comercio, Mercosur y Comunidad Europea: Solución de controversias e interpretación uniforme. McGraw-Hill, Madrid

Amoroso Botelho J C (2013) La creación y la evolución de Unasur. Juruá Editora, Curitiba

Avery W P and Cochraine J D (1973) Innovation in Latin American Regionalism: The Andean Common Market. International Organisation 27(2): 181–223

Fernández F (2012) Alba-TCP et CELAC: instruments d'une politique indépendante et souveraine. Revue générale de droit international public 116: 557–563

Ferrer Vieyra E (2003) Reflexiones sobre la integración de America Latina (ALADI). In: Comité Jurídico Interamericano (ed), Cursos de derecho internacional: serie temática. UNAM, Instituto de Investigaciones Jurídicas, México DF, pp. 529–542

Fisher G C (1967) The "Most Favored Nation" Clause in GATT: A Need for Reevaluation? Stanford Law Review 19: 841–855

Klabbers J (2009) International Institutional Law. Cambridge University Press, Cambridge

Lamrani S (2012) The Bolivarian Alliance for the Peoples of Our America: The Challenges of Social Integration. The International Journal of Cuban Studies 4(3–4): 347–365

Lorenzo F and Vaillant M (2005) The MERCOSUR and the Creation of the Free Trade Area of the Americas. In: Lorenzo F and Vaillant M (eds), Mercosur and the Creation of the Free Trade Area of the Americas. Woodrow Wilson International Center for Scholars, Washington DC, pp. 1–28

Manzolillo C (2011) Il trattato costitutivo dell'Unione delle Nazioni Sudamericane (Unasur). In: La protezione dell'ambiente e la collaborazione fra l'Unione europea e il Mercosur: Atti del seminario (Sassari, 10–11 ottobre 2008), Jovene, Napoli

Milensky E (1973) The Politics of Regional organization in Latin American Free Trade Association. Praeger, New York

Nicolaides P (2013) Withdrawal from the European Union: a typology of effects. Maastricht Journal of European and Comparative Law 20: 209–219

Oelsner A (2005) International Relations in Latin America: Peace and Security in the Southern Cone. Routledge, Abingdon

O'Keefe T A (2009) Latin American and Caribbean Trade Agreements: Keys to a Prosperous Community of the Americas. Martinus Nijhoff Publishers, Leiden

Oliver P (ed) (2010) Oliver on Free Movement of Goods in the European Union. Hart Publishing, Oxford

Opertti Badán D (2006) Globalización e integración: presente de la Asociación Latinoamericana de Derecho Internacional (Aladi). In: AA.VV. Curso de Derecho Internacional: organizado por el Comité Juridico Interamericano y la Secretaría General de la OEA en agosto de 2005. OEA, Washington, DC, pp. 213–256

Perry G (2014) The Pacific Alliance: A Way Forward for Latin American Integration? Centre for Global Development, Washington DC, at http://www.cgdev.org/sites/default/files/pacific-alliance-way-forward-latin-american-integration.pdf. Accessed 5 November 2014

Polanco R (2013) The Trans-Pacific Partnership Agreement and Regulatory Coherence. In: Voon T (ed) Trade Liberalisation and International Co-operation: a Legal Analysis of the Trans-Pacific Partnership Agreement. Edward Elgar, Cheltenham

Ramírez S (2013) Regionalism: The Pacific Alliance, special issue: Latin America Goes Global. Americas Quarterly, at: http://www.americasquarterly.org/content/regionalism-pacific-alliance. Accessed 22 March 2014

Reinalda B (2009) Routledge History of International Organizations: From 1815 to the Present Day. Routledge, Abingdon

Rivarola Puntigliano A and Briceño-Ruiz J (eds) (2013) Resilience of Regionalism in Latin America and the Caribbean: Development and Autonomy. Palgrave MacMillan, London:

Saltamacchia Ziccardi N (2014) The Mexican Agenda in Latin America: the Pacific Alliance, paper delivered at the Mexican Week, London School of Economics, 11–13 March 2014, at: http://www.academia.edu/7176070/The_Mexican_Agenda_in_Latin_America_the_Pacific_Alliance. Accessed 11 November 2014

Santulli C (2012) Retour à la théorie de l'organe commun: réflexions sur la nature juridique des organisations internationales à partir du cas de l'Alba et de la Celac, comparées notamment à l'Union européenne et à l'O.N.U. Revue générale de droit international public 116: 565–578

Seatzu F (2014) The Legal Mandates of the CABEI and of the CAF as Agents of Economic Growth in Latin America. Korean Journal of International and Comparative Law 2(2):164–192

Valvis A I (2008) Regional Integration in Latin America, Institute of International Economic Relations, at: http://idec.gr/iier/new/Valvis-_Latin_America_regionalism.pdf. accessed 11 November 2014

Vincent D P (2013) The Trans-Pacific Partnership: Environmental Savior or Regulatory Carte Blanche? *Minnesota Journal of International Law* 23:1–46

Williamson E (2003) The Penguin History of Latin America. Penguin Books, London

Chapter 8
The Caribbean Community (CARICOM)

Francesco Seatzu

Abstract The contribution of Caribbean countries to global commerce has not been impressive. To this end, when the Treaty of Chaguaramas establishing the Caribbean Community and Common Market (CARICOM) became operative in August 1973, there were great expectations that at long last there was in place an institutional framework for economic integration in the Caribbean. This invariably implied that the challenge of market fragmentation would be an issue of the past and intra-regional commerce would also be enhanced. Forty years and more after the entry into force of the Treaty of Chaguaramas (and 12 years after the entry into force of the Revised Treaty of Chaguaramas), not much progress has been made in terms of the economic integration and de-fragmentation of Caribbean markets. Issues abound at present as to whether the CARICOM, one of the world's oldest still-functioning regional economic institutions, would ever be able to survive and if it does, whether it would at last plug the Caribbean region into the grid of global commerce. This chapter holds that there are still some weak areas in the institutional and normative framework of the Revised Treaty of Chaguaramas that could not properly support market integration. It suggests that the CARICOM needs to play a greater role in ensuring that this weak framework is strengthened.

Keywords CARICOM · Revised Treaty of Chaguaramas · CARICOM single market and economy (CSME) · CARICOM legal system

F. Seatzu (✉)
International and European Union Law, University of Cagliari, Cagliari, Italy
e-mail: seatzu@hotmail.com

© T.M.C. ASSER PRESS and the authors 2015
M. Odello and F. Seatzu (eds.), *Latin American and Caribbean International Institutional Law*, DOI 10.1007/978-94-6265-069-5_8

Contents

8.1 Introduction

Economic integration in the Caribbean is set within the larger framework of regional integration. In its report of April 2011 the Institute of International Relations (IIR) at The University of the West Indies (UWI), an interdisciplinary Caribbean regional centre for the analysis and advancement of international relations, has identified various areas of concern in terms of the framework for regional integration in the Caribbean.[1]

These concerns can be summarized as follows: (1) the normative and institutional framework for regional integration in the Caribbean region is imprecise and ambiguous; (2) the continental blueprints for regional integration do not match the existing reality; (3) there is a limited national capacity to implement and follow up CARICOM decisions and little capacity of enforcement[2]; (4) there is institutional stagnation within the CARICOM Secretariat, and possible fragmentation and incoherence in the system of complementary institutions and agencies; (5) there is the continued retention of the character of CARICOM as a 'community of sovereign States', with reluctance to pool sovereignty at the sub-regional level by moving towards the supra-nationality of the legal regime and governance arrangements. Though these areas of concern have been identified for the whole process of integration, they are also relevant in the specific discourse on economic integration.

Careful examination of these areas of concern will show that the first gives rise to the other three. The reason behind this is that if the legal framework is unambiguous and precise, it will most likely address existing realities. In so doing, it would put in place a tool to harmonize the continental and sub-regional agenda. In order to achieve this goal, the normative framework will formulate legal rules to bind all the parties involved as a matter of necessity. On the other hand, a weak normative framework will give rise to all the concerns identified by the IIR in its above-mentioned report.

The chapter is structured into two parts. Following this introduction, and after the background on integration processes in the Caribbean, the first section

---

[1]References can be found at: https://sta.uwi.edu/iir/documents/IIR_Research_Documents/IIRRegionalIntegrationReportFINAL.pdf. Accessed 11 September 2014.

[2]For general commentary on the political and legal problems with enforcement see: Mills et al. 1990, pp. 30–33; Geiser et al. 1976, pp. 158–173.

(Sects. 8.2 and 8.3) analyses the current state of Caribbean legal integration, mindful of the meaning of the EU model as a frame of reference. Following the consideration of some gaps in the CARICOM's institutional and normative framework, the second and final section (Sects. 8.4 and 8.5) offers conclusions and suggestions for additional studies and research. Throughout this chapter, the European Union is used as a yardstick for CARICOM's implementation of its stated integration purpose and its institutional structure. The question then arises: Is the European Union the most appropriate yardstick for CARICOM?[3] The vast disparity between the two regional organizations with respect to the size of population and geographic area, the potential for intra-regional trade, and the development status of the Member States begs the question. Despite these and other disparities, the usefulness of the European Union as a yardstick is strongly convincing due to the importance of the following: (1) in the author's opinion, it is the most successful regional integration experiment of sovereign States on the planet; (2) a comparison of the CARICOM and European Union treaties reveals that the CARICOM drafters have been inspired by (and on occasion rejected) salient features of the European Union structure (see Sect. 8.5 for discussion); and (3) like the European Union, the CARICOM treaties provide for the foundation of a single market, a single economic space outside the context of a federation of States. However, this does not lead to the conclusion that CARICOM will always follow the EU pattern. Contrary to this idea, this chapter argues that CARICOM must formulate its own original process of integration that does not necessarily follow a methodology like the one applied in the European experience.

8.2 Background of Integration Processes in the Caribbean

The short-lived West Indies Federation can be considered as the starting point of the sub-regional integration processes in the Caribbean. This Federation was established in 1958 with a federal Government drawn from 10 Member States, and it was operational until 1962. With the independence of both Jamaica and Trinidad and Tobago in 1962, the Federation came to an end. A less ambitious project of integration, the Caribbean Free Trade Association (CARIFTA), was established only 6 years later.[4] But it was quickly replaced in 1973 by a further-reaching treaty of regional integration, the Chaguaramas Agreement, which was signed by the four Commonwealth Caribbean independent States (Barbados, Guyana, Jamaica and Trinidad and Tobago) at Chaguaramas, Trinidad and Tobago on 4 July 1973.

The Chaguaramas Agreement, which sought to establish a customs union and policy and functional cooperation and that formally established the Caribbean

---

[3]It is worth stressing that the EU has been instrumental in providing aid to CARICOM and to individual Member States in many functional areas. *Amplius* Krämer and Krajewski 2011, p. 422 ff.

[4]The original plan to establish a Caribbean Free Trade Association was announced in July 1965, and an agreement to this effect was signed by Antigua, Barbados and Guyana in December 1965. However, this 1965 Agreement was never implemented. See also Pollard 2003, pp. 5–8.

Community and Common Market, later known as CARICOM, concluded that CARIFTA had ceased to exist on 1 May 1974 and recognized the right of any: 'State of the Caribbean region, mentioned in para 1(b) of Article 2 of the Annex establishing the Caribbean Common Market to become a Member of the Common Market on such terms and conditions as the Conference may determine'. The four original signatories were subsequently joined by the other eight Caribbean territories. The Bahamas became the thirteenth Member State of the Community on 4 July 1983. In July 1991, the British Virgin Islands and the Turks and Caicos Islands became associated members of CARICOM. Twelve other States from Latin America and the Caribbean enjoy observer status in various institutions of the Community and CARICOM ministerial bodies. Suriname became the fourteenth Member State of the Caribbean Community on 4 July 1995. All the heads of government of the CARICOM unanimously adopted the Grand Anse Declaration, confirming the intention of establishing the CARICOM Single Market and Economy (CSME) by 4 July 1993. Of special significance is that CARICOM signed an agreement with Cuba: this established the CARICOM-Cuba Joint Commission, which aims to promote cooperative relations between the Caribbean Community and Cuba in economic, social, cultural and technological fields in the same year. In this regard, it was agreed that the members of CARICOM and Cuba would seek a greater understanding of each others' views and positions on issues which may arise in the various regional and international forums, in an effort to promote closer relations. It was further agreed that the Joint Commission would meet once a year alternately in a CARICOM Member State and Cuba.

In 2001, the CARICOM countries signed a new version of the Treaty (by means of nine separate Protocols), formally called the Revised Treaty of Chaguaramas (RTC). This Treaty introduced a number of changes to the institutional structure of CARICOM which were aimed at making CARICOM more efficient and streamlining the decision-making process, though the overall balance of power between the Member States and the organs and institutions of CARICOM was largely left untouched. Moreover, the Revised Treaty committed the CARICOM States to the gradual creation of an Economic Union (i.e. the CARICOM Single Market and Economy). The new Treaty envisioned this Union's creation through a multistage process, starting with the removal of legal, regulatory and technical barriers to the movement of production and of goods and services within CARICOM and culminating in a single market and economy.

Nevertheless, from its very inception CARICOM was plagued by in-fighting between Member States and a disregard for written declarations. By 1999–2001 it was clear that further integration in the framework of CARICOM was possible only at different levels. Formally established in 2001 the Caribbean Court of Justice (CCJ), which represents a 'unicum' among regional and international courts in having both an appellate and an original jurisdiction, became one of those levels where the sub-regional integration processes proceeded. The trend to ensure sub-regional integration through cooperation continued until 2009 when the Member States of the CARICOM signed a Protocol amending the Revised Treaty to incorporate both the Council for National Security and Law Enforcement (CONSLE) as an organ of the Community, and the CARICOM Implementation

Agency for Crime and Security (IMPACS). The Protocol envisioned extending the scope of the integration and transforming the CARICOM into an organization that includes not only economic issues but also social, scientific and technical, and political relations on its integration agenda.

On January 2006 the Declaration bringing into being the CARICOM Single Market and Economy was signed by the representatives of the CARICOM countries. The Declaration set forth the following basic purposes of the CARICOM: (1) coordination of efforts in the stepwise formation of a common economic space; (2) cooperation in tariff policies; (3) coordination of border and customs control policies; (4) contribution to the growth of a skills-sharing perspective for the region whilst simultaneously facilitating those seeking improved standards of living and better employment prospects away from their domestic spheres; (5) progressive insertion of the region into the global trading and economic system by strengthening trading links with non-traditional partners; (6) full use of labour (full employment) and full exploitation of the other factors of production (natural resources and capital); (7) competitive production leading to a greater variety and quantity of products and services to trade with other countries.

Although the Declaration mentioned the idea of forming a common economic space, it could hardly be qualified as a regional integration agreement (RIA), since it did not strive to—even partially—eliminate trade tariffs and barriers and provided merely for—though advanced—cooperation and coordination in the sphere of the borders and customs. With respect to its implementation, at the eighteenth Inter-Sessional CARICOM Heads of Government Conference in St. Vincent and the Grenadines on 12–14 February 2007, it was agreed that the Single Economy was expected to be implemented in two phases, the second of which would take place between 2010 and 2015 and consist of the consolidation and completion of the Single Economy.

8.3 The Current Normative Framework for Economic Integration in the Caribbean

The normative framework for economic integration in the Caribbean can be examined from two different angles. The first entails examining economic integration at the whole regional level while the second involves examining it from the sub-regional level. At the regional level Caribbean countries (or at least the majority of them) belong to the CARICOM, and at the sub-regional level countries from the eastern part of the Caribbean belong to the Organization of Eastern Caribbean States (OECS).[5]

---

[5]It is worth noting that a third regional organization named the Association of Caribbean States (ACS) was established in 1994 with the primary and specific aims of developing greater commerce between its members, enhancing transportation, developing sustainable tourism, and easing greater and more effective responses to local natural disasters. The Convention Establishing the Association of Caribbean States, signed at Cartagena de Indias, Colombia, on 24 July 1994, can be accessed online at http://www.acs-aec.org/Legal/Convention.htm. The ACS home page is located at: http://www.acs-aec.org. Accessed 14 November 2014. See Chap. 9 in this book.

At the regional level, the Revised Treaty of Chaguaramas lays the foundation for a regional approach to economic integration (the Revised Treaty). The Revised Treaty has the integration of Caribbean economies as part of its primary objectives, in order to increase economic self-reliance, self-sustained development and coordinating policies among economic communities so as to foster the gradual establishment of the Caribbean Single Market and Economy (CSME).[6] Member States undertake to create favourable conditions for the development of the CSME, which was perceived as a historic necessity that must be brought to full fruition,[7] and enact legislation in accordance with their constitutional procedures to ensure the implementation of the Revised Treaty. This is indirectly confirmed by Article 27(4), according to which: 'Subject to the agreement of the Conference, a Member State may opt out of obligations arising from the decisions of competent Organs provided that the fundamental objectives of the Community, as laid down in the Treaty, are not prejudiced thereby'.[8] The Revised Treaty also introduced a number of changes to the institutional structure of CARICOM, which were aimed at making CARICOM more efficient and streamlining the decision-making process. However, this Treaty left the overall balance of power between the Member States and the organs and institutions of CARICOM basically untouched. The Revised Treaty also creates Community organs to oversee and to implement the objectives of the Community. Of special significance is the establishment and implementation of the Caribbean Court of Justice (CCJ).

The Revised Treaty adopts an economic integration approach that primarily depends on the success of intra-commerce and the convergence of macro-economic

---

[6]After 15 years of delay, the Caribbean Single Market and Economy (CSME) was finally scheduled for launch in January 2005. The date of launch was further delayed to December 2005. On the issue, see: Bravo 2005. See also Prime Minister of Barbados, Owen Arthur, who stresses that the CSME offers the societies of the region, individually and collectively, the only realistic and viable option by which to achieve sustainable development, and in the process the prospect of erasing the two great economic deficits which confront the region at the start of this new century ('Today, the task of our generation is to see to the implementation (of the CSME) through to finality, and we can afford no slippage' quoting Secretary General of CARICOM, Mr. Edwin Carrington), Single Market, Global Cooperation Highlighted at Suriname Meeting (CARICOM) Press Release, 16 February 2005 at: http://www.crnm.org/documents/press_release_2005/16th_intersessional/opening_ceremony_16intersessional_suriname.pdf. Accessed 18 November 2014.

[7]Article 9 of the Revised Treaty reads as follows: 'Member States shall take all appropriate measures, whether general or particular, to ensure the carrying out of obligations arising out of this Treaty or resulting from decisions taken by the Organs and Bodies of the Community. They shall facilitate the achievement of the objectives of the Community. They shall abstain from any measures which could jeopardize the attainment of the objectives of this Treaty'. See also Bernal 2006, p. 13 ff.

[8]Analogous conclusions are suggested by Article 48 that deals with the right of a Member State to apply to the Community Council for a waiver of the requirement to grant any of the rights mentioned in para 1 of Article 30 in respect of any industry, sector or enterprise. See also Article 115 (Consequences of Failure to Eliminate or Establish Adverse Effects of Subsidies) which provides that: 'If the offending Member State fails to implement the recommendations of COTED within 6 months of the date of issue of the report referred to in para 2 of Article 114, COTED shall authorize the aggrieved Member State to impose appropriate countervailing duties commensurate with the nature and degree of serious adverse effects determined to exist'.

policies. Confirmation is to be found in Article 14, para 2(a) of the Revised Treaty, which expressly refers to the: 'establish*ment* and promot*ion of* measures for the co-ordination and convergence of national macro-economic policies of the Member States and for the execution of a harmonized policy on foreign investment'. In other words, the convergence of macro-economic policies is designed to serve as a building block for regional economic integration and is an intrinsic component of the Caribbean agenda for economic integration. The success or failure of economic integration at the regional level largely depends on the realization of this convergence. Measures have been put in place to ensure the success of economic integration but not much progress has been made on this front. This slow progress may be attributed to some inherent weaknesses or gaps in the legal framework for economic integration.

8.4 Some Gaps in the Institutional and Normative Framework

First, the economically wealthier countries of the Caribbean such as Bermuda, the British Virgin Islands and the Cayman Islands, which are deemed to be the pillars for economic integration in the Caribbean, are not CARICOM members but only associate members. The implication is that these countries are not bound by the obligations of membership, as defined by Article 3, para 2 of the Revised Treaty.[9] The absence of some of the most economically powerful countries of the region in the treaty drafting process may indicate that the specific interests of each Caribbean country were not taken into consideration within the framework of the Revised Treaty. Each Caribbean country is unique and has its specific agenda, which ought to have been considered when the Revised Treaty was negotiated.

In a bid to establish strategic partnerships between the CARICOM and the Bahamas and Cayman Islands, two agreements were adopted, in 2002 and 2006 respectively.[10] The first is the 2002 Agreement with the Cayman Islands and the second is the 2006 Agreement with the Bahamas. These Agreements function as the operative documents that highlight specific duties and strengthen relations between the CARICOM and these two countries which were outside the treaty drafting process.

Nevertheless, the two agreements do not create the basis for a binding duty on the part of the Bahamas and Cayman Islands. With the sole exception of the obligation to pay an appropriate contribution to the budget of the CARICOM Secretariat, the 2002 Agreement with the Cayman Islands stipulates that it applies to guarantee the Cayman Islands' right of participation (without the right to

---

[9]Article 3, para 2 of the Revised Treaty reads as follows: 'Membership of the Community shall be open to any other State or Territory of the Caribbean Region that is, in the opinion of the Conference, able and willing to exercise the rights and assume the obligations of membership'.

[10]For the texts of the agreements see the Caribbean Community Secretariat's official webpage at: http://www.caricom.org/jsp/secretariat/legal_instruments/agreement_caricom_caymanislands.jsp ?menu=secretariat. Accessed 8 April 2014.

vote) in the deliberations of the organs and subsidiary bodies of the Community (with the exception of the Council for Foreign and Community Relations), the right of accession to the Protocol on Privileges and Immunities of the Caribbean Community and other relevant Community instruments, and the acceptance by the Cayman Islands of the Caribbean Community travel document. The 2006 Agreement also refers to the right of participation in the deliberations of the organs and subsidiary bodies of the Community. Clearly, these articles were drafted on the assumption that Articles 3 and 14, para 2(a) of the Revised Treaty create binding obligations on its Contracting States.

Another weakness in the normative framework for economic integration in the Caribbean is the inability of the Revised Treaty to prevent Member States from belonging to more than one sub-regional economic institution.[11] Records have it that 100 % of the Caribbean countries belong to more than one sub-regional economic institution[12] and this makes it difficult for them to honour their duties.[13] While it is recognized that some Caribbean countries might have already been members of more than one sub-regional economic institution before the Revised Treaty came into force, the normative framework would have been strengthened if the drafters of the Revised Treaty or subsequent protocols had expressly prohibited overlapping membership. The absence of such prohibition continues to be a great challenge to attaining economic integration at the regional and sub-regional level as Member States are sometimes caught in between conflicting obligations.[14]

The framework is further weakened by a combination of circumstances: the fact that the Caribbean's history and geography are simultaneously incentives and disincentives to integration; the fact that some of the wealthier countries of the Caribbean are only associate members of the CARICOM; the comparatively small size of the CARICOM market; the lack of an independent supra-national authority to enact the policies with which the CARICOM countries were entrusted[15]; and the delay (or failure altogether) of some CARICOM members to ratify the CARICOM treaties, protocols and agreements in their national parliaments. The danger is that the CARICOM's institutions might not be able to effectively accomplish its mandates. Moreover, Article 27(4) of the Revised Treaty, albeit indirectly, highlights compliance with the CARICOM legal system as one of its core principles. But complying with such a legal system could be hard, if not even impossible, due to both the lack of elements of supra-nationality (with the only exception of the CCJ) and the

---

[11]See: Brewster 2012, p. 441 ff.

[12]I use the term "regional economic organizations" in place of the commonly used regional trade agreements or preferential trade agreements (PTAs) because the chapter refers specifically to organizations that have a secretariat and staff. Many of the world's 400-odd PTAs are simply paper agreements, which also may become obsolete, but through different mechanisms than those advanced in this piece.

[13]Every single country in the OECS is also a member of Caricom and the ACS. On the issue, see generally Girvan 2013, p. 303 ff.

[14]*Amplius* Brewster 2012.

[15]See also Kiplagat 1994, p. 39.

inability of the CARICOM to keep the critical—albeit fragile—sense of regional unity originally forged in the crucible of the colonial period. Furthermore, technical organs like the four ministerial councils—namely, the Council for Finance and Planning, the Council for Trade and Economic Development, the Council for Foreign and Community Relations, and the Council for Human and Social Development (COHSOD)—that have replaced the complex of ministerial committees under the Revised Treaty are not granted enough powers to drive the process of economic integration and guarantee compliance. The situation might have been different if the CARICOM had had its own Secretariat which dealt with purely economic matters.

8.5 What Role Can the CARICOM Play in Economic Integration?

The provisions of the Revised Treaty as a whole show that member countries purport to establish a community of independent sovereign states grounded on the rule of law. These provisions are aimed at leading the process of economic integration in the Caribbean. For these provisions to be adequately developed and enforced, functional and competent bodies need to be in operation to monitor the integration process. The CARICOM and its organs—in particular its two main organs that are the Conference of Heads of Government (the Conference), and the Community Council of Ministers (the Community Council)—are currently endowed with the power to pursue the aims of the Revised Treaty.

The CARICOM is going to modify the Revised Treaty in order to strengthen the current normative and institutional framework. Reform of the Revised Treaty will help to resolve at least some of the challenges pinpointed above. However, this will only be possible if steps are taken to remedy the 'information deficit' and the disconnect between the ordinary people and the CSME.[16] In other words, steps need to be taken to enhance the democratic character of the CARICOM to ensure that people are put at the centre of integration to promote participation and greater social cohesion and security. Second, the reform of the Revised Treaty will help to strengthen the framework if it is directed mainly at ensuring an approach to integration that combines issues of 'inter-governmentalism' (which recognizes the enduring importance of individual member countries in determining the path of the integration process), and issues of neo-functionalism (which is premised on the principle of shared sovereignty or the collective exercise of such sovereignty in specified sectors). On this ground, the two priorities of regionalism and nationalism could be reconciled,

---

[16]Accordingly, see: WC Grenade, Caricom: Coming of Age? Jean Monnet/Robert Schuman Paper Series, April 2007, at: http://www.as.miami.edu/eucenter/papers/GrenadeEU50yrs_long07_edi.pdf. Accessed 8 April 2014, who stresses that: 'This is one similarity that CARICOM shares with the EU and it is one feature that CARICOM should not emulate from the EU'.

based on a distribution of responsibility between the two levels of decision-making. All the Caribbean countries must take all the necessary steps that are indispensable for becoming contracting parties to the Revised Treaty and the process of amendment has to be all encompassing. Involving all the Caribbean countries in the process of amendment will allow the Revised Treaty to take into consideration the different phases of development of each Caribbean country. It will also build up a better sense of community and integrity of aim among the member countries.

The revision should clearly forbid member countries to adhere to more than one regional economic organization. The revision must also require the CARICOM Secretariat to ensure monitoring of the integration process. Indeed, although the CARICOM Secretariat has on several occasions played a noteworthy role in CARICOM's history, it has never acted as an independent body.[17] A feasible and active Commission, as envisaged by the West Indian Commission (WIC) in its 1992 report 'Time for Action',[18] is indispensable for supervising the economic integration process in the Caribbean. This is indirectly confirmed by the fact that the CARICOM Bureau—which has responsibility for initiating proposals for development and approval by the ministerial councils, and facilitating implementation of community decisions at both the regional and national levels[19]—is a poor substitute for the CARICOM Commission. In particular, like its counterpart in the European Union, the CARICOM Commission must be allowed to hold member countries accountable if they fail to comply with their legal duties in the Revised Treaty. In this regard, the CARICOM Commission, in the exercise of its powers, should have the authority to intervene within individual national systems and at the level of regional entities on behalf of the collective political directorate (Heads of Government and Ministerial Councils), in the drafting and implementation of agreed decisions. In other words, the CARICOM Commission should be able to mobilize the CARICOM to have a single negotiating position and a single attitude in the international negotiations. Moreover, the future Commission should establish a mandatory reporting system that will allow it assess the progress that a member country is making. Specifically, consideration must be devoted to the enactment of a mechanism that is able to legally distinguish between the specific types of Community decision-making: viz. directives, regulations, decisions, opinions and recommendations.[20] It is very much to be hoped that with the future revision of the CARICOM, the mandate and role of the CARICOM Commission will be provided for and clearly defined in order to deal with the monitoring of economic integration.

The pattern proposed by the Revised Treaty for achieving economic integration is such that it requires the strengthening of the Assembly of Caribbean Community Parliamentarians to address the democratic deficiencies in the CARICOM and

---

[17]See: O'Brien 2011, p. 631 ff.

[18]See: Ramphal 1993, p. 18 ff.

[19]CARICOM Bureau has been established, composed of the current chairman and the immediately outgoing and incoming chairmen of the conference.

[20]See: O'Brien 2011, p. 631 ff.

automaticity of financing to enhance the CARICOM's financial arrangements, as is the case in the EU. To this end, it is important for the parliaments of Member States to introduce an implementation mechanism (i.e. a Single Caribbean Act) to allow the reception of CARICOM law in the jurisdictions of member countries. The latter is both important and urgent since Member States have generally so far failed to implement their commitments—consistently, wholly and in a timely way—under the various schemes.[21] Yet it is equally important for the CCJ to reverse its consolidated jurisprudence which argues that the Revised Treaty cannot have a direct effect on Member States' legal systems: this is based on the principle that only the CCJ can interpret and apply the Revised Treaty (the exclusive jurisdiction principle). The enforcement mechanism under the Revised Treaty as it currently stands may not properly serve the purpose of economic integration because of this limitation. Imposing (as Article 214 does)[22] that national courts are obliged to refer all questions of interpretation and application of the RTC to the CCJ (so making the CCJ dependent upon Member States and individuals for its caseload) may not only not be beneficial to the enforcement of CARICOM law in domestic legal systems, but may also not be beneficial to economic integration in the Caribbean.[23]

Since serious uncertainties persist about whether individuals will be willing to bring proceedings before a regional court (the CCJ) with all the further expense and time that this is likely to entail, the Community Council of Ministers should amend the Revised Treaty to grant individuals the possibility to bring proceedings before their own national courts.

8.6 Final Remarks

This chapter has highlighted three areas of weakness in the CARICOM's normative and institutional framework for economic integration. The areas indicated are not exclusive and if resolved they would not entirely ensure that economic integration is obtained. Nevertheless, were these areas to be strengthened, this could work as a platform for filling other gaps. From the discussion on the role of the CARICOM, it is clear that an amendment of the Revised Treaty is urgently required.

Because the process of amendment can only be carried out by the Community Council of Ministers, political will is indispensable to expedite action. The political will required cannot stop at the stage of revision, but it should go on to ask member countries to comply with their duties under the Revised Treaty. Due to

---

[21]On the issue, see: Grenade, n. 16 above.

[22]Article 214 reads as follows: 'Where a national court or tribunal of a Member State is seized of an issue whose resolution involves a question concerning the interpretation or application of this Treaty, the court or tribunal concerned shall, if it considers that a decision on the question is necessary to enable it to deliver judgment, refer the question to the Court for determination before delivering judgment'.

[23]On this issue, see: Pollard 2004, p. 95 ff; Cherubini 2010, p. 71 ff. See also Virzo 2010, p. 345 ff.

the energy, cost and time that have been expended so far, it is safe to state that Member States entered into the process with the willingness to comply with the Revised Treaty. So that this work may not have been in vain, it is important for Member States to take the necessary steps that will give effect to their action.

References

Bernal R (2006) Nano-Firms, Regional Integration, and International Competitiveness: The Experience and Dilemma of the CSME. In: Production Integration in CARICOM: From Theory to Action. Ian Randle Publishers, Kingston, pp. 90–115

Bravo K E (2005) CARICOM, The Myth of Sovereignty, and Aspirational Economic Integration. North Carolina Journal of International Law and Commercial Regulation 31(1): 146–205

Brewster H R (2012) The Future of CARICOM in A Changing International Environment. In: The Pertinence of CARICOM in the 21st Century: Some Perspectives. Trafford Publishing, Indiana, pp. 441–466

Cherubini F (2010) La Corte caraibica di giustizia. In: Pennetta P (a cura di) L'evoluzione dei sistemi giurisdizionali regionali e influenze comunitarie. Cacucci, Bari, pp. 71–98

Geiser H J, Alleyne P, Gajraj C (1976) Legal Problems of Caribbean Integration: A Study of the Legal Aspects of CARICOM. Sijthoff, Leyden

Girvan N (2013) Alba, Petrocaribe and CARICOM: Issue in a New Dynamic. In: Hall K O, Chuck-A-Sang M (eds) Coping With The Collapse of The Old Order: CARICOM's New External Agenda. Ian Randle Publishers, Kingston, pp. 303–325

Kiplagat P K (1994) An Institutional and Structural Model for Successful Economic Integration in Developing Countries. Texas International Law Journal 29: 39–68

Krämer R and Krajewski M (2011) State Aid (Subsidies) in International Trade Law. In Szyszczak E (ed) Research Handbook on European State Aid Law. Edward Elgar Publisher, Cheltenham, pp. 404–424

Mills G E et al (1990) Report on Review of Regional Programmes and Organisation of the Caribbean Community. Caribbean Community Secretariat, Georgetown, Guyana

O'Brien D (2011) CARICOM: Regional Integration in a Post-Colonial Word. European Law Journal 5: 630–648

Pollard D E (2004) The Caribbean Court of Justice: Closing the Circle of Independence. Caribbean Law Publishing Company, Kingston

Pollard D E (ed) (2003) The CARICOM System: Basic Instruments. The Caribbean Law Publishing Company, Kingston

Ramphal S S (1993) Time for Action: Report of the West Indian Commission. The Press, University of the West Indies, Kingston

Virzo R (2010) Le procedure di rinvio pregiudizial ai tribunali internazionali regionali. In: Pennetta P (a cura di) L'evoluzione dei sistemi giurisdizionali regionali e influenze comunitarie. Cacucci, Bari, p. 317–344

Chapter 9
The Organisation of Eastern Caribbean States

Alana Lancaster and Jill St George

Abstract This chapter looks at the Organisation of Eastern Caribbean States (OECS) and at its institutional evolution. The 1981 original agreement was not conceived as a platform for a political or economic union, and consequently did not commit its Member States to achieving such a union in time. By the year 2000, however, OECS states began to explore the fundamentals of some form of economic union, as well as a closer integration in other policy areas. In January 2011, this vision became a reality, with the entry into force of the 2011 Revised Treaty of Basseterre, which transformed the structure and operation of the union into a modern regional trade agreement (RTA), which may be viewed as a variant of the Treaty of the European Union.

Keywords Organisation of Eastern Caribbean States · Caribbean States · Treaty of Basseterre · Regional trade agreement (RTA) · Economic union · Protocol of Eastern Caribbean economic union · Dispute settlement

Contents

A. Lancaster (✉) · J. St George
Faculty of Law, University of the West Indies, Cave Hill Campus, Cave Hill, Barbados
e-mail: alana.lancaster@cavehill.uwi.edu; alana.lancaster@gmail.com

J. St George
e-mail: jill.stgeorge@cavehill.uwi.edu

© T.M.C. ASSER PRESS and the authors 2015
M. Odello and F. Seatzu (eds.), *Latin American and Caribbean International Institutional Law*, DOI 10.1007/978-94-6265-069-5_9

9.1 An Overview of the OECS

9.1.1 History

The Organisation of Eastern Caribbean States is a regional trading agreement within the Caribbean region, born of the 1981 Treaty of Basseterre,[1] and continued under Article 2 of the 2011 Revised Treaty of Basseterre (Revised Treaty).[2] The 1981 agreement was based on a report which recommended joint overseas representation for the islands after independence. The union grew out of the desire of the then non-independent Eastern Caribbean Islands, whose leaders, under the aegis of the West Indies Associated States (WISA) Council of Ministers, set about to establish an arrangement in which they could cooperate in external affairs representation after independence, given their limited human and financial resources.[3] The objectives of the Organisation are illustrated in Article 3.1 of the 1981 Treaty of Basseterre, and give primacy to cooperation in the international relations of its Member States, the coordination of foreign policy by the Member States of the OECS.

When the OECS was formed, the Member States had already been involved in an economic integration scheme called the East Caribbean Common Market (ECCM) which was formed in 1968, one year after the establishment of the

---

[1]Treaty Establishing the Organisation of Eastern Caribbean States, Basseterre, 18 June 1981, 1338 UNTS 97. See: Emmanuel 1989, Menon 1995, Gibbins 2002, Simmonds 2006, Girvan 2012, Ishmael 2014.

[2]Revised Treaty of Basseterre Establishing the Organisation of Eastern Caribbean States Economic Union, signed on 18 June 2010 in St. Lucia, during the 51st Meeting of the Authority of Heads of Government of OECS Member States, entered into force on 21 January 2011, at: http://www.oecs.org/publications/treaties-agreements/506-revised-treaty-of-basseterre-establishing-the-oecs-economic-union/file. Accessed 15 December 2014.

[3]E Huntley, The Treaty of Basseterre and OECS Economic Union (Paper No. 17, doc. OECS/AUT/03/38/17). http://www.sice.oas.org/ctyindex/OECS/Treaty_e.pdf. Accessed 9 October 2014.

WISA Council. The membership of the ECCM was the same as that of the WISA Council, but the two organisations operated as separate entities. The 1981 Treaty of Basseterre was not conceived as a platform for building a deeper form of union—either political or economic—and consequently did not commit its Member States to achieving such a union in time. By 2000 however, OECS states began to explore the fundamentals of a new treaty on closer union, containing the ingredients for the formation of an economic union, as well as for closer integration in other policy areas. This was in the form of an economic union of Member States encompassing a unified economic territory out of the separate economic entities that constitute the OECS. Consequently, this would include the application of the common external tariff by the members, the free movement of labour, free movement of goods of trade and services, and free movement of capital.

In January 2011, this vision became a reality, with the entry into force of the 2011 Revised Treaty, which transformed the structure and operation of the union into a modern regional trade agreement (RTA), which may be viewed as a hybrid variant of the Treaty of the European Union.

9.1.2   Geographic Coverage

The OECS currently comprises nine members, spread across the Eastern Caribbean, forming a near-continuous archipelago across the Leeward Islands and Windward Islands. The membership is divided between seven full members and two associate members, but all Member States are either former colonies or current overseas territories of the United Kingdom. All members of the OECS are either full or associate members of the Caribbean Community (CARICOM),[4] and the two Regional Trade Agreements (RTAs) share a close relationship (Map 9.1).

9.1.3   Membership

Article 1 of the 2011 Revised Treaty of Basseterre defines a Member State of the OECS as a Full Member State or an Associate Member State of the Organisation. There are seven full members—Antigua and Barbuda, The Commonwealth of Dominica, Grenada, Saint Christopher and Nevis, Saint Lucia, Saint Vincent and the Grenadines and Montserrat[5]; Montserrat being an overseas territory of the United Kingdom. As a result, there are some provisions—for example those concerning the competence of the Union—which may apply differentially for Montserrat.

---

[4]See Chap. 8 in this book.

[5]Revised Treaty (n. 2 above) Article 3.1.

Map 9.1 OECS Group of States (*Source* http://apps.who.int/medicinedocs/en/d/Js4940e/4.html)

All seven full members are also the founding members of the OECS, having been a part of the organisation since its creation on 18 June 1981. The two associate members are the most geographically distant states of Anguilla and the British Virgin Islands,[6] which joined in 1995 and 1984 respectively. The rights and obligations of Associate Member States are reserved within the purview of Authority.[7] The bifurcated categorisation of the membership of the Organisation, manifests in the structure, competences and decision-making processes of the Union, and will be discussed in this chapter.

The Revised Treaty makes provision for the Caribbean states or territories, which are not members under the current arrangement, to become full or associate members,[8] and over the years, Trinidad and Tobago, Venezuela, Saba, St. Eustatius and St. Maarten have made varying attempts to seek membership of the union.

---

[6]Ibid., Article 3.2.

[7]Ibid., Article 3.3.

[8]Ibid., Article 3.3.

There are also policy areas in which the union collaborates with other Caribbean states—for example Forum of Tourism Ministers of the Eastern Caribbean, which includes members of the French and Dutch overseas territories.[9]

9.2 Legal Capacity, Privileges and Immunities

According to Abass[10] there are four general features which are considered necessary for the existence and operation of an international governmental organisation. They include membership, a constitutive instrument, legal personality and privileges and immunities. The 2011 Revised Treaty serves as the constituent instrument for the OECS, and Article 21.1 prescribes that the organisation shall enjoy legal personality, but does not specify whether the OECS is to be accorded international legal personality. However, the Revised Treaty specifically accords the organisation legal personality required for the performance of its functions,[11] as well as with respect to real, personal, movable and immovable property.[12] Berry posits that the possibility of the Organisation also possessing international legal personality is raised by the designation of the OECS as an international organisation, as well as several express competences granted to the OECS under the Revised Treaty.[13] These include the ability of the Authority to conclude treaties on behalf of the Organisation and enter into relationships with other international organisations and third countries,[14] passive legation and competences and functions which contemplate foreign and international roles.[15]

Article 22 provides for the establishment of the headquarters of the Organisation, which while currently located in Castries, St. Lucia, can be moved on the decision of the Authority. The Headquarters hosts the Commission, which as discussed in Sect. 9.4, is the administrative centre of the union. The members of the Commission and the senior officials of the Organisations at its headquarters and in Member States are vested with privileges and immunities as accorded to members of diplomatic missions accredited at the Organisation and in Member States under the 1961 Vienna Convention on Diplomatic Relations. Other

---

[9]Organisation of Eastern Caribbean States, 'OECS Tourism Ministers End Successful Meeting', 12 April, 2006, at: http://www.oecs.org/media-center/press-releases/trade,-economics-statistics/14-tourism/203-oecs-tourism-ministers-end-successful-meeting. Accessed 1 January 2015.

[10]Abass 2014, p. 162.

[11]Revised Treaty (n. 2 above) Article 21.2(a).

[12]Ibid., Article 21.2.

[13]Berry 2014, p. 112.

[14]Revised Treaty (n. 2 above) Article 8.13.

[15]Berry 2014, pp. 112–113.

privileges and immunities to be recognised and granted by Member States in connection with the Organisation will be determined by the Authority.[16]

9.3 The Objectives and Functions of the Organisation

The objectives and functions of the OECS were dramatically transformed with the 2011 Revised Treaty, and largely aimed at transforming the union into a modern and progressive economic union. The main purposes, as set out in Article 4, include inter alia, cooperation between Member States at the regional and international levels,[17] harmonisation of foreign policy,[18] and the establishment of an Economic Union as a single economic and financial space.[19] The Union is envisioned as an institutional forum to discuss constitutional, economic, political and other policies of interest to Member States,[20] to serve as a conduit to harmonise and undertake joint policies, specifically in 23 fields,[21] coordinate foreign policy,[22] as well as any other activities calculated to further the purposes of the Organisation.[23] In addition, the Revised Treaty provides for participation with other trading arrangements,[24] other international organisations and other countries.[25] These objectives are expected to be pursued by the Organs and Institutions of the Organisation.[26]

9.4 The Structure and Function of the Organisation

The OECS has transformed its organisational structure under the new revised treaties, by simplifying and substituting organs, clarifying competencies and increasing the efficiency of decision-making processes, by allowing greater use of the qualified majority voting procedures for binding decisions.[27]

---

[16]Revised Treaty (n. 2 above) Article 21.4.

[17]Ibid., Article 4.1(a).

[18]Ibid., Article 4.1(d).

[19]Ibid., Article 4.1(e).

[20]Ibid., Article 4.1(f).

[21]Ibid., Article 4.2(a)–(w).

[22]Ibid., Article 15.

[23]Ibid., Article 4.2(x).

[24]Ibid., Article 19.

[25]Ibid., Article 20.

[26]Ibid., Article 4.1(g).

[27]Berry 2014, p. 68.

Accordingly, under the 2011 Revised Treaty, there are three Institutions[28] and five Organs.[29] The Institutions are the Eastern Caribbean Supreme Court—one of the main dispute settlement mechanisms of the Organisation,[30] the Eastern Caribbean Central Bank[31] and the Eastern Caribbean Civil Aviation Authority.[32] The OECS Authority, which is the principal organ of the Organisation, can expand this list of Institutions to include any inter-Governmental entity whose functions relate to at least all the full members,[33] as is deemed necessary for achieving the purposes of the Organisation.[34]

At present, the five Organs of the Organisations are the Authority of the Heads of Government of the Member States (the Authority),[35] the Council of Ministers,[36] the OECS Assembly,[37] the Economic Affairs Council[38] and the OECS Commission.[39] Of these, the Authority may be considered a primary organ[40] while the others are secondary organs. This is essentially because of the Authority's role as the supreme, policy-making organ, which is responsible for overall guidance of the Organisation.[41]

The Authority is responsible for the policy direction of the union,[42] the budget[43] of the Organisation, making final decisions on financial matters[44] and concluding international agreements on the Organisation's behalf.[45] Decisions, recommendations and directives of the Union are made exclusively at this level. By Article 8.5, all substantive decisions—unless otherwise provided for in the Revised Treaty—will have no force and effect unless there is an affirmative vote of all full members at the meeting at which the decision was taken. The Revised Treaty however provides for a consideration period of 30 days for Parties which are absent, to provide an indication of their support of abstention of the decision. A no-response by the Party at the

---

[28]Revised Treaty (n. 2 above) Article 6.1.

[29]Ibid., Article 7.1.

[30]Ibid., Article 6.1(a).

[31]Ibid., Article 6.1(b).

[32]Ibid., Article 6.1(c).

[33]Ibid., Article 7.2.

[34]Ibid., Article 8.12.

[35]Ibid., Article 7.1(a).

[36]Ibid., Article 7.1(b).

[37]Ibid., Article 7.1(c).

[38]Ibid., Article 7.1(d).

[39]Ibid., Article 7.1(e).

[40]Berry 2014, p. 76.

[41]Ibid.

[42]Revised Treaty (n. 2 above) 8.4.

[43]Ibid., Article 17.

[44]Ibid., Article 8.14.

[45]Ibid., Article 8.13.

end of 30 days is recorded as an abstention. Procedural decisions on the other hand, require a majority of all full members present and voting at the meeting at which such decisions were taken.[46] Decisions by the OECS Authority are binding on all Member States, as well as all Organs of the Organisation, provided that the decision was within the sovereign competence of Member States to implement them.[47]

The Authority comprises the Heads of Government of the Member States,[48] who can designate a Minister to represent them at any meeting.[49] This delegation seems to be qualified to circumstances which are deemed as appropriate, and to a Minister of Government, as opposed to any other functionaries of the Government. This is perhaps because of the scope and binding nature of the decisions taken by the Authority. There are further restrictions in both deliberations and decision-making at the Authority, in relation to the specific matter under deliberation. Thus a Member State must have the necessary competence in respect to matters under consideration[50]—a restriction which permeates to the other Organs of the Organisation.[51] Berry opines that this requirement may in part have been necessitated by the foreign affairs limitations encumbering its non-independent full member—Montserrat.[52]

The Council of Ministers, which is responsible to the Authority,[53] comprises Ministers of Government selected by Heads of Governments as representatives.[54] Its main role is to consider, report and enact law, regulations and other implementing instruments which are adopted by the Authority.[55] Although remaining subject to any directives passed by the Authority, the Council has the competence under the Revised Treaty to determine its own procedure.[56] Voting of the Council follows the same guidelines as those of the Authority,[57] and regulations made by the Council have the same binding force as the Acts of the Organisation which authorises them, but are subject to judicial review.[58]

The OECS Assembly is meant to be a forum where each member elects representatives—a total of eight, reflecting both members of the Executive[59] and the

---

[46]Ibid., Article 8.6.

[47]Ibid., Article 8.8.

[48]Ibid., Article 8.1.

[49]Ibid., Article 8.2.

[50]Ibid., Article 8.3.

[51]Ibid., Articles 9.6 and 13.6.

[52]Berry 2014, p. 76.

[53]Revised Treaty (n. 2 above) Article 9.2.

[54]Ibid., Article 9.1.

[55]Ibid., Article 9.3.

[56]Ibid., Article 9.10.

[57]Ibid., Articles 9.6 and 9.7.

[58]Ibid., Article 9.5.

[59]Five in total, reflecting as nearly as possible the proportionate representation of government and opposition representative of the elected government and opposition.

Legislature[60]—for a 2-year period or the next general election of the Executive, whichever comes first.[61] The Assembly's role is to report to the Authority on any proposal to enact an Act under their legislative competence,[62] consider matters referred to the Assembly by the Authority[63] and report to the Council on any proposal to make regulations which have been referred to the Assembly by the Council.[64] The Assembly may determine its own procedure, except where the Authority has given directions by either the Authority or the Council.[65]

The Economic Affairs Council is the principal organ of the Economic Union, and is earmarked to play a pivotal role in the establishment of a single economic and financial space provided for by Article 11 of the Revised Treaty and Article 28 of the Protocol of Eastern Caribbean Economic Union (the Protocol)[66] which was adopted at the same time as the Revised Treaty. As set out, the Protocol is the main tool for closer economic, financial and social relations among OECS states. The Economic Affairs Council comprises at least one Minister of Government appointed by the Heads of the Member States—each of which has one vote.[67] Article 11 precludes any Member State from participating in deliberations of the Council where the Member State is deemed to be without competence in the matter at hand.[68] Decisions are made by unanimous voting unless the Protocol details otherwise.[69] The Affairs Council serves the economy in a variety of ways, including the supervision of the functioning and application of the Protocol, reviewing the operation of the Protocol,[70] considering whether action should be taken by Protocol Member States to promote the Protocol, and facilitating links with other countries, groups of countries or international organizations.[71] The Economic Affairs Council is responsible for the implementation of the Economic Union, acting under the direction of the Authority but with the capacity to direct and delegate to the OECS Commission where it deems appropriate. With Authority approval, the Economic

---

[60]On the basis of Articles 10.1 and 10.2 of the Revised Treaty (n. 2 above) the representatives of the Legislature are to comprise at least two elected members chosen by the elected government members and one elected member chosen by the elected opposition members.

[61]Revised Treaty (n. 2 above) Article 10.5.

[62]Ibid., Article 10.13(a)(i).

[63]Ibid., Article 10.13(a)(ii).

[64]Ibid., Article 10.13(b).

[65]Ibid., Article 10.14.

[66]Protocol of the Eastern Caribbean Economic Union (entered into force 21 January 2011), The Revised Treaty of Basseterre includes an Annex on the Settlement of Disputes, and a Protocol which formally established the Economic Union.

[67]Revised Treaty (n. 2 above) Article 11.1.

[68]Ibid., Article 11.2.

[69]Protocol (n. 66 above) Article 28.

[70]Ibid. 28., Article 1(b).

[71]Ibid. 28., Article 1(c).

Affairs Council has the capacity to take decisions which are binding on Protocol Member States, and to make recommendations to Protocol Member States.

The OECS Commission is the principal administrative organ of both the OECS in general[72] and the Economic Union.[73] It is headed by a Director General, who is appointed by the Authority to serve for a 4-year term,[74] and is responsible for the day-to-day administration of the OECS.[75] The full suite of powers and responsibilities of the Director General is outlined in Article 13, and most notably the Revised Treaty asserts that independence is vital in the role of Director General.[76] Accordingly, it expressly prohibits the Director General from accepting instructions from any Government, since the post is as an international official and not as the representative of any State. The staff of the Commission comprises Commissioners, who hold an ambassadorial rank and represent each Member State and the OECS Commission in their respective Member States.[77] Decisions of the Commission are made by a simple majority vote,[78] and the Commission's functions with respect to the Organisation are specified in Article 12.2 of the Revised Treaty, and those with respect to the Economic Union in Article 29.

The Commission, through the office of the Director General, has mandate over various units, including those on legal matters, research communication and information services, regional integration, internal audit, functional cooperation services and overseas diplomatic and technical missions. At present, the OECS is represented by diplomatic and technical missions in Brussels[79] Geneva[80] and Puerto Rico.[81]

The other main components of the OECS are its institutions, whose purpose it is to support the functioning of the OECS. At present there are three institutions of the Organisation—the Eastern Caribbean Supreme Court, the Eastern Caribbean Central Bank and the Eastern Caribbean Civil Aviation Authority,[82] but the Authority by unanimous decision can add to this list, provided that the entity is inter-governmental, and its functions relate at least to all the full Member States.[83]

---

[72]Revised Treaty (n. 2 above) Article 12.1.

[73]Protocol (n. 66 above) Article 29.1.

[74]Revised Treaty (n. 2 above) Article 13.1.

[75]Ibid. 12.2.

[76]Ibid. 13.6.

[77]Ibid., Article 12.2.

[78]Ibid., Article 12.3.

[79]A diplomatic mission to ensure political and diplomatic representation at the EU.

[80]A technical mission to ensure effective representative at the WTO.

[81]A honourary consulate.

[82]Revised Treaty (n. 2 above) Article 6.1.

[83]Ibid., Article 6.2.

9.5 Legislative Competence

9.5.1 The Legislative Regime of the OECS

The OECS derives its ability to pass legislation, binding on all Members States, from Article 5.3. The Revised Treaty details areas of law and policy in which states are required to ensure OECS legislation has direct effect without the need for enabling acts. Member States are required to continue to engage the public in discussion and participation in the legislative process, despite the direct effect of OECS legislation.[84]

Notwithstanding the broad nature of the OECS legislative competence, the Revised Treaty protects the Constitution as the supreme law of each Member State,[85] and Member States are not required to amend their constitutions in order to ensure compliance with the OECS. However, Article 5 contains general undertaking provisions, which require Member States to ensure the carrying out of obligations under the Treaty, delegating to the Organisation authority to legislate in the areas of competence,[86] as well as enacting domestic laws to give direct effect to Acts, Regulations and Orders of the Organisation in the areas of competence outlined in Article 14.[87] The expression 'direct effect', as used in Article 5.3, is borrowed from the law of the European Union,[88] and time will tell how the doctrine will evolve in the OECS.[89] These provisions are mandatory for independent states, while non-independent states of the union are not required to delegate legislative authority to the Organisation.[90] They are however required to pass legislation which enables Acts, Orders and Regulations passed by organs of the OECS to be received into their laws without need for enactment by the states legislature.[91]

9.5.2 Areas of Legislative Competence of the OECS

By Article 14 of the Revised Treaty, states grant the Organisation legislative competence in accordance with Article 5.3 and subject to Article 5.4 in a total of 8 areas. The first 5 areas, namely—the common market, including customs union; monetary policy, on the recommendation of the Monetary Council; trade policy; maritime

---

[84]Ibid., Article 5.5.

[85]Ibid., Article 5.4.

[86]Ibid., Article 5.3(i).

[87]Ibid., Article 5(a)(ii).

[88]Berry 2014, p. 142.

[89]For a discussion of direct effect in the OECS, see Berry 2014, Chap. 8.

[90]Revised Treaty (n. 2 above) Article 5.3(b).

[91]Ibid., Article 5.3(b)(i), (ii).

jurisdiction and maritime boundaries; and civil aviation[92]—appear to grant the Organisation superior competence after the coming into effect of the Revised Treaty in 2011. Berry points out that while the article does not on the face of it grant exclusive competence to the Organisation, when read in conjunction with Article 5.3 and a reservation made under Article 14.4, Article 14.1 may best be described as setting out areas of potentially exclusive competence for the OECS.[93] The 3 remaining areas—common commercial policy, environmental policy and immigration policy—are meant to be shared or administered concurrently between the Organisation and Member States, subject to pre-emptive acts on the part of the Organisation. Accordingly, states can reserve the right to legislate in relation to these matters, or make a reservation in respect of the area of competence. The Article also provides for the Authority to expand these areas of competence to areas which may best be addressed at the Organisational level, as opposed to the national level.[94]

9.6 Economic Union

9.6.1 The Monetary Union

The Eastern Caribbean Currency Union (ECCU) comprises eight states in the OECS whose official currency is the Eastern Caribbean dollar (EC dollar, XCD). Established in 1965 and pegged at $2.70EC-$1US, the EC dollar replaced the West Indies Federation dollar. The only OECS state which is not a member of the currency union is the British Virgin Islands, which continues to use the US dollar.

Prior to independence in the 1970s and 1980s, economic activity in the OECS was determined in most part by colonial policies. Such policies were centred in the agricultural sector concerning primary commodities such as sugar and bananas.

Post-independence, the International Monetary Fund (IMF) noted that the 'region became the testing ground for a wide range of economic theories and ideologies that shaped its social, political, and economic history; these include the plantation economy model, industrialisation by invitation, small open economy models, and diversification into tourism'.[95]

Between 1965 and 1983, the Eastern Caribbean Currency Authority was responsible for issuing the EC dollar. In July 1983, the Eastern Caribbean Central Bank (ECCB) was established by the Eastern Caribbean Central Bank Agreement (ECCBA)[96] to replace the Eastern Caribbean Currency Authority. Signatories to

---

[92]Ibid., Article 14.1.

[93]Berry 2014, pp. 146–147.

[94]Revised Treaty (n. 2 above) Article 14.3.

[95]Schipke et al. 2013.

[96]Eastern Caribbean Central Bank Agreement Act, 5 July 1983, passed into law by the eight Participating Governments, at: http://www.eccb-centralbank.org/PDF/bank_agreement1983.pdf. Accessed 5 January 2015.

the ECCBA were Antigua and Barbuda, Dominica, Grenada, Montserrat, St Kitts and Nevis, Saint Lucia, and St Vincent and the Grenadines, with Anguilla ratifying the Agreement in 1987.[97]

As a common currency existed in the OECS prior to the establishment of the EC dollar, the ECCBA did not elaborate on the operation of the monetary union. The Agreement acknowledged the previous operations of the Eastern Caribbean Currency Authority, acknowledging all assets and liabilities together with all its rights and obligations were now transferred to the Eastern Caribbean Bank under the Agreement.[98]

The primary objective of the ECCB is to 'maintain the stability of the Eastern Caribbean Currency and the integrity of the banking system'.[99] Functions and services offered by the ECCB include issuing and management of the EC dollar, management of the OECS foreign reserves, provision of policy advice to Governments of Member States, regulation and supervision of commercial banks in the Currency Union and the monitoring of economic and financial conditions locally, regionally and internationally.

In compliance with the Agreement, the monetary policy of the Union is executed by the Monetary Council through the ECCB.[100] The IMF describes the OECS as being 'among the world's most highly monetized regions',[101] with well-developed banking and insurance sectors, a number of credit unions[102] and small but functioning offshore activities, including international banking for corporations and individuals and direct foreign investment. The IMF categorises the OECS economies as 'small, open, middle-income, and tourism-dependent island economies'.[103]

The Monetary Council, created under the ECCB Agreement[104] is the highest decision-making body for the ECCB.

9.6.2 Economic Union

In January 2001, the nine OECS Member States moved to establish an economic union. The core elements of the proposed union were approved in 2002, and the drafting of the proposed treaty began in 2004. Following mass national and

---

[97]A full chronology of the history of the ECCB from 1981 until 2010 is available at http://www.eccb-centralbank.org/PDF/chronology.PDF. Accessed 9 October 2014.

[98]ECCBA (n. 96 above) Article 3(1).

[99]See http://www.eccb-centralbank.org/PDF/fact%20sheet.pdf. Accessed 9 October 2014.

[100]Revised Treaty (n. 2 above) 14.

[101]Schipke et al. 2013.

[102]The IMF identified 61 in 2013.

[103]Ibid.

[104]ECCBA (n. 96 above) Article 7.

regional educational programmes, the Revised Treaty of Basseterre Establishing the Organisation of Eastern Caribbean States Economic Union, came into force in January 2011, with the Economic Union being governed by the Protocol of Eastern Caribbean Economic Union (the Protocol). To enter into force, the treaty required four ratifications by 21 January 2011, which it achieved on 20 January 2011.[105] In 2013, Montserrat passed the Revised Treaty of Basseterre Establishing the Organisation of Eastern Caribbean States Economic Union Act 2013, thereby ratifying the treaty establishing the economic union of the OECS into their domestic legislation.

Following the decision to establish an economic union, discussion led to the conclusion that the objective of the Union was to ensure 'all legal and administrative impediments to the most efficient allocation of factors of production (with the obvious exception of land) and the fruits of production within this economic space are removed'.[106]

The establishment of an economic union deepened the integration between already very close and interdependent states. The preamble to the Protocol refers to establishing the foundations of a closer union, the elimination of barriers which divide Member States and the contribution which an economic union will make to 'the rapid growth of these States and to the ultimate creation of a viable economic community of Caribbean countries'.[107]

The Protocol sought to establish strong economic relationships between Member States, in order to facilitate and ensure that the objectives of the union were achieved. In order to achieve the objectives, Member States were required to establish a single financial and economic space. This space is the Eastern Caribbean Economic and Currency Union (OECS/ECCU), one of only four regional currency unions in the world. Unless the Authority decides otherwise, the expense of administering the economic union is to be borne by Protocol Member States in equal shares.[108]

The broad aim of a single financial and economic space is to establish an area in which persons, goods and capital can move freely within the zone, while harmonising policies which affect such movements. The Revised Treaty establishes a customs union which prohibits the imposition of import duties on eligible goods which are traded between Member States and a common customs tariff with third countries.[109] In order for goods to be deemed 'eligible', they must: be consigned from a Protocol Member State to a consignee in the importing Protocol Member State

---

[105]Ratification dates were as follows: Antigua and Barbuda (30th December 2010); St Vincent and The Grenadine (12th January 2011); St Kitts and Nevis (20th January 2011); Grenada (20th January 2011); Dominica (21st January 2011).

[106]Progress Report 1 on the OECS Economic Union Project, p. 1, cited in Huntley, n. 3 above, p. 3.

[107]Protocol (n. 64 above) Preamble.

[108]Ibid., Article 18.

[109]Ibid., Article 5.

and meet the requirements of rules of origin under the 2001 Revised Treaty of Chaguaramas.[110]

A common customs tariff is the applicable tariffs placed on goods entering into the economic union across external borders. The tariff is set by an Act of the Organisation; however, where such a tariff has not been set, the Common External Tariff under the Revised Treaty of Chaguaramas applies.[111] Member States are prohibited from imposing any tariff higher than that set as the Common Customs Tariff. Further, any goods imported from outside of the Union which have complied with customs duties and charges and thus are in free circulation within the Union, enjoy the privilege of any goods produced within the area,[112] subject to Article 9.1.[113]

Free movement of citizens is secured within the Union,[114] allowing persons to live and work freely in any member state within the Union. Member States are required to abolish any discriminatory practices which may exist as regards employment, and the OECS Authority and Commission are charged with monitoring compliance. This is distinguished from CARICOM, where the free movement of labour under the Revised Treaty of Chaguaramas is restricted to those designated as 'Skilled Community Nationals' under the Treaty.[115] Such skilled nationals include university graduates, sportspersons, artists and musicians.

There must also be fair and equitable access to education across Member States, with the Protocol calling on states to endeavour to harmonise the accreditation of education and standardising both curriculum and assessment,[116] along with the harmonisation of human and social development.[117]

The Protocol calls for the abolition of any obstacles to the free movement of capital. Such freedom of capital allows not only for physical money to be moved, but also the investment of capital into ventures, buying of property and purchasing of shares in any other Protocol Member State. In order to assist the freedom of movement of capital, the Protocol calls for the harmonisation of investment, taxation and incentive policies, in addition to the coordination of both monetary and fiscal policies. Furthermore, the Protocol calls for Member States to harmonise

---

[110]Revised Treaty of Chaguaramas Establishing the Caribbean Community including the CARICOM Single Market and Economy, adopted 7 May 2001, entered into force 4 February 2002, 2259 UNTS 293; this treaty is the successor to the 1973 Treaty of Chaguaramas which established the Caribbean Community and the CARICOM Single Market and Economy. The Revised Treaty creates the framework for the removal of legal, regulatory and technical barriers to the movement of factors of production and of goods and services within CARICOM.

[111]Ibid., Article 81.

[112]Ibid., Article 10.1.

[113]Concerning dumped or subsidised imports.

[114]Revised Treaty of Chaguaramas (n. 110 above) Article 12.

[115]Ibid., Article 46.1.

[116]Protocol (n. 66 above) Article 22.

[117]Ibid., Article 23.

policies in a number of key social and development policy areas, including service sectors, telecommunications and information technologies sector; tourism development, agriculture; social policy and common competition policy.

Agreements made by Member States prior to the Protocol coming into force remain in force, and any associated rights and obligations as regards such pre-Protocol treaties were not affected by the Protocol.[118] However, while respecting pre-Protocol agreements, the Revised Treaty calls upon Member States to 'take any steps at their disposal which are necessary to reconcile the provisions of any such agreements with the basic objectives of this Protocol'.[119] Such necessary steps are monitored annually by the Economic Affairs Council.[120]

9.7 Dispute Settlement

The OECS treaty regime provides an interesting variety of dispute settlement options. Parties have three clear routes of dispute settlement—through the organs of the Organisation by means of the Protocol of the Economic Union, and by ad hoc methods and judicial mechanisms set up jointly under Article 18 of the 2011 Revised Treaty and the Annex on Dispute Settlement.

9.7.1 Non-judicial Dispute Settlement Options

Both the 2011 Treaty, and the Protocol to the Economic Union establish the basis for non-judicial settlement through the Organs. On the other hand, the Annex on Dispute Settlement, in conjunction with Article 18 establishes a variety of ad hoc methods varying from good offices through to mediation, consultations, conciliation, arbitration and culminating with adjudication in the original jurisdiction of the Eastern Caribbean Court of Appeal (ECCA).

9.7.2 Dispute Settlement Under the Organs of the OECS

The Protocol of the Economic Union provides for dispute settlement for the Protocol Member States to address issues arising under the Protocol.[121] This process cannot be challenged by conciliation or arbitration set up pursuant to paras 4 or 5 of the

---

[118]Ibid., Article 11.1.

[119]Ibid., Article 11.2.

[120]Ibid., Article 11.6.

[121]Ibid., Articles 30 and 31.

Dispute Settlement Annex. Article 30 outlines a general consultation and complaints procedure if the objectives of the Protocol are or may be frustrated. Under this Article, an aggrieved State has several options, ranging from negotiations with the State it alleges the breach,[122] to an investigatory process, failing which an adjudicatory processes to resolve the dispute.

If consultations and negotiations—which are the first course of action fail, the matter may be submitted to the Economic Affairs Council.[123] The Council first refers the matter to an examining committee[124] set up under Article 31, which is furnished with relevant facts and assistance by parties,[125] that can be compiled into a report that can be utilised by the Economic Affairs Council to decide whether a breach or frustration of the purpose of the Protocol has occurred.[126] Consequently, by means of a majority vote, the Council can make recommendations,[127] institute or authorise sanctions if the recommendations are not complied with,[128] and if requested by a Protocol State, institute interim measures[129] on the issue. Interim measures may be requested by a party to safeguard their position, and if successful, may even have their obligations suspended for a period deemed appropriate by the Council.[130] Finally, a State which is aggrieved by a decision, or actions of the Economic Affairs Council, can invoke the original jurisdiction of the ECCA, without waiting the 3-month period mandated in Article 18.2 of the Revised Treaty.[131] This procedure, which may be considered the expedited route to the Court, requires the party to bring the claim against the Organisation, and other parties to the dispute, and the Court will re-examine the issue afresh on its own merit.

9.7.3 Ad Hoc Dispute Settlement Mechanisms

Disputes which are not resolved by means of the Economic Affairs Council may then be resolved by the ad hoc dispute settlement mechanisms or by judicial dispute settlement as set out in Article 18 of the Revised Treaty and the Dispute Settlement Annex. These procedures address disputes arising specifically under the 2011

---

[122]Ibid., Article 30.1.

[123]Ibid.

[124]Ibid., Article 30.2.

[125]Ibid.

[126]Ibid., Article 30.3.

[127]Ibid.

[128]Ibid., Article 30.4.

[129]Ibid., Article 30.5.

[130]Ibid.

[131]Ibid., Article 30.6.

Treaty,[132] and can also be particularly important if a party is a member of either the Revised Treaty or Protocol, but not both. Eligible parties to these disputes are either full or associate Member States, or the Organisation.[133] Therefore, like the International Court of Justice, but unlike the 2001 Revised Treaty of Chaguaramas to which all nine OECS states belong, individuals cannot bring claims directly to the Court, but can presumably do so in national courts, or by the State on their behalf.[134]

In the instance a dispute arises between eligible parties, Article 18.1 of the Revised Treaty enjoins them to utilise a minimum of 3 months[135] to settle disputes amicably, failing which they can submit a request to the Director General[136] or Chief Registrar of the ECCA[137] to pursue any of the ad hoc methods outlined in the Annex on Dispute Settlement.[138] Parties can however circumvent the 3-month minimum period by either utilising the procedure under the Protocol of the Economic Union[139] discussed in the previous section, or by applying to the Chief Registrar of the ECCA for the Court to grant a waiver based on circumstances of urgency.[140]

Utilising the Annex on Dispute Settlement, eligible parties can subject to Article 30 of the Protocol of the Economic Union make use of five modes of dispute settlement—ranging from the non-adversarial measures of good offices and consultation; alternative dispute settlement mechanisms of conciliation and arbitration; to the adversarial option of adjudication.[141] The rules and procedures regarding good offices and consultation; alternative dispute settlement mechanisms of conciliation and arbitration are set out in paras 2 through 5 of the Annex on Dispute Settlement, respectively, while that on adjudication is set out in para 6.

9.7.4 Judicial Settlement of Disputes

The forum designated by the Revised Treaty for the judicial settlement of disputes is the ECCA. The Court was established in 1967 as the superior court of record for the nine OECS members[142] to hear appeals from lower courts in these States.

---

[132]Revised Treaty (n. 2 above) Article 18.1. Disputes existing prior to the coming into force of the Revised Treaty in 2011, shall according to Article 18.6 be governed by the 1981 Treaty.

[133]Ibid., Article 18.5.

[134]For example the *LaGrand case (Germany v. U.S)*, [2001] ICJ Rep 466 or by utilising the *Mavrommatis* test (*Mavrommatis Palestine Concessions) (Greece v. U.K.)* [1924] PCIJ (ser. B) No. 3.

[135]Revised Treaty (n. 2 above) Article 18.2.

[136]For disputes between parties.

[137]Where the Organisation is a party to the dispute.

[138]Revised Treaty (n. 2 above) Article 18.2.

[139]Ibid., Article 18.4.

[140]Ibid., Article 18.3.

[141]Annex on Dispute Settlement, para 1.

[142]West Indies Associated States Supreme Court Order 1967 SI 223/1967.

Under the Revised Treaty, it is anticipated that this jurisdiction will need to be transformed into a treaty-interpreting jurisdiction as outlined in para 6 of the Annex on Dispute Settlement. This expands significantly the scope of the Court from the second highest appeal court of the nine OECS States to one with a bifurcated jurisdiction. In this regard it is similar to its regional counterpart—the Caribbean Court of Justice (CCJ), which is also set up in a similar manner. The record of the courts varies, however, because while the CCJ has produced a number of high quality judgements in its original jurisdiction,[143] the ECCA is still to receive a claim. Conversely, because the ECCA has been established as an appellate court since 1967, it has a rich and varied jurisprudence of appeals from its Member States.

While in its appellate jurisdiction the Court is meant to pronounce on domestic legal issues, as a treaty-interpreting tribunal with competence to interpret and apply the Revised Treaty, it will have to be *au fait* with international law, specifically with the law of treaties.[144] In its original jurisdiction, as outlined in the Annex and in the Protocol, the Court will play an integral role in dispute settlement for the union. The reference in Article 18.1 of the Revised Treaty and para 1(b) of the Annex, make it the default dispute settlement mechanism and for allowing unilateral referral to matters of the Court, makes its jurisdiction compulsory. The Court can hear contentious cases, either between Member States, or between States and the Organisation or vice versa, as well as issue advisory opinions. Advisory opinions can be requested by the Authority or any other organ of the Organisation, and can relate to the interpretation and application of the Revised Treaty. Finally, para 8 of the Annex provides for a kind of appellate jurisdiction from decisions of tribunals in the Organisation as part of its treaty jurisdiction. As Berry outlines, this is a unique role since it combines both original and appellate forms of jurisdiction.[145]

9.8 Relationship with the CARICOM Regional Trade Advisor

The six full members of the OECS are also full members of CARICOM. Montserrat is a full member of CARICOM, while Anguilla and the British Virgin Islands (BVI) are both associate members of CARICOM. Member States of the OECS are permitted qualified free movement of labour and the rights of establishment within the Caribbean Single Market Economy (CSME).[146] Passports issued in OECS states are passports of the Caribbean Community, bearing the 'CC' logo. Under the 2001 Revised Treaty of Chaguaramas, all OECS Member States are less developed countries for the purposes of the Treaty. This status, as less developed

---

[143]See Caribbean Court of Justice, at: http://www.caribbeancourtofjustice.org/judgments-proceedings. Accessed 17 December 2014.

[144]Berry 2014, pp. 394–395.

[145]Ibid.

[146]Lewis 2006.

countries, affords OECS Member States a level of protection and a number of benefits as regards tariffs and trade within the CSME.

Part Three of the Revised Treaty of Chaguaramas creates a 'special regime' for less developed countries, through Articles 160–166. Privileges afforded to less developed countries include making available technological and research facilities, special needs to be considered with regard to the imposition of the common external tariff, establishing any programmes for incentives within the community and the imposition of import duties where states have suffered or are likely to suffer loss of revenue as a result of the importation of goods from CARICOM.

Although all Member States are members of CARICOM, none of the states has recognised the appellate jurisdiction of the Caribbean Court of Justice. Therefore, all OECS Member States use the Privy Council as their final appellate court, and the CCJ is used only for the interpretation of the Revised Treaty of Chaguaramas, in its original jurisdiction. As a result, OECS states have recourse to two fora in the original jurisdiction—the Eastern Caribbean Supreme Court for matters arising under the 2011 Revised Treaty or the Protocol, and the Caribbean Court of Justice for matters arising under the 2001 Revised Treaty. Presumably, therefore, a non-OECS/CARICOM Member State can have recourse to both courts if a matter arises as a direct result of the 2011 Treaty.

References

Abass A (2014) International Law: Text, Cases and Materials, 2nd ed. Oxford University Press, Oxford.

Berry D (2014) Caribbean Integration Law. Oxford University Press, Oxford.

Emmanuel P A M (1989) Community within a Community: The OECS Countries. In: Ramcharan B G and Francis L B (eds), Caribbean Perspectives on International Law and Organizations. Nijhoff, Dordrecht, pp. 402–416.

Gibbins W (2002) OECS at the Centre. The Integrationist 1(3): 8–11.

Girvan N (2012) Caribbean Community: The Elusive Quest for Economic Integration by Regional Integration. In Hall K and Chuck-A-San M (eds), Key to Caribbean Survival and Prosperity. Trafford Publishing, Bloomington, pp. 34–67.

Ishmael L (2014) The OECS Model of Integration in the Context of Caribbean Regionalism. Pensamiento Propio Publicación Trilingüe de Ciencias Sociales de América Latina y el Caribe, at: <http://www.cries.org/contenidos/pp23.pdf#page=37. Accessed 14 October 2014.

Lewis V (2006) The Caribbean Single Market and Economy (CSME): The International Environment and Options for CARICOM and the OECS Countries. In: Hall K and Chuck-A-Sang M (eds), CARICOM Options: Towards Full Integration Into the World Economy. Ian Randle Publishers, Kingston.

Menon P K (1995) Sub-regional Integration in the Caribbean: The OECS Experience. Revue de droit international, de sciences diplomatiques et politiques 73(1): 1–44.

Schipke A, Cebotari A and Thacker N (eds) (2013) The Eastern Caribbean Economic and Currency Union Macroeconomics and Financial Systems. International Monetary Fund, Washington DC.

Simmonds K C (2006) Financing Growth in the 1990s: New Challenges for OECS Countries. Public Administration and Development 14(5): 439–449.

Selected Bibliography

Compiled by Marco Odello and Francesco Seatzu

General Works on Institutional Cooperation and Integration in Latin America

Barbosa R. A., *América Latina em Perspectiva: A integração regional, da retórica á realidade* (São Paulo, Aduaneiras, 1991).

Blouet W. and Olwyn M. (eds), *Latin America and the Caribbean: A Systematic and Regional Survey* (J. Wiley & Sons: New York, 2011).

Börzel T. A., Goltermann L., Lohaus M. (eds), *Roads to Regionalism: Genesis, Design, and Effects of Regional Organizations* (Farnham: Ashgate, 2011).

Briceño Ruiz J. and Marleny Bustamante A. (eds), *La integración latinoamericana: entre el regionalismo abierto y la globalización* (Mérida, Venezuela: Universidad de Los Andes, Consejo de Publicaciones, 2002).

Bulmer Thomas V. (ed), *Regional Integration in Latin American and the Caribbean* (Latin American Studies, University of London, 2001).

Dabène O., *The Politics of Regional Integration in Latin America: Theoretical and Comparative Explorations* (New York: Palgrave Macmillan, 2009).

Hurrell A., 'Regionalism in the Americas', in L. Fawcett and A. Hurrell (eds), *Regionalism in World Politics: Regional Organization and International Order* (New York: Oxford University Press, 1995).

Kühnhardt L., *The Global Proliferation of Regional Integration* (New York: Berghan Books, 2010).

Lacasse N. and Perret L. (eds), *Le libre-échange dans les Amériques: (une perspective continentale* (Montréal: Wilson & Lafleur, 1994).

Laursen F. (ed.), *Comparative Regional Integration: Europe and Beyond* (Abingdon, Ashgate, 2010).

León Li J. M., *Regional Integration Process in South America: Analysis of Institutions and Policies under the EU Framework* (Hamburg: Diplomica Verlag, 2001).

Lewis D. E., 'The Latin Caribbean and Regional Cooperation: A Survey of Challenges and Opportunities' (1995) 4 *Journal of Interamerican Studies and World Affairs*, pp. 25–55.

Mace G., 'Regional Integration in Latin America: A Long and Winding Road' (1988) 43(3) *International Journal*, pp. 404–427.

Mossman K. F., *Regional Economic Integration in Latin America* (PhD thesis. Harvard University, 1997).

O'Keefe T. A., *Latin American and Caribbean Trade Agreements: Keys to a Prosperous Community of the Americas* (The Hague, Martinus Nijhoff Publishers, 2009).

© T.M.C. ASSER PRESS and the authors 2015

M. Odello and F. Seatzu (eds.), *Latin American and Caribbean International Institutional Law*, DOI 10.1007/978-94-6265-069-5

Paredes B., 'El parlatino y la integración latinoamericana' (2000) 8 *Revista del Senado de la República*, pp. 13–17.

Ribeiro Hoffmann A., van der Vleuten A. (eds.), *Closing or Widening the Gap?: Legitimacy and Democracy in Regional Integration Organizations* (Abingdon, Ashgate, 2007).

Sampson G. P., Woolcock S. (eds.), *Regionalism, Multilateralism, and Economic Integration: The Recent Experience* (Tokyo: United Nations University Press, 2003).

Sánchez-Ancochea D., Shadlen K. C., *The Political Economy of Hemispheric Integration: Responding to Globalization in the Americas* (Abingdon, Ashgate, 2008).

Santulli C., 'Retour à la théorie de l'organe commun: réflexions sur la nature juridique des organisations internationales à partir du cas de l'Alba et de la Celac, comparées notamment à l'Union européenne et à l'O.N.U.' (2012) 116 *Revue générale de droit international public*, pp. 565–578.

Pennetta P. (a cura di), *L'evoluzione dei sistemi giurisdizionali regionali e influenze comunitarie* (Bari: Cacucci, 2010).

Pennetta P., *Integraciòn e integraciones. Europa, Amèrica Latina y el Caribe* (Bogotà, Planeta, 2011).

Pennetta P., 'Consideraciones sobre los procesos de integración regional en Europa y América Latina' (2013) 15 *Cultura Latino Americana. Annali*, pp. 181–206.

Phillips N., 'Hemispheric Integration and Subregionalism in the Americas' (2003) 79(2) *International Affairs*, pp. 327–349.

Shaw T. M., Andrew Grant J., Cornelissen S. (eds.), *The Ashgate Research Companion to Regionalisms* (Farnham: Ashgate, 2011).

Sánchez Sánchez R. A., *The Politics of Central American Integration* (Abingdon: Routledge, 2009).

Santiso J., *The Decade of the Multilatinas* (Cambridge: CUP, 2013).

Latin American Economic System (SELA)

Bond R. D., 'Regionalism in Latin America: Prospects for the Latin American Economic System (SELA)' (1978) 32 *International Organization*, pp. 401–423.

Diaz Müller L., *El SELA y las empresas multinacionales latinoamericanas en el marco del desarrollo regional* (México D.F.: UNAM, Instituto de Investigaciones Jurídicas, 1981).

Marinas Otero L., 'El sistema económico latinoamericano (SELA)' (1978) 159 *Revista de política internacional*, pp. 137–143.

Zagaris B., 'The Economic System of Latin America (SELA): An Innovative Mechanism for Less Developed Countries' (1978) 2 *Comparative Law Yearbook*, pp. 117–148.

Latin American Integration Association (ALADI)

Ferrer Vieyra E., 'Reflexiones sobre la integración de America Latina (ALADI)', in: Organización de los Estados Americanos, *Cursos de Derecho Internacional*, Comité Jurídico Interamericano, vol. 2, n. 1, 2003, pp. 529–542.

Garré Copello B., 'Las soluciones paralelas al Mercosur: el nuevo rol de la Aladi', in *Estudios multidisciplinarios sobre el Mercosur* (Montevideo: Universidad de la República, Facultad de Derecho, 1995) pp. 245–303.

Niaradi G. A., 'A intergração econômica nas Américas: ALADI e ALALC, MERCOSUR, NAFTA, ALCA', in: *Estudos de direito internacional: anais do 2° Congresso Brasileiro de Direito Internacional* (Curitiba: Juruá, 2001) pp. 419–425.

Rojas Penso J., 'New Dispute Settlement Perspectives in the Latin American Integration Assocuation (ALADI)', in: Lacarte J. and Granados J (eds), *Inter-governmental Trade Dispute Settlement : Multilateral and Regional Approaches* (London: Camoeron May, 2004) pp. 207–213.

UNASUR

Allen D. N., 'The Union of South American Nations, the OAS and Suramérica' (2010) 1(1) *ILSA Journal of International & Comparative Law*, pp. 44–58.

Botelho, J. C. A., 'La creación y la evolución de Unasur' (Curitiba: Juruá Editora, 2013).

Cano Linares M. A. 'La Unión de Naciones Suramericanas: un ambicioso e innovador proceso de construcción de integración regional' (2010) 4(1) *Revista Electrónica Iberoamericana*, pp. 9–37.

Díaz Barrado C.M., 'La Comunidad Suramericana de Naciones: propuestas y realizaciones', *Revista Española de Derecho Internacional* (2005) 57(2), pp. 639–663.

Saludjian A., *Hacia otra integración sudamericana* (Buenos Aires: Libros del Zorzal, 2004).

Serbin A., 'Entre UNASUR y ALBA: ¿otra integración (ciudadana) es posible?' (2007–2008) 1 *Anuario CEIPAZ*, pp. 183–288.

Wade A., 'The Union of South American Nations ("UNASUR"): Challenges and Opportunities for States pursuing Regional Integration', (Master Thesis) The Elliot School of International Affairs, George Washington University, May 2010.

Latin American Sub-regional Development Institutions

Cevallos R., 'The Central American Bank for Economic Integration', (1995–1996) 4 *Tul. J. Int'l & Comp. L.*, pp. 245–274.

Culpeper R., *The Multilateral Development Banks: Titans Or Behemoths?*, (Boulder: Lynne Rienner Publishers, 1997).

Syz J., *International Development Banks*, (Leiden: Oceana Publications, 1974).

Michaelowa K., Humphrey C., Strong C., *The Business of Development: Trends in Lending by Multilateral Development Banks to Latin America, 1980–2009*, CIS Working Paper No. 65 (16 November 2010).

Andean Community

Alter K. J. and Helfer L. R., 'Legal Integration in the Andes: Law-Making by the Andean Tribunal of Justice' (2011) 17 *European Law Journal*, pp. 701–715.

Kearns K. C., 'The Andean Common Market: A New Thrust at Economic Integration in Latin America' (1972) 14(2) *Journal of Interamerican Studies and World Affairs*, pp. 225–249.

O'Leary T. F., 'The Andean Common Market and the Importance of Effective Dispute Resolution Procedures', (1984) 2 *Int'l l Tax & Bus. Law*, pp. 101–128.

Suárez Mejías J. L., *Integración y supranacionalidad en la Comunidad andina proceso decisorio, sistema jurisdiccional y relación con los derechos nacionales* (PhD thesis. Universidad Complutense de Madrid, 2006).

Southern Common Market (Mercosur)

Borba Casella P. (ed.), *Mercosul: Integração Regional e Globalização* (Rio de Janeiro: Renovar, 2000).

Bouzas R., da Motta Veiga P., Torrent R., *In-Depth Analysis Mercosur Integration, Its Prospectives And The Effects Thereof on The Market Access of EU Goods, Services And Investment* (Barcelona: Observatory of Globalisation, 2002).

Domínguez F., Guedes de Oliveira M. A. (eds), *Mercosur: Between Integration and Democracy*, (Oxford, Bern, Berlin, Bruxelles, Frankfurt/M., New York, Wien: Peter Lang, 2004).

Estrella Faria J. A., *O Mercosul: princípios finalidade e alcance do Tratado de Assunção*, (Brasília DF: Ministerio das Relaçoes Exteriores, 1993).

Foders F., *MERCOSUR: a new approach to regional integration?* (Universität Kiel. Institut für Weltwirtschaft, 1996).

Gardini G. L., *The Origins of Mercosur: Democracy and Regionalization in South America* (New York: Palgrave Macmillan, 2010).

Haines-Ferrari M., 'MERCOSUR: A New Model of Latin American Economic Integration' (1993) 25 *Case W. Res. J. Int'l L.*, pp. 413–48.

Lorenzo F., Vaillant M. (eds), *Mercosur and the Creation of the Free Trade Area of the Americas*, (Washington DC: Woodrow Wilson International Center for Scholars, 2005) pp. 1–28.

Olavo Baptista L., *O Mercosul, Suas Institutuições e Ordenamento Jurídico*, (São Paulo: LTr, 1998).

Pérez Otermin J., *El Mercado Común Del Sur: Desde Asunción a Ouro Preto* (Montevideo: Fundación de Cultura Universitaria, 1995).

Porrata-Doria R. A., *MERCOSUR: The Common Market of the Southern Cone* (Carolina Accademic Press, 2005).

Toscano M, Filho F, Lixinski L, Olmos Giupponi M B (eds), *The Law of MERCOSUR* (Oxford: Hart publishing, 2010).

Vervaele J.A.E., 'Mercosur and regional integration in Latin America', (2005) 4 *The International and Comparative Law Quarterly*, pp. 387–409.

Pacific Alliance

Ramirez S., 'Regionalism: The Pacific Alliance', (2013) *Americas Quarterly*, available at: http://www.americasquarterly.org/content/regionalism-pacific-alliance (last accessed on 3 December 2014).

Caribbean Community (CARICOM)

Berry D., *Caribbean Integration Law* (Oxford: Oxford University Press, 2014).

Emmanuel P. A. M., 'Community within a Community: The OECS Countries', in: Ramcharan B. G. and Francis L. B. (eds), *Caribbean Perspectives on International Law and Organizations* (Dordrecht: Nijhoff, 1989) pp. 402–416.

Geiser H. J., Alleyne P., Gajraj C., *Legal Problems of Caribbean Integration: A Study of the Legal Aspects of CARICOM* (Leyden: Sijthoff, 1976).

Hall K. O. (ed.), *The Pertinence of CARICOM in the 21st Century: Some Perspectives: Some Perspectives* (Indianan: Trafford Publishing, 2012).

Hall K. O., Chuck-A-Sang M. (eds), *Coping with the Collapse of the Old Order: CARICOM's New External Agenda* (Kingston: Ian Randle Publishers, 2013).

O'Brien D., 'CARICOM: Regional Integration in a Post-Colonial Word' (2011) 5 *European Law Journal*, pp. 630–648.

Pollard D.E.E., *The Caribbean Court of Justice: Closing the Circle of Independence* (Kingston: Caribbean Law Publishing, 2004).

Cherubini F., 'La Corte caraibica di giustizia', in P. Pennetta (a cura di), *L'evoluzione dei sistemi giurisdizionali regionali e influenze comunitarie* (Bari: Cacucci, 2010), pp. 71–98.

Index

© T.M.C. ASSER PRESS and the authors 2015

M. Odello and F. Seatzu (eds.), *Latin American and Caribbean International
Institutional Law*, DOI 10.1007/978-94-6265-069-5

Printed by Printforce, the Netherlands